Religious Diversity in Ancient Israel and Judah

Religious Diversity in Ancient Israel and Judah

Edited by

Francesca Stavrakopoulou and John Barton

t&t clark

Published by T&T Clark International
A Continuum Imprint
The Tower Building, 11 York Road, London SE1 7NX
80 Maiden Lane, Suite 704, New York, NY 10038

www.continuumbooks.com

British Library Cataloguing-in-Publication Data
A catalogue record for this book is available from the British Library

Typeset by Pindar NZ, Auckland, New Zealand
Printed and bound in Great Britain by CPI Antony Rowe, Chippenham, Wiltshire

ISBN13:   9780567032157 (Hardback)
           9780567032164 (Paperback)

Contents

Editors' Note   vii
Abbreviations   viii
Notes on Contributors   xiv

Chapter 1
INTRODUCTION: RELIGIOUS DIVERSITY IN ANCIENT ISRAEL AND JUDAH   1
Francesca Stavrakopoulou and John Barton

PART I
CONCEPTUAL DIVERSITIES

Chapter 2
EXPERIENCING THE DIVINE: HEAVENLY VISITS, EARTHLY ENCOUNTERS
AND THE LAND OF THE DEAD   11
Susan Niditch

Chapter 3
'ISRAELITE' RELIGION AND 'CANAANITE' RELIGION   23
Herbert Niehr

Chapter 4
'POPULAR' RELIGION AND 'OFFICIAL' RELIGION: PRACTICE, PERCEPTION,
PORTRAYAL   37
Francesca Stavrakopoulou

PART II
SOCIO-RELIGIOUS DIVERSITIES

Chapter 5
ROYAL RELIGION IN ANCIENT JUDAH   61
Nicolas Wyatt

Chapter 6
CULTIC SITES AND COMPLEXES BEYOND THE JERUSALEM TEMPLE   82
Diana Edelman

Chapter 7
URBAN RELIGION AND RURAL RELIGION   104
Philip Davies

Chapter 8
HOUSEHOLD RELIGION   118
Carol Meyers

Chapter 9
PERSONAL PIETY   135
Rainer Albertz

PART III
GEOGRAPHICAL DIVERSITIES

Chapter 10
SOUTHERN, NORTHERN AND TRANSJORDANIAN PERSPECTIVES   149
Jeremy M. Hutton

Chapter 11
'MANY NATIONS WILL BE JOINED TO YHWH IN THAT DAY': THE
QUESTION OF YHWH OUTSIDE JUDAH   175
Lester L. Grabbe

PART IV
POSTSCRIPT

Chapter 12
REFLECTING ON RELIGIOUS DIVERSITY   191
John Barton

Index of Authors   194
Index of Ancient Sources   197
Index of Subjects   201

EDITORS' NOTE

It is usual in editing a volume such as this to smooth contributors' differing writing styles towards a more coherent presentation by standardizing the use of key terms. Though we have taken some measures to produce a stylistically consistent collection of essays (such as referring to the inhabitants of Judah as 'Judahites' rather than 'Judaeans'), we have, however, decided against standardizing the way in which authors refer to Yhwh (aka YHWH, Yahweh, JHWH . . .). This is, after all, a book about diversity.

ABBREVIATIONS

AASOR	Annual of the American Schools of Oriental Research
AB	Anchor Bible
ABD	*The Anchor Bible Dictionary* (6 vols; edited by D.N. Freedman. New York, NY: Doubleday, 1992).
ABRL	Anchor Bible Reference Library
ABS	Archaeology and Biblical Studies
ADAJ	Annual of the Department of Antiquities of Jordan
AfOB	Archiv für Orientforschung: Beiheft
AfR	*Archiv für Religionsgeschichte*
AHI	*Ancient Hebrew Inscriptions* (2 vols; edited by G. Davies. Cambridge: Cambridge University Press, 1991–2004.)
AJA	*American Journal of Archaeology*
AJBA	*Australian Journal of Biblical Archaeology*
AJSL	*American Journal of Semitic Languages and Literatures*
ALASP	Abhandlungen zur Literatur Alt – Syrien – Palästinas
ANEP	*The Ancient Near East in Pictures Relating to the Old Testament* (edited by J.B. Pritchard, 2nd edn. Princeton, NJ: Princeton University Press, 1969).
ANESS	Ancient Near Eastern Studies Supplement Series
ANET	*Ancient Near Eastern Texts Relating to the Old Testament* (edited by J.B. Pritchard, 3rd edn. Princeton, NJ: Princeton University Press, 1969).
AnOr	Analecta Orientalia
AOAT	Alter Orient und Altes Testament
AP	*Aramaic Papyri of the Fifth Century BC* (edited by A.E. Cowley. Oxford: Clarendon Press, 1923).
ASOR	American Schools of Oriental Research
ASORMS	American Schools of Oriental Research Monograph Series
ASV	American Standard Version
AThANT	Abhandlungen zur Theologie des Alten und Neuen Testaments
AulOr	Aula Orientalis
BA	*Biblical Archaeologist*
BAIAS	*Bulletin of the Anglo-Israel Archaeological Society*
BAR	*Biblical Archaeology Review*
BASOR	*Bulletin of the American Schools of Oriental Research*
BBS	*Bulletin of Biblical Studies*
BEAT	Beiträge zur Erforschung des Alten Testaments
BETL	Bibliotheca ephemeridum theologicarum lovaniensium
BFChTh	Beiträge zur Förderung christlicher Theologie

BHH	*Biblische-historisches Handwörterbuch: Landeskunde, Geschichte, Religion, Kultur* (4 vols, edited by B. Reicke and L. Rost. Göttingen, 1962–66).
BHS	*Biblia Hebraica Stuttgartensia* (edited by K. Elliger and W. Rudolph. Stuttgart: Deutche Bibelstiftung, 1983).
Bib	*Biblica*
BibB	Biblische Beiträge
BibInt	*Biblical Interpretation*
BibOr	Biblica et orientalia
BIS	Biblical Interpretation Series
BJRL	*Bulletin of the John Rylands University Library of Manchester*
BJS	Brown Judaic Studies
BN	*Biblische Notizen*
BO	*Bibliotheca orientalis*
BR	*Bible Review*
BS	Biblical Seminar series
BWANT	Beiträge zur Wissenschaft vom Alten (und Neuen) Testament
BZ	*Biblische Zeitschrift*
BZAR	Beihefte zur Zeitschrift für altorientalische und biblische Rechtgeschichte
BZAW	Beihefte zur Zeitschrift für die alttestamentliche Wissenschaft
CAT	Commentaire de l'Ancien Testament
CB	Century Bible
CBET	Contributions to Biblical Exegesis and Theology
CBQ	*Catholic Biblical Quarterly*
CBQMS	Catholic Biblical Quarterly Monograph Series
CHM	*Cahiers d'Histoire Mondiale*
CIS	*Corpus inscriptionum semiticarum*
CIS	Copenhagen International Seminar series
ConBOT	Coniectanea biblica: Old Testament series
COS	*The Context of Scripture* (3 vols, edited by W.W. Hallo. Leiden: Brill, 1997–2002).
CRAIBL	*Comptes rendus de l'Académie des inscriptions et belles-lettres*
CSA	Copenhagen Studies in Assyriology
CSF	Collezione di studi fenici
CTA	*Corpus des tablettes en cunéiformes alphabétiques découvertes à Ras Shamra-Ugarit de 1929 à 1939* (edited by A. Herdner. Mission de Ras Shamra 10. Paris: Imprimerie nationale, 1963).
DaF	Damaszener Forschungen
DDD	*Dictionary of Deities and Demons in the Bible* (edited by K. van der Toorn, B. Becking and P. W. van der Horst. 2nd extensively rev. edn. Leiden: Brill, 1999).
DISO	*Dictionnaire des inscriptions sémitiques de l'ouest* (edited by Ch.F. Jean and J. Hoftijzer. Leiden: Brill, 1965).
DJD	Discoveries in the Judaean Desert
DNWSI	*Dictionary of North-West Semitic Inscriptions* (2 vols, J. Hoftijzer and K. Jongeling. Leiden: Brill, 1995).
DULAT	*A Dictionary of the Ugaritic Language in the Alphabetic Tradition*

	(2 vols, edited by G. del Olmo Lete and J. Sanmartín. Translated by
	W.G.E. Watson. HdO 67; Leiden: Brill, 2003).
EdF	Erträge der Forschung
EPROER	Etudes preliminaries aux religions orientales dans l'empire romain
ErIsr	*Eretz Israel*
ESHM	European Seminar in Historical Methodology
ET	English Translation
ETL	*Ephemerides theologicae lovanienses*
ExpTim	*Expository Times*
FAT	Forschungen zum Alten Testament
FOTL	Forms of the Old Testament Literature
FRLANT	Forschungen zur Religion und Literatur des Alten und Neuen
	Testaments
FZPhTh	*Freiburger Zeitschrift für Philosophie und Theologie*
GUS	Gorgias Ugaritic Series
HAE	*Handbuch der althebräischen Epigraphik* (3 vols, J. Renz and
	W. Röllig. Darmstadt: Wissenschaftliche Buchsgesellschaft,
	1995–2003.
HALOT	*The Hebrew and Aramaic Lexicon of the Old Testament* (4 vols,
	L. Koehler, W. Baumgartner and J.J. Stamm. Translated and edited
	under the supervision of M.E.J. Richardson. Leiden: Brill, 1994–99).
HAR	*Hebrew Annual Review*
HAT	Handbuch zum Alten Testament
HdO	Handbuch der Orientalistik
HI	*Hebrew Inscriptions: Texts from the Biblical Period of the Monarchy*
	with Concordance (F.W. Dobbs-Allsopp, J.J.M. Roberts, C.L. Seow
	and R.E. Whitaker. New Haven, CT: Yale University Press, 2005).
HSM	Harvard Semitic Monographs
HTR	*Harvard Theological Review*
HUCA	*Hebrew Union College Annual*
ICC	International Critical Commentary
IEJ	*Israel Exploration Journal*
IES	Israel Exploration Society
JA	*Journal Asiatique*
JAEI	*Journal of Ancient Egyptian Interconnections* (online)
JANER	*Journal of Ancient Near Eastern Religions*
JANESCU	*Journal of the Ancient Near Eastern Society of Columbia University*
JAOS	*Journal of the American Oriental Society*
JBL	*Journal of Biblical Literature*
JCS	*Journal of Cuneiform Studies*
JESHO	*Journal of the Economic and Social History of the Orient*
JETS	*Journal of the Evangelical Theological Society*
JHS	*Journal of Hebrew Scriptures*
JJS	*Journal of Jewish Studies*
JNES	*Journal of Near Eastern Studies*
JNSL	*Journal of Northwest Semitic Languages*
JPOS	*Journal of the Palestine Oriental Society*
JPS	Jewish Publication Society

JPSTCS	Jewish Publication Society Torah Commentary Series
JQR	*Jewish Quarterly Review*
JSJ	*Journal for the Study of Judaism in the Persian, Hellenistic and Roman Period*
JSOT	*Journal for the Study of the Old Testament*
JSOTS	Journal for the Study of the Old Testament Supplement Series
JSS	*Journal of Semitic Studies*
JTS	*Journal of Theological Studies*
K	Ketib
KAI	*Kanaänaische und aramäische Inscriften* (H. Donner and W. Röllig, 2nd edn. Wiesbaden: Harrassowitz, 1964–66).
KTU	*Die keilalphabetischen Texte Ugarit* (edited by M. Dietrich, O. Loretz and J. Sanmartin. AOAT 24/1. Neukirchen-Vluyn: Neukirchener Verlag, 1976).
LHBOTS	Library of Hebrew Bible/Old Testament Studies
LSTS	Library of Second Temple Studies
LXX	Septuagint
MARI	*Mari: Annales des Recherches Interdisciplinaires*
MRS	Mission de Ras Shamra
MT	Masoretic Text
NCB	New Century Bible
NCBC	New Cambridge Bible Commentary
NEA	*Near Eastern Archaeology*
NEAEHL	*The New Encyclopaedia of Archaeological Excavations in the Holy Land* (4 vols, edited by E. Stern. Jerusalem: Magnes Press, 1993).
NEB	New English Bible
NRSV	New Revised Standard Version
OBO	Orbis Biblicus et Orientalis
OEANE	*The Oxford Encyclopedia of Archaeology in the Near East* (edited by E.M. Meyers. New York, NY: Oxford University, 1997).
OLA	Orientalia lovaniensia analecta
OrAnt	*Oriens antiquus*
OTE	*Old Testament Essays*
OTL	Old Testament Library
OTP	*The Old Testament Pseudepigrapha* (2 vols, edited by J.H. Charlesworth. New York, NY: Doubleday, 1983).
OTS	Oudtestamentische Studiën
OTWSA	*Die Outestamentiese Werkgemeenschap in Suid-Afrika*
PEQ	*Palestine Exploration Quarterly*
POLO	Proche-Orient et littérature ougaritique
Q	Qere
QDAP	*Quarterly of the Department of Antiquities in Palestine*
RB	*Revue biblique*
RBS	Resources for Biblical Study
RdA	*Revue d'assyriologie et d'archéologie orientale*
RES	*Répertoire d'épigraphie sémitique*
RHR	*Revue de l'histoire des religions*
RivB	*Rivista biblica*

RlA	Reallexikon der Assyriologie und vorderasiatischen Archäologie (edited by E. Ebeling, *et al.* Berlin: de Gruyter, 1928–).
RPARA	*Rendiconti della Pontifica Accademia Romana di Archeologia*
RQum	*Revue de Qumrân*
RSO	Ras-Shamra – Ougarit
RSO	*Rivista degli studi orientali*
RSR	*Religious Studies Review*
RSV	Revised Standard Version
SAAB	*State Archives of Assyria Bulletin*
SBAB	Stuttgarter biblische Aufsatzbände
SBLMS	Society of Biblical Literature Monograph Series
SBLWAW	Society of Biblical Literature Writings from the Ancient World
SBS	Stuttgarter Bibelstudien
SHAJ	*Studies in the History and Archaeology of Jordan*
SHANE	Studies in the History of the Ancient Near East
SHCANE	Studies in the History and Culture of the Ancient Near East
SHR	Studies in the History of Religions
SJOT	*Scandinavian Journal of the Old Testament*
SJSJ	Supplements to the *Journal for the Study of Judaism*
SS	Studi semitici
SWBAS	Social World of Biblical Antiquity Series
TA	*Tel Aviv*
TAD	B. Porten and A. Yardeni, *Textbook of Aramaic Documents from Ancient Egypt: 1–4* (Hebrew University, Department of the History of the Jewish People, Texts and Studies for Students; Jerusalem: Hebrew University Press, 1986–99).
TBü	Theologische Bücherei
TDOT	*Theological Dictionary of the Old Testament* (15 vols, edited by G.J. Botterweck and H. Ringgren. Translated by J.T. Willis, G.W. Bromiley and D.E. Green. Grand Rapids: Eerdmans, 1974–).
ThLZ	*Theologische Literaturzeitung*
TQ	*Theologische Quartalschrift*
TRE	*Theologische Realenzyklopädie* (edited by G. Krause and G. Müller. Berlin: de Gruyter, 1977–).
TynBul	*Tyndale Bulletin*
TZ	*Theologische Zeitung*
UBL	Ugaritisch-biblische Literatur
UCOP	University of Cambridge Oriental Publications
UF	*Ugarit-Forschungen*
UUÅ	*Uppsala Universitets Årskrift*
VT	*Vetus Testamentum*
VTS	Vetus Testamentum Supplements
WBC	Word Biblical Commentary
WDSP	*Wadi Daliyeh II: The Samaria Papyri from Wadi Daliyeh* (D.M. Gropp) and *Qumran Cave 4: XXVIII Miscellanea, Part 2* (M. Bernstein, *et al.*) (DJD 28; Oxford: Clarendon Press, 2001).
WZKM	*Wiener Zeitschrift für die Kunde des Morgenlandes*
ZA	*Zeitschrift für Assyriologie*

ZAR	*Zeitschrift für altorientalische und biblische Rechtsgeschichte*
ZAW	*Zeitschrift für die alttestamentliche Wissenschaft*
ZDMG	*Zeitschrift der deutschen morgenländischen Gesellschaft*
ZDPV	*Zeitschrift des deutschen Palästina-Vereins*

Notes on Contributors

Rainer Albertz was Professor of Old Testament in the Protestant Theological Faculty of the University of Münster until his retirement in 2008. He now works as a Senior Professor in the 'Religion and Politics in Pre-Modern and Modern Times' Cluster of Excellence in Münster. He received his Dr theol. and *venia legendi* (Habilitation) from Heidelberg University. His primary area of research is the social and religious history of ancient Israel, including the history of literature. His books include *A History of Israelite Religion in the Old Testament Period* (Westminster John Knox, 1994; German edition 1992) and *Israel in Exile: The History and Literature of the Sixth Century B.C.E.* (Society of Biblical Literature, 2003; German edition 2001).

John Barton is Oriel & Laing Professor of the Interpretation of Holy Scripture in the University of Oxford. His most recent publications are *The Nature of Biblical Criticism* (Westminster John Knox, 2007), *The Old Testament: Canon, Literature and Theology* (Ashgate, 2007), and *The Bible: The Basics* (Routledge, 2009). His interests include biblical hermeneutics, prophecy in the Hebrew Bible, and biblical ethics.

Philip Davies is Professor Emeritus of Biblical Studies at the University of Sheffield. He has written on many aspects of the Hebrew Bible/Old Testament, with a special interest in history, prophecy and canon formation. His books include *Scribes and Schools: The Canonization of the Hebrew Scriptures* (Westminster John Knox, 1998) and *The Origins of Biblical Israel* (T&T Clark, 2007). He is also the author of several books on the Dead Sea Scrolls.

Diana Edelman is a Reader in the History, Archaeology and Literature of the Southern Levant in the Department of Biblical Studies at the University of Sheffield. She has published widely on King Saul as a literary and historical figure, and more recently has proposed the Persian-era temple was built under Artaxerxes I, not Darius I, in *The Origins of the 'Second' Temple* (Equinox, 2005). Her research currently is focused on the emergence of monotheism in the Persian period and the effect that has had on the production of many of the books in the Hebrew Bible. Her work regularly integrates critically evaluated textual and artefactual materials into historical recreations of the past in the southern Levant.

Lester L. Grabbe is Professor of Hebrew Bible and Early Judaism at the University of Hull. He is founder and convener of the European Seminar in Historical Methodology. His publications include *Judaic Religion in the Second Temple Period* (Routledge, 2000) and *Ancient Israel: What Do We Know and How Do We Know It?* (T&T Clark, 2007).

Jeremy M. Hutton is Assistant Professor of Old Testament at Princeton Theological Seminary. His research interests include the history of Israelite religion(s), historical and symbolic geography of the southern Levant, Northwest Semitic philology, and the formation and structure of the Deuteronomistic History. His recent publications include numerous essays and articles and his book *The Transjordanian Palimpsest: The Overwritten Texts of Personal Exile and Transformation in the Deuteronomistic History* (de Gruyter, 2009).

Carol Meyers holds the Mary Grace Wilson Professorship in the Department of Religion at Duke University. She has been a staff member or co-director of many archaeological field projects and has served as a consultant for numerous media productions focusing on the Bible. Her research interests include the social world of ancient Israel, biblical archaeology, and gender in the biblical world. She has authored or co-authored ten books and has edited or co-edited five others; she has also written hundreds of articles and reviews. Her recent books include *Exodus*, for a Cambridge University Press commentary series (2005), and *Households and Holiness: The Religious Culture of Israelite Women* (Fortress Press, 2005).

Susan Niditch is the Samuel Green Professor of Religion at Amherst College. She completed her undergraduate and graduate degrees at Harvard University. Her research interests include the study of oral tradition as relevant to ancient Israelite literature and culture; biblical ethics with a special focus on war in the Hebrew Bible; and issues pertaining to the body and gender in biblical literature. Her most recent books are *Judges: A Commentary* (Westminster John Knox, 2008) and *'My Brother Esau Is a Hairy Man': Hair and Identity in Ancient Israel* (Oxford University Press, 2008). Her new project deals with personal religion in the Second Temple period.

Herbert Niehr studied Catholic Theology and Ancient Near Eastern languages at the universities of Bonn and Würzburg. Since 1992 he has been Professor of Biblical Introduction and History of the Biblical Period at the University of Tübingen. He is also a Professor in the Department of Ancient Studies at the University of Stellenbosch. His research focuses on the languages and religions of West Semitic cultures in the Ancient Near East. Among his publications are *Der höchste Gott* (de Gruyter, 1990), *Religionen in Israels Umwelt* (Echter, 1998) and *Ba'alšamem* (Peeters, 2003).

Francesca Stavrakopoulou is Senior Lecturer in Hebrew Bible in the University of Exeter. Her research focuses primarily on ancient Israelite and Judahite religions and biblical portrayals of the religious past. She is the author of *King Manasseh and Child Sacrifice: Biblical Distortions of Historical Realities* (de Gruyter, 2004) and *Land of Our Fathers: The Roles of Ancestor Veneration in Biblical Land Claims* (T&T Clark, forthcoming). She is also co-editor of the Biblical Refigurations series (Oxford University Press).

Nicolas Wyatt is Emeritus Professor of Ancient Near Eastern Religions in the University of Edinburgh. He taught at the Universities of Glasgow and Edinburgh, with briefer stints at Stirling, Ibadan, and as visiting reader at the EPHE (Ecole Pratique des Hautes Etudes) in Paris. His research has been mostly devoted to the interface between Ugaritic and biblical studies, and in particular to the themes of cosmology, mythology and royal ideology. His authored books include *Myths of Power* (Ugarit-Verlag, 1996), *Religious Texts from Ugarit* (Sheffield Academic Press, 1998), '*There's Such Divinity Doth Hedge a King*' (Ashgate, 2005) and *The Mythic Mind* (Equinox, 2005), and he co-edited *Ugarit, Religion and Culture* (Ugarit-Verlag, 1996) and the *Handbook of Ugaritic Studies* (Brill, 1999).

Chapter 1

Introduction: Religious Diversity in Ancient Israel and Judah

Francesca Stavrakopoulou and John Barton

Scholarly perceptions of ancient Israelite and Judahite religions have changed considerably in recent years. Indeed, most scholars of generations past would have thought it unusual, and perhaps even confusing or misguided, to distinguish between the religions of Israel *and* Judah, as though in essence the two might be considered somewhat distinct. And it is only in the last decade or so that references to the religions of these ancient societies have become a more common characteristic of scholarly discourse about Israel and Judah.[1] This deliberate pluralization acknowledges that 'religion' is not uniform but pluriform, and can vary from place to place – whether temple, tomb or home – and within and among different groups of people – from rural households to royal households, from garrison troops to women's local networks. Indeed, it is now understood that the religious worlds of these groups were likely populated by different combinations of various deities and divine beings, such as Yhwh, Asherah, Baal, specialized craft deities and household ancestors (cf. van der Toorn, Becking and van der Horst 1999). Moreover, despite certain shared features, there was likely notable diversity across various cults, so that, for example, the Yhwh worshipped in the temple in Samaria was not the same deity as the Yhwh worshipped in the Jerusalem temple (which suggests that while it is now quite usual to speak of polytheism in ancient Israel and Judah, it is also appropriate to speak more specifically of poly-Yahwism).

These changing scholarly perceptions thus reflect a now widespread recognition that the biblical presentation of the religious past is often at odds with the likely religious realities of ancient Israel and Judah. But they also attest to an increasingly nuanced engagement with the idea that – whatever else they may be – religious beliefs and practices are social and cultural activities. Put crudely, people 'do' religion, and religion cannot be divorced from those 'doing' it. Accordingly, scholarly reconstructions of ancient Israelite and Judahite religions have become much more context-specific in dealing with the social dynamics and locations of religious activity, so that in paying closer attention to the many diversities and varieties inherent within and among different social groups (such as royal households, agrarian families, or local mantic specialists), the diversities and varieties of religious expression within a given society are more readily acknowledged, addressed and understood.

This volume seeks to explore some of these diversities by drawing together specialists in the field to examine and analyse key aspects of religious diversity in ancient Israel

---

1.   Consider, for example, the plural forms employed in the volume titles of Edelman 1995, Zevit 2001 and Hess 2007.

and Judah. The book falls into four sections. The first focuses on conceptual diversities. It seeks to deconstruct persistent and misleading assumptions about Israelite and Judahite religions and reconstructs Israelite and Judahite perceptions of the nature of the religious world. The second section deals with socio-religious diversities. It examines some of the varied social contexts of Israelites and Judahites, exploring the relationship between worshippers' social locations and their perceptions and experiences of the divine. The third section deals with geographical diversities. It seeks to understand how geographical distinctions may engender certain characteristics within religious practice and the extent to which certain shared aspects of Israelite and Judahite religions might be limited by their geographical reach. The last section reflects upon the complex relationship between the Hebrew Bible and the religious past it seeks to portray. Underpinning each essay in this volume is a shared concern to explore the ways in which worshippers' socio-cultural contexts shape and colour their religious beliefs and practices, and to assess the roles, benefits and limitations of the Hebrew Bible in reconstructing and understanding ancient Israelite and Judahite religions.

This last point is an important one. Scholars frequently wrestle with the problems inherent in using the Hebrew Bible for historical reconstruction, for it is often recognized that the biblical literature is both selective and ideological in telling its story of Israel and Judah. Indeed, for many generations now, biblical scholars have looked to the material remains not only of these cultures, but of other ancient West Asian/Near Eastern cultures in order to piece together a more historically reliable portrait of the past. In dealing more specifically with the religious beliefs and practices of Israel and Judah, scholars have similarly contextualized and critiqued biblical portrayals of religious activity in the light of archaeological and cross-cultural comparative evidence. Recent examples of this important work include the volumes by Ackerman (1992), Keel and Uehlinger (1998), Zevit (2001) and Smith (2001, 2002), and those edited by Dietrich and Klopfenstein (1994), Edelman (1995), van der Toorn (1997), Gittlen (2002), Beckman and Lewis (2006) and del Olmo Lete (2008). To varying degrees, these studies have shown that the Hebrew Bible's imaging of what it presents as religious norms is at best particularized, and at worst highly unreliable.

As outlined above, the present volume takes seriously the *social* contexts and dynamics of religious beliefs and practices, which can go a considerable way in accounting for some of the key diversities evident in Israelite and Judahite religions. Many of the contributions here thus build upon work undertaken by biblical scholars engaging with social-scientific perspectives on religious activity and its socio-cultural frames. These include important studies by Jay (1992), Albertz (1994), van der Toorn (1996, 1997), Niditch (1997), Olyan (2000, 2004) and Meyers (2005), and the excellent volume edited by Bodel and Olyan (2008). Each of these works demonstrates the importance of considering not only the participants involved in (or excluded from) a particular ritual or practice, but also the spatial and temporal contexts of religious activities, which also play a crucial role in shaping and reflecting religious preferences.

Understanding the religious culture of any ancient society is a difficult task, not only because of the limitations in the nature and content of literary accounts and material remains of societies long since past, but also because of the researcher's own perceptions of his or her cultural distance from, or nearness to, the chosen subject. One of the benefits of an edited collection of this sort is that it brings together a variety of different perspectives. Thus, while this volume is intended to be neither comprehensive nor exhaustive in its exploration of religious diversities in ancient Israel and Judah, it is hoped that its own diversities in foci and opinions will prove stimulating and rewarding to its readers, prompting further enquiry.

One of the points on which several of our contributors are agreed is that it is important not to oversimplify the range of diversity in the beliefs and practices of ancient Israel and Judah. Indeed, the three chapters in Part I, 'Conceptual Diversities', emphasize how complex it can be. Susan Niditch takes as an example of this the accounts of direct experience of the divine found in the Hebrew Bible. A later idea of orthodox Judaism as focused on correct praxis, with a consequent downplaying of mystical experience, can easily lead one to imagine that accounts of dreams, visions and visits to the land of the dead belong exclusively to 'popular' religion, frowned on by the representatives of the 'official' cult. But, as Niditch shows, the boundaries between 'popular' and 'official' religion are highly porous on this issue throughout the period covered by the Hebrew Bible. All sorts of people are portrayed as having direct visions of God or as undergoing the more oblique experience of coded, symbolic dreams and showings. And contact with the dead, though forbidden by a few elite groups, was obviously a widely shared interest: everyone needed to ensure, for example, that their parents had a proper burial and so could rest in Sheol rather than wander on earth. The story of Saul at Endor does indeed say that Saul had banned the practice of communing with the dead, but it illustrates at the same time just how far everyone believed that such communing was possible, and efficacious in revealing the future. The seemingly weird and paranormal were part of life for a wide range of people, not restricted to 'popular' religious experience. We have diversity, but not a dichotomy.

Herbert Niehr demolishes another widely believed dichotomy, between the religion of 'Canaan' and that of 'Israel'. Traditionally Israelite religion is understood as a pure monotheistic faith which, on the entry of the tribes into Canaan, became corrupted by the abominable fertility cults of the Canaanites. Recent scholarship has shown that the Israelites were in any case Canaanites themselves, and it has also demonstrated that their religion was simply a subset of West Semitic religion more generally. Something distinctive did eventually emerge, the monotheism that is the ancestor of Judaism, Christianity and Islam. But this is a late arrival (no earlier than the sixth century BCE). In earlier times Israelites and Judahites were polytheists like any other Canaanites and worshipped Yhwh as a god of weather and of fertility. 'The Canaanites' as a group quite distinct from 'Israel' is an artificial construct, an invented 'other' that serves as a foil for all that is supposed to be good and noble in Israelite religion. So there is great diversity within the religious customs of the land of Canaan, but it cannot be mapped accurately in terms of a simple Israelite/Canaanite dichotomy.

Francesca Stavrakopoulou, like Niditch, focuses on the alleged distinction between 'official' and 'popular' religious practice as it affects especially death cults and the worship of goddesses. These are often understood, respectively, as examples of 'folk' religion and the religion of women, but, as she shows, both are amply attested for all strata of the population. Treating them as the religion of marginalized people (the 'common folk' and women) results not from actual study of the archaeological and textual evidence but from a set of assumptions that derive from the later monotheistic 'religions of the book', in which there is to be no dealing with female deities or dead ancestors. Significantly, these assumptions have been reinforced by 'modernist' concerns to separate the dead from the living and to reject anything that smacks of a religion of 'nature'. But to ancient Israelites and Judahites the world of the living and the dead formed a continuum, so that communication could take place across the boundaries of embodied life, while it was taken for granted at all levels of society that the divine realm had both male and female elements. It was not 'elite' or 'official' religion that sought to undermine these assumptions, but the later work of the scribes who produced the Hebrew Bible in its finished form, and these should not be assumed to be continuous with the upper classes of historical Israel and Judah. The perceived dichotomy between 'official' and 'popular' religions is arguably a false one.

The second section, 'Socio-Religious Diversities', again seeks to demonstrate that the religions of ancient Israel and Judah can best be understood as a series of spectra, rather than in terms of either/or distinctions. Nicolas Wyatt examines royal religion in Judah, which was in some ways distinct from the religion of the average person, yet permeated the wider culture. He rejects the idea that Judahite conceptions of monarchy were distinctive within the ancient Near Eastern context, arguing for close resemblances to the monarchic ideology of Ugarit in particular. If the cult of the dead was omnipresent in the Hebrew kingdoms, the cult of dead kings was a crucial element in Judahite worship. And once again the centrality of women can be seen in the role of the *gĕbîrâ*, often the queen mother, who was the source of legitimate dynastic succession, and far more important than the patriarchalized and Deuteronomized Hebrew Bible now allows. The suggestion that monarchy was an alien imposition on Israelite and Judahite culture is quite mistaken: it belongs to the ideology of the Deuteronomists who in this as in other things wanted to portray 'Israel' as a wholly distinctive kind of nation.

Where cultic sites are concerned, the Deuteronomists have again influenced all subsequent generations by asserting that there was essentially only one legitimate sanctuary for Yhwh, by implication the temple in Jerusalem. In fact this was in origin simply a royal chapel: the worship of the vast majority of the population of the two kingdoms took place at other locations, including people's homes, tombs and local shrines or 'high places' (*bāmôt*), at which other gods than Yhwh were also widely worshipped. Diana Edelman points to the extensive biblical evidence for the existence of many shrines, and also surveys the archaeological evidence for Israelite and Judahite complexes for worship other than the Jerusalem temple. Such complexes include shrines in fortresses and at trade centres (most famously, the shrine at Kuntillet 'Ajrud) as well as temples in the everyday sense of the word. One of the markers of worship centres tends to be the presence of figurines, suggesting that imageless worship is a theoretical requirement of the Hebrew Bible rather than a reflection of practice on the ground in ancient Judah and Israel. The idea that any variation from worship concentrated at the single central sanctuary represented apostasy from Yhwh stems from a small coterie within Judah, the Deuteronomists, and does not correspond to what was believed by most people, though it has had an unfortunate effect on most later readers of the Bible: 'there is,' Edelman writes, 'an understandable tendency to depict in the mind's eye the other holy sites and complexes mentioned as being contemporaneous with the temple in Jerusalem as minor, insignificant outlying institutions of dubious pedigree'.

The presence of so many places for worship suggests that it ought in principle to be possible to contrast the religion of small rural sanctuaries with the religious life of cities such as Jerusalem and Samaria. But Philip Davies shows that this is one area of diversity in which evidence is largely lacking: the Hebrew Bible presents almost entirely an urban view, being written by scribes in cities – almost exclusively, indeed, in Jerusalem. Where rural religion is mentioned, we get an urbanite's view of it. There must have been differences between the city and the countryside where religious practice is concerned, but we do not know what they were. What this does not authorize us to do is to generalize from the evidence we have about Jerusalem, as though its urban religion was typical of the country as a whole. From the Psalms, for example, we might think that the religion of Judah was greatly focused on divine kingship, but this may well be an accidental impression deriving from the fact that the Psalms are liturgical texts from the royal sanctuary, and may be wholly atypical of the religion of the people at large.

If the Jerusalem cult was not representative of the religion of other sanctuaries, it was also only a part of religious practice in that it was a set of public and civic rites; and Carol Meyers points out that there must also have been religious practices that concerned people in their homes, away from sanctuaries whether central or local. Such practices, indeed, may underlie the great central liturgies portrayed in the Hebrew Bible, having been transferred from the home to the public shrine – a 'bottom-up' origin for grand public religious observance. (The Passover, in origin a household observance, was apparently thus elevated into a public rite – later, of course, to revert to the domestic domain.) The primary evidence for household religion is archaeological, but the biblical text also offers a measure of information, and both sources suggest that the religion of the Israelite or Judahite household had two primary foci: the cycles of time (daily, weekly, monthly), connected to the agricultural year, and the cycles of human life – rites of passage, and care for the dead. The last is yet another area where later 'official' religion opposed immemorial custom in forbidding various mourning rites, which however surely continued unabated in most households. A major difficulty in studying the variety of household rituals is dating: we can pinpoint many rites as having been practised in 'ancient Israel', but tracing development over time is extremely hard. Later Jewish domestic life is strongly characterized by the food laws, for example, and though these certainly go back into 'biblical times' we do not know exactly when they originated or how they developed.

Can we move to an even more limited level than that of the single household, and speak of the piety or religious practice of the individual? Rainer Albertz argues that there is evidence for the religious life of individual persons, and that it is notably uncoordinated with the salient features of the so-called 'national' religion portrayed in the Hebrew Bible. Individual psalms, for example, hardly mention the great 'acts of God' such as the Exodus or the giving of the Land, and concentrate rather on salvation and blessing as known or sought in the personal life of the worshipper, while the wealth of theophoric names concentrate on the divine care for the individual being named. Personal piety was by no means always directed to Yhwh – indeed, the biblical prophets attest that people often prayed to other gods, perhaps in some cases local or household gods, seeing Yhwh as the god of the nation rather than of the individual. (Albertz points out, however, that no theophoric names occur with Asherah or any other goddess as an element – a feature Israel and Judah share with some of their neighbours, including the Moabites, Ammonites and Aramaeans.) Evidence of personal piety can also be found in wisdom collections, especially Proverbs, which also has scarcely anything to say about the 'national' religion. Biblical scholarship has sometimes seen the individual as merely part of a larger collectivity, and has thought it anachronistic to see him or her as having a life apart from the group; but the evidence for individual piety tends in the opposite direction, suggesting that many individuals had a distinctive kind of religious belief and practice, radically different from the national cult and focused on living a good life and trusting in divine power in times of crisis. Archaeology supports this picture, with amulets attesting to the belief in divine aid in trouble and the many figurines of nude women holding their breasts mediating prayers to the divine realm to ensure conception and safe delivery. It is only after the Exile that we can talk of 'piety' developing into 'theology', as religious conceptuality becomes overt in biblical books such as Job and Ecclesiastes.

The third type of diversity addressed in this book is geographical, and on this there are two essays. Jeremy Hutton discusses the different perspectives on religion in the north and south of Palestine and in Transjordan. He argues that even this is over-simple: religion in the ancient cultures of Palestine is a set of micro-religions. But the threefold division does correspond to genuine family likenesses within these broad areas. For example, domestic use of altars seems to have been less common in the south (Judah) than in the other two areas, suggesting a higher degree of dominance by so-called 'official' religion there, at least in some periods; while a higher proportion of theophoric names with the element *ba'al* in the north may imply – as the biblical text itself suggests – that Israelites were more likely than Judahites to worship deities with Baal-names, perhaps because of their contiguity to the Aramaeans. But we must exercise great care in using biblical sources: the Deuteronomists have been at work everywhere, and have often smoothed out local diversity in favour of their 'normative' version of Yahwism, and given tendentious interpretations of features such as the cult of the 'calves' (really bulls) at northern shrines as indications of apostasy from Yhwh. Hutton offers a full discussion of Transjordanian religious practice: the evidence is scanty (the finds at Deir 'Alla represent the major material for reconstruction), and there are some parallels between religions here and in Israel and Judah. But there is also reason to think that there were distinct differences from the situation in both Israel and Judah. For example, there was a plethora of minor deities, 'shaddays', and the name Yhwh does not occur, though El does. It is unclear whether the peoples of Transjordan should be seen as also 'Israelites' in some sense – indeed, the question may not be a real one. But the region certainly shows that there was variety in the religious practices of Palestine in 'biblical' times.

Lester Grabbe then examines evidence for the worship of Yhwh outside the areas covered by the kingdoms of Israel and Judah. He finds no convincing evidence that Yhwh was worshipped anywhere before the first millennium BCE: alleged occurrences in the Ebla and Ugaritic texts are improbable. But Yhwh certainly continued to be worshipped by the Jewish diaspora communities that arose in the Neo-Babylonian, Persian and Greek periods, both in Mesopotamia and in Egypt, and probably also in Idumaea. Yhwh was exclusively the God of Israel and Judah and continued to be recognized only by the descendants of these peoples: he was never 'exported' to other ethnic groups. So there is a limit to the geographical variety of Yhwh religion.

The book closes with a postscript by John Barton, who reflects on the nature of the diversities raised in this volume and its implications for our understanding of the Hebrew Bible's portrait of the religious past. While the studies of diversity in the present book might be perceived by some readers as too provocative a challenge to biblical accounts, the Hebrew Bible itself also depicts the religions of Israel and Judah as diverse and changing beliefs and practices. In particular, Barton points to certain aspects of religious diversity only lightly touched on by other contributors but heavily emphasized in the biblical literature: expressions of monolatrous and monotheistic beliefs, and the elevation and veneration of the written word.

As Barton points out, diversity need not imply a set of bipolar contrasts, but a spectrum of infinite variety. It is hoped that this volume will go some way to better understanding just a handful of religious diversities in ancient Israel and Judah.

Bibliography

Ackerman, S.
1992 *Under Every Green Tree: Popular Religion in Sixth-Century Judah* (HSM 46; Atlanta, GA: Scholars Press).

Albertz, R.
1994 *A History of Israelite Religion in the Old Testament Period* (2 vols; trans. J. Bowden. OTL; London: SCM Press).

Beckman, G.M. and T.J. Lewis (eds)
2006 *Text, Artifact, and Image: Revealing Ancient Israelite Religion* (BJS 346; Providence, RI: Brown University).

Bodel, J. and S.M. Olyan (eds)
2008 *Household and Family Religion in Antiquity* (Oxford: Blackwell).

Dietrich, W. and M.A. Klopfenstein (eds)
1994 *Ein Gott allein? JHWH-Verehrung und biblischer Monotheismus im Kontext der israelitischen und altorientalischen Religionsgeschichte* (OBO 139; Fribourg: Universitätsverlag; Göttingen: Vandenhoeck & Ruprecht).

Edelman, D.V. (ed.)
1995 *The Triumph of Elohim: From Yahwisms to Judaisms* (CBET 13; Kampen: Kok Pharos).

Gittlen, B.M. (ed.)
2002 *Sacred Time, Sacred Place: Archaeology and the Religion of Israel* (Winona Lake, IN: Eisenbrauns).

Hess, R.
2007 *Israelite Religions: An Archaeological and Biblical Survey* (Grand Rapids, MI: Baker Academic).

Jay, N.
1992 *Throughout Your Generations Forever: Sacrifice, Religion, and Paternity* (Chicago, IL: University of Chicago Press).

Keel, O. and C. Uehlinger (eds)
1998 *Gods, Goddesses, and Images of God in Ancient Israel* (trans. T.H. Trapp. Edinburgh: T&T Clark).

Meyers, C.L.
2005 *Households and Holiness: The Religious Culture of Israelite Women* (Facets; Minneapolis, MN: Fortress Press).

Niditch, S.
1997 *Ancient Israelite Religion* (Oxford and New York, NY: Oxford University Press).

Olmo Lete, G. del (ed.)
2008 *Mythologie et religion des Sémites Occidentaux* (2 vols; OLA 162; Leuven: Peeters).

Olyan, S.M.
2000 *Rites and Rank: Hierarchy in Biblical Representations of Cult* (Princeton, NJ: Princeton University Press).
2004 *Biblical Mourning: Ritual and Social Dimensions* (Oxford and New York, NY: Oxford University Press).

Smith, M.S.
2001   *The Origins of Biblical Monotheism: Israel's Polytheistic Background and the Ugaritic Texts* (Oxford and New York, NY: Oxford University Press).
2002   *The Early History of God: Yahweh and the Other Deities in Ancient Israel* (2nd edn; Grand Rapids, MI: Eerdmans).

Toorn, K. van der
1996   *Family Religion in Babylonia, Syria and Israel: Continuity and Change in the Forms of Religious Life* (SHCANE 7; Leiden: Brill).
1997   (ed.), *The Image and the Book: Iconic Cults, Aniconism, and the Rise of Book Religion in Israel and the Ancient Near East* (CBET 21; Leuven: Peeters).

Toorn, K. van der, B. Becking and P.W. van der Horst (eds)
1999   *Dictionary of Deities and Demons in the Bible* (2nd extensively rev. edn; Leiden: Brill).

Zevit, Z.
2001   *The Religions of Ancient Israel: A Synthesis of Parallactic Approaches* (London and New York, NY: Continuum).

PART I

CONCEPTUAL DIVERSITIES

Chapter 2

EXPERIENCING THE DIVINE: HEAVENLY VISITS, EARTHLY
ENCOUNTERS AND THE LAND OF THE DEAD

Susan Niditch

Building on the work of Rudolph Otto (1958) who explores the nature of 'the numi-
nous', the electric, evocative and transformative presence of the divine, Ninian Smart
(1983: 8, 62–78) describes 'the experiential dimension' of religion: the ways in which
human beings experience the divine on emotional, visceral and intellectual planes.
Judaism and its ancient precursors in biblical tradition are sometimes described as
pragmatic, this-worldly in orientation, concerned with behaviour and with what Smart
would call the ethical dimension of religious orientation. The experiential, however,
shimmers in the writings of the Hebrew Bible and is the focus of this chapter on religious diversity in ancient Israel and Judah. Three sets of biblical texts provide case
studies: descriptions of visits to God's realm; reports of symbolic visions; and descriptions of the underworld, Sheol, and references to appearances of the dead on earth.
These manifestations of the experiential dimension reflect patterns and changes in
Israelite and Judahite social, political and intellectual history as well as aesthetic and
theological developments. They testify to the richness and diversity of the tradition
even while serving as proof of a remarkable wholeness and continuity that is the mark
of traditional-style cultures and their literatures.

Popular Religion

As Susan Ackerman noted in her 1992 monograph on popular religion in sixth-century
BCE Judah, it has long been axiomatic in biblical studies to draw a sharp contrast
between the religion of the commoners and the religion of the elite, a position which
Ackerman deftly contests (1992: 1–3, 213–17). Similarly problematical is a related
dichotomy between 'official' and 'unofficial' religion. It might be suggested, for
example, that during the Judahite monarchy, the official Jerusalem cult was centralized whereas other sacred spaces exemplified unofficial religion or that institutional
religion professed by priestly sources was strongly aniconic whereas unofficial or
popular religion included the use of icons. Various biblical polemics have been seen
as condemnations of popular religious practices viewed as renegade by mainstream
or official biblical writers. As Ackerman (1992), Peter Brown (1981: 19), Arnaldo
Momigliano (1971: 18), Lester Grabbe (2004: 253) and others have noted, however,
the boundary between official and unofficial, popular and institutional, vulgar and
elite is a porous and artificial one (see Chapter 4 in this volume). To suggest a clear
demarcation is to deny the overlap, synergy and diversity in modes of ancient Israelite

religious expression. Then as now, popular and even peripheral practices influence and inform 'central' ritual while elites or representatives of central religious leadership in turn do influence and no doubt participate in popular belief and practice. Biblical polemics may well reveal the views of the few, preservers of particular biblical texts. Israelite religion as lived, however, may have included the very beliefs and behaviours condemned by the writers. By the same token, many key features of worldview and practice were no doubt shared by Israelites, rural and urban, commoners and aristocrats, those outside of the power structure and political insiders.

Individual and Cultural, Unique and Formulaic

Immersion into the realm of the divine, and descriptions of it, suggest a paradox. On the one hand they reflect unique, individual, powerful experience. On the other, they reflect a culturally shared conception of what such religious experiences entail and connote. Reports of visions or descriptions of the land of the dead reveal and reinforce socially embraced expectations concerning the otherworldly. Moreover imagery, events and responses are expressed in conventionalized or formulaic language. They are products of culture and of tradition.

In exploring religious symbols, Gananath Obeyesekere (1981) emphasizes the complex ways in which the personal intertwines with the public and the cultural. For the female mystic he interviewed in Sri Lanka, her long matted hair is 'personal' and has to do with that person's life experience, her 'anxieties', 'psychology', and 'idiosyncrasies' (1981: 7, 37, 40). Social context, however, is also critical to the meaning of the hair; were there not certain assumptions and expectations concerning hairstyle in Sri Lanka, where the mystic has lived and developed, her personal response to her own hair might differ considerably (1981: 11–12).

The workings of religious symbols, patterns and language thus reveal an interplay between the personal and the socio-cultural. A symbol such as the divine throne, an image of the deity or an angel, a chain of events such as an initiation process, and the words in which these may be described by the seer as well as the words he or she may hear in the vision all have personal meaning. They are mediated through individual consciousness, emotions and life-experience. Nevertheless, from the language itself to imagery and constellations of motifs, the individual experience is also mediated through culture and tradition.

When exploring a biblical vision text, for example, rich in the experiential, we do well to ask about the emotional and personal experience of the seer as well as the cultural media that make such an experience believable to him and to the audience that receives his report. This suggestion raises other related questions. Did ancient Israelites believe in the possibility of vision experiences? Did the writers and receivers of vision reports consider them to be records of 'real' visionary events or staged media used to frame certain kinds of meanings and messages? One cannot be certain about the answer to these questions, but believability is not incompatible with conventions of content, language and plot (see Brakke, Satlow and Weitzman 2005b: 5; Olyan 2005: 40–41).

Stephen T. Katz's comments (1983) on the new and yet derivative aspects of mystical experiences and reports provide a relevant parallel. On the one hand the mystical experience can be viewed as radical, powerfully personal and a challenge to religion as usual. On the other hand, in a rather conservative way, tradition influences the contents and form of the mystical experience and the very language in which it is described (Katz 1983: 5–6). Indeed many mystics study canonical literature whose form and content makes its way into mystical experience. In a largely oral culture in which texts as texts are not studied, the oral tradition has an equally strong if not stronger influence on what a vision is meant to be or upon the way the underworld looks. John Miles Foley (1991) has pointed to the 'immanently referential' quality of language and experience in traditional societies in which the deity looks a certain way, in which certain phrases evoke certain emotional responses, and in which the larger tradition bears upon any smaller piece of it that is employed or recreated. Thus as we trace some of the recurring literary forms in which these visions are preserved, we will point to specific, individual and sometimes innovative scenes and messages that are nevertheless clothed in the imagery, the meaning-world, and the linguistic expectations of the visionary tradition.

Divining the Otherworldly: Beginning with Dreams

The closest most of us come to experiencing visions of the otherworldly in our daily lives may be in dreaming. Even for contemporary, rationalistic post-Freudians, dreams can be transformative experiences that immerse the dreamer into an alternative reality that may shed light upon and influence waking experience. In the cultures of the ancient Near East, dreams were accorded varying degrees of respect as divinatory and prophetic media. As noted with religious symbols, the contents of dreams are rooted in individual life experience, in the very nature of human psychology and in the dreamer's culture. Symbols and scenes recur in people's dreams allowing ancient scholars of Assyria, Egypt and elsewhere to prepare lists of dream omens so that the interpretation of dreams became a divinatory science, as were the reading of flight patterns of birds, the entrails of animals and the shapes of rising smoke (see Niditch 1980: 15–16). Specific techniques of interpretation include idea association and word association, as dream interpretation shares a border with the later Rabbinic activity of Midrash whereby the words and imagery of biblical texts provide the medium to be decoded. One sees glimpses of this mantic activity in tales of Joseph, a wise man who himself has dreams that relate to his and his family's future and who has the ability to interpret the dreams of others. In the beautifully composed *Bildungsroman* about Joseph in Genesis, dreams have an important narrative function, foreshadowing the hero's career and leading directly to his elevation as Pharaoh's vizier and saviour of his own people. To have and understand dreams is presented as positive, a sign of God-sent wisdom connoting a special connection with the deity who makes possible both the dreams and the capacity to interpret them. This set of stories is in the 'official' canon and also reflects general beliefs about the efficacy and usefulness of dreams in popular cultures. Abraham, another venerable patriarch, is pictured in Genesis to receive God-sent messages and visions in a divinely induced deep sleep, a trance-like state (14.12). Jacob receives important information from God via dreams (Gen. 28.12; 46.2). Positive assessments of dreams as having prophetic content and indicating communication with the deity are, however, not uniform in Hebrew Scriptures. And as one might expect, dreams share a conceptual border with visions that are received in a waking state, paranormal experiences or events. Both mark a boundary between reality and meta-reality, the earthly and the divine, and both are sudden intrusions into the mundane, uncontrollable in content, often richly symbolic in meaning, and open to interpretation. A thread of biblical texts belittles or condemns dreamers, dream interpreters and visions. Attitudes to visual experiences of the otherworldly, in fact, reveal interesting ambivalences and tensions among biblical writers.

Numbers 12.6-8 serves in context as propaganda in favour of Mosaic Levitical power and over against both Aaronides and priestly groups claiming descent from Miriam, the female Levitical sibling. A message about leadership intertwines with one about forms of revelation. Speaking 'face to face', as God does with Moses in direct word oracles, is preferable to other forms of divine communication, that is, messages mediated by dreams and visions, visual rather than auditory media. Implicitly, overt messages are preferable to symbolic content, to 'riddles' (literally that which is turned aside or indirect, dark speech), visions and dreams, which are grouped together as media that need to be interpreted to be understood. The direct speech mode of experiencing the divine dominates in the preserved oracles of the so-called classical prophets who speak in richly formulaic speech and patterns of content. Dreams and visions, however, are not entirely rejected. Warnings to beware of these visual forms of divine communication suggest, in fact, their cultural vibrancy and currency throughout the history of Israel and Judah. Criticisms are levelled by biblical writers against the improper use of dreams and visions, singling out those whose visions and dreams reveal only their own imagination or mind, literally their 'heart' rather than the message of God (Jer. 23.16; Ezek. 13.2, 17). False seers produce vapour or delude (NRSV Jer. 23.16). Their message is 'wrong', that is, it does not reflect the critic's own view of God's wishes (Jer. 27.9). Their dreams misinform: 'In falsehood they prophecy to you in my name. I did not send them' (Jer. 29.8; see also Ezek. 13.6, 7).

Deuteronomy 13.2, 4, 6 equates the prophet with the dreamer. If this person, prophet or diviner of dreams, tempts you to go after other gods, you must not follow. These dreamers and prophets are deserving of death for speaking treason (13.6), but all depends on the content of the dream and its application. The scene in 1 Kgs 22.19-23 underscores some of these issues in true and false prophecy as they emerge in a vision experience. The spectrum that spans the official and the unofficial, the individual and the cultural, and the unique and the formulaic is also at play in this passage, an example of the visit to the divine council, a case study in experiencing the divine.

Experiencing the Divine Council

One important set of biblical material dealing with the experiential dimension describes the physical presence of human beings inside the divine court or hall. Divine council scenes are common stock in the epic literature of the ancient Mediterranean world. In its most frequent form, the chief deity who makes decisions regarding groups or individuals, war and peace, is surrounded by fellow celestial beings, including his advisors and sometimes his adversaries or rivals. This cross-cultural constellation of motifs, including the divine king-like figure, his retainers and their conversation/actions, is specified in a prophetic medium. The seer, a human being, is transported to the heavenly realm where he observes the scene or hears the conversation and often participates himself in the action. Isaiah 6, Ezekiel 1-3 and Daniel 7 likely offer a chronological trajectory from the eighth to the second centuries BCE. 1 Kings 22 and Exodus 24 are more difficult to date, but it does seem clear that all of these texts offer a shared type; that greater complexity comes to characterize the style of datable versions; and that certain variations and trends emerge in views of the deity and the experience of the seer or human participant.

The simplest (though not necessarily earliest) version is found in Exod. 24.9-11 in which Moses, Aaron, Nadab, Abihu and 70 of the elders ascend to the divine realm after the escape from Egypt and the formative scene at Sinai. Exodus 24.9-11 alludes to a banquet, an appropriate motif to conclude the victory-enthronement pattern that characterizes the escape from Egypt, the defeat of the Egyptian enemy, and the enthronement on the mountain, 'God's sanctuary', as described poetically in Exodus 15. This same pattern is found in ancient Near Eastern epic creation texts, such as the Mesopotamian *Enuma elish* and the Ugaritic tale of Baal and Anat in which the enemy is chaos or death and the new order is celebrated by a gathering of deities and feasting. In Exodus 24, the world of God is 'above' – one ascends (24.9). The deity is visible – he has feet (24.10) – and the human guests behold him. The seeing is described in two verbs (24.10, 11), one of which, *ḥzh*, is related to an ancient term for prophet as suggested by the biblical author at 1 Sam. 9.9. The environment appears to be palpable if more luminously pure than anything on earth – 'like the image of sapphire tile-work', like the 'very substance of heaven' (24.10). A feast is provided with eating and drinking as the guests commune with God. Shared, communal eating is an important symbolic representation of a relationship. The deity, the powerful warrior seen in the electric volcanic presence at Sinai where the people and even ritually pure priests are warned to keep their distance lest he lash out against them, here welcomes the feasters without warning. The author emphasizes that God does not lay a hand upon them although they are in his very realm. Indeed no supra-mundane counsellors are present. Human beings play the role of those invited to dine at God's table, but this is no randomly selected set of people; they are leaders, people of inherited status. The image and role of the elites, Levites and elders, is thereby asserted and enhanced. Such establishment authors may well lie behind this particular use of the traditional scene.

The divine council appears again in 1 Kgs 22.19-23 in a more theatrical version. An auditory as well as visual dimension is included, and the narrator is not the anonymous biblical voice but the prophet himself who is lifted into the scene of the deity surrounded by heavenly beings and who reports what he observes. This version of the type as contextualized points to the sliding scale between central and peripheral, establishment and anti-establishment (see Wilson 1980) as it emerges in descriptions of the experiential.

The author pictures a contest between royal prophets, who predict victory and urge the Israelite king, Ahab, and his Judahite ally, Jehoshaphat, to go to war against the Aramaeans, and the outsider Micaiah who predicts military failure. Micaiah establishes his divinatory credentials by revealing an experience of the divine council in which he learns about the inevitable defeat. The experiential thus validates his message. The council scene is clearly imagined to be culturally recognizable and believable by all who hear the report; it is capable of providing spiritual capital and has efficacy. There is no bifurcation between 'popular religion' and 'official religion'. Ahab at first resists hearing from the anti-establishment prophet Micaiah, and as the king had feared, the scene provides the prophet's *bona fides*. He is a 'fly on the wall' who observes the archetypal king-deity enthroned, surrounded by his heavenly courtiers, the hosts or army of heaven to his right and left. The spirits speak, revealing the divine plan to entice Ahab to battle via a lying spirit placed in the mouth of the king's prophets in order to kill him. The message of the vision suggests that the prophets such as Zedekiah, whom Ahab trusts and wants to believe, are wrong. It is Micaiah's vision experience that both accurately predicts the future and in a sympathetically magical way helps to bring it about. As in the case of dreams and visions, not all prophecies are accurate. God himself may send miscues in order to fulfil his larger purpose. While validating the role of the peripheral prophet Micaiah whom the royal leaderships hates, the vision as a whole casts doubt on the prophetic enterprise itself. There is no sure way to know the will of God. The connection with the divine realm is thus always tenuous and fraught with uncertainty.

In Isaiah 6, the divine council experience serves as the eighth-century BCE prophet's initiation as a seer of God. This more expansive version of the scene outlined for Exodus 24 and 1 Kings 22 includes a dateline and seeing the anthropomorphized deity sitting on his throne, the ample train of his robe filling the temple or palace. His courtiers are six-winged seraphim who cover his (or their) face and feet, and can fly. They call to one another in divine song. There is loud noise, smoke and vibration, and finally a purification ceremony in which the prophet is cleansed of his sin via a burning coal to his mouth. He then volunteers to deliver the deity's message of doom. A human being not only speaks in the first person as in 1 Kings 22 and serves as a witness, but also participates in the activities of the divine realm. The divine realm and the heavenly leader evoke not only the powerful fiery forces of nature but also the architecture, dress and retinue of earthly monarchs. Human institutions thus parallel the divine while the heavenly realm gives validation to the earthly; special people are acknowledged to be immersed in the very essence of the heavenly realm. The scene is more baroque than those in Exodus 24 and 1 Kings 22, and a greater role is provided for the human participant. Pietistic and mystical experience is implicit. He has been personally transformed. These traits are even more pronounced in Ezekiel 1-3, the vision of the sixth-century BCE prophet-priest Ezekiel.

The pattern of content seen in Isaiah 6 recurs. There is a dateline (Ezek. 1.1), a rubric indicating encounter with the divine (Ezek. 1.3), a vision of the deity enthroned (Ezek. 1.26), a description of his courtiers and surroundings (Ezek. 1.4-28), a commission (Ezek. 2.1-7), and a ritual initiation or transformation (Ezek. 2.8–3.1-3). The prophet speaks in the first person. The recurring core not only reflects a shared tradition but also is flexibly adapted to suit the prophet's sixth-century BCE message and aesthetics, his individual experience and personal orientation to life. Ezekiel's use of this form reflects and shapes a particular view of the prophetic role and an attitude to the relationship between the divine realm and the human realm.

The scene is altogether more baroque than previous examples. God's chariot throne is described in mesmerizing, mystical detail, and understandably becomes an iconic focus of later Jewish mystical speculation. We see its whirling wheels with rumbling sounds, the rims full of eyes (Ezek. 1.18). The divine courtiers are similarly detailed in description, wings brushing (Ezek. 3.12-14), mysteriously moving, associated with fire and shiny materials such as burnished bronze; alternatively, the wings sound like mighty waters, thunder, an army (Ezek. 1.24). Sounds are more lushly described and less controlled than the artful singing in Isaiah. The author revels in metaphor and simile. The creatures are artful combinations of beings, dream-like and reminiscent of ancient Near Eastern iconography. God is tactile and felt (Ezek. 3.14). Emotion and the experiential dimension are enhanced (Ezek. 1.28; 2.2; 3.12-14). At the same time, the divine realm is more transcendent and distant from human cognition and capacity to comprehend. The vision reveals 'something like four living creatures' (Ezek.1.5), the wheels have 'an appearance like the gleaming of beryl' (Ezek. 1.16), above the dome over the heads of the living creatures was 'something like a throne' and above the likeness of a throne is 'something that seemed like a human form' (Ezek. 1.26). All is indefinite: something like, something having the appearance of, something that looked like. As Robert R. Wilson (1984) has noted, this very indefiniteness is central to Ezekiel's worldview. There is no direct encounter as in Exodus 24, 1 Kings 22 and Isaiah 6. Rather, the sacred realm is seen through a glass darkly; it is utterly 'Other', distant, a meta-historical reflection of reality. The prophet's immersion in this other world has a trance-like quality. God is further away from human comprehension and the son of man can only obliquely describe the ineffable quality of the heavenly realm, reporting of the encounter in the pathetic and limited medium of human perception and speech. Even so, he interacts with the scene as shown above, becoming part of this mythic reality.

This trajectory of visions of the divine council beautifully reinforces suggestions gleaned from the studies of the experiential dimension of religion explored at the opening of this chapter. The constellation of motifs is rooted in a formulaic conventionalized set of material and yet each contributor to the tradition draws upon this set even while creatively adapting it to his message as set in a particular socio-historical context. Thus we see Ezekiel reflecting the uncertainty of the period of the exile of elites such as himself; the Babylonian threat is perceived as punishment and alienation from God. God is harder to perceive than ever. The emotional dimension is enhanced, reflecting a different aesthetic than that of the eighth-century BCE prophet; a more baroque aesthetic is at play and a more personal engagement. The narrative dimension of the visionary experience is also deepened with descriptions of the place where the prophet sees the vision (Ezek. 1.1-3) and with the wind-swept, stormy setting of the scene (Ezek. 1.4). The physicality of being lifted up (Ezek. 3.12), of feeling God's hand (Ezek. 3.14), of experiencing emotions of bitterness and heat (Ezek. 3.14) all point to the way in which the tradition is rendered personal and internalized.

There is, moreover, no divide between official and unofficial religion throughout the use of this form. Exodus 24 pictures the quintessential community leaders mystically taken up, the kings of 1 Kings 22 fear and implicitly believe what the peripheral prophet Micaiah sees, the eighth-century BCE Isaiah, a central prophet with close ties to the monarchy, offers his *bona fides* in a visionary report, and Ezekiel, a priest of the Jerusalem establishment, receives the most baroque and otherworldly visions of all. The medium itself thus spans dichotomies between official and unofficial religion, unique and formulaic, personal and cultural, even while serving as a mirror of the history of ideas reflected in and shaped by Israelite literary tradition. A similar conceptual framework informs a trajectory of symbolic visions.

Symbolic Visions

An essential pattern of content characterizes each example, one rooted in a larger ancient Near Eastern tradition of divination. Texts from the eighth-century BCE Amos, the sixth-century BCE prophet Jeremiah, the late sixth-century BCE Zechariah, second-century BCE Daniel, and a host of post-biblical pseudepigraphic works include shorter and longer versions of the following motifs: an indication that a vision experience is taking place with language of seeing or showing; a description of certain objects or images; questions asked about what is seen; and a response that explicitly interprets or more obliquely comments upon the significance of sights of the opening vision. This trajectory of texts, however, offers a similar challenge to the dichotomies between official and non-official religion, elite and popular religion, discussed in connection to the divine council scenes, and also points to the spectrum from personal to cultural, unique to formulaic that encompasses and frames the broader visionary tradition. The increasingly emotive, baroque and narrative qualities of these examples of the experiential dimension point to the aesthetic and socio-historical developments seen in our first case study. A key theme is the increasing hiddenness of God with the accompanying election of the seer and his group who are uniquely and selectively allowed knowledge of the machinations of the divine realm as they apply to the future of the cosmos.

The pattern of this literary form exhibits stages from simpler to more complex. Amos 8.13 provides a good example of a simplest stage (see also Jer. 1.11-12; 24; Amos 7.7-9). God himself is the interlocutor in this version; he asks the question allowing the seer to repeat the description of the seen objects, and God himself provides the interpretation. The seen objects are simple everyday items, in this case a harvest basket or a basket of summer fruit, and the interpretation is achieved via the divinatory technique of word-play as the term for summer plays upon the word for end: 'Come has the end to my people Israel' (8.2). Repetition of language is dense in the brief format, the style economical. The interpretation of the vision helps in a sympathetically magical way to bring about its prediction; meanings are clear and the symbols have direct correspondence to their interpretation.

Zechariah 6.1-8, exemplifying a second stage in the development of this form, introduces further complexity and important nuances (see the other visions in Zechariah 1–8 for variations). Questions and answers play a role, but now an angelic interpreter is introduced. It is the more interactive seer who asks the questions. What is initially seen, moreover, is no mere mundane basket as in Amos 8.1-3 or plumb-line as in Amos 7.7-9 or basket of figs as in Jeremiah 24 but dramatic, motion-filled horse-drawn chariots coming forth from cosmic mountains of bronze (Zech. 6.1). These are interpreted to be synonymous with the four winds of the earth who 'wait upon the Lord of the whole earth', a phrase suggestive of the divine council. Whereas Isaiah 6 and Ezekiel 1–3 suggest an ascent to the divine council, Zechariah 6 suggests the descent of divine emissaries to earth. Having been given leave, they are going forth to traverse the world and set down God's spirit in the land of the north, a possible reference both to actual historical enemies and to a more mythical netherland. The seer thus describes his hopes for a rehabilitated Judahite kingdom, made possible by the defeat of Babylon and the return of elites to their land in the late sixth century BCE. He pictures himself made aware of the activities of divine servants in the cosmos, and he interacts with an angelic messenger. The relationship between symbol and meaning is integral and deeply mythological.

Daniel 7 and 8 exemplify the most ornate version of this form in Hebrew Scriptures and anticipate late usages in works such as 4 Ezra and 2 Baruch. The opening symbols of Daniel 7 provide not merely a cameo scene but a cosmogonic narrative in which dream-like beasts emerge from a troubled sea. The beasts are meta-historical representations, some of which scholars have linked to a shared stock of ancient Near Eastern astrological and other iconic symbols (see Niditch 1980: 203–4). The visionary is immersed in a divine council scene at v. 9 so that symbolic vision and divine council scene combine as anticipated in the visions of Zechariah. Once again, we see the deity on a throne. As in Ezekiel 1–3, motifs of fire and the wheels are present and the deity, pictured in Daniel as a white-haired Ancient One, reminiscent of El, head of the Canaanite pantheon (Niditch 1980: 196), sits in judgement surrounded by his thousands of minions. The beasts are interpreted to mean four kingdoms, as the author/ seer employs a stock motif found as well in ancient Persian and Greek sources (Niditch 1980: 207–9). The passage of kingdoms describes a historical trajectory leading down to the actual time of the composition. It is a fiction of the past. Daniel 7, a work of the Hellenistic era, assumes a date as if anticipating the coming of each of these historically antecedent kingdoms. It is important for our purposes to note, however, that the given interpretation of the vision's scenes of enthronement and judgement is as difficult to understand as the dream symbols; correspondences between symbol and interpretation are not simple or direct. The message of the symbolic vision is even more encoded than in Amos and Zechariah; the interpretation raises as many questions as it answers. Who exactly are the holy ones, for example? The increasingly complex symbols and difficult-to-comprehend interpretations are a filtering medium suggesting great distance between the unknown and the knowable. Meanwhile, narrative detail and emotional dimensions are greatly enhanced. The dream nuance is more explicit when compared with the brief mention of seeing in the night in Zechariah, and this nuance provides more of a setting to the narrative. The seer, moreover, expresses fear (7.15, 28; see also 8.27), as one begins to get a sense of the lead character in this narrative. The vision thus incorporates and extends a motif of theophany, an ancient experiential form.

Whereas the symbolic vision form clearly exists in its simplest version in so-called classical prophecy, it becomes a much more common medium in post-exilic material, dominating Zechariah and playing an important role in Daniel and a number of post-biblical examples of the experiential including 4 Ezra and 2 Baruch. Why and how this particular revelatory medium becomes so popular in the Second Temple period and beyond reflects changing setting, worldview and aesthetic sensibilities.

The symbolic vision emphasizes that God is more distant; visual messages must be decoded to be understood. The seer himself becomes part of the vision, the mythic realm implicit in the scene ever more present and visceral. In the latest examples we have explored from the book of Daniel, only the select few receive these visions. Rather than shout forth revelation as in the case of earlier prophets, the seer keeps the matter in his mind (Dan. 7.28) or is told explicitly to 'seal up the vision' (8.26). The message is for the saved alone, and 'Israel' is no longer perceived as a whole community who rise or fall together. The real 'Israel' who receives revelation is thus perceived as more and more circumscribed, as symbolic visions become the medium of apocalyptic.

The trauma of exile as experienced by elites, the perceived potential of God to hide himself, increasing sectarianism in Israelite self-definition, an increasing emphasis on the religious experience of individuals, and perhaps also a loss of those institutions that supported the passing down of techniques of creating poetic oracles all lead to the popularity and preservation of symbolic visions. As noted above, even the most ornate versions of the symbolic vision are not a wholly new form. They are a medium found in the writings of the prophet Amos and reach back into the phenomenon of divination practised in a variety of ancient Near Eastern cultures over a lengthy period of time. Divination itself in certain forms was the purview of learned elites, but we would be mistaken if we saw any of the visionary material shaped and preserved by scribal elites as merely reflecting their own circumscribed worldview without reference to ancient Israelite and Judahite religion as lived by ordinary people.

The texts were contoured within a written, literary tradition preserved by the few, but they testify to a host of general perceptions of the divine world and its relationship to the lives of people across the social spectrum who participate in and contribute to Israelite culture: there is a heavenly realm that parallels in many ways the sacred spaces created by human beings on earth. God is not alone in that realm but has a retinue. Seers are capable of envisioning the heavenly throne room and of experiencing divinely sent visions on earth. Some visions like the many biblical theophanies, divine appearances on earth, are non-symbolic whereas others require interpretation to be understood. The interpretative technique is related to the use of dream omens to divine the future, a specialized skill, but one about which all Israelite dreamers were no doubt aware. There is moreover a large fund of culturally shared, traditional patterns and motifs: the way that vision experiences go, the sort of symbols that have meanings. The council scenes and the symbolic visions and their contents are pan-cultural communicative phenomena. In exploring genres in the experiential dimension we thus point to a border shared by popular and elitist cultural threads, by uniquely individual sensibilities and socially shared expectations. These forms allow us to trace theological and intellectual currents among the framers of the Hebrew Bible while pointing to shared aspects of Israelite belief. These vision forms may be, at the same time, both radical and conservative, built as they are on long-standing, traditional motifs and patterns of thought.

Our third case study is perhaps the most relevant to religion as lived and Israelite belief. We all dream, but we all do not see visions even if we believe in the possibility of experiencing them and in their significance. We do all die. The Hebrew Bible is not completely uniform in what it suggests concerning beliefs about death, the dead and the underworld, but there are some shared contours: there is an underworld; the dead have some sort of sentience; there exists the possibility of dead people's continued engagement in the world of the living; for most of the biblical period the state of death is permanent. Late in the biblical period, however, there is also hope that life can be eternal or that those who have died may return to the status of living beings.

The Realm of the Dead

In ancient Israel, those who die pass into an underworld across the river to take up a shadowy existence as a shade or ghost (Job 33.18). Biblical authors describe the underworld, Sheol, 'the recesses of the Pit' (Isa. 14.15), as a gloomy, dark place (Job 10.22, 26) where all hierarchy and claims to former status are erased (Isa. 14.9-11). This levelling paradoxically may be a welcome change in status, a relief, for members of the underclass who toiled endlessly and suffered in life (Job 3.15-19). The peace of the underworld is afforded only to those who have received proper burial. Ideally, the living oversee rituals allowing the transition between life and death and keep watch over the tomb. Other contributors to this volume discuss the material culture of death in ancient Israel and Judah, rituals for the dead, and debates among modern scholars concerning the evidence for these dimensions of ancient Israelite religion as lived (see Chapters 4, 5 and 8). Interest in the experiential dimension of Israelite religion leads to a discussion of the congress between the realm of the dead and the realm of the living. Those who die may continue to have some sort of sentience and influence in the cosmos.

It should be said at the outset that some ancient contributors to the tradition, those who present themselves as the voice of 'official' religion, seek to sever ties between the realm of the living and the realm of the dead, while death itself is a source of uncleanness to be safely circumscribed, purified and avoided by the priestly elites. God is a god of the living, and the dead cannot praise the Lord (Ps. 115.17). Various forms of propitiation for the dead and consultation of the dead for divinatory purposes seem to be forbidden (see Lev. 20.6, 27; Deut. 18.9-14; 26.12-15; 2 Kgs 21.6; Isa. 57.3-13; Niditch 1997: 65–66).

The scene in 1 Samuel 28 illustrates a number of the themes we have explored in religion as lived across the span of Israelite social history and preserved tradition. The narrator indicates that Samuel the prophet has died and adds that Saul has expelled ghost-raisers and the familiars of spirits from the land, as if he followed the warnings and polemics found in Leviticus and Deuteronomy. This Deuteronomic-style voice probably dates the composition to the late monarchy. Saul, threatened by the forces of the Philistines, finds himself deserted by God. He 'makes inquiry of the Lord', formulaic language indicating the request for an oracle; such requests for divine guidance are typical before battles in ancient Near Eastern war accounts. God will not answer him via dreams or Urim, divinatory means, or by prophecy. The assumption is that various divinatory media are efficacious means of receiving information about the future. Saul decides to turn to what the Deuteronomic framers regard as forbidden divinatory means, the consultation of the dead. He seeks a woman who is 'a mistress of ghosts', and his servants tell him there is such an adept in Endor. Disguised, Saul presents himself as a potential client, and the woman insists that such divinatory practices have been outlawed by the king himself, echoing the 'official' line, the line that the composer wants to present as official. Saul, however, convinces her to raise the spirit of Samuel. The narrator does not describe the ritual process, but she succeeds, and seeing the image of the old man in a robe, 'a divinity', she screams loudly and becomes aware that the client is Saul. Samuel delivers a message of doom after complaining that Saul had disturbed him, indicating that Sheol is a place of rest.

The scene suggests belief in the sentience of the departed, in their capacity to know the future, and in the possibility of their communicating with the living. Professionals moreover engage in mediation between the living and the dead. The 'official' religion and central religious authority are said to condemn the practice of ghost-raising, but the official Scripture beautifully portrays the mediating activity. Perhaps it is this long-term belief in the continued connection between the departed and the living that makes possible belief in bodily resurrection alluded to in a few late texts (Isa. 26.19; Dan. 12.2). There is no sharp divide between 'popular' religion and 'true' religion, except in the polemics of the few, given lip service in 1 Samuel 28. There is rather religion as lived, a worldview in which human beings are regarded as capable of experiencing divine presence on earth in palpable and visceral visions. They can imagine being transported to the heavenly realm itself, becoming witness to the machinations of the divine council and they can receive visits from those in Sheol, the world of the dead. In late biblical tradition, the possibility of bodily resurrection for the 'saved' anticipates a formative thread in early Judaism. Imagery is rooted in a shared cultural fund, and descriptions of such experiences and places are conventionalized, but each example bears the stamp of the unique voices and orientations of individual contributors to the tradition who arise in particular socio-historical settings.

Bibliography

Ackerman, S.
1992   *Under Every Green Tree: Popular Religion in Sixth-Century Judah* (HSM 46; Atlanta, GA: Scholars Press).

Brakke, D., M.L. Satlow and S. Weitzman (eds)
2005a   *Religion and the Self in Antiquity* (Bloomington, IN: Indiana University Press).

Brakke, D., M.L. Satlow and S. Weitzman
2005b   'Introduction', in D. Brakke, M.L. Satlow and S. Weitzman (eds), *Religion and the Self in Antiquity* (Bloomington, IN: Indiana University Press), 1–11.

Brown, P.
1981   *The Cult of the Saints: Its Rise and Function in Latin Christianity* (The Haskell Lectures on History of Religions, New Series 2; Chicago, IL: University of Chicago Press).

Foley, J.M.
1991   *Immanent Art: From Structure to Meaning in Traditional Oral Epic* (Bloomington, IN: Indiana University Press).

Grabbe, L.L.
2004   *A History of the Jews and Judaism in the Second Temple Period 1: Yehud: A History of the Persian Province of Judah* (LSTS 47; London and New York, NY: T&T Clark International).

Katz, S.T.
1983   'The "Conservative" Character of Mystical Experience', in S.T. Katz (ed.), *Mysticism and Religious Traditions* (Oxford and New York, NY: Oxford University Press), 3–60.

Momigliano, A.D.
1971   'Popular Religious Beliefs and Late Roman Historians', *Studies in Church History* 8: 1–18; repr. in *Essays in Ancient and Modern Historiography* (Oxford: Blackwell, 1977), 141–59.

Niditch, S.
1980   *The Symbolic Vision in Biblical Tradition* (HSM 30; Chico, CA: Scholars Press).
1997   *Ancient Israelite Religion* (Oxford and New York, NY: Oxford University Press).

Obeyesekere, G.
1981   *Medusa's Hair: An Essay on Personal Symbols and Religious Experience* (Chicago, IL: University of Chicago).

Olyan, S.M.
2005   'The Search for the Elusive Self in Texts of the Hebrew Bible', in D. Brakke, M.L. Satlow and S. Weitzman (eds), *Religion and the Self in Antiquity* (Bloomington, IN: Indiana University Press), 40–50.

Otto, R.
1958   *The Idea of the Holy: An Inquiry into the Non-Rational Factor in the Idea of the Divine and its Relation to the Rational* (trans. J.W. Harvey; New York, NY, and Oxford: Oxford University Press).

Smart, N.
1983   *Worldviews: Crosscultural Explorations of Human Beliefs* (New York, NY: Charles Scribner's Sons).

Wilson, R.R.
1980   *Prophecy and Society in Ancient Israel* (Philadelphia, PA: Fortress Press).
1984   'Prophecy in Crisis: The Call of Ezekiel', *Interpretation* 38: 117–30.

Chapter 3

'ISRAELITE' RELIGION AND 'CANAANITE' RELIGION

Herbert Niehr

1
Introduction

According to the narrative tradition of the Hebrew Bible, especially as found in Deuteronomy and in the work of the Deuteronomistic historians (Joshua–2 Kings), the history of the people Israel is marked throughout by a fundamental opposition between 'Israel' and 'Canaan'. Israel entered the Promised Land from the desert, bringing with it the uncorrupted cult of YHWH as its only god. Having entered the Promised Land, Israel came into contact with the gods and goddesses of Canaan, thus perverting its Yahwistic religion. The central implication of this biblical view of Israel's religion is that Israel's religion differs fundamentally from Canaanite religion and that YHWH has nothing to do with the gods of Canaan.

This biblical perspective was particularly perpetuated in modern research by two very influential scholars and their followers. William Foxwell Albright published a book called *Yahweh and the Gods of Canaan* with the loaded subtitle 'A Historical Analysis of Two Contrasting Faiths' (1968). Several years before, he had already disqualified the religion of Canaan as abominable (Albright 1961 [1942]).[1] Similarly, Albrecht Alt and the scholars influenced by him claimed the incompatibility of Israelite and Canaanite societies (e.g. Alt 1953 [1930]; Schmitt 1970)[2] and thus asserted the existence of two totally distinct social layers in Judah and Israel during the Iron Age (Dietrich 1979; see the critique in Uehlinger 1999: 562–65). The climax of this kind of research was reached in a dissertation by Ulf Oldenburg (1969), whose author stated even in its preface: 'The more I studied pre-Israelite religion, the more I was amazed with its utter depravity and wickedness. Indeed there was *nothing* in it to inspire the sublime faith of Yahweh. His coming is like the rising sun dispelling the darkness of Canaanite superstition' (1969: xi).

However, as a result of excavations in Syria and Palestine, and particularly the textual finds made during these excavations, overall perceptions of Syrian religion totally changed. These finds enabled scholars to view Marduk, Ishtar, El, Baal and other deities not through the lens provided by the Hebrew Bible but from the standpoint of independent evidence from Assur, Nineveh, Babylon, Mari, Ebla, Emar and various minor sites in Phoenicia and Syria. The excavations in Ugarit turned out to be of special

1. On Albright's treatment of Canaanite religion, see Hillers 1985: 259–61.
2. Note the critical response of Whitelam 1997: 129–35.

importance for the reconstruction of the religious history of Syria and Palestine during the Late Bronze Age. For the first time, mythological and ritual texts in a Northwest Semitic language were in the hands of biblical scholars, and these texts inevitably had a strong impact upon research into Israelite religion of the first millennium BCE.[3]

One should not overlook totally that there were also some scholars of the Albright school who undertook different approaches. Frank Moore Cross (1973, 1998) showed that the Israelites were, in some respects, Canaanite too[4] and Delbert Hillers (1985) has demonstrated the serious shortcomings in treating Canaanite religion as 'analyzing the abominable'. But all this textual and archaeological material did not yet suffice to bring about a total turn in biblical research.

During recent decades, however, two important changes have taken place in our reconstructions of the religion and history of Judah and Israel. It is without exaggeration that we can speak about a real paradigm shift. The first change came with the discovery of the inscriptions from Kuntillet 'Ajrud in the Negev in 1975/6. This discovery helped to interpret another inscription, which had already been found in 1967 in Khirbet el-Qom (inscription no. 3) in the vicinity of Hebron. These inscriptions associate YHWH with the goddess Asherah as his *paredros*, and both deities, YHWH and his Asherah, are invoked to bestow blessings on those bearing Israelite and/or Judahite names (cf. Hadley 2000: 84–155). The decipherment of the inscriptions and their subsequent discussion sparked new interest in the history of Israelite religion which was, in the wake of this discussion, increasingly judged to be Canaanite too.

The second change concerns reconstructions of the history of Judah and Israel. In this respect too, many critical insights had been brought forth, all of which deconstructed a simple, biblically based and coherent picture of Israel's past. Consequently, it was no longer possible to offer simple paraphrases of Hebrew Bible texts, furnished with bibliographical notes, and to declare this product a 'history' of Israel. It is only recently that a comprehensively critical reconstruction of the history of Israel has been written. Indeed, Mario Liverani's book, first published in 2003, is of particular significance for our perceptions of 'Israelite' and 'Canaanite' religions. It is divided into two parts, the first of which bears the title 'Una storia normale' ('A Normal History'), while the second part is entitled 'Una storia inventata' ('An Invented History') (Liverani 2006 [2003]: 37–220, 275–398). In the wake of the above-mentioned works of deconstruction it does not come as a surprise that the 'Canaanites' are dealt with only in the second part of Liverani's book.

Following this paradigm shift, biblical scholars can now no longer continue to speak about 'Israel and Canaan' in the ways in which their predecessors had done (cf. Lemche 1991: 13–24, 151–73; Smith 2001: 195–200).

2

Israel and Canaan: Historical Aspects

Before approaching the realm of religions we should contextualize our discussion by first focusing on the geographic and historical concepts of Canaan and Israel during

---

3.   The history of research of biblical and Ugaritic studies has been sketched by Smith 2001.
4.   See further Hillers 1985: 265–66; Smith 2001: 156.

the Late Bronze Age.[5] The earliest reference to Canaanites occurs in the Mari letters (c. 1750 BCE), and Canaan itself is first mentioned c. 1500 BCE in the inscription on the statue of King Idrimi from Alalach. Further attestations stem from Egyptian inscriptions, letters from Hattusha and Ugarit, and above all from the El-Amarna archive. On the basis of all these texts a certain circumscription of Canaan becomes visible. It would appear that during the Amarna Age Canaan comprised Palestine and Lebanon. It stretched from the area of Gaza in the southwest to the region north of Byblos. Here Canaan was bordered by Amurru, while to the east it was contained by the province of Upe and the Dead Sea.

The earliest mention of Israel occurs in the stela inscription of Pharaoh Merneptah (c. 1210 BCE).[6] The formal structure of this inscription suggests that Canaan and Israel were regarded as subdivisions of Palestine. Gösta Ahlström says, 'Remembering that in its extended meaning Canaan referred to the cultural and urban areas of the country, the name Israel logically refers to the remaining sparsely populated hill country area where few cities were located' (Ahlström 1986: 40). In the light of recent research, it has become increasingly clear that Israel did not immigrate as a whole people into Canaan, but that – contrary to biblical claims – Israel came into existence *within* Canaan. So a concept not of immigration, but of ethnogenesis is needed to explain the early history of Israel (cf. Halpern 1983; Liverani 2006 [2003]: 37–87, esp. 66–68).

When Egypt had to leave its dominions in the Levant, the province of Canaan became subject to a vacuum of power. Consequently, the Phoenician royal cities and their hinterland, as well as the kingdoms of Israel and Judah, and the Philistine pentapolis, became the dominant powers in the region. Nevertheless, the Hebrew Bible has retained a memory of the old land of Canaan, using it as a designation for Palestine (Gen. 10.19; 37; Num. 34.2-12; cf. Deut. 1.7). 'Israel', on the other hand, became the name of the northern kingdom, which lasted from the tenth century BCE until its annexation as an Assyrian province in 720 BCE. After this date, the name of Israel became part of the literature of the southern kingdom of Judah, a change we will now discuss.

3
Israel and Canaan: Literary Aspects

The Hebrew Bible contains two originally distinct stories of origin: the patriarchal narratives (Genesis 12–36) and the story of the Exodus (Exodus 1–12). The common denominator of both traditions is the statement that Israel's origins lie outside Canaan and is therefore not autochthonous (cf. Schmid 2008: 86–93, 124–26). For this reason, apart from 'Canaan' in the narrative of the book of Genesis (which can only be mentioned here),[7] the second starting point for the literary history of 'Canaan' in the Hebrew Bible is the story of the Exodus. According to this narrative, Israel had been living in Egypt from the time of the patriarchs until the time of Moses. In the wake of

5. For the details of the following paragraph, see the overviews given by Weippert 1976–80; Lemche 1991: 25–52; Na'aman 1994, 1999; Finkelstein 1996; Rainey 1996, 2003: 169–72; Uehlinger 2000: 175–79; Tammuz 2001; Liverani 2006 [2003]: 5–33.
6. Cf. Ahlström 1986: 37–43; Görg 1997: 58–63; Rainey 2003: 180–84; Hasel 2004.
7. Cf. Lemche 1991: 75–79; Uehlinger 1999: 567–70.

the Exodus, Israel remained in the desert for 40 years before the people were allowed to enter the Promised Land under the leadership of Joshua. In the book of Exodus, Israel is invented as a non-autochthonous people, a people who had nothing in common with the Canaanites. All in all, the patriarchal narratives and the Exodus story serve to separate Israel from the Canaanites.

According to the books of Joshua and Judges, the Canaanites were already living in the Promised Land when, under Joshua's leadership, Israel arrived. In this tradition, the Canaanites were not totally driven away by the Israelites but remained there (Joshua 1–12; Judges 1; 2.1-5, 20-23; 3.1-6; 4–5). Memories of a 'land of Canaan' comprising Palestine and the Lebanon thus appear to have survived in the Hebrew Bible. But the biblical literature also marks a decisive difference as compared to the political and social situation of the Late Bronze Age: it insists that the Israelites were not Canaanites. Indeed, they differed entirely from the Canaanites – ethnically, politically, ethically and in terms of religion. This biblical distinction had several consequences. For example, marriages between Canaanites and Israelites were strictly forbidden (e.g. Gen. 24.3-4, 37; 26.34-35; 27.46–28.5, 6-9; Deut. 7.3). Furthermore, Israelites were not allowed to make alliances with the Canaanites (Exod. 23.23-24, 28-33; 33.2; 34.11-16; Num. 33.51-56; Deut. 7.1-5; 20.10-18; cf. Schmitt 1970) or to behave like the inhabitants of Canaan (Leviticus 18). Instead, they were to kill the Canaanites and eradicate their cults (e.g. Deut. 7.1-6, 17-26; 20.16-17; 12; Exod. 34.13-15). Thus, on the basis of the textual evidence in the Hebrew Bible, Nadav Na'aman is certainly right when he states that 'the idea that the Canaanites were the former inhabitants of Palestine is not a literary construction nor is the description of their land a late scribal invention' (Na'aman 1998: 415). On the other hand, however, he also states: 'The image of the Canaanites as it appears in the Old Testament and its heavy theological overlay are certainly the product of biblical auithors [*sic*] and are greatly divorced from historical reality' (Na'aman 1998: 415).

It has gradually been acknowledged that the 'Canaanites' in the literature of the Hebrew Bible were invented in the counter-image of what Israel claimed to be – a precise antithesis of Israelite society (Lemche 1991: 20). So 'Canaan' is an ideological term, coined by biblical writers in order to create an 'anti-people' to stand in contrast to 'Israel' (Lemche 1991: 101–20). Accordingly, the notion of 'Israel' should also be recognized as an ideological term serving as the positive complement to 'Canaan' (Ahlström 1986: 101–18). This insight is especially important if we want to understand the exilic and post-exilic narrative literature of the Hebrew Bible. But how can we explain the literary invention of Canaan as an anti-people by the Hebrew Bible authors? There are several historical analogies that help us to understand this feature.

In Egypt during the Saitic and Persian periods, a cultural construction of 'the other' was undertaken in order to mark a clear difference between the Egyptians (who were considered to be pure) and the non-Egyptians (who were judged as being unclean and who were rejected as potential enemies). Jan Assmann notes:

> The sacred objects and rites were protected not so much from the impure and the uninitiated but from the foreigner. Foreigners symbolized the ultimate in impurity and noninitiation and also stood for the threat posed by Seth, the sacrilegious will to destruction, desecration, and plunder – the vandalistic, iconoclastic impulse. Late period cult texts also occasionally articulate the rule forbidding foreigners entry to the sanctuary and attendance at the sacred rites.
>
> (Assmann 2002: 395)

Concerning the case of Greece, Edith Hall argues:

> Greek writing about barbarians is usually an exercise in self-definition, for the barbarian is often portrayed as the opposite of the ideal Greek. It suggests that the polarization of Hellen and barbarian was invented in specific historical circumstances during the early years of the fifth century BC partly as a result of the combined Greek military efforts against the Persians . . . The image of an enemy extraneous to Hellas helped to foster a sense of community between the allied states.
>
> (E. Hall 1989: 1–2)[8]

Benjamin Isaac has argued convincingly for the large-scale 'invention' of racism in Antiquity, including the racist attitudes of Greece and Rome against the Phoenicians, Carthaginians and Syrians (Isaac 2004: 324–51). They were all, says Isaac, 'the target of particularly fierce forms of dislike and disapproval. Their merits and gifts are regarded as morally dubious, their faults are the opposite of the merits decent people ought to display . . . They practice cannibalism and human sacrifice' (Isaac 2004: 350).

In the Hebrew Bible, the most important difference between Canaan and Judah/ Israel is claimed to be a religious one. We have already noted that the construction of an *ethnos* 'Israel' as opposed to an *ethnos* 'Canaan' was an ideological fiction. Similarly, the biblical claim that a pure 'Israelite' religion was imported from outside Canaan is a fiction without religio-historical reality, just as the biblical claim that a Canaanite religion in opposition to the religion of Israel and Judah once existed is also fictional. All this is not to deny that there were, indeed, Judahite and Israelite religions. Nevertheless, these religions have to be judged as local variants of Canaanite religions in Palestine during the first millennium BCE. So we should not take a literary device simply at face value, nor build a complete social and religious history on it.

4
Israel and Canaan: Religio-Historical Aspects

Set against this background, the religio-historical reality of the religion of ancient Judah and Israel is quite different from a simple 'Israel-versus-Canaan' pattern. Consequently, Michael Coogan's characterization of 'Israelite religion as a subset of Canaanite religion' (Coogan 1987: 115) can be fully maintained, as can the logical implications of this position. Coogan continues:

> From a historical perspective it is more appropriate . . . to speak of the special development of the religion of ancient Israel, rather than of the ways in which it was influenced by other cultures, as though it were a static, fully formed reality subject only to tangential modification. To be sure, by the beginning of the first millennium B.C.E. Israel, like its neighbors Phoenicia, Ammon, Moab, Edom, and Aram, had begun to show distinctive traits in religious as well as in other aspects of its life. But this was a development from a Canaanite matrix and can be

8.   On the forming of ethnic identity and the shaping of ethnic consciousness in ancient Greece, see J.M. Hall 2000.

understood only by the reconstruction of that matrix from all available evidence and by the analysis of parallel developments in neighboring states.

(Coogan 1987: 115–16)

In this light, is easy to understand why Gregorio del Olmo Lete has most appropriately described Israelite religion as 'La religion cananéenne des Anciens Hébreux' ('the Canaanite religion of the ancient Hebrews') (del Olmo Lete 2008a; see also the programmatic approach in del Olmo Lete 1994).

Given that the term 'Canaanite' is highly controversial in its Hebrew Bible usage, the proposal has been made to replace it with the more neutral 'West Semitic' (Grabbe 1994: 121; Smith 2001: 196–97; Niehr 2003b: 715). Indeed, the religions of Israel and Judah are best viewed as typical West Semitic religions of the first millennium BCE. But what does the label 'West Semitic religions' actually signify? In order to answer that question, we must note that a range of West Semitic religions existed during the Late Bronze and Iron Ages. The most prominent aspects of their shared features will now be discussed.[9]

Polytheism

As a rule, ancient Near Eastern religions were polytheistic, and the religions of Judah and Israel were no exception to this rule. Polytheistic conceptions of the divine cannot be understood merely as a collection of several gods and goddesses; rather, they are best interpreted as systems of ordered interaction within the divine world, in which every god and goddess has a dominion for which he or she is responsible. Importantly, this system also helps to organize the worlds of the living and the dead, as we shall see. It is clear that these panthea, with their concepts of domination and order, mirrored Northwest Semitic societies.

The Hierarchy of Gods

Lowell Handy (1994: 65–167) has demonstrated that West Semitic panthea of the Late Bronze and Iron Ages displayed a four-tiered hierarchy:

1. Authoritative deities
2. Major active gods
3. Artisan deities
4. Messenger deities

Since life in Syria-Palestine depended on rainfall, the most important role within the panthea was held by the weather god, who was responsible for the lives of human beings, animals and vegetation (Schwemer 2001, 2008, 2009). Well-known names of the weather god included Baal, Addu/Haddu and also YHWH. The female companion of the weather god was conceived as a mother goddess: here the goddesses Hepat, Shala and Asherah can be named.

Other important deities included Dagan, a god of the underworld and of grain; Rashpu, who was responsible for pestilence and also for protecting against pestilence; the sun god or sun goddess, who was the god of justice and righteousness; and the

---

9.   For overviews of West Semitic religions see van der Toorn 1996; Niehr 1998, 2003b; Cornelius and Niehr 2003; Johnston 2004; Xella 2007; del Olmo Lete 2008b.

moon god, who was responsible for all aspects of fertility. Deities of minor rank included artisan gods, messenger gods, spirits and demons, and also the kings who underwent divinization after their death (see Chapter 5 in this volume).

The king was believed to be the son of the highest god and, as such, functioned as the deity's earthly governor. He was thus responsible for the establishment and maintenance of the divine order. The king accomplished his responsibility via the temple cults and by his function as supreme judge of his kingdom. The protection of widows, orphans and the poor were especial royal duties. Significantly, the king was also the bond between heaven and earth: he conveyed divine blessing and salvation for the land and the people, and built the temples, organized the priesthoods and presided over the cults dedicated to the service of the gods. During his lifetime the king was not regarded as a divine being, but after his death, divine honours were bestowed upon him and he was worshipped within the royal cult of the dead. As such, the dead king was taken up into the number of the gods and represented in the cult place by a statue in order to receive offerings.

The Divine Abode

The deities were believed to dwell in their temples and sanctuaries, where they were worshipped in the form of their cult images or cult symbols. The king and his priests were responsible for providing everything necessary to the gods. There were therefore rituals to ensure the deities were treated properly and that no important aspect of their provision was neglected. The priests had to take care of nourishing the deities through slaughtering and presenting animal offerings and pouring out libations. They also served the gods by washing, clothing, incensing and adorning their statues. Although the deity was present in his or her cult statue, he or she could also leave it. This would occur if a deity had not received the prescribed offerings or if the statue had suffered neglect. Offences committed against the deity could also provoke the departure of the god from the cult statue.

Besides the cults held in the temples, there were also household cults presided over by the paterfamilias. Important indications for these kinds of cults include terracotta and metal figurines of deities and ancestors, and miniature temples modelled in clay. The main concerns of domestic cults were problems surrounding health and fertility, the quest for children, and important life events such as marriage, childbirth and death (see Chapters 8 and 9 in this volume). As the families of the Semites not only comprised the living but also the dead, the care of the dead – among all households, including that of the royal family – was an important characteristic of the domestic and state cults. Beyond the domestic sphere, there were other cults located in the city gates and in open air sanctuaries outside the cities and villages (see Chapters 6 and 7 in this volume).

Sacred Times

The first, seventh and fifteenth days of a month were of special importance for the ancestral cults. The most important feast during the year was the New Year, the beginning of which was celebrated in autumn. According to rituals and myths, on this day the weather god returned from the underworld so that the vegetation could set in anew. During the year, the celebration of the equinox separated the year into two halves.

Magic and Divination

As everything which happened could be ascribed to divine will, it was crucial to know what the divine will was. Pestilence, famine and war, or childlessness in the personal sphere, were indications of divine wrath. In order to remedy this, diviners sought to discern both the reasons for this wrath and the means by which the gods might be reconciled. Special techniques of divination included the scrutiny of the livers and lungs of slaughtered sheep, the interpretation of birds' flights and birth omens, and also necromancy. By this use of magic people tried to improve their situations.

Mythology

Myths provided this religious world with a narrative unity. Some myths had functions of legitimation or aetiology; others complemented rituals. Myths also communicated the cosmologies necessary for understanding the world, including the interrelation of life and death both within and between the divine and earthly realms. The best-known myth from second-millennium Syria, the Ugaritic Baal Cycle, deals with the struggle of the weather god Baal against the god of death and the underworld, Mot, and with Baal's deliverance from the underworld.

5
Judahite and Israelite Religions as Subsets of West Semitic Religion

As observed above, the religions of the kingdoms of Judah and Israel can only be understood as being West Semitic religions. However, we should not neglect the fact that each West Semitic religion also has its own characteristics, only some of which can be discussed here.

Contrary to what is often claimed in the secondary literature, YHWH was a weather god even until post-exilic times, as is shown by several Hebrew Bible texts (e.g. Judg. 5.4-5; Pss. 18.8-16 = 22.8-16; 29; 65.10-14; 104; Jer. 10.13 = 51.16; 14.22; 31.12; Hos. 2.10; Hab. 3.3; Hag. 1.2-12; 2.15-19; Zech. 8.9-12; 10.1). That is why YHWH could also be called 'Bull' or 'Baal' (e.g. Num. 23.22; Ps. 68.5), and why he was depicted as a 'rider of the clouds' (Deut. 33.26; Pss. 18.10-11; 68.5-34; Isa. 19.1). In the sanctuaries of Bethel and Dan, YHWH appears to have been represented by a bull figurine (e.g. 1 Kgs 12:28-30). Moreover, like Baal, YHWH was also a god of war who protected his people from its enemies and waged war against them, as suggested in texts including Judges 4–5; Pss. 18.8-16; 21.9-13; 29.3-9; 46.7-12; 65.10-14; 68.15-22; 83.14-18; 144.5-8 (cf. Klingbeil 1999).

Nevertheless, the Hebrew Bible makes a strict separation between YHWH on the one hand and gods like Baal and Hadad on the other, as the story of Elijah on Mount Carmel illustrates (1 Kings 18). According to the Hebrew Bible, YHWH did not tolerate the cults of other gods – although their actual existence is not denied. As such, YHWH is sometimes qualified as a jealous god (e.g. Exod. 20.5; Deut. 5.7).

However, epigraphy tells us a different story. As seen above, in the inscriptions from Kuntillet 'Ajrud and Khirbet el-Qom, YHWH was invoked together with a divine *paredros*, the goddess Asherah. According to the Elephantine papyri (from the latter half of the fifth century BCE), YHWH (here called Yahu) was worshipped together with the goddess Anat-Yahu, a goddess who had been conceived of after the Aramaean goddess Anat-Bethel (van der Toorn 1992). Astonishing as it might seem, then, the religions of Judah and Israel were *not* monotheistic right from their beginnings, but were as polytheistic as the Canaanite religions of the Late Bronze and Iron Ages. Monotheism is best seen as a late-comer onto the stage of religious history in the ancient Near East.

There is no common consensus on how monotheism developed in Judah. For this reason, only some of the steps leading to monotheism can be discussed here.[10] As we saw earlier, YHWH was not the only god worshipped either in Judah or in Israel. Belief in a divine assembly surrounding the supreme god is a distinctive trait of ancient Near Eastern religions and can also be observed in the West Semitic religions of the first millennium BCE. YHWH's rise to the position of highest god in Judahite and Israelite religion made him the chief of a divine assembly in Jerusalem and Samaria (e.g. 1 Kgs 22.19-22; Isaiah 6; Job 1; Psalms 82; 89). But during the Achaemenid period and even later, the second and third levels of the above-mentioned polytheistic hierarchy were gradually discarded as increasing emphasis was placed on YHWH as an authoritative deity and on the messengers as YHWH's servants. Handy states:

> Thus, when Yahweh is taken as the sole deity to have any power in the cosmos, the messenger deities may be allowed to exist since they have no power at all. All other deities, from Asherah through the Craft-Gods, could disagree with Yahweh and thereby diminish the centrality of power in the single deity. By retaining the messenger level of the Syro-Palestinian pantheon, the theologians have managed to retain for Yahweh the full extent of divine authority and still allow 'the' God rule over a heavenly 'host' which could do nothing but what its ruler desired.
>
> (Handy 1990: 29)

Extra-biblical evidence shows that there were different manifestations of the god YHWH: inscriptions from Kuntillet 'Ajrud refer to 'YHWH from Shomron' and 'YHWH from Teiman' (Hadley 2000: 121–36), while the Khirbet Beit Lei inscription mentions the 'God of Jerusalem' (see the text in Gibson 1981: 57–58). When viewed against this background of 'poly-yahwism', the claim in Deut. 6.4 that YHWH is 'one' (*'eḥad*) can be seen as an emphasis on the unity of YHWH. In post-exilic times, Deutero-Isaiah focused creation and salvation exclusively in YHWH by denying the power of all other gods (Isa. 40.12-26; 41.21-29; 42.8; 43.8-16; 44.6-7; 45.5-7, 18; 46.9-10). During the same period, YHWH is described in the so-called priestly code as *'ĕlōhîm*, attesting to the emergence of the concept of an inclusive monotheism.

Due to its prestige in the Late Bronze Age, Mount Zaphon to the north of Ugarit had become the divine mountain par excellence in West Semitic religions and remained so even until the Iron Age. That is why in several Syro-Palestinian religions the weather god or the supreme god was said to have been enthroned on Mount Zaphon. Consequently, while YHWH's divine abode in Jerusalem was Mount Zion, it is not surprising that in Ps. 48.3 it is stated that 'Mount Zion is [on] the summit of Zaphon' (cf. Isa. 14.13-14; Job 26.7; 37.22; see also Niehr 1995: 63–64). Jerusalem's sacred mountain is here called Zaphon because, as weather god and supreme god of Judah, YHWH could only be enthroned on the divine mountain par excellence.

The YHWH cult in Jerusalem was also in keeping with its West Semitic religio-cultural context in other ways. The description in 1 Kings 6–8 of the temple supposedly

---

10.   See further the articles assembled in Dietrich and Klopfenstein 1994; Becking, *et al.* 2001; Krebernik and van Oorschot 2002; Oeming and Schmid 2003.

built by King Solomon clearly follows a North Syrian temple type. We know temples of similar size and arrangement from Tell Tayinat on the Orontes (Busink 1970: 558–62) and from 'Ain Dara in the Afrin valley (Abū-'Assāf 1990). During recent years it has come to be thought that YHWH was represented in Jerusalem by a statue or a cultic symbol and not only by an empty throne (Niehr 1997, 2003a; Becking 2001; Köckert 2008). So in this case, too, Judahite and Israelite religions were normal West Semitic religions. But what was new in the Judahite and Israelite cults was the prohibition of religious images (e.g. Exod. 20.3-5; 34.13; Deut. 4.16-19, 23-26; 5.7-9) and the polemics against them (e.g. Isa. 40.18-20; 41.6-7; 44.9-20; 46.1-7) in exilic and post-exilic times. This prohibition was likely motivated by priestly attempts to establish a cult monopoly in the Second Temple in Jerusalem. This may be related in part to biblical traditions insisting that the only legitimate cult place of YHWH was the temple in Jerusalem. All other sanctuaries (including, for example, the sanctuary in Bethel) were heavily condemned, or portrayed in a negative sense as *bāmôt*. In a similar manner, other sanctuaries – including the YHWH temple in Samaria – were subjected to a *damnatio memoriae*, which is at least attested in epigraphy.[11] The centralization of cults in Jerusalem aimed at prohibiting the cults of all the other deities ever worshipped in Judah. Although ascribed to Josiah (2 Kings 22–23), this programme was only realized in post-exilic times.

As for the Israelite and Judahite festival calendar, it is unlikely that it ever underwent a denaturalization or historicization as is often claimed. Rather, an influence from the Babylonian festival calendar can be seen (Wagenaar 2005).

6
Summary

The religions of Judah and Israel did not develop in splendid isolation from Canaanite religions. On the contrary, they were part and parcel of West Semitic culture and religion. This is not, however, to deny a specific character to the religions in Israel and Judah, for some differences between Israel and Judah and the religions of their neighbours can be discerned. But the genealogy of Jerusalem as given by Ezekiel is fully understandable: 'By origin and by birth you are of the land of the Canaanites' (Ezek. 16.3; cf. 16.29; 17.4). In its biblical context, though, this was, of course, meant not in a religio-historical sense, but rather in a negative manner in order to criticize Jerusalem and Judah.

We should not overlook the fact that only since the second half of the nineteenth century have extra-biblical texts become available to the historians of religions. This is why, in the recent past, an independent view on the sources for religion given in the Hebrew Bible has had to be learned.

---

11.   See Hadley 2000: 123–25 for the Kuntillet 'Ajrud inscriptions mentioning 'YHWH from Samaria'.

Bibliography

Abū-'Assāf, A.
1990   Der Tempel von 'Ain Dāra (DaF 3; Mainz: Von Zabern).

Ahlström, G.W.
1986   Who Were the Israelites? (Winona Lake, IN: Eisenbrauns).

Albright, W.F.
1961 [1942]   'The Role of the Canaanites in the History of Civilization', in G.E. Wright (ed.), The Bible and the Ancient Near East: Essays in Honor of William Foxwell Albright (Garden City, NY: Doubleday), 328–62.
1968   Yahweh and the Gods of Canaan: A Historical Analysis of Two Contrasting Faiths (London: Athlone Press).

Alt, A.
1953 [1930]   'Die Staatenbildung der Israeliten in Palästina', in Kleine Schriften zur Geschichte des Volkes Israel II (München: Beck), 1–65.

Assmann, J.
2002   The Mind of Egypt: History and Meaning in the Time of the Pharaohs (New York, NY: Henry Holt).

Becking, B.
2001   'The Gods, in Whom They Trusted . . . Assyrian Evidence for Iconic Polytheism in Ancient Israel', in B. Becking, M. Dijkstra, M.C.A. Korpel and K.J.H. Vriezen, Only One God? Monotheism in Ancient Israel and the Veneration of the Goddess Asherah (BS 77; London: Continuum, 2001), 151–63.

Becking, B., M. Dijkstra, M.C.A. Korpel and K.J.H. Vriezen
2001   Only One God? Monotheism in Ancient Israel and the Veneration of the Goddess Asherah (BS 77; London: Continuum).

Busink, T.
1970   Der Tempel von Jerusalem I (Leiden: Brill).

Coogan, M.D.
1987   'Canaanite Origins and Lineage: Reflections on the Religion of Ancient Israel', in P.D. Miller, P.D. Hanson and S.D. McBride (eds), Ancient Israelite Religion: Studies in Honor of Frank Moore Cross (Philadelphia, PA: Fortress Press), 115–24.

Cornelius, I. and H. Niehr
2003   Götter und Kulte in Ugarit (Mainz: von Zabern).

Cross, F.M.
1973   Canaanite Myth and Hebrew Epic: Essays in the History of the Religion of Israel (Cambridge, MA: Harvard University Press).
1998   From Epic to Canon: History and Literature in Ancient Israel (Baltimore, MD, and London: The Johns Hopkins University Press).

Dietrich, W.
1979   Israel und Kanaan. Vom Ringen zweier Gesellschaftssysteme (SBS 94; Stuttgart: Katholisches Bibelwerk).

Dietrich, W. and M. Klopfenstein (eds)
1994   Ein Gott allein? JHWH-Verehrung und biblischer Monotheismus im Kontext der israelitischen und altorientalischen Religionsgeschichte (OBO 139; Freiburg: Universitätsverlag; Göttingen: Vandenhoeck & Ruprecht).

Finkelstein, I.
1996   'The Territorial-Political System of Canaan in the Late Bronze Age', UF 28: 221–55.

Gibson, J.C.L.
1981   Textbook of Syrian Semitic Inscriptions I. Hebrew and Moabite Inscriptions (Oxford: Clarendon Press).

Görg, M.
1997   *Die Beziehungen zwischen dem Alten Israel und Ägypten* (EdF 290; Darmstadt: Wissenschaftliche Buchgesellschaft).

Grabbe, L.L.
1994   '"Canaanite": Some Methodological Observations in Relation to Biblical Study', in G.J. Brooke, A.H.W. Curtis and J.F. Healey (eds), *Ugarit and the Bible: Proceedings of the International Symposium on Ugarit and the Bible* (UBL 11; Münster: Ugarit-Verlag), 113–22.

Hadley, J.
2000   *The Cult of Asherah in Ancient Israel and Judah: Evidence for a Hebrew Goddess* (UCOP 57; Cambridge: Cambridge University Press).

Hall, E.
1989   *Inventing the Barbarian: Greek Self-Definition through Tragedy* (Oxford: Clarendon Press).

Hall, J.M.
2000   *Ethnic Identity in Greek Antiquity* (Cambridge: Cambridge University Press).

Halpern B.
1983   *The Emergence of Israel in Canaan* (SBLMS 29; Chico, CA: Scholars Press).

Handy, L.K.
1990   'Dissenting Deities or Obedient Angels: Divine Hierarchies in Ugarit and the Bible', *BR* 35: 18–35.
1994   *Among the Host of Heaven: The Syro-Palestinian Pantheon as Bureaucracy* (Winona Lake, IN: Eisenbrauns).

Hasel, M.G.
2004   'The Structure of the Final Hymnic-Poetic Unit on the Merenptah Stela', *ZAW* 116: 75–81.

Hillers, D.R.
1985   'Analyzing the Abominable: Our Understanding of Canaanite Religion', *JQR* 75: 253–69.

Isaac, B.H.
2004   *The Invention of Racism in Classical Antiquity* (Princeton, NJ: Princeton University Press).

Johnston, S.I. (ed.)
2004   *Religions of the Ancient World – A Guide* (Cambridge, MA: Belknap Press of Harvard University Press).

Keel, O. and C. Uehlinger
1998   *Gods, Goddesses, and Images of God in Ancient Israel* (trans. T.H. Trapp; Minneapolis, MN: Fortress Press).

Klingbeil, M.
1999   *Yahweh Fighting from Heaven: God as Warrior and as God of Heaven in the Hebrew Psalter and Ancient Near Eastern Iconography* (OBO 169; Freiburg: Universitätsverlag; Göttingen: Vandenhoeck & Ruprecht).

Köckert, M.
2008   'Suffering from Formlessness – The Prohibition of Images in Exilic Times', *JNSL* 34: 21–37.

Krebernik, M. and J. van Oorschot (eds)
2002   *Polytheismus und Monotheismus in den Religionen des Vorderen Orients* (AOAT 298; Münster: Ugarit-Verlag).

Lemche, N.P.
1991   *The Canaanites and Their Land: The Tradition of the Canaanites* (JSOTS 110; Sheffield: Sheffield Academic Press).

Liverani, M.
2006 [2003] *Oltre la Bibbia: Storia antica di Israele* (3rd edn; Roma-Bari: Laterza).

Na'aman, N.
1994 'The Canaanites and Their Land: A Rejoinder', *UF* 26: 397–418.
1999 'Four Notes on the Size of Late Bronze Age Canaan', *BASOR* 313: 31–37.

Niehr, H.
1995 'The Rise of YHWH in Judahite and Israelite Religion: Methodological and Religio-Historical Aspects', in D.V. Edelman (ed.), *The Triumph of Elohim: From Yahwisms to Judaisms* (CBET 13; Kampen: Kok Pharos), 45–72.
1997 'In Search of YHWH's Cult Statue in the First Temple', in K. van der Toorn (ed.), *The Image and the Book: Iconic Cults, Aniconism, and the Rise of Book Religion in Israel and the Ancient Near East* (Leuven: Brill), 73–95.
1998 *Religionen in Israels Umwelt. Einführung in die nordwestsemitischen Religionen Syrien-Palästinas* (NEB ErgBd. 5; Würzburg: Echter).
2003a 'Götterbilder und Bilderverbot', in M. Oeming and K. Schmid (eds), *Der eine Gott und die Götter. Polytheismus und Monotheismus im antiken Israel* (AThANT 82; Zürich: Theologischer Verlag), 227–47.
2003b 'Westsemitische Religion', *TRE* 35: 715–23.

Oeming, M., and K. Schmid (eds)
2003 *Der eine Gott und die Götter. Polytheismus und Monotheismus im antiken Israel* (AThANT 82; Zürich: Theologischer Verlag).

Oldenburg, U.
1969 *The Conflict between El and Ba'al in Canaanite Religion* (Dissertationes ad Historiam Religionum pertinentes III; Leiden: Brill).

Olmo Lete, G. del
1994 'Approaching a Description of the Canaanite Religion of Ancient Israel: Methodological Issues', in G.J. Brooke, A.H.W. Curtis and J.F. Healey (eds), *Ugarit and the Bible: Proceedings of the International Symposium on Ugarit and the Bible* (UBL 11; Münster: Ugarit-Verlag), 259–73.
2008a 'La religion cananéenne des Anciens Hébreux', in *Mythologie et religion des Sémites Occidentaux II: Émar, Ougarit, Israël, Phénicie, Aram, Arabie* (OLA 162; Leuven: Peeters), 165–265.
2008b (ed.), *Mythologie et religion des Sémites Occidentaux* (2 vols; OLA 162; Leuven: Peeters).

Rainey, A.F.
1996 'Who is a Canaanite? A Review of the Textual Evidence', *BASOR* 304: 1–15.
2003 'Amarna and Later: Aspects of Social History', in W.G. Dever and S. Gitin (eds), *Symbiosis, Symbolism, and the Power of the Past: Canaan, Ancient Israel, and Their Neighbors from the Late Bronze Age through Roman Palestinia* (Winona Lake, IN: Eisenbrauns), 169–87.

Schmid, K.
2008 *Literaturgeschichte des Alten Testaments. Eine Einführung* (Darmstadt: Wissenschaftliche Buchgesellschaft).

Schmitt, G.
1970 *Du sollst keinen Frieden schließen mit den Bewohnern des Landes. Die Weisungen gegen die Kanaanäer in Israels Geschichte und Geschichtsschreibung* (BWANT 91; Stuttgart: Kohlhammer).

Schwemer, D.
2001 *Die Wettergottgestalten Mesopotamiens und Nordsyriens im Zeitalter der Keilschriftkulturen* (Wiesbaden: Harrassowitz).
2008 'The Storm-Gods of the Ancient Near East: Summary, Synthesis, Recent Studies (Part I)', *JANER* 7: 121–68.

2009   'The Storm-Gods of the Ancient Near East: Summary, Synthesis, Recent Studies (Part II)', *JANER* 8: 1–44.

Smith, M.S.
2001   *Untold Stories: The Bible and Ugaritic Studies in the Twentieth Century* (Peabody, MA: Hendrickson).

Tammuz, O.
2001   'Canaan – A Land without Limits', *UF* 33: 501–43.

Toorn, K. van der
1992   'Anat-Yahu, Some Other Deities, and the Jews of Elephantine', *Numen* 34: 80–101.
1996   *Family Religion in Babylonia, Syria and Israel* (SHCANE 7; Leiden: Brill).

Uehlinger, C.
1999   'The "Canaanites" and Other "Pre-Israelite" Peoples in Story and History (Part I)', *FZPhTh* 46: 546–78.
2000   'The "Canaanites" and Other "Pre-Israelite" Peoples in Story and History (Part II)', *FZPhTh* 47: 173–98.

Wagenaar, J.A.
2005   *Origin and Transformation of the Ancient Israelite Festival Calendar* (BZAR 6; Wiesbaden: Harrassowitz).

Weippert, M.
1976–80 'Kanaan', *RlA* V: 352–55.

Whitelam, K.W.
1997   *The Invention of Ancient Israel: The Silencing of Palestinian History* (London and New York, NY: Routledge).

Xella, P.
2007   *Religione e religioni in Siria-Palestina* (Rome: Carocci).

Chapter 4

'POPULAR' RELIGION AND 'OFFICIAL' RELIGION:
PRACTICE, PERCEPTION, PORTRAYAL

Francesca Stavrakopoulou

The scholarly distinction between 'popular' religion and 'official' religion has tended to function within biblical, religious, sociological and cultural studies as a means of reconciling preconceived notions of religious norms with the diversities evident within religions. This distinction recognizes that not all people within the seemingly same cultural community share the same religious perspectives or practices, but ostensibly ranks these diversities in relation to one another by marginalizing those beliefs and rituals perceived to fall beyond the bounds of 'normative' practice. Accordingly, 'formal' forms of religion, such as those associated with culturally authoritative religious specialists, state-sponsored places of worship or politically dominant institutions, tend to be cast as 'official' and differentiated from 'popular' forms of religion, which are often perceived to represent localized traditions, or the beliefs and practices of non-specialists (often labelled the 'masses' or the 'laity'), or a type of religiosity unendorsed or opposed by 'formal' religious groups (Davis 1974, 1982; Vrijhof and Waardenburg 1979; Williams 1980).[1]

For biblical scholars and historians of ancient Israel and Judah, a distinction between 'official' religion and 'popular' religion is particularly encouraged by the Hebrew Bible itself, in which the religious past is portrayed not as an age of cultic uniformity, but as a time of great variety, competition and division within and among different socio-religious groups. A similar – though crucially, neither directly parallel nor identical – impression of diversities within ancient Israelite and Judahite religious practices is also suggested (albeit in a fragmented way) by the material remains of these cultures, from temples in urban areas and cult rooms in city gates, to incense stands amidst olive presses and amulets in tombs and homes (see Chapters 6, 8 and 9 in this volume). Consequently, many scholars have sought to 'manage' biblical and archaeological indications of religious diversities in ancient Israel and Judah by assuming a firm distinction between 'popular' religion and 'official' religion. But this distinction is often drawn relatively uncritically on theological grounds – which risks misrepresenting or distorting the likely religious realities of ancient Israel and Judah.

Indeed, in exploring precisely what is meant by the phrase 'popular' religion in biblical scholarship, it quickly becomes evident that it tends not to be used to refer merely to widespread, shared practice. It is rarely employed, for example, of Passover, despite its biblical portrayal as a cult in which most people participated. Rather, in biblical scholarship, 'popular' religion tends to refer to certain practices assumed to be

---

1. These distinctions might be broadly aligned with the differentiation of 'Great Traditions' and 'Little Traditions' within some anthropological and socio-religious studies of cultures.

unendorsed or unregulated by representatives of 'normative' or 'centralized' religion, and often sounds a pejorative tone in consequently characterizing these practices as 'deviant'. This chapter will explore some of the ways in which assumptions about religious norms in ancient Israel and Judah have contributed to the scholarly imaging of certain religious diversities as 'deviant' forms of practice, focusing particularly on so-called 'women's religion' and death cults as case studies to demonstrate the limitations and distortions arising from adopting a dichotomous distinction between 'official' and 'popular' forms of religion.

Theological Constructs of 'Popular' Religion and 'Official' Religion

The scholarly distinction between 'popular' religion and 'official' religion has often been assumed and defined in broad agreement with biblical portrayals of religious practices, which themselves frequently impose a sharp, polemical distinction between 'legitimate' (Torah-endorsed) activities and 'illegitimate' activities (those condemned as deviant, or not legislated for in Torah). As such, many scholars have constructed their views of 'popular' religion and 'official' religion on the basis of the theological preferences of the biblical writers, so that the forms of Yhwh worship represented by the prophets, priesthoods and temple cults approved by the biblical writers have been broadly cast as 'formal', 'state', 'orthodox' or 'official' religion in Israel and Judah (e.g. Bright 1981: 218, 320; McNutt 1999: 176; Miller 2000: 47–51). In its turn, 'popular' religion (also described as 'folk', 'non-orthodox', 'heterodox' or 'non-conformist' religion) has been identified with the practices falling beyond the biblical bounds of this 'official' religion, so that it is held to include worship at the *bāmôt* (e.g. Zevit 2001: 470; Smith 2002: 11), sacrificing to deities other than Yhwh (e.g. Vorländer 1986: 69), and performing rituals deemed inappropriate for Yhwh (e.g. Miller 2000: 59).

But this biblically based, theological distinction is problematic. It is constructed in part upon a relatively uncritical acceptance of the historical reliability of the biblical texts – a position which has been seriously and persuasively challenged (e.g. P.R. Davies 1992; Grabbe 1997; Lemche 1998; Liverani 2005). But it also reflects the related perception that the 'official' theological and religious preferences of the biblical writers are intellectually and even morally superior to the forms of religious belief and practice deemed 'popular'. This distinction is widely attested in the scholarship of generations past: William Albright, for example, suggested that the uncompromising and 'abstract' theological perspective of 'the religion of Yahweh' was beyond the intellectual grasp of those at the 'popular level', who participated in those 'objectionable pagan practices' he identified as 'Canaanite' (1968: 199) and characterized as 'primitive' and 'demoralizing' (1961: 338; cf. Labuschagne 1966: 123). This derogatory contrast was brought into sharp focus by J.B. Segal, who in 1976 published a now well-known article in which he wrote:

> Outside the borders of the established cult lies the shadowy region of popular superstition, of actions that arise from the vague, half-conscious feelings of fear and anticipation that have been summed up in the not ill-chosen term of 'Nature religion'.
>
> (Segal 1976: 1)

In identifying 'popular' religion with 'superstition', 'paganism' and 'Canaanite' religion (itself often caricatured as 'nature' worship and 'fertility' religion), scholars tended to

present and favour biblical monotheism as the religion of the spiritually and intellectually enlightened – an elite with whom they could perhaps themselves identify. The
differentiation of biblical monotheism from 'popular' religion was thus symptomatic of
a confessional bias within scholarship (van der Toorn 2002: 225; cf. J.Z. Smith 1978:
107–8; Barton 2007: 167–71), a scholarly differentiation particularly well rehearsed
in the part-competitive, part-symbiotic interrelation of Western Christianity and the
indigenous religions of pre-Modern and Early Modern Europe (Vrijhof 1979; Jolly
1996; cf. Ebertz and Schultheis 1986) but also further fuelled by eighteenth- and
nineteenth-century Rationalism and the application of Hegelian principles to biblical
history and religion (van der Toorn 2002: 225; Gomes 2003: 32; Hess 2007: 45).

Broadly speaking, these biblically-based perspectives have persisted into the present,
for some scholars continue to distinguish 'Canaanite' religion or polytheism from biblical Yhwh religion by aligning it with 'folk' or 'popular' religion. Ephraim Stern, for
example, defines the iconic polytheism of ancient Israel and Judah as 'folk religion' and
'pagan Yahwism' (Stern 2001); John Day describes the worship of the Queen of Heaven
(Jer. 7.16-20; 44.15-19, 25) as 'a popular folk custom, that is, she was a Canaanite
goddess' (Day 2000: 148), while Stephen Cook's favouring of biblical monotheism over
'popular' polytheism is evident in his claim that, 'Before the reforms of Hezekiah and
Josiah, at least, Sinai theology had to *struggle* against popular religion and its polytheistic beliefs and practices' (Cook 2004: 143, emphasis added). His loaded language is
reminiscent of Albright's portrayal of what he designated the 'Struggle between Yahweh
and the Gods of Canaan' (1968: 153), which draws a distinction between religions
that is itself reflected in the self-consciously referential title Day selected for his own
book, *Yahweh and the Gods and Goddesses of Canaan* (2000).

Given its confessional heritage and cultural contexts, the distinction assumed by
many scholars between 'popular' or 'folk' religion and 'official' or biblical 'Yhwh'
religion was likely also – and arguably remains – informed by a qualitative differentiation between 'high' culture and 'popular' (or 'low') culture, whereby the former is
associated with the dominant but elitist power groups within society (groups with
which some scholars can perhaps self-identify), while the latter is associated with
those who have relatively less social power (cf. Hall 1981; Bourdieu 1984). Elites are
thus often held to exemplify the highest religio-cultural values within a society (Sharot
2001: 11), values which are themselves frequently aligned with what might be loosely
termed 'written' religion (sacred texts and other religious writings), while the perceived
low-value religion of non-elites (or even 'sub-elites') is frequently caricatured as 'non-
written' or 'practised' religion (cf. Goody 1986: 20–26). Viewed from this perspective,
then, scholarly constructs of 'popular' religion and 'official' religion in ancient Israel
and Judah are frequently problematic because they are all too often value-laden with
the theological or cultural preferences of (primarily Western) scholars themselves,[2]

---

2.   As Benson Saler observes, scholarly constructs of 'religion' as a category are themselves
potentially deeply problematic:

> Western scholars who study religion develop some understanding of what is meant by religion
> in their society long before they become scholars . . . Long before European scholars of religion
> become scholars of religion, they have fairly well developed ideas of what to look for in searching
> the world for religions. In large measure, indeed, their scholarly efforts to define or characterize
> religion are efforts to . . . foreground what they deem most salient or important about religion.
>
> (Saler 1997: 28; cf. Fitzgerald 2000, 2003)

preferences which continue to be shaped in part by the 'models' of monotheism and religious expression promoted and endorsed in the biblical texts.

Social-Scientific Constructs of 'Popular' Religion and 'Official' Religion

Some scholars, however, seek to nuance the perceived dichotomy between 'official' religion and 'popular' religion in ways intended to avoid oversimplification by engaging more directly with the cultural roles and social locations of various socio-religious groups in ancient Israel and Judah. This endeavour has been helped by the more broadly sociological and anthropological reframing of ancient Israelite and Judahite religions and their composite groups, so that most scholars now distinguish many more forms of religion in these societies, including personal piety, 'family' or 'household' religion, and 'local', 'community' or 'non-elite' religion, as well as 'national' or 'state' religion (e.g. Albertz 1978, 1994, 2008; Ahlström 1982; Lang 1983, 2002: 109–38; van der Toorn 1996, 2003; Miller 2000; Hutter 2004; Olyan 2008). Within this context, 'official' religion continues to be aligned with those groups perceived to be superior, dominant or elitist, whether socially, politically or theologically. Thus in historical reconstructions, temple or bureaucratic religion in Judah and Israel tends to be defined (often problematically) as 'state' and therefore 'official' religion (e.g. Ahlström 1982; Tsumura 1993; McNutt 1999; Rogerson 2007; cf. Greenberg 1983), while within a biblical frame, the 'priestly' and 'Torah' theologies shaping the Hebrew Bible are frequently held to represent socially sanctioned and hence 'official' or 'normative' expressions of Yhwh religion, often on the assumption that these texts were produced by palace and/or temple scribes (cf. Weinfeld 1972; Schniedewind 2004).

In view of the aligning of 'official' religion with the beliefs and practices of elite or dominant power groups in ancient Israel and Judah, 'popular' religion is now increasingly defined in social opposition to it (e.g. Berlinerblau 1996). It is thus constructed not only as the religion of 'ordinary' people (Dever 2005), nor merely (and now more commonly) as 'family' religion (Albertz 1994, 2008; van der Toorn 1996; Olyan 2008), but also as the religion of the disenfranchised, the marginalized, or those who have been excluded or suppressed by dominant Israelite and Judahite elites and/or the biblical writers (Ackerman 1992; cf. Rose 1975; Gerstenberger 2002: 258–62). These might be thought to include polytheistic Yhwh worshippers (e.g. 2 Kgs 21.2-8; Jer. 11.12-13), religious specialists at the margins of 'mainstream' society (e.g. 1 Sam. 28.3-25; 2 Sam. 14.2), indigenous groups rejected by the 'establishment' (e.g. Deut. 7.1-5), and the priests of cult places beyond the 'state' temples (2 Kgs 17.32).

The socio-political agendas of twentieth-century feminist, liberation and post-colonial theologies have played a particularly influential role (both directly and indirectly) in casting the practitioners of various (particularly modern) forms of 'popular' religion as the marginalized or oppressed (Carroll R. 2000), encouraging a more critical sensitivity to the derogatory connotations of the term 'popular'. Stephen Sharot comments:

The dichotomization is seen to lead to caricatured portrayals of popular religion as magic, oriented solely to practical and materialistic ends, without any ethical, philosophical, or soteriological concerns . . . [It is t]he religion of the masses, who were unable to acquire the understandings and complex formulations of the enlightened elite . . .

(Sharot 2001: 13)

Within biblical studies, similar concerns about the pejorative connotations of the dichotomy between 'popular' and 'official' religions have been voiced (e.g. Ackerman 1992: 1–3; Berlinerblau 1996: 17–18), so that those marginalized or denounced in the Hebrew Bible for their religious practices are now increasingly rehabilitated in scholarly reconstructions of the religious past. In particular, the beliefs and practices frequently categorized as 'women's religion' have reframed the debate about the nature of 'official' religion and 'popular' religion in ancient Israel and Judah. As most scholars now recognize, women are the major group for whom male-dominated 'official' religion – as typically constructed – might have been relatively inaccessible, irrelevant, alien, or even (for the majority) unknown (cf. Bird 1987, 1991; Jay 1992; Meyers 1988, 2002, 2003).[3] Instead, most women's religious practice was carried out in their domestic and local settings and was seemingly bound up with fertility, fecundity and productivity rituals associated with the household and agrarian activities (such as childrearing, healing, spinning, weaving and grain processing) in which most women likely participated, probably within the contexts of informal inter-household social networks (van der Toorn 1994, 2003; Meyers 2002, 2003, 2005; Ackerman 2008). Once the more usual focus of scholarly discussions of 'popular' religion, the proverbial 'man in the street' has now given way to 'women in the home'.

The recognized need for a more precise socio-cultural contextualization of 'popular' religious groups has discouraged the scholarly tendency to polarize 'official' and 'popular' forms of religion. In particular, it is now increasingly emphasized that 'official' and 'popular' manifestations of religion co-exist within a complex dynamic relationship, reflecting the dynamism of the cultural system in which religious practice must be located (e.g. Carroll R. 2000; cf. C. Geertz 1973, 1983). This perspective necessarily highlights the reciprocal relationship between 'official' and 'popular' socio-religious groups, encouraging the recognition that the power groups with whom 'official' religions are often aligned depend to a certain extent on the compliance and consent of those they seek to 'dominate' (cf. Berlinerblau 1996, 1999; Büchner 2008). Much of this compliance is constructed upon what is shared by all socio-religious groups, elite and non-elite, 'official' and 'popular' – despite the differences and variations between and among them and their symbols, rituals and the meanings manifested within them. Aspects of 'popular' religion might thus be exhibited (intentionally or not) in 'official' religion, while aspects of 'official' religion might feature in 'popular' religion (Routledge 2006). Set within the cultural matrix, all socio-religious groups and their beliefs and practices are thus inextricably interrelated, so that imposing a dichotomous or polarized distinction between 'official' religion and 'popular' religion risks misrepresenting the essentially *social* context and function of religious practice. As M. Daniel Carroll R. comments:

---

3.   Although this is not to deny the place of some high-status women in the sorts of religious environments commonly designated 'elite' or 'official'; see further Marsman 2003 and Ackerman 2008.

> From this perspective, 'popular religion' would refer to the religion of the general population and would not be limited to certain subgroups. It is not to be reduced to religious phenomena which are in opposition to 'official religion', nor is the latter simply defined as the ideological weapon of the dominant classes. There is a recognition that what is professed and practiced by the people as a whole includes elements of both official religion and what lies beyond its purview . . . Some might suggest that this more phenomenological take on 'popular religion' is sociologically imprecise, but I am persuaded that it is *culturally realistic*.
>
> (Carroll R. 2002: 156–57; emphasis in original)

Scholars of ancient Israelite and Judahite religions are thus encouraged to engage with the social specifics of various religious groups, their beliefs and practices, while at the same time recognizing the interrelation of these groups and their religiosity within the cultural matrix. But the sharpened social-scientific interrogation of ancient Israelite and Judahite religions has transformed the debate about the dichotomy between 'official' and 'popular' religions so much that the scholarly value of the distinction between them has steadily cheapened. Not only is the once-accepted caricature of 'popular' religion as a corrupt, perverse and degenerate form of Yhwh worship (Labuschagne 1966: 123) no longer intellectually acceptable, but the increasingly nuanced variegation of ancient Israelite and Judahite religions calls into question the appropriateness of the distinction itself.

A Limiting Model?

One of the most significant illustrations of the limiting dichotomy between 'popular' and 'official' religions pertains to the study of ancient Israelite and Judahite goddess worship, the widespread existence of which is now generally accepted by most biblical scholars, who tend to associate or identify it very closely (though not unproblematically) with women's religious practice.[4] Understood as a form of women's cult, some scholars thus tend to categorize goddess worship (and particularly Asherah worship) as a form of 'popular' religion (e.g. Ikeda 1993; Bach 1999; Dever 2005). But if women's religion is to be regarded as a widespread form of 'popular' religion, under-represented by or excluded from 'official' religion, how then should scholars best account for indications of goddess worship and other expressions of women's religion within 'elite' or 'official' or 'state' contexts? For example, in the Hebrew Bible, Asherah worship and weaving cults are located in the Jerusalem temple (e.g. 2 Kgs 21.7; 23.4, 6-7), and some women are portrayed as high status worshippers of Asherah (1 Kgs 15.13; 18.19). In Jeremiah 7 and 44, the household worship of the Queen of Heaven, in which children, husbands and wives appear to participate (7.16-18; 44.15-19, 24-25), is imaged as a cult of a goddess credited with a 'state' level function (protection from military attack in 44.18) and 'state' level worshippers (political elites in 44.17). Even when taken in isolation from the extant material remains of Israelite and Judahite religions – which, some have argued, similarly attest to the widespread worship of goddesses across

---

4.   Goddess worship should not be caricatured simply as 'women's religion' (Bird 1991: 107), just as men's religious practice need not be equated purely with the worship of male deities. Women likely worshipped male deities and/or deified male ancestors within their households (cf. van der Toorn 2008: 29). On women's Yhwh worship, see most recently Ackerman 2006 and 2008.

'official' and 'popular' boundaries (Byrne 2004; Büchner 2008) – these biblical portrayals of women's religious behaviour challenge the sharp differentiation of 'popular' religion from 'official' religion. As Susan Ackerman observes:

> Asherah worship – which is frequently described using this rubric of 'popular religion' – is hardly restricted to the non-elite . . . the special role of women within Asherah's cult is best understood by seeing a close interrelationship between the Asherah cult as it was practiced in the temple, as it was practiced in the palace, and as it was practiced in private Israelite households. 'Popular religion', at least in this one case, needs to be understood as transcending any elite versus non-elite divide.
>
> (Ackerman 2003: 465; cf. Olyan 1988)

In similarly recognizing the presence of supposedly 'popular' religious practices in 'official' contexts, some scholars seek to counter the problematic distinction between 'official' religion and 'popular' religion by refining and redefining these awkward categories. Jacques Berlinerblau, for example, calls for a greater recognition of the diverse forms of 'popular' religion within their precise social contexts, arguing that scholarly enquiry should focus on distinct 'popular religious groups' made up of '"adjectived" Israelites' as 'bearers of precise economic, social, sexual and geographic attributes' (Berlinerblau 1993: 17; 1996). Rainer Albertz (1994, 2008) and Karel van der Toorn (1996, 2008) have chosen not to employ the designation 'popular' religion, preferring to speak instead of 'family' religion or 'local' religion (cf. Lewis 2008), though perhaps at the risk of being misunderstood to simply substitute one moniker for another.

William Dever has similarly sought to change the language of the contemporary debate altogether. He returns to older formulations by shifting from the designation 'popular religion' (used, for example, in his 1994 and 2002 publications) to primarily refer instead to ancient Israelite 'folk religion' (Dever 2005; cf. Stern 2001). While this shift in terminology may reflect to a degree the more inclusive readership of his recent discussion – pitched, as he says, at 'ordinary people' (Dever 2005: ix, 314; cf. 1997) – it also marks his discomfort with the distinction between 'official' and 'popular' religions:

> . . . speaking of 'popular' religion implies that it constituted a form of religious life that was not represented in the priestly and court circles in Jerusalem but was widespread only in the countryside. And that cannot be the case . . .
>
> (Dever 2005: 7; cf. 1994)

And yet, despite Dever's apparent discomfort, there remains a reluctance to abandon the underlying dichotomy and its prevailing ideological assumptions altogether. He self-consciously assumes it in sketching some of the distinctive differences between 'state' religion and 'folk' religion, differences that include the theoretical antithetical pairing of literate/popular, texts/artefacts, mythology/magic, dogma/praxis, national/local and state/family (2005: 5–6). Indeed, Dever's discussion ultimately endorses the old stereotype of 'popular' or 'folk' religion as the simplistic practices of rural communities, describing ancient Israelite folk religion as 'simple, but adequate for the needs of a simple agrarian society' (2005: 273–74; cf. Gomes 2003: 49). And despite his explicit attempt to critique scholarly constructs of 'ordinary people in ancient Israel and their everyday religious lives' (2005: ix), Dever's description of these people and their practices perpetuates some of the more derogatory assumptions recent sociolo-gical and anthropological critiques have sought to counter. This is particularly evident in his contextualizing of 'folk religion' within its 'everyday' 'traditional' village set-ting (2005: 18–20), which he describes as 'kin-based, and thus in a sense inbred . . . As in an Arab village of 100–300 [people] today, everyone was related by blood to everyone else' (2005: 18), so that the social setting of 'traditional' family life and its 'folk religion' is, claims Dever, very much like that of *'primitive* Arab villages in the Hebron hills' in the twentieth century (2005: 19, emphasis added). This derogatory sketch of 'folk' religion and its practitioners can only undermine the intellectual basis on which socio-cultural distinctions between 'official' and 'popular' forms of religion might be made.

Regrettably, the Western, orientalizing tone of Dever's discussion shares much in common with many other studies of 'indigenous' or 'traditional' or even 'primitive' religions of non-Western cultures – ancient and modern (cf. Cox 1996, 2007; A.W. Geertz 2004). It is possible that a deeply embedded cultural and/or theological dis-comfort with the 'other' continues to encourage the caricaturing of certain religious practices as 'popular' within some scholarly circles.

'Popularizing' Practices

The scholarly rehabilitation of both the goddess Asherah and 'women's religion' in ancient Israel and Judah has gone some way to expose some of the problems inher-ent within assumptions about 'official' and 'popular' religion. Mainstream biblical scholarship tends now to be far more comfortable in recognizing the wide-ranging place of goddess worship in ancient Israel and Judah, and is consequently less likely to relegate this type of religious activity to the realm of mere 'popular' practice. While this shift owes much to the well-known debates concerning the interpretation of arte-facts and inscriptions associated with women and/or Asherah worship, it also reflects, to a notable degree, the present-day prominence of gender as a matter of continued social and academic concern. The religious behaviour of ancient Israelite and Judahite women, and the cults of female deities, can no longer be marginalized or dismissed as 'popular' piety. But there remains a tendency within scholarship to 'popularize' other religious practices, which are not so easily mapped onto the contours of contemporary Western socio-cultural concerns and preferences. This is particularly evident within discussions of mortuary rituals, ancestor cults and other practices associated with the dead in ancient Israel and Judah.

Religious practices dealing with the dead have long functioned as fodder for schol-arly accounts of 'popular' religion. Until recently, the so-called cult of the dead was typically characterized in this context as a practice associated with 'primitive and uncivilized races' (Paton 1921: 248) and disparaged as a 'black art' (Frazer 1923: 295). Perhaps somewhat unsurprisingly, J.B. Segal agreed that 'popular' religion included death cult rituals comprising mourning and interment activities and the 'black arts' of 'witchcraft and the summoning of twittering and moaning ghosts and familiar spirits' (Segal 1976: 6; cf. Bright 1981: 450–51). Although some of the more pejorative pre-suppositions have given way to a sharpened critical perspective (cf. Lewis 2002), there remains a widespread scholarly assumption that mortuary cults, ancestor worship and necromancy were a part of ancient Israel and Judah's 'popular' religion, influenced by

Canaanite practices and opposed by the 'official' religion of orthodox Yahwism (e.g. Xella 1982, 1995; Spronk 1986; Mendenhall 1992; Milgrom 2000: 1375–82; King and Stager 2001: 376–80).

Even those who appear to be more careful in their handling of the dichotomy between 'official' and 'popular' forms of religion in Israel and Judah quickly designate ancestor veneration, cults of the dead and other post-mortem rituals as 'popular' practices (e.g. Lewis 1989: 176–77; Ackerman 1992: 214–15; Bloch-Smith 1992: 150–51; Schmidt 1996: 236; Rogerson 2007: 230–31). Mark Smith offers a pointed critique of scholarly constructs of 'official' Yahwism and 'popular' practice, urging a more nuanced and critical application of these categories – including when used in discussions of mortuary cults and post-mortem practices (Smith 1998, 2002: xx–xxi, 162–63; cf. Smith and Bloch-Smith 1988). And yet, despite his apparent reservations, he nevertheless holds firm to the dichotomy between 'official' and 'popular' religions, resorting to the familiar, seemingly default position established by earlier generations of scholars, which assumes that cults of the dead were a part of Canaanite-influenced 'popular' religion; they were 'traditional' practices, performed within all sectors of society, and were essentially distinct from Yhwh worship (Smith 2002: 162–63).

Despite the recent paradigm shifts that have transformed scholarly reconstructions of the religious cultures of ancient Israel and Judah – particularly concerning the false contrasting of 'Canaanite' and 'Israelite' cultures (see Chapter 3 in this volume) – scholarly debates about Israelite and Judahite mortuary cults thus remain stubbornly sluggish in adopting the newer perspectives more readily employed in other areas of enquiry. Indeed, the persistent 'popularizing' of rituals associated with the dead is particularly curious given the near certainty that mortuary practices of some sort or another were performed at all levels of society by all social groups, however configured. After all, everybody dies. It might thus be expected that death cults would be treated as a more normative and mainstream aspect of religious practice, so that the only justification for their being termed 'popular' would be their widespread, common occurrence. In most discussions, however, the 'popular' label affixed to Israelite and Judahite death cults reflects the perception that they fall beyond the bounds or interests of mainstream Yhwh religion and its sanctuaries (e.g. Zevit 2001: 664; Johnston 2002). This view is particularly encouraged by the biblical condemnation of practices associated with the dead (e.g. Lev. 19.28, 31; Deut. 14.1; 18.11; 26.14; Isa. 8.19-20; 57.3-13; 65.1-5), suggesting that these rituals were incompatible with 'official' or 'establishment' religion, whether for theological reasons (e.g. Johnston 2002), socio-political reasons (e.g. Blenkinsopp 1995; van der Toorn 1996: 318–19), or both (e.g. Halpern 1991, 2003; Milgrom 2000: 1776–77).

Social-scientific analyses of death cults are often thought to complement this biblical perspective, for these practices are usually located within the seemingly private sphere of household religion, rather than the apparently more public spaces of 'local' or 'establishment' religion – a distinction which is itself often mapped directly onto the dichotomous 'popular'/'official' paradigm. This assumed distancing of the dead from 'establishment' or 'public' religion is also thought to be supported by archaeological investigations of burial sites in ancient Judah, which attest to an apparent tendency to locate graves and tombs outside settlements (see Bloch-Smith 1992, 2002). This for some is suggestive of a continued socio-religious anxiety about the ritual impurity of the dead and their burial places (see Pitard 2002: 150–51; contra Wenning 1997), an anxiety, which, in its turn, is used to bolster the biblically-based assumption that practices pertaining to the dead were necessarily peripheral or 'foreign' aspects of normative religious concerns (see Johnston 2002: 44–45; cf. Schmidt 1996: 289–92). For many, then, activities dealing with the dead are best characterized as 'popular' forms of religion.

However, there are reasons to avoid 'popularizing' death rituals. While some biblical texts appear to assert that religious practices pertaining to the dead are 'foreign' to mainstream Yhwh worship (e.g. Deut. 18.9-12; Ps. 106.28), others suggest that mortuary rituals and death cults played a more prominent and central role at its state-sponsored sanctuaries, including Yhwh's temple in Jerusalem. For example, Ezek. 43.7-9 indicates that a royal cult of the dead was maintained here (Ebach 1971; Niehr 2003), while Isa. 56.5 images Yhwh himself performing mortuary rituals (setting up a memorial monument, invoking the name of the dead) in his temple (cf. 2 Sam. 18.18; Stavrakopoulou forthcoming: ch. 5). In 2 Sam. 21.9-14 the public performance of mortuary rituals is held to secure Yhwh's blessings upon the land, blessings that could also be transformed into curses through the ritual reversal of these public practices, as indicated in Jer. 8.1-3 (cf. Lightstone 2006: 44–48). The close interrelation of Yhwh worship and rituals bound up with the dead is also evident in inscriptions from Khirbet Beit Lei and Khirbet el-Qom (see Zevit 2001: 359–70, 405–37) and the inscribed silver amulets from Ketef Hinnom (see Barkay 1992), which attest to the invocation of Yhwh's blessings upon – and perhaps protection of – the dead in their tombs. Thus, in the light of this biblical and non-biblical material, it would appear that practices pertaining to the dead were not necessarily distinct from Yhwh worship, nor were they necessarily confined to the 'private' sphere of the house or family tomb, but might also have found more public expression at larger sanctuaries too (van der Toorn 1996: 211–18; Olyan 2008: 115, 118–20). As such, the common assumption that mortuary rituals and ancestor cults were socially, spatially and conceptually peripheral to mainstream or normative Yhwh worship – and thus in essence 'popular' – is difficult to defend.

The caricaturing of these practices as 'popular' religion is likely due in part to an assumption that 'family' or 'household' religion (in which death cults played a central role) was distinct from and unrelated to public or 'elite' or 'establishment' forms of religion, and it also owes something to a relatively uncritical assessment of the complex social dynamics of these practices. The scholarly 'popularizing' of rituals dealing with the dead might also be shaped to a degree by a cultural or intellectual difficulty in understanding the ritualized interrelation and interaction of ancestors and descendants – or even a discomfort with the perceived otherness of these beliefs and practices. Rituals including feeding the dead (Deut. 26.14; Ps. 16.3-4; 106.28; Tob. 4.17; Sir. 30.18) and consulting the dead (1 Sam. 28.3-25; Isa. 8.19-20; 29.4) are well known features of ancient West Asian ancestor and mortuary cults (Lewis 1989; Fleming 2008; van der Toorn 2008) and reflect a widespread belief in the post-mortem life of the dead. These rituals might be felt to be alien to contemporary – ostensibly secularized – Western responses to the dead, for in most parts of the UK, Western Europe and the US today, the dead tend to be far more marginalized, isolated or separated from the living (Barley 1995; Foltyn 1996; Parker Pearson 1999: 40–49). This is bound up with the modernist notion that assumes that death irrevocably breaks the active social relationship between the newly deceased individual and the living community of which they were a part, so that the living are unable to communicate with the dead, and the dead are unable to communicate with the living (cf. Klass, Silverman and Nickman 1996; Bennett and Bennett 2000; Francis, Kellaher and Neophytou 2001).[5] Thus a modernist emphasis on a perceived disconnect between the living and the dead – notably perpetuated in Western academia (Valentine 2006; cf. Klass and Goss 1999) – may perhaps underlie the scholarly diminishing of the religious value and status of mortuary and ancestor cults in ancient Israel and Judah.

This preference is also likely shaped by a persistent religio-cultural scepticism about these particular sorts of religious beliefs and practices, for ancestor worship and cults of the dead (ancient and modern) have been heavily caricatured in Western intellectual discourse since the nineteenth century as 'primitive' or 'exotic' forms of religion (e.g. Paton 1921; Frazer 1923; Tromp 1969; Mendenhall 1992) and continue to be regarded by many as inferior to the ('orthodox') monotheisms dominating religious perspectives today (e.g. Milgrom 2000: 1783–84). This position is closely related to a deeply rooted intellectual and theological othering of non-Western attitudes to the dead (cf. Hockey 1996), which may go some way to explaining why some biblical scholars are careful to distance certain ancient Israelite and Judahite practices dealing with the dead from contemporary Christian death rituals and their accompanying beliefs (e.g. Schmidt 1996: 9–11), and why others seek to minimize the religious role of the dead in Israel and Judah in favour of crediting Christianity with a unique and exclusive claim to agency beyond the grave (e.g. Johnston 2002: 239). It is thus not surprising that these views are often accompanied by an assumption that many rituals dealing with the dead were 'popular', 'foreign' or 'pagan' aspects of the religious worlds giving rise to the Hebrew Bible.

Thus, the scholarly 'popularizing' of practices might at times harbour an uneasiness about religious practices felt by some to be incompatible or disharmonious with more familiar or contemporary constructs of 'appropriate' religio-cultural beliefs and behaviours. This in its turn can encourage a pejorative distinction between 'popular' and 'official' religious practices, which risks further undermining or discrediting the polarized categories of this dichotomous model.

Abandoning the Model

The Western perspectives of biblical scholars dealing with 'popular' religion have been highlighted in different ways by Ziony Zevit (2001: 658–64; 2003), who argues that the scholarly framing of 'official' and 'popular' religions is inappropriately dichotomous for the socio-cultural and archaeological study of what he broadly terms ancient Israelite religion. The reasons for this, he suggests, are essentially rooted in the social and cultural differences between Western Christianity – which (as discussed above) has so heavily influenced the scholarly categorization of 'official' and 'popular' forms of religion – and ancient Israelite religion, which, like other non-Western (particularly polytheistic) religions, exhibits 'nested' socio-cultic groups too dissimilar to those

---

5.   This is not to suggest that contemporary Western societies exhibit 'shallow' death cultures (cf. Robben 2004: 1), for as numerous studies show, death rituals and attitudes to the corpse continue to perform a richly profound and transformative function within seemingly secularized societies (e.g. D.J. Davies 2002; Foltyn 2008). The dead are accepted and socially active members of the living community in many non-Western cultures, in which they are often venerated as ancestors or the sacred dead. For a recent ethnographic study, see Prendergast 2005.

comprising Western Christianity. Accordingly, Zevit argues, the 'digitized dichotomies' of 'official' and 'popular' religion 'lack a social or ideological referent in the culture of ancient Israel' (2003: 232). He says:

> There was no state or elite or official or popular religion in ancient Israel. There was a political body that we may label 'state'; there were social and economic elites; there were sacerdotal and royal officials; there was a populace; and there was the so-called 'man in the street'. But data do not support the proposition that a particular type of pattern or credo or praxis may be associated with them.
>
> (Zevit 2003: 232)

Instead, Zevit proposes that scholars employ not their own models of socio-religious organization to describe ancient Israelite and Judahite religious practices, but the model of a nested social hierarchy to which the Hebrew Bible itself alludes (cf. Stager 1985; Albertz 1994; cf. Saler 1993). Collectively, the biblical texts image five inter-related levels of social stratification, a system succinctly illustrated in Josh. 7.13-14, in which the following social units appear, each comprising the next: *geber* ('individual male'), *bayit* ('house' or 'extended family'), *mišpāḥâ* ('clan'), *šēbeṭ* ('tribe') and *'ām* ('people'). These are the categories, Zevit suggests, by which scholars should describe and analyse religious practice in ancient Israel and Judah, for they are the '*known* ancient social realities' of Israelite religion (Zevit 2003: 233, emphasis added).

In the light of the preceding discussion, Zevit's reasoned rejection of the designations 'official' and 'popular' is certainly attractive. Indeed, there are good reasons to avoid 'projecting' contemporary (and primarily Western, Christianizing) labels and their accompanying assumptions onto the religious cultures of ancient Israel and Judah – not the least of which is the well-practised anthropological principle that the study of specific features of any culture is likely enriched by the analytical use of constructs 'indigenous' to that culture.

However, Zevit's model also has its weaknesses. Though it is appropriately sensitive to the social diversities of ancient religions, it is perhaps over-confident in assuming biblical portrayals of socio-religious stratification as discernable historical realities. Some forms of socio-religious diversity might feasibly be identified by means of archaeo-anthropology and other social-scientific approaches, without recourse to the Hebrew Bible (for example, 'household' religion, 'urban' religion, or even 'royal' religion), but other forms are not so easily discerned beyond their portrayals in the biblical literature – including 'clan' religion, 'tribal' religion, and indeed the religion of the 'people'.[6] This essentially limits the critical value of Zevit's proposed model.

Indeed, in adopting the biblical portrayal of socio-religious stratification, Zevit also relies upon biblical portrayals of socio-religious practice as the template for historical reconstructions of religious realities in ancient Israel and Judah: 'A range of biblical texts drawn from both narrative and legal genres . . . indicate that Israelite

---

6.   Given their interrelation, there has been some difficulty in discerning and distinguishing between socio-religious groups and their practices, particularly at the levels of family and/or household and local and/or regional practice (cf. van der Toorn 1996). Recent studies, however, exhibit a growing confidence in distinguishing between these groups – primarily, it would seem, in terms of the social spaces in which they functioned (such as the home, tomb, local or regional sanctuary, or even temple). See further Ackerman 2008; Albertz 2008: 96–97; Lewis 2008: 72–80; Olyan 2008.

writers described cultic activities occurring at each level of social organization' (Zevit 2003: 230). But, as already noted, biblical descriptions are themselves inherently problematic: they are written from the likely specialized (scribal) and elite perspectives of the biblical writers, whose representations of certain socio-religious groups may intentionally or unintentionally misrepresent the religious beliefs and practices of those groups (Berlinerblau 1993; cf. Ackerman 1992: 213–17). While this is not to dismiss the usefulness of the biblical texts altogether, it remains that they must be handled cautiously and carefully in historical reconstructions of the religious past. As such, Zevit's assumption that the Hebrew Bible's categories and characterizations of socio-religious diversity are the 'known' realities (2003: 233) of ancient Israelite and Judahite religions is perhaps over-optimistic.

Further undermining what may or may not be 'known' from biblical texts about the socio-religious realities of the past is the 'configured' nature of the Hebrew Bible itself. The self-legitimizing presentation of the biblical texts (particularly Torah) as authoritative religious teaching renders the Hebrew Bible itself a construct of a later type of religion *unlike* the religions of the social groups that probably comprised the nested social matrix of ancient Israel and Judah. Though its writings might draw somewhat selectively upon a variety of traditions deriving from different socio-religious contexts, the Hebrew Bible essentially presents and represents a 'book religion' too dissimilar to the religious realities of ancient Israel and Judah to offer a reasonably unproblematic template for scholarly reconstructions of the socio-religious past (*pace* Zevit 2003: 230–33). Instead, and at best, the religion of the Hebrew Bible likely reflects the idealized religious preferences of the scribal elites and their textual communities of the Persian and Hellenistic periods, the groups for whom 'written religion' is self-referentially promoted in texts including Exod. 24.12; 2 Kings 22–23; Jeremiah 29; Nehemiah 8; and the book of Deuteronomy. The dynamic of social power created and sustained by this specialist-dominated religion is well described by Jan Assmann, who writes:

> The characteristics of a textual community are, on the one hand, the use of a basic text to define identity, and, on the other hand, to structure the authority and leadership that arises from the ability to handle texts. Philological and political competence come together here. Leadership falls to the person who possesses the most comprehensive knowledge and the most illuminating interpretation of the texts.
>
> (Assmann 2006: 73)

Viewed from this perspective, the 'book religion' of the Hebrew Bible masquerades as an archaic 'official' religion, seemingly intended to transform or eclipse the religions practised by other groups within the broader cultural community, so that they become 'improper', 'illegitimate' or even 'deviant' religions. Karel van der Toorn similarly observes:

> This religion of the book was designed to take the place of both family religion and state religion, since the father in the family would read the Torah to his son, just as the king would read the Torah to himself. From now on, there would be an official religion, and all forms of religious life departing from its doctrine would be unofficial – and be referred to in later times as popular religion.
>
> (van der Toorn 1996: 379)

Despite the biblical portrayal of an age-old written religion, this 'official' religion promoted in the biblical texts was not a religious reality of ancient Israel or Judah, but a literary construct, built on the later elitist framing and prioritization of the written 'revelation' of Yhwh (cf. van der Toorn 1997, 2007: ch. 8). This self-proclaimed 'book religion' would only begin to be become aligned with sanctioned and 'normative' religious preferences in the latter centuries of the first millennium BCE, when it was used as a powerful tool in shaping the more dominant religious aspects of early Judaisms (cf. P.R. Davies 1995, 1998). While, then, the Hebrew Bible cannot be assumed to directly reflect religious reality, to a degree it nonetheless came to play a crucial role in determining it during the Hellenistic and later periods.

The dichotomy between 'popular' religion and 'official' religion is thus neither straightforward, nor easily defined, nor indeed easily applied to the likely religious realities of ancient Israel and Judah. As social-scientific interrogations of ancient and modern religions have shown, concepts of 'popular' religion are inherently tied to, and necessarily defined by, concepts of 'official' religion; accordingly, concepts of 'popular' religion are of most relevance to religions in which a prevailing, culturally accredited and dominant source of religious legitimation (usually written) is aligned with and regulated by a socially and/or religiously specialized elite and their institutions (Vrijhof and Waardenburg 1979; Williams 1980). While some early Judaisms appear to have functioned in this way, the religions of ancient Israel and Judah did not (cf. van der Toorn 2002: 228). Thus, if any broad distinction between types of religion is to be assumed within discussions of religious diversities in ancient Israel and Judah, it seems prudent to abandon the categories of 'popular' religion and 'official' religion altogether, and instead to distinguish between biblical portrayals of the religious past on the one hand, and the likely religious realities of ancient Israel and Judah, on the other. Beyond that, ancient Israelite and Judahite religious diversities are perhaps best managed on a case-by-case basis, framed within the context of their cultural, social, anthropological, geographical, economic, political and temporal specifics – to the extent that these can be reasonably reconstructed without undue, uncritical reliance upon the Hebrew Bible. This 'particularization' of religious diversities remains a difficult task, but is intellectually preferable to what was a default and is now an increasingly discredited dependence upon a polarizing, misrepresentative paradigm.

Bibliography

Ackerman, S.
1992   *Under Every Green Tree: Popular Religion in Sixth-Century Judah* (HSM 46; Atlanta, GA: Scholars Press).
2003   'At Home with the Goddess', in W.G. Dever and S. Gitin (eds), *Symbiosis, Symbolism, and the Power of the Past: Canaan, Ancient Israel, and Their Neighbors from the Late Bronze Age through Roman Palestinia* (Winona Lake, IN: Eisenbrauns), 455–68.
2006   'Women and the Worship of Yahweh in Ancient Israel', in S. Gitin, J.E. Wright and J.P. Dessel (eds), *Confronting the Past: Archaeological and Historical Essays on Ancient Israel in Honor of William G. Dever* (Winona Lake, IN: Eisenbrauns), 189–97.
2008   'Household Religion, Family Religion, and Women's Religion in Ancient Israel', in J. Bodel and S.M. Olyan (eds), *Household and Family Religion in Antiquity* (Oxford: Blackwell), 127–58.

Ahlström, G.W.
1982   *Royal Administration and National Religion in Ancient Palestine* (SHANE 1; Leiden: Brill).

Albertz, R.
1978   *Persönliche Frömmigkeit und offizielle Religion: Religionsinterner Pluralismus in Israel und Babylon* (Calwer Theologische Monographien A 9; Stuttgart: Calwer Verlag).
1994   *A History of Israelite Religion in the Old Testament Period* (2 vols; trans. J. Bowden. OTL; London: SCM Press).
2008   'Family Religion in Ancient Israel and its Surroundings', in J. Bodel and S.M. Olyan (eds), *Household and Family Religion in Antiquity* (Oxford: Blackwell), 89–112.

Albright, W.F.
1961   'The Role of the Canaanites in the History of Civilization', in G.E. Wright (ed.), *The Bible and the Ancient Near East: Essays in Honor of William Foxwell Albright* (Garden City, NY: Doubleday), 328–62.
1968   *Yahweh and the Gods of Canaan: A Historical Analysis of Two Contrasting Faiths* (London: Althone Press).

Assmann, J.
2006   *Religion and Cultural Memory: Ten Studies* (trans. R. Livingstone; Palo Alto, CA: Stanford University Press).

Bach, A.
1999   'Man's World, Woman's Place: Sexual Politics in the Hebrew Bible', in A. Bach (ed.), *Women in the Hebrew Bible: A Reader* (New York, NY, and London: Routledge), xiii–xvi.

Barkay, G.
1992   'The Priestly Benediction on Silver Plaques from Ketef Hinnom in Jerusalem', *TA* 19: 139–92.

Barley, N.
1995   *Dancing on the Grave: Encounters with Death* (London: John Murray).

Barton, J.
2007   *The Nature of Biblical Criticism* (Louisville and London: Westminster John Knox).

Bennett, G. and K.M. Bennett
2000   'The Presence of the Dead: An Empirical Study', *Mortality* 5.2: 139–57.

Berlinerblau, J.
1993   'The "Popular Religion" Paradigm in Old Testament Research: A Sociological Critique', *JSOT* 60: 3–26.
1996   *The Vow and the 'Popular Religious Groups' of Ancient Israel: A Philological and Sociological Inquiry* (JSOTS 210; Sheffield: Sheffield Academic Press).
1999   'Preliminary Remarks for the Sociological Study of Israelite "Official Religion"', in R. Chazan, W.W. Hallo and L.H. Schiffman (eds), *Ki Baruch Hu: Ancient Near Eastern, Biblical, and Judaic Studies in Honor of Baruch A. Levine* (Winona Lake, IN: Eisenbrauns), 153–70.

Bird, P.
1987   'The Place of Women in the Israelite Cultus', in P.D. Miller, P.D. Hanson and S.D. McBride (eds), *Ancient Israelite Religion: Essays in Honor of Frank Moore Cross* (Philadelphia, PA: Fortress Press), 397–419.
1991   'Israelite Religion and the Faith of Israel's Daughters: Reflections on Gender and Religious Definition', in D. Jobling, P.L. Day and G.T. Sheppard (eds), *The Bible and the Politics of Exegesis: Essays in Honor of Norman K. Gottwald on his Sixty-Fifth Birthday* (Cleveland, OH: Pilgrim Press), 97–108.

Blenkinsopp, J.
1995   'Deuteronomy and the Politics of Post-Mortem Existence', *VT* 45: 1–16.

Bloch-Smith, E.
1992   *Judahite Burial Practices and Beliefs about the Dead* (JSOTS 123; Sheffield: JSOT Press).
2002   'Life in Judah from the Perspective of the Dead', *NEA* 65.2: 120–30.

Bourdieu, P.
1984   *Distinction: A Social Critique of the Judgement of Taste* (trans. R. Nice; London: Routledge).

Bright, J.
1981   *A History of Israel* (3rd edn; OTL; London: SCM Press).

Büchner, D.
2008   '*Boshet* in Jeremiah 3:24: Disenfranchisement and the Role of the Goddess in Seventh Century Judah', *JTS* 59: 478–99.

Byrne, R.
2004   'Lie Back and Think of Judah: The Reproductive Politics of Pillar Figurines', *NEA* 67.3: 137–51.

Carroll R., M.D.
2000   'Re-examining "Popular Religion": Issues of Definition and Sources. Insights from Interpretive Anthropology', in M.D. Carroll R. (ed.), *Rethinking Contexts, Rereading Texts: Contributions from the Social Sciences to Biblical Interpretation* (JSOTS 299; Sheffield: Sheffield Academic Press), 146–67.

Cook, S.L.
2004   *The Social Roots of Biblical Yahwism* (Atlanta, GA: Society of Biblical Literature).

Cox, J.L.
1996   'The Classification "Primal Religions" as a Non-empirical, Christian Theological Construct', *Studies in World Christianity: The Edinburgh Review of Theology and Religion* 2.1: 55–76.
2007   *From Primitive to Indigenous: The Academic Study of Indigenous Religions* (Aldershot: Ashgate).

Davies, D.J.
2002   *Death, Ritual and Belief* (2nd edn; London and New York, NY: Continuum).

Davies, P.R.
1992   *In Search of 'Ancient Israel'* (JSOTS 148; Sheffield: JSOT Press).
1995   'Scenes from the Early History of Judaism', in D.V. Edelman (ed.), *The Triumph of Elohim: From Yahwisms to Judaisms* (CBET 13; Kampen: Kok Pharos), 145–82.
1998   *Scribes and Schools: The Canonization of the Hebrew Scriptures* (Library of Ancient Israel; Louisville, KY: Westminster John Knox).

Davis, N.Z.
1974   'Some Tasks and Themes in the Study of Popular Religion', in C. Trinkaus and H.A. Oberman (eds), *The Pursuit of Holiness in Late Medieval and Renaissance Religion* (Studies in Medieval and Religious Thought 10; Leiden: Brill), 307–36.
1982   'From "Popular Religion" to Religious Cultures', in S. Ozment (ed.), *Reformation Europe: A Guide to Research* (St Louis, MO: Center for Reformation Research), 321–41.

Day, J.
2000   *Yahweh and the Gods and Goddesses of Canaan* (JSOTS 265; Sheffield: Sheffield Academic Press).

Dever, W.G.
1994   'The Silence of the Text: An Archaeological Commentary on 2 Kings 23', in M.D. Coogan, J.C. Exum and L.E. Stager (eds), *Scripture and Other Artifacts: Essays on the Bible and Archaeology in Honor of Philip J. King* (Louisville, KY: Westminster John Knox), 143–68.
1997   'Folk Religion and Early Israel: Did Yahweh Have a Consort?', in H. Shanks (ed.), *Aspects of Monotheism: How God is One* (Washington, DC: Biblical Archaeology Society), 27–56.

2002   'Theology, Philology, and Archaeology: In Pursuit of Ancient Israelite Religion', in B.M. Gittlen (ed.), *Sacred Time, Sacred Place: Archaeology and the Religion of Israel* (Winona Lake, IN: Eisenbrauns), 11–33.
2005   *Did God Have a Wife? Archaeology and Folk Religion in Ancient Israel* (Grand Rapids, MI: Eerdmans).

Ebach, J.H.
1971   'PGR = (Toten-)opfer? Ein Vorschlag zum Verständnis von Ez. 43, 7.9', *UF* 3: 365–68.

Ebertz, M.N. and F. Schultheis (eds)
1986   *Volksfrömmigkeit in Europa* (München: Kaiser).

Fitzgerald, T.
2000   *The Ideology of Religious Studies* (Oxford: Oxford University Press).
2003   'Playing Language Games and Performing Rituals: Religious Studies as Ideological State Apparatus', *Method & Theory in the Study of Religion* 15.3: 209–54.

Fleming, D.E.
2008   'The Integration of Household and Community Religion in Ancient Syria', in J. Bodel and S.M. Olyan (eds), *Household and Family Religion in Antiquity* (Oxford: Blackwell), 37–59.

Foltyn, J.L.
1996   'Dead Beauty: The Preservation, Memorialization, and Destruction of Beauty in Death', in G. Howarth and P. Jupp (eds), *Contemporary Issues in the Sociology of Death, Dying and Disposal* (London: Macmillan), 72–83.
2008   'The Corpse in Contemporary Culture: Identifying, Transacting, and Recoding the Dead Body in the Twenty-First Century', *Mortality* 13.2: 99–104.

Francis, D., L. Kellaher and G. Neophytou
2001   'The Cemetery: The Evidence of Continuing Bonds', in J. Hockey, J. Katz and N. Small (eds), *Grief, Mourning and Death Ritual* (Buckingham: Open University Press), 226–36.

Frazer, J.G.
1923   *Folklore in the Old Testament: Studies in Comparative Religion, Legend and Law* (abridged edn; London: Macmillan).

Geertz, A.W.
2004   'Can We Move Beyond Primitivism? On Recovering the Indigenes of Indigenous Religions in the Academic Study of Religions', in J.K. Olupona (ed.), *Beyond Primitivism: Indigenous Religious Traditions and Modernity* (New York, NY, and London: Routledge), 37–70.

Geertz, C.
1973   *The Interpretation of Cultures: Selected Essays* (New York, NY: Basic Books).
1983   *Local Knowledge: Further Essays in Interpretative Anthropology* (New York, NY: Basic Books).

Gerstenberger, E.S.
2002   *Theologies in the Old Testament* (trans. J. Bowden; Edinburgh: T&T Clark).

Gomes, J.
2003   'Popular Religion in Old Testament Research: Past, Present and Future', *Tyndale Bulletin* 54: 31–50.

Goody, J.
1986   *The Logic of Writing and the Organization of Society* (Cambridge: Cambridge University Press).

Grabbe, L.L. (ed.)
1997   *Can a 'History of Israel' be Written?* (JSOTS 245/ESHM 1; Sheffield: Sheffield Academic Press).

Greenberg, M.
1983   *Biblical Prose Prayer as a Window to the Popular Religion of Ancient Israel* (Berkeley, CA: University of California Press).

Hall, S.
1981   'Notes on Deconstructing "the Popular"', in R. Samuel (ed.), *People's History and Socialist Theory* (London: Routledge), 227–40.

Halpern, B.
1991   'Jerusalem and the Lineages in the Seventh Century BCE: Kingship and the Rise of Individual Moral Liability', in B. Halpern and D.B. Hobson (eds), *Law and Ideology in Monarchic Israel* (JSOTS 124; Sheffield: JSOT Press), 11–107.
2003   'Late Israelite Astronomies and the Early Greeks', in W.G. Dever and S. Gitin (eds), *Symbiosis, Symbolism, and the Power of the Past: Canaan, Ancient Israel, and Their Neighbors from the Late Bronze Age through Roman Palestinia* (Winona Lake, IN: Eisenbrauns), 323–52.

Harvey, G.
1994   'Death and Remembrance in Modern Paganism', in J. Davies (ed.), *Ritual and Remembrance: Responses to Death in Human Societies* (Sheffield: Sheffield Academic Press), 103–22.

Hess, R.
2007   *Israelite Religions: An Archaeological and Biblical Survey* (Grand Rapids, MI: Baker Academic).

Hockey, J.
1996   'The View from the West', in G. Howarth and P.C. Jupp (eds), *Contemporary Issues in the Sociology of Death, Dying and Disposal* (Basingstoke: Macmillan), 3–16.

Hutter, M. (ed.)
2004   *Offizielle religion, locale Kulte und indiviuelle Religiosität: Akten des religionsgeschichtlichen Symposiums 'Kleinasien und angrenzende Gebiete vom Beginn des 2. bis zur Mitte des 1. Jahrtausends v. Chr.'* (AOAT 318; Münster: Ugarit-Verlag).

Ikeda, Y.
1993   'Because Their Shade is Good – Asherah in the Early Israelite Religion', in E. Matsushima (ed.), *Official Cult and Popular Religion in the Ancient Near East: Papers of the First Colloquium on the Ancient Near East – The City and Its Life* (Heidelberg: Universitätverlag C. Winter), 56–80.

Jay, N.
1992   *Throughout Your Generations Forever: Sacrifice, Religion, and Paternity* (Chicago, IL: University of Chicago Press).

Johnston, P.S.
2002   *Shades of Sheol: Death and Afterlife in the Old Testament* (Leicester: Apollos).

Jolly, K.L.
1996   *Popular Religion in Late Saxon England: Elf Charms in Context* (Chapel Hill, NC: University of North Carolina Press).

King, P.J. and L.E. Stager
2001   *Life in Biblical Israel* (Library of Ancient Israel; Louisville, KY: Westminster John Knox).

Klass, D. and R. Goss
1999   'Spiritual Bonds to the Dead in Cross-Cultural and Historical Perspective: Comparative Religion and Modern Grief', *Death Studies* 23: 547–67.

Klass, D., P. Silverman and J. Nickman
1996   *Continuing Bonds* (Philadelphia, PA: Francis and Taylor, 1996).

Labuschagne, C.J.
1966   'Amos' Conception of God and the Popular Theology of His Time', *OTWSA* 7–8: 122–33.

Lang, B.
1983   'Persönlicher Gott und Ortsgott', in M. Görg (ed.), *Fontes atque Pontes: Eine Festgabe für Hellmut Brunner* (Wiesbaden: Harrassowitz), 271–301.

2002   *The Hebrew God: Portrait of an Ancient Deity* (New Haven, CT: Yale University Press).

Lemche, N.P.
1998   *The Israelites in History and Tradition* (Louisville, KY: Westminster John Knox Press).

Lewis, T.J.
1989   *Cults of the Dead in Ancient Israel and Ugarit* (HSM 39; Atlanta: Scholars Press).
2002   'How Far Can Texts Take Us? Evaluating Textual Sources for Reconstructing Ancient Israelite Beliefs about the Dead', in B.M. Gittlen (ed.), *Sacred Time, Sacred Place: Archaeology and the Religion of Israel* (Winona Lake, IN: Eisenbrauns), 169–217.
2008   'Family, Household, and Local Religion at Late Bronze Age Ugarit', in J. Bodel and S.M. Olyan (eds), *Household and Family Religion in Antiquity* (Oxford: Blackwell), 60–88.

Lightstone, J.N.
2006   *The Commerce of the Sacred: Mediation of the Divine among Jews in the Greco-Roman World* (2nd edn; New York, NY: Columbia University Press).

Liverani, M.
2005   *Israel's History and the History of Israel* (trans. C. Peri and P.R. Davies; London: Equinox).

McNutt, P.
1999   *Reconstructing the Society of Ancient Israel* (Louisville, KY: Westminster John Knox).

Marsman, H.J.
2003   *Women in Ugarit and Israel: Their Social and Religious Position in the Context of the Ancient Near East* (OTS 49; Leiden: Brill).

Mendenhall, G.E.
1992   'From Witchcraft to Justice: Death and Afterlife in the Old Testament', in H. Obayashi (ed.), *Death and Afterlife: Perspectives of World Religions* (London: Praeger), 67–81.

Meyers, C.L.
1988   *Discovering Eve: Ancient Israelite Women in Context* (Oxford: Oxford University Press).
2002   'From Household to House of Yahweh: Women's Religious Culture in Ancient Israel', in A. Lemaire (ed.), *Congress Volume: Basel, 2001* (VTS 92; Leiden: Brill), 277–304.
2003   'Material Remains and Social Relations: Women's Culture in Agrarian Households of the Iron Age', in W.G. Dever and S. Gitin (eds), *Symbiosis, Symbolism, and the Power of the Past: Canaan, Ancient Israel, and Their Neighbors from the Late Bronze Age through Roman Palestinia* (Winona Lake, IN: Eisenbrauns), 425–44.
2005   *Households and Holiness: The Religious Culture of Israelite Women* (Facets; Minneapolis, MN: Fortress Press).

Milgrom, J.
2000   *Leviticus 17–22: A New Translation with Introduction and Commentary* (AB 3A; New York, NY: Doubleday).

Miller, P.D.
2000   *The Religion of Ancient Israel* (LAI; Louisville, KY: Westminster John Knox).

Niehr, H.
2003   'The Changed Status of the Dead in Yehud', in R. Albertz and B. Becking (eds), *Yahwism After the Exile: Perspectives on Israelite Religion in the Persian Era* (Assen: Van Gorcum), 136–55.

Olyan, S.M.
1988   *Asherah and the Cult of Yahweh in Israel* (SBLMS 34; Atlanta, GA: Scholars Press).
2008   'Family Religion in Israel and the Wider Levant of the First Millennium BCE', in J. Bodel and S.M. Olyan (eds), *Household and Family Religion in Antiquity* (Oxford: Blackwell), 113–26.

Parker Pearson, M.
1999   *The Archaeology of Death and Burial* (Stroud: Sutton).

Paton, L.B.
1921   *Spiritism and the Cult of the Dead in Antiquity* (London: Hodder and Stoughton).

Pitard, W.T.
2002   'Tombs and Offerings: Archaeological Data and Comparative Methodology in the Study of Death in Israel', in B.M. Gittlen (ed.), *Sacred Time, Sacred Place: Archaeology and the Religion of Israel* (Winona Lake, IN: Eisenbrauns), 145–68.

Prendergast, D.
2005   *From Elder to Ancestor: Old Age, Death and Inheritance in Modern Korea* (Folkstone: Global Oriental).

Robben, A.C.G.M.
2004   'Death and Anthropology: An Introduction', in A.C.G.M. Robben (ed.), *Death, Mourning and Burial: A Cross-Cultural Reader* (Oxford: Blackwell), 1–16.

Rogerson, J.
2007   'Ancient Israel to the Fall of the Second Temple', in J.R. Hinnells (ed.), *A Handbook of Ancient Religions* (Cambridge: Cambridge University Press), 214–65.

Rose, M.
1975   *Der Ausschliesslichkeitsanspruch Jahwes: Deuteronomische Schultheologie und die Volksfrömmigkeit in der späten Königszeit* (BWANT 106; Berlin: de Gruyter).

Routledge, C.
2006   'Parallelism in Popular and Official Religion in Ancient Egypt', in G.M. Beckman and T.J. Lewis (eds), *Text, Artifact, and Image: Revealing Ancient Israelite Religion* (BJS 346; Providence, RI: Brown University), 223–38.

Saler, B.
1993   *Conceptualizing Religion: Immanent Anthropologists, Transcendent Natives, and Unbounded Categories* (Leiden: Brill).
1997   'Conceptualizing Religion: The Matter of Boundaries', in H.-J. Klimkeit (ed.), *Vergleichen und Verstehen in der Religionswissenchaft* (Wiesbaden: Harrassowitz Verlag), 27–35.

Schmidt, B.B.
1996   *Israel's Beneficent Dead: Ancestor Cult and Necromancy in Ancient Israelite Religion and Tradition* (reprinted edn; Winona Lake, IN: Eisenbrauns; originally published as FAT 11; Tübingen: J.C.B. Mohr, 1994).

Schniedewind, W.M.
2004   *How the Bible Became a Book: The Textualization of Ancient Israel* (Cambridge: Cambridge University Press).

Segal, J.B.
1976   'Popular Religion in Ancient Israel', *JJS* 27: 1–22.

Sharot, S.
2001   *A Comparative Sociology of World Religions: Virtuosos, Priests, and Popular Religion* (New York, NY: New York University Press).

Smith, J.Z.
1978   *Map Is Not Territory: Studies in the Histories of Religions* (Studies in Judaism in Late Antiquity 23; Leiden: Brill).

Smith, M.S.
1998   Review of J. Berlinerblau, *The Vow and the 'Popular Religious Groups' of Ancient Israel*, *JSS* 43: 148–51.
2002   *The Early History of God: Yahweh and the Other Deities in Ancient Israel* (2nd edn; Grand Rapids, MI: Eerdmans, 2002).

Smith, M.S. and E. Bloch-Smith
1988   'Death and Afterlife in Ugarit and Israel', *JAOS* 108: 277–84.

Spronk, K.
1986   *Beatific Afterlife in Ancient Israel and in the Ancient Near East* (AOAT 219; Neukirchen-Vluyn: Neukirchener Verlag).

Stager, L.E.
1985   'The Archaeology of the Family in Early Israel', *BASOR* 260: 1–35.

Stavrakopoulou, F.
Forthcoming   *Land of Our Fathers: The Roles of Ancestor Veneration in Biblical Land Claims* (New York, NY, and London: T&T Clark).

Stern, E.
2001   'Pagan Yahwism: The Folk Religion of Ancient Israel', *BAR* 27.2: 21–9.

Toorn, K. van der
1994   *From Her Cradle to Her Grave: The Role of Religion in the Life of the Israelite and the Babylonian Woman* (trans. S.J. Denning-Bolle; BS 23; Sheffield: JSOT Press).
1996   *Family Religion in Babylonia, Syria and Israel: Continuity and Change in the Forms of Religious Life* (SHCANE 7; Leiden: Brill).
1997   'The Iconic Book: Analogies between the Babylonian Cult of Images and the Veneration of the Torah', in K. van der Toorn (ed.), *The Image and the Book: Iconic Cults, Aniconism, and the Rise of Book Religion in Israel and the Ancient Near East* (CBET 21; Leuven: Peeters), 229–48.
2002   'Recent Trends in the Study of Israelite Religion', in G. Wiegers (ed.), *Modern Societies and the Science of Religion: Studies in Honour of Lammert Leertouwer* (Leiden: Brill), 223–43.
2003   'Nine Months among the Peasants in the Palestinian Highlands: An Anthropological Perspective on Local Religion in the Early Iron Age', in W.G. Dever and S. Gitin (eds), *Symbiosis, Symbolism, and the Power of the Past: Canaan, Ancient Israel, and Their Neighbors from the Late Bronze Age through Roman Palestinia* (Winona Lake, IN: Eisenbrauns), 393–410.
2007   *Scribal Culture and the Making of the Hebrew Bible* (Cambridge, MA: Harvard University Press).
2008   'Family Religion in Second Millennium West Asia (Mesopotamia, Emar, Nuzi)', in J. Bodel and S.M. Olyan (eds), *Household and Family Religion in Antiquity* (Oxford: Blackwell), 20–36.

Tromp, N.J.
1969   *Primitive Conceptions of Death and the Nether World in the Old Testament* (BO 21; Rome: Pontifical Biblical Institute).

Tsumura, D.T.
1993   'The Interpretation of the Ugaritic Funerary Text KTU 1.161', in E. Matsushima (ed.), *Official Cult and Popular Religion in the Ancient Near East: Papers of the First Colloquium on the Ancient Near East – The City and Its Life* (Heidelberg: Universitätverlag C. Winter), 40–55.

Valentine, C.
2006   'Academic Constructions of Bereavement', *Mortality* 11.1: 57–78.

Vorländer, H.
1986   'Aspects of Popular Religion in the Old Testament', in N. Greinacher and N. Mette (eds), *Popular Religion* (Concilium 186; Edinburgh: T&T Clark), 63–70.

Vrijhof, P.H.
1979   'Conclusion', in P.H. Vrijhof and J. Waardenburg, J. (eds), *Official and Popular Religion: Analysis of a Theme for Religious Studies* (Religion and Society 19: The Hague: Mouton), 668–99.

Vrijhof, P.H. and J. Waardenburg (eds)
1979   *Official and Popular Religion: Analysis of a Theme for Religious Studies* (Religion and Society 19: The Hague: Mouton).

Weinfeld, M.
1972   *Deuteronomy and the Deuteronomic School* (Oxford: Clarendon Press).

Wenning, R.
1997   'Bestattungen im königszeitlichen Juda', *TQ* 177: 82–93.

Williams, P.W.
1980   *Popular Religion in America: Symbolic Change and the Modernization Process in Historical Perspective* (Englewood Cliffs, NJ: Prentice-Hall).

Wolff, S.R.
2002   'Mortuary Practices in the Persian Period', *NEA* 65.2: 131–37.

Xella, P.
1982   'Il "culto dei morti" nell' Antico Testamento', in V. Lanternari, M. Massenzio and D. Sabbatucci (eds), *Scritti in memoria di Angelo Brelich* (Rome: Dedalo), 645–66.
1995   'Death and the Afterlife in Canaanite and Hebrew Thought', *COS*, 4.2059–70.

Zevit, Z.
2001   *The Religions of Ancient Israel: A Synthesis of Parallactic Approaches* (London and New York, NY: Continuum).
2003   'False Dichotomies in Descriptions of Israelite Religion: A Problem, Its Origin, and a Proposed Solution', in W.G. Dever and S. Gitin (eds), *Symbiosis, Symbolism, and the Power of the Past: Canaan, Ancient Israel, and Their Neighbors from the Late Bronze Age through Roman Palestinia* (Winona Lake, IN: Eisenbrauns), 223–35.

Part II

Socio-Religious Diversities

Chapter 5

Royal Religion in Ancient Judah[1]
Nicolas Wyatt

1
Introduction

The destruction of the state of Judah, brought about by the Babylonians in the early sixth century BCE, effectively marked the end of the monarchy, until the rise of the Hasmoneans in the second century BCE. A flurry of expectation at the time of Zerubbabel was disappointed. Yet the king in the abstract continued to play a part in futuristic expectation of a saviour who would liberate the people. In this we have the roots of messianism, which should initially be assessed within the context of royal ideology, and was not originally eschatological. Limitations of space preclude discussion of this aspect here.[2]

We should begin our discussion with a brief consideration of the problems facing an enquiry of this sort. Apart from general issues of particularity and comparability, on which many opinions are held, we have the fundamental issue of the nature of our sources as regards the matter of history. In what sense, if any, are these historical documents? How trustworthy are they for the reconstruction of real sequences of events, and of real historical institutions? We can no longer ignore the critique of the conventional approach of generations of scholars, already thoroughly deconstructionist towards the text, at the hands of the minimalists. The safest position to adopt in a study of this sort is to attempt an interpretation of the literature (for it is at least that,

---

1.   'Judah' versus 'Israel': a note on usage. From the demise of the northern kingdom, 'Israel', in about 720 BCE, the term appears to have taken on an ideological role in the southern kingdom, 'Judah', as the 'true' against the 'false' (secessionist) Israel; and the term is also commonly used indiscriminately by scholars to cover a blend of beliefs and practices. More confusingly, 'Israel' is sometimes used to denote the southern kingdom while the northern was still in existence. My discussion is directed primarily to Judah. It may be taken that analogous forms and developments (apart from dynastic stability) also obtained in Israel. But in my view Jeroboam's secession involved the rejection of Yahweh as royal god; see Wyatt 2005b: 72–91.

2.   The royal roots of messianism are evident from the discussions in Day (ed.) 1998: 209–400. It was essentially a development of the old royal ideology. Gillingham (1998: 209) noted the tendency to eisegesis in Christian interpretation of the witness of the Hebrew Bible. In view of the thrust of the present discussion, I would tend to downplay the eisegetical element (while not entirely denying it): it is rather an exegetical dimension to which biblical scholarship, particularly 'Old Testament' scholarship, and more particularly still that of a more 'neutral' kind, which disparaged Christian interpretations of the tradition, has been purblind for too long.

even if we have to stop short of calling it history) which is faithful to the evidence. Its bearing on historical matters will then need to be assessed by those concerned with the reconstruction of historical events. It seems to me that the maximalists expect too much, and the minimalists too little,[3] from the evidence before us. But we have no magic wand to resolve the problems, except perhaps the vague default position of 'legend', or a relative agnosticism.[4]

The literature accepts that there was a time before monarchical rule. Kingship in Israel and Judah had a specific beginning, according to our sources. These tell how the Israelite tribes – not originally a unity, though later tradition added this gloss[5] – made common cause in the face of the threat posed by Philistine settlement in the Shephelah and expansion eastwards. A charismatic leader, Saul, was chosen to meet the threat, though he proved inadequate for the sustained management of the new state of Israel. The tradition knows of two accounts of his rise to power, firstly as a divine choice to resolve the political crisis (1 Sam. 9.15–10.16), and secondly as representing a man-made institution set up against the divine will (1 Sam. 8.1-22) to conform to the norm among neighbouring peoples.[6] First Samuel 10.17–11.15 harmonizes these two accounts with military action against the Ammonites. Another charismatic leader, David, anointed as an alternative to Saul in 1 Sam. 16.1-13, became king in Judah and, by some clever footwork, king of Israel too (2. Sam. 1.4; 3.12-19; 5.1-3). It is with the figure of David that kingship seems[7] to begin to conform to older patterns of royal ideology and practice, as already experienced in the earlier and contemporary Levantine kingdoms, and usually explained as the adoption of 'Jebusite' traditions in Jerusalem.[8] However, the record cannot be taken at face value. George Athas noted that:

> In c. 800 BCE [supposedly c. 200 years after David!] Jerusalem [was] . . . little more than a fortified compound belonging to an ancient family. It did however form its own political unit

3.   The terms 'minimalist' and 'maximalist' are labels used of the opposing outlook by parties to the somewhat polarized positions currently adopted with regard to the interpretation of the Hebrew historiographical texts (above all Joshua–2 Kings – the so-called 'Deuteronomistic History' – and 1–2 Chronicles).

4.   For a good recent discussion of the methodological problems see Grabbe 2007.

5.   Tribal unity came to be expressed in genealogical terms by the welding of the diverse peoples into one family, the descendents of Jacob, and in modern assessment as the so-called amphictyony, a cultic federation proposed on the analogy of Greek amphictyonic leagues, though this model is no longer used.

6.   Caquot 1990: 40–43 thought that the negative aspect is a later addition.

7.   We are speaking in literary terms. The issue of David's position in history remains difficult to assess, the Tel Dan stela notwithstanding. Athas cautiously wrote that 'the inscription has increased the likelihood of a historical David' (Athas 2003: 317). That falls short of being confident of his existence! For a survey of recent disagreements on the possibility of historical reconstruction, and with a different assessment of David, see Knoppers 1997. He remarked 'although the inscription proves neither the existence of the united monarchy nor the existence of Solomon, it does point to David as a historical figure. The use of the expression "house of David" evinces the importance of this figure as the founder of a dynasty' (Knoppers 1997: 39). See also the useful dialogue between Finkelstein and Mazar in Schmidt 2007, in which the former is generally more restrained than the latter in conceding historicity to the account of the early monarchy. See also Ussishkin 2003.

8.   See for example Day 1998: 73–75, who appears to give credence to the view that Melchizedek (of Genesis 14 and Psalm 110) was a real historical precursor of David. I find this an improbable viewpoint.

and was recognized as a distinct unit by Bar Hadad. We cannot talk of a unified Judaean state at this time. At best, Jerusalem was a principality with very limited sovereignty. Yet in less than a century . . . this small estate had gained suzerainty over the entire region of Judah and so evolved into a fully fledged state entity.

(Athas 2003: 316)

If we accept this scenario, then the monarchy we see reflected in the narrative concerning David and his successors down to this period is seen as largely the construction of later historiographers who either invented David or at least heroized and epicized a local bandit in presenting him as archetypal king. It is more likely that the monarchy they were actually reflecting was that of Manasseh's period. This of course is not a worthless assessment of the earlier tradition, for we can still identify in the presentation of David the values and ideology of the later time – rather as Geoffrey of Monmouth's Arthur reflected Norman values, or Sir Thomas Malory's Arthur those of Tudor England – reflected in the Deuteronomists' treatment of Manasseh.[9] The present discussion therefore attempts an evaluation of the literary evidence as a reflection of general historical realities, while remaining non-committal on specific historical questions. But even fiction reflects somebody's values.

Since the Saulide monarchy, which must also be seen through the perspective of these remarks, was instituted precisely to provide Israel with a king 'like their neighbours' (1 Sam. 8.5) – that is, they wanted to conform to a norm – it is reasonable to consider its monarchical system (and more specifically that of Judah) in comparison with neighbouring ones, though our knowledge of these is inevitably sketchy where we know anything at all, because of the fragmentary historical record. We know of local kingdoms, at least so far as biblical literature goes, in Ai (Josh 8.23), Arad (Num. 21.1), the 'Amorites' of Heshbon (e.g. Num. 21.21) and Bashan (e.g. Num. 21.33),[10] Edom (Num 20.14), Jericho (Josh. 2.3), Moab (Num. 22.4), Tyre (e.g. 2 Sam. 5.11) and so on; the summary of Josh. 12.9-24 lists 17. Others are attested for the Late Bronze Age (mid-fourteenth century BCE) in the Amarna archives. These range from northern Syria (Ugarit, Nuhašše and Amurru), through the central region (Beirut, Qatna, Sidon, Tyre) to the southern settlements of Lachish, Megiddo, Shechem, Taanach and Jerusalem. Jerusalem features in both lists, and Amarna letters EA 285–90[11] are from its ruler Abdi-Ḫeba, whose theophoric name attests the Hurrian goddess Ḫeba in the local pantheon, a point of some historical interest, and a tenuous link with later tradition, to which we shall return. These local kings were perhaps in many cases little more than clan chieftains, and their designation as 'king' in many cases probably reflects the imposition of standard patterns of political classification for literary or administrative purposes respectively in the two bodies of literature.

By far the most useful of all these local states from the historian's perspective was Ugarit (Ras Shamra), which though at the far end of the Levant, and thus furthest removed within the region from Israel and Judah, has yielded by far the most extensive archive. Most of the written evidence dates from the Late Bronze Age, in the period

---

9.   See Stavrakopoulou 2004 for an evaluation of the tendentious nature of the treatment of Manasseh.

10.   Og, King of Bashan, is a mythical rather than historical figure, with cosmological overtones. For a recent assessment and bibliography see Wyatt 2009.

11.   See Moran 1992: 325–34 for translations.

c. 1400–1190 BCE, in the era when the so-called Israelite communities were suppos-edly establishing themselves in Palestine. Although it is thus too early to give us direct contact with the kingdoms of Israel and Judah, there are a remarkable number of direct correspondences in structure, and it is probably fairly accurate to speak of a common ideology (with of course local variations and special emphases) across the region, so that making cautious comparisons is a legitimate procedure. There are also some specific literary links, such as concern the Ugaritic *Rāpi'ūma*, corresponding to the biblical Rephaim, which will be discussed below.

One of the problematic perspectives of biblical scholarship has been a tendency to understand that its disciplinary boundaries correspond to real boundaries in the ancient world. But these latter boundaries were not only infinitely complex, but also historically and regionally porous. One example of the way in which the reality was more internationally minded than we are apt to acknowledge may be seen in the incidence of griffins in the art of the ancient Near East. Attested already in the fourth millennium as far apart as Egypt and Susa, we can trace the path and ideology of the Egyptian forms continuously from the Predynastic period down through the Pharaonic era, into the Levant (and from there into Assyrian art) and on to the Cypriot, Minoan and Mycenaean palace cultures. And the griffin retained its royal and solar symbolism, however attenuated, throughout its long journeys, and frequently appeared on Israelite seals.[12] This should give us pause before making snap judgements about discontinuity between cultures.

With this in mind, we may quite legitimately look to Ugarit for analogues of and parallels to Judahite phenomena, and this line of enquiry has long been pursued (Kapelrud 1963; Craigie 1983; Brooke, Curtis and Healey 1994; Smith 2007).[13] The temporal and geographical distance is not great in terms of the military, diplomatic and commercial history of the region. Both areas belong to the Northwest Semitic language zone, and though Ugarit was not 'Canaanite', and biblical tradition rejected 'Canaanite' values, we may reasonably speak of a Canaanite cultural sphere. All those listed above were minor kingdoms on the international scale; while Ugarit and Israel benefited from their location along transnational trade routes, Judah was relatively isolated in its highland terrain. While our knowledge of Israel and Judah comes from historiographical sources, which may be regarded as romancing the tradition to produce a variety of national epic, Ugaritic literature also exhibited epic traits (Wyatt 2005d), and the portrayal of kingship we encounter in *Baal*, *Kirta* and *Aqhat* is certainly comparable to that found in Judah and among the other kingdoms of the region of which we hear. Thus the epic assessment of Kirta as failing in the duties of kingship, and of his son as insubordinate, is echoed in the Deuteronomistic assessment of kings, and of the portrayal of David's sons. One of the great benefits of the Ugaritic evidence is its window into the ritual life of the king, of which we catch only glimpses in the biblical material. Much of the ritual material is admittedly exceedingly opaque,[14]

---

12.   For examples of these see Keel and Uehlinger 1998: §§228 (Hazor); 231a, b (both Megiddo); 248 (Tell Dan); 250a, b, c (respectively unprovenanced, Megiddo, Tell el Farah south); 252 (Samaria); 253 (Tell el Farah south); 254a, b (both Megiddo); 258c, 259b (both Samaria); 282c (Megiddo); 292 (Samaria); and 293a (Gezer). For discussion see Wyatt 2008.

13.   For royal ideology see Day (ed.) 1998; Wyatt 1996, 2005a:191–220, 2005b: 72–91.

14.   For the material and its analysis see in particular del Olmo Lete 1999; Pardee 2000, 2002. The apparent bias to royal involvement in the cult is understandable in official archives. The popular

but enough can be seen to give some idea of the calendrical programme, and of the king's explicit role in the pantheon – since he went in procession with the images of the gods, his activity in sacrifice, his involvement with the royal ancestors and his role as intermediary between the gods and the community at large. The mythic language used of him in the literature enables us to perceive the mythic dimension of royal ideology (that he was a god, a son of El, born of Athirat and Rahmay, avatars of Shapsh the sun goddess, and was suckled by them).[15] All this material finds an echo in biblical texts, though these have often been misconstrued by tradition, or even deliberately changed in transmission. The accumulating evidence suggests that allowing for local variations and emphases, we should postulate a broadly similar ideology of kingship throughout the region. It would be most unusual if any particular social group had a radically different perception of kingship from its neighbours. Constant interaction in trade, diplomacy and war would constantly reinforce the common elements.[16]

2
The Ritual Duties of the King

Kingship in the ancient world was universally a complex institution. As the ruler of a city or nation, the king fulfilled religious and ceremonial duties, as well as administrative, legal and political roles. He was a figurehead, a representative figure, albeit generally with absolute power, though this would normally be tempered by a council of advisors and elders. Even a usurper, whose ambition may have been simply the exercise of power, would inevitably find himself circumscribed by a kingly role he was obliged to fulfil. The rough division between religious functions taken as normative in the Hebrew Bible, of prophet, priest and king, as exemplified by Zadok, Nathan and Solomon all playing their parts at the king's enthronement (1 Kgs 1.45), disguises the fact that these other religious functionaries generally held their office at the pleasure of the king. He was the essential figure, who in effect delegated aspects of his role.

In the Hebrew Bible, early kings certainly perform ritual actions, to the point of themselves conducting sacrifices. Thus Saul offers a holocaust at Gilgal (1 Sam. 13.9), David at Jerusalem (2 Sam. 6.13, 17-18; 24.25), and Solomon at Gibeah (1 Kgs 3.4, 15) and Jerusalem (1 Kgs 8.5, 62–64; 9.25). Jeroboam (1 Kgs 12.33; 13.1-2) and Ahaz (2 Kgs 16.4, 12-15) are also described as themselves offering cult. This is in accordance with the pattern we find throughout the Levant. The king in Ugarit is described (KTU 1.41)[17] as being ritually purified and later desacralized (we shall see the significance

religion has left virtually no record. On distinctions between 'popular' and 'official' religion, see Chapter 4 in this volume.

15.   In KTU 1.23.23–24, a text dealing *inter alia* with a royal birth, the princes born (Shahar and Shalim = Athtar geminated) are described as sucking the breasts of Athirat and Rahmay (cf. Ps. 110.3, LXX!), avatars of Shapsh, and in KTU 1.15.ii.26–28, Kirta's heir does the same, being 'the suckling of goddesses'.

16.   This similarity is borne out by the use of an international repertoire of iconography (cf. the griffin noted above), and it is surely significant that the common denominator in all this appears to be Egyptian. Thus the Samarian ivories, for example, which illustrated the main heraldic themes of kingship, with sphinxes, griffins, falcons, Nefertem figures, lotus flowers and cartouches, were all inspired by Egyptian forms, if not directly manufactured by Egyptian craftsmen.

17.   Translations in Pardee 2002: 56–65; Wyatt 2002: 348–55.

of this below); between these two rites he himself performed numerous offerings to various gods, a pattern repeated in several texts. Ethbaal of Tyre (Ahab's father-in-law, 1 Kgs 16.31) in the ninth century BCE, was priest of Ashtart,[18] as were Tabnit and Eshmunazar, kings of Sidon in the fifth century BCE (*COS* 2.182 [sarcophagus of Tabnit]; Day 1998: 75). Such roles were probably *ex officio*, though their mention in monumental inscriptions may be to record the personal devotion of a king to a specific deity. We have no reason to doubt that other kings of Judah and Israel also served as priests. This would not of course entail their involvement in day-to-day priestly ritual obligations, but they would officiate at national festivals and great public sacrifices, and perhaps at the beginning of important enterprises, such as military campaigns, or dedications and rededications of temples (cf. 1 Kgs 8.62-64). The episode at Gilgal (1 Sam. 10.8; 13.7-15) when Saul failed to wait for Samuel before sacrificing, and incurred the latter's anger, is not to be understood as disqualifying kings from the performance of sacrifices: Saul's error was in not waiting the allotted period of seven days for Samuel, as instructed.

The cult of Yahweh in Judah appears from some parts of the literary record to have been an innovation of David's. This estimation should perhaps receive some explanation. The motive given for the reform of Jeroboam (I), when shortly after Israel's secession from the united kingdom he instituted the bull cult in Israel, with images at Dan and Bethel (1 Kgs 12.26-33), was stated thus:

> Then Jeroboam said to himself, 'Now the kingdom will return to David's dynasty, if the people (continue to) go up to offer sacrifices in Yahweh's temple in Jerusalem, and the people's allegiance will revert to their lord Rehoboam king of Judah: they will kill me and return to Rehoboam king of Judah.'
>
> (1 Kgs 12.26-27)

Jeroboam's action is usually taken to be a deliberate act of apostasy, turning his back on the true religion, and imposing his perverse reform on his people. This is certainly the Deuteronomists' perspective. A more likely historical situation, if recoverable as an event, is rather different. A religious reform could only be made in good faith. And what Jeroboam was doing was not inventing a new cult, but reviving an old one, largely displaced by the royal ideological cult of Jerusalem (Wyatt 2005b: 75–86, with assessment of earlier treatments). The antiquity of this cult – of a bull god, rather than the calf of the parody – may be seen within the tradition, for many passages indicate that it was El who had brought Israel out of Egypt,[19] to use the formulation of the nationalistic biblical myth (itself probably of northern origin). If the Jerusalem cult of Yahweh had been imposed on the nation (as David's personal devotion) – and it would certainly need to have been imposed on Israel, coming into David's realm secondarily – then it is not hard to imagine ears being sympathetic to Jeroboam's call, especially in view of claims about Solomon's and Rehoboam's forced labour policies. This allows for Jeroboam's reform to be equally biased towards royal ideology, for in the Ugaritic tradition El was seen mythologically as the king's father. As for David's

18.   Josephus, *Contra Apionem* 1.18, noted in Day 1998: 75.

19.   See Exodus 18; Num. 23.22; 24.8; Ps. 106.19-22; Hos. 8.6 (following Tur-Sinai and NEB, reading *kî mî šōr'ēl* rather than *kî miyyiśrā'ēl*: 'for who is Bull El?' instead of 'for from Israel'), discussed in Wyatt 2005b: 83–88. See also Smith 2001: 142–45.

cult, it is possibly its first biblical mention when he consulted Yahweh about settling in Judah, and was told by the oracle to go to Hebron (2 Sam. 2.1-4). Of course the whole pre-Davidic tradition is now couched in Yahwist terms, but this could be explained as retrospectively introduced. There is certainly a problem concerning the origin of the cult if it did not go back to an Exodus tradition. And this is reinforced by the almost complete absence of Yahwist theophoric personal names before the putative time of David, and by its implicit status as a newly introduced cult if we read between the lines of Jeroboam's words. There is a historical problem to be answered here. David's cult probably had its origin, or at least its earlier history, in the two towns associated with his rule, Hebron and Jerusalem.[20] Certainly the idea of this cult as a royal innovation makes sense of the evidence noted here, and considered further below, which cannot really be convincingly harmonized with the alternative biblical models, of a primordial Kenite (Genesis 4!) or patriarchal origin (Genesis 12, 15, 17), or of the Mosaic model (Exodus 3, 6). And there is no intrinsic reason why these alternatives should be privileged as historical sources.

We drew attention above to the name of the Late Bronze Age ruler of Jerusalem, Abdi-Ḥeba. This provides evidence of a Hurrian presence in the city in that earlier period.[21] Another important piece of evidence in the David traditions for a residual Hurrian dimension is the name of two persons mentioned, Uriah the Hittite and Araunah the Jebusite. The second, occurring several times in the threshing-floor negotiations in 2 Samuel 24, appears to be a title rather than a name, as is hinted at by the Qere *'ăwarnâ* in the margin wherever the form *'ărawnâ* appears in the text, and its occurrence in v. 16 with the article. Particularly noteworthy is v. 23, which states that *hakkōl nātan'ărawnâ* (read <*hā*>*'ăwarnâ*) *hammelek lammelek*: 'the Awarnah – the king – gave everything to the king'. The second 'king' here is David; the first is an explanatory gloss on the unusual term *'ăwarnâ*. This is best explained as a local form of the Hurrian term *ewir, iwer*, 'lord' (perhaps related to Hittite *arawanniaš*), here translated into its Hebrew equivalent as 'king'.[22] This could be construed as a little piece of evidence supporting the antiquity of the Hebrew Bible's David traditions, or at least David's verisimilitude within an early (e.g. tenth-century BCE) setting, since we have no obviously first millennium evidence for the survival of Hurrian cultural elements. 'Araunah the Jebusite' appears to have been the king of the city, with whom David now negotiated to acquire the site for a temple. As for Uriah the Hittite, in

20.   Discussion of this sort can no longer be carried on against a supposed background of Israelite or Judahite monotheism. As Mark Smith remarked, 'Israelite religion in its earliest form did not contrast markedly with the religions of its Levantine neighbors in either number or configuration of deities. The number of deities in Israel was relatively typical for the region' (Smith 2002: 64). The whole of this study (on which see the useful review in Sanders 2002–3) is an important revision of earlier views of Israelite religion. Also germane to the discussion are Wyatt 1996; Keel and Uehlinger 1998; Day 2000; Smith 2001, reviewed Gnuse 2002–3, Trapp 2002–3 and Wyatt 2004. On the broad issue of how polytheism functioned, see Wyatt 2007: 47–84.

21.   Not direct involvement by Mittanni, which had been destroyed; but Hurrian elements in the population, and elements of Hurrian culture, is entirely possible. Cf. the extensive archival evidence for Hurrian elements in the populations of Alalakh and Ugarit, and note references in n. 24.

22.   See discussion in Wyatt 2005a: 1–2, with reference to earlier treatments by Maisler (Mazar) and Ahlström. Wyatt 2005a: 2 n. 7 lists the occurrence of *iwr* in Hurrian personal names from Ugarit, Alalakh and Qatna.

whose name, scarcely Hebrew if he was a 'Hittite',[23] the same element *iwer* may be present, together with *yau*: thus 'The Lord is king'. We shall return to him and his wife Bathsheba in our later discussion.

We may also mention here the term *hayyĕbusî*, 'Jebusite', occurring in 2 Sam. 24.18, as an epithet. While the term appears in the 'lists of nations', its independent existence is unknown, so that it cannot be confirmed as a genuine gentilic form, and it seems probable that it was a title of the Jerusalemite king. The toponym 'Jebus' (e.g. Judg. 19.10-11) can hardly exist independently of it, is unattested extra-biblically, and may be explained as a back-formation from the former term. A Hittite origin has been proposed,[24] which could also have been mediated through Hurrian. Hurrians were also associated with Hebron and several other Levantine cities in the Amarna period.[25] For our purposes, the possibility exists that it was the Hurrian dimension linking Hebron and Jerusalem that had a bearing on David's choice of action. The reason for this is the potential solution to the etymology of the divine name Yahweh that this presents. The form *yau*, variously transcribed, occurs in a number of contexts, from Mesopotamia, Ugarit, Hamath, and Tell en-Nasbeh in Palestine (Vanderhooft and Horowitz 2002: 318–27),[26] and has been proposed as offering an explanation for the Hebrew tetragrammaton *yhwh* and its other forms *yāh* and *yāhû*. Whichever specific solution is agreed (see Wyatt 1989: 21–27), it seems that we have here not a Semitic lexeme, but a foreign one, which is glossed in the dictionary of rare words BM 93035 as DINGIR/*ilu*, 'god'.[27]

Attested sporadically around the ancient Near East, its putative transmission by Hurrian elements is entirely plausible, and in my view more probable than any alternatives thus far proposed. The situation envisaged therefore is that David went to Hebron, and naturally adopted the local deity, presumably a form of El, with the local cult title Yau, as his patron.[28] This would have been a means of expressing his solidarity with his new subjects.[29] Upon assuming the kingship over Israel as well, he then took Jerusalem (2 Sam. 5.1-10), which became a royal fief under the specific tutelage of the deity, now Hebraized as Yahu (later form Yahweh).[30] The rest is history (larded with legend). While there is no mention of it in the text, it is scarcely likely that he advanced on Jerusalem without an oracle from Yahu.

Some anachronisms in the tradition are implausible as coincidence. So in the present instance, the tradition which tells of this earlier dimension in the Hebron and

---

23.   Note Van Seters 1972 and his analysis of the term.

24.   *HALOT* 2.382, citing *BHH*, 806. No proposal as to its meaning is forthcoming.

25.   See Wyatt 1989, esp. 7 n. 9, where I cited Alalakh, Aleppo, Beerot, Ebla, Gibeon, Hebron, Jerusalem, Megiddo, Qatna, Shechem, Taanach, Tunip and Ugarit. Discussion in Speiser 1931–32 = 1953 = 1967: 256–69; Albright 1935: 17; O'Callaghan 1948: 54.

26.   Information courtesy of Stephanie Dalley. See also Dalley 1990 on the Yaudic royal name which also uses the element *yau*: Yau-bi'di (var. Ilu-bi'di: the variant shows the equivalence of *yau* and *ilu*).

27.   Published in CT XII, 4, and discussed in Murtonen 1952: 48.

28.   El would have been the head of most or all the local pantheons, so that this would not really be a new departure for David.

29.   And as Henri de Navarre remarked, 'Paris vaut bien une messe'.

30.   I suggested that the formula *yw il[m]* in the Ugaritic text KTU 1.1.iv.14 means 'lord of the gods' (Wyatt 2002: 48). While the adoption of the perpetual Qere of *yhwh* as *'ădōnāy* is to be dated much later, it is striking that the identical formula in Genesis 2–3, Ketib *yhwh 'ĕlōhîm* (Qere *'ădōnāy 'ĕlōhîm*) appears to have the same force.

Jerusalem political world, which shows signs of being continuous with the realities of the Amarna period, *must* have its roots in that period. Beyond that, we cannot write with any certainty.

The temple and palace complex which David is described as intending to build (2 Sam. 7.1-17), but which was constructed under his successor Solomon (1 Kgs 5.17–9.14), was primarily a statement of royal power, expressed in architectural form. An interesting reflexion of its political significance were the relative dimensions of the temple (60 by 20 by 25 cubits, 1 Kgs 6.2) and the 'House of the Forest of Lebanon' (100 by 50 by 30 cubits, 1 Kgs 7.2; the House is also mentioned at 10.17, 2 Chron. 9.16 and Isa. 22.8), which served as a ceremonial armoury (Wyatt 2005a: 182–84; Geyer 2007: 101–9).[31] The dimensions of the royal palace, in which this House appears to have been incorporated (1 Kgs 7.1-12a) are nowhere given, but it took 13 years to build, which suggests huge expenditure; whether or not it reflects a tenth-century BCE or a later construction, it is eloquent of the massive investment in the ritual trappings of royalty. The relationship of the buildings indicate that the temple was essentially a royal chapel, a place devoted in some way to the cult of the king (or at least 'the cult of kingship') as well as of his patron deity. We cannot be certain from its description how the House of the Forest functioned, but it seems likely that it was somehow involved in the widely attested ritual use of 'divine' weapons, which sacralized the king's military undertakings and promised him divine protection and victory in the field (Wyatt 2005a: 151–89). The 'divine' arms used in the investiture of Zimri-Lim of Mari (ARM A 1968) were kept in the shrine at Terqa, having been brought for the occasion from Aleppo (ARM A 1858). The former text contains the following remarkable sequence:

> Thus speaks Adad: . . .
>
> I have brought you back to the throne of your father, and have given you the arms with which I fought against Tiamat. I have anointed you with the oil of my victory, and no one has withstood you.[32]

That a similar ritual tradition may have been observed in Judah is supported circumstantially by the wording of such passages as Pss. 72.8 and 89.26 (read *nahar* as singular), which wish a rule of cosmic range on the king at his enthronement (Wyatt 2001: 118–19), such language presupposing the ritual tradition I have catalogued (Wyatt 2005a: 151–89). This could account for the peculiar importance accorded the House of the Forest. Most importantly, the conception of the deity as warrior, shown here, modelled on the conception of warrior-kings, assimilates the king to divine activity and implicitly, ontology: a king who performs a god's role shares in his divinity (a theme discussed below).

The fact that the temple was part of the same architectural complex of House and royal palace is crucial for our overall understanding of the cult. Jerusalem no doubt had, like other ancient cities, a number of sanctuaries dedicated to the cult of various deities. That the worship of Yahweh, as so commonly represented in modern

---

31.   This building may of course be projected back into the Solomonic period, but was undoubtedly a historical construction.

32.   Durand 1993: 45, cited Wyatt 2005a: 159. By a delicious historical irony, Hammurabi of Babylon very quickly demonstrated the hollowness of this prayer!

scholarship, was the 'national', or indeed the only cult in the city and country at large, is unlikely (see Chapters 4, 7 and 8 in this volume). It was essentially the dynastic cult. This is borne out by Jeroboam's reaction. He was not interested in arcane theology, but with the basic issue of loyalty to a dynasty and its symbols. Yahwism became over the centuries increasingly intolerant of other cults, a development possibly first occurring in a small proto-Deuteronomic clique isolated by Jeroboam's policies in Israel,[33] and erupting into the open in Judah in Josiah's reign and his reform, and vigorously supported by Yahweh's prophets.

David's reputation for music (1 Sam. 16.14-23 and the traditional attribution to him of many psalms, many with explicit musical elements) suggests a particular importance for music in the royal cult. The formula *lĕdāwîd* in a psalm introduction may signal not so much authorship as an indication of royal application. The number of 'royal psalms' is certainly higher than most conservative estimates. I have identified two new ones (Psalms 8 and 19), which had never appeared in scholars' lists.[34]

3
The Living King as the Object of Ritual Behaviour

The clearest examples of this are the anointing (de Vaux 1961: 104–5) and enthronement of the king. We could wish for more details, but have sufficient to recover the rough outlines of procedure. The first two instances of unction cited, Saul (1 Sam. 9.14–10.16) and David (1 Sam. 16.1-13), are not strictly representative of the established norm, since both are the anointing of charismatics chosen outside a hereditary system. They are contrasted: Saul's 'ecstasy' is of short duration; David's (1 Sam. 16.13) is permanent, a coded reference to its authenticity in the writer's view. However, Saul's sacrality persists, as indicated by David's words to the Amalekite (2 Sam. 1.14). Further charismatic unctions are mentioned, of Absalom in 2 Sam. 5.3 and Jehu in Israel in 2 Kgs 9.1-10. David was anointed at Hebron over Israel in 2 Sam. 19.11, but otherwise we may assume that the rite was performed within the palace-temple complex when the next succession was settled, or at least before a king's enthronement, as with Solomon in 1 Kgs 1.39, Jehoash in 2 Kgs 11.12 and Jehoahaz in 2 Kgs 23.30. For details of unction practice, having no direct information, we should compare priestly procedure in Exod. 29.20-21. This describes the anointing of various parts of the high priest's body. I have suggested (Wyatt 2005a: 103–31) that in Psalm 19 we have an account of the mythic birth of the king (vv. 2–7, ET vv. 1–6), followed (vv. 8–11, ET vv. 7–10) by the liturgy of unction, identifying parts of the king's body, and (vv. 12–15, ET vv. 11–14) by words spoken by the king on assuming his new office. The Psalm appears to envisage unction at the time of the enthronement.

The coronation may be tentatively reconstructed from a number of biblical passages: Isaiah 14, Ezek. 28.2-11 and 28.12-18, and verses in Exodus 19, 20 and 24 and

---

33.   The putative existence of a post-Jeroboamid sectarian minority remaining loyal to Yahweh in Israel would nicely explain both the shrillness of Deuteronomic rhetoric and the discovery of the 'Book of the Law' (2 Kgs 22.3-10) taken southwards by refugees in about 720 BCE.

34.   See Wyatt 2005a: 95–131, and Caquot 1990: 45–48 on the underestimation of this aspect. Cf. Mithen 2005: 266: 'With the emergence of religious belief, music became the principal means of communicating with the gods'. (My thanks to Simon Wyatt for this reference.)

Deuteronomy 9 and 10, evidently in keeping with a widespread pattern attested in Ugarit in KTU 1.6.i.43–65 and in the account of the enthronement of Enmeduranki of Sippar.[35] We have two accounts of coronations from Judah, of Solomon (1 Kgs 1.38-39) and Joash (2 Kgs 11.12). Both take place in special circumstances, and differ in details (Widengren 1950; von Rad 1965: 222–31; Caquot 1990: 52–53; Wyatt 2005a: 46 n. 67). We may tentatively reconstruct a synoptic account from the partial details of each narrative. Thus the king was taken to the Gihon spring, source of Jerusalem's water supply, and a feature in the cosmology of Eden (Gen 2.13),[36] surely a reference to its ideological importance; from thence he proceeded to the temple, where he mounted and stood on a pillar; he was anointed; he was enthroned and crowned (according to 1 Chron. 28.5; 29.23, it was Yahweh's throne that was used; cf. Ps. 110.1); he was given the 'testimony' (a written contract of kingship?); he received the sceptre; he was acclaimed; he came down from the throne. The pillar (Jachin or Boaz? See 1 Kgs 7.21), like the throne, no doubt represented a 'high point', the summit of the king's ascent, and a symbol of the cosmic mountain (as in Moses' ascent, below). The two pillars perhaps corresponded to the two peaks of the cosmic mountain, stylized into an architectural form (Dijkstra 1991).[37]

Seemingly independently of these initiatory rites, the general ritual practice in which the king was subject, as functionary, in sacrifices, also implied his continuing role as perpetually reaffirming his peculiar status. This comes out very clearly in the texts from Ugarit. In *Kirta*, the passages KTU 1.14.ii.9–26 and 1.14.iii.52–iv.8 list instructions for the king's ritual activity, which Kirta then duly performed. The programme involved a number of stages: ritual washing, rouging, entry into the sanctuary, ritual performances, ascent to the highest part of the temple, raising of hands to heaven, formal offering of victims and descent. There were seven stages to the culmination of the rite, and an eighth that led to its resolution. This looks very like a re-enactment of the royal ascent; that is, it appears to be a constant reaffirmation of the king's supernatural status as intermediary with the gods. This is reproduced in the ritual texts, in which many of those in which the king himself performed explicitly state that he was 'sacralized' and 'desacralized' at the beginning and end of the services (Wyatt 2005a: 196–202). The biblical tradition offers no direct parallel to this information, but if the king in his ritual performances was set apart, we should expect analogous beliefs.

---

35.   Enoch was modelled on Enmeduranki. For the Akkadian text see Widengren 1950: 7–8. All these texts are discussed in Wyatt 2005a: 35–46. The Ugaritic text is now seen to contain an account of the preparation for Athtar's unction (Wyatt 2002: 132, following Emerton 1965: 441–43 and Day 1998: 81). See also the apotheosis of Tuthmosis III, described in a Karnak temple inscription (*ANET*, 446–47). The roots of the pattern are probably to be seen in shamanism (see Davila 2001). A graphic illustration of the ascent motif (*ANEP* §529), though in a different context, appears on a building inscription of Nabu-apal-iddina (c. 870 BCE). The king enters the heavenly shrine of Shamash at Sippar, accompanied by the goddess Aya (l.) and Nabunadinšumi (r.), who stands before an altar with offerings and sun-disc. The *apsu* appears below, with a row of stars separating it from the scene above, indicating that the scene is 'in heaven', before the celestial throne of the god, though from an etic perspective the events take place in the Sippar temple. The text (in *COS* 2.364–68, §2.135) is a record of the king's restoration of the image of the god.

36.   Note that Solomon's rival Adonijah went to a 'spurious' spring, down the valley at Ein Rogel (1 Kgs 1.9) as a part of his conspiracy to win the throne.

37.   The Egyptian horizon sign (a twin-peaked mountain), which may have influenced West Semitic convention (on which see Wyatt 2005b: 102–24) also featured in Aegean and early Greek iconography as a symbol of kingly power.

4
The Question of the Divinity of the King

The rites performed on the king were transformative ('performative actions'), and raise issues of his subsequent metaphysical status. A crucial passage for understanding the status of the king deals with Moses at Sinai, Exod. 34.29-30:

> Now when Moses came down from Mount Sinai, with the two tablets of the testimony in his hand(s) as he came down the mountain, Moses did not know that he had horns on his face after speaking to (Yahweh). And when Aaron and all the Israelites saw that Moses had horns on his face, they were afraid to go near him . . .

The significance of this becomes clear from comparative study, for this is the archetypal biblical passage for the royal ascent, seen above in enthronement rites. Moses' action is modelled on the royal ascent, and like an enthroned king he comes down from the mountain (the dwelling of the god, the temple sanctuary representing it in the cult) transfigured. This is to be understood as the transformation of Moses into a god. This is clear from the horns appearing on his temples, conceptually modelled on those of Mesopotamian divine images (Propp 1987; Dozeman 2000; Sanders 2002; Wyatt 2005a: 208–11).[38] King Naram-Sin had had himself similarly portrayed on his victory stela. Psalm 132.17 is sometimes cited in the context of this discussion:

> There shall I cause a horn to sprout for David
> I shall trim a lamp for my anointed.

There may well be some subtle wordplay here,[39] but it can certainly be understood in the light of our understanding of Moses' apotheosis to refer to the divinization of the king.[40] This was also clearly intended in the king's ascent onto Yahweh's throne, noted above. The language of various royal psalms, which reiterates such points – Ps. 2.7 speaks of sonship, of the king being begotten now, in the act of consecration;[41] Ps. 8.5 (ET v. 4) speaks of the man (sc. the king) as divinely begotten (Cooke 1961; Wyatt 2005a: 95–100),[42] Ps. 45.7 (ET v. 6) addresses the king as 'god' (*ĕlōhîm*), as does

---

38.   William Propp concluded 'that the skin of Moses' face *qāran* is unlikely to be a sign of virtual apotheosis' (Propp 1987: 386). But in the implicit ritual context, and in view of the Ugaritic evidence, I disagree. His earlier question, 'Why should Moses be manifest as a pagan deity after meeting Yahweh?' (Propp 1987: 383) is naïve. It already exhibits the prejudices of monotheism. Dozeman championed Gressmann's old view that Moses was masked.

39.   Sanders's explanation of the Exodus passage by reference to the ambiguity of Sumerian SI, meaning both 'horn' and 'radiance', 'light', etc., already noticed but not developed by Propp, seems almost tailor-made for commentary on the Psalm.

40.   There are two strands to Mosaic tradition, the Exodus, wilderness-wandering and conquest, a national origin myth; and the giving of Torah on Sinai and the apotheosis of Moses, a royal myth. Post-exilic redaction has more or less fused the two.

41.   While Day is broadly sympathetic to the notion of the king's divinity, his estimate that this is to be taken not literally, but metaphorically (Day 1998: 82), begs the question. *All* theological language is metaphorical, but it is unlikely that the psalmist distinguished the two categories: to do so here is to introduce a false dichotomy. Cf. Wyatt 2007: 13 n. 24.

42.   The psalm also reflects the tradition behind KTU 1.23.

110.1, 5 (*'ădōnāy*); Ps. 110.1 has the king sit *beside* Yahweh on his throne, and v. 3 (LXX) speaks of divine birth in the courts of the holy ones (= gods!),[43] which echoes the mythology of Psalm 19 – cannot seriously be downgraded as so often in modern estimation to the merely metaphorical, the legal language of adoption, and so forth. This is theological language used of the king, and implies a theological status. In some manner, the king was perceived as divine. And if my explanation of Psalm 82 (Wyatt 1996: 357–65) is cogent, the 'demotion' of unrighteous Judahite kings implies their prior divine status.

But we need to understand precisely what was meant by such a concept, if it is the correct interpretation. It is wrong to begin with any modern presuppositions about the nature of deity: we should start from the realities of ancient practice. The Egyptian king was declared in his titulary to be identified with a range of royal deities,[44] and such titularies have been claimed for Ugaritian and Judahite kings.[45] The view that there must be evidence of cult to justify the term 'god' is not a disqualification here if our estimate that the king was indeed treated as one of the gods is just. Many ancient gods were 'conceptual', reifying metaphysical ideas, as in Hesiod's *Theogony*, though not offered cult. For all its vaunted monotheism, the Hebrew Bible is remarkably abundant in references to a perfectly acceptable polytheism: the expression *běnê 'ēlîm* occurs in Pss. 29.1 and 89.7 (ET v. 6); the variant *běnê 'ĕlōhîm* is found in Gen 6.1, 2, Job 2.1 and 38.7; the term meant originally not 'angels', as commonly understood, but 'gods'; *'ēlîm* is to be construed as an archaic genitive singular (with the *m* perhaps as intensive), the Hebrew equivalent of Ugaritic *bn il*. This latter term is a standard designation of the gods of the pantheon, sons of El.[46] When the king was called 'son of God', it means that he was a god. The radical ontological difference moderns presuppose to obtain between divine and natural probably did not obtain. The gods were very like humans, with parts, passions and biographies.

5
The Function of Dead Kings

There is evidence for a ritual involving dead kings in Judah, similar to that in Ugarit. Isaiah's satirical poem in Isaiah 14, which mocks a Babylonian king (v. 4), appears to

---

43. After Wyatt 1996: 271, reading:

From the Uterine* at dawn,
Like dew I begot you . . .

(LXX ἐκ γαστρός, presupposing *merehem*, as MT: I understand an allusion to Ugaritian *rahmay*, an avatar, with Athirat, of the goddess Shapshu in KTU 1.23). I think this approach preferable to that of Day 1998: 83.

44. The full fivefold titulary identified the king as (i) Horus; (ii) the Two Ladies (Wadjet and Nekhbet as the deified crowns); (iii) the 'golden Horus' (or possibly, Horus-and-Seth); (iv) the *ka* of various deities; (v) the son of Ra. In addition, the formula *mri*-DN (Amun, Ptah, etc.) used in conjunction with the fifth title meant either 'beloved of DN' or 'begotten of DN'. For discussion of the connection with Solomon's cognomen Jedidiah, see Wyatt 2005a: 13–22.

45. For Ugarit, see del Olmo Lete 1999: 168–84; Wyatt 2002: 48–9 nn. 50, 54 (KTU 1.1.iv.12–20); 2005a: 19–20. For Judah, see Cazelles 1957.

46. For the Ugaritic evidence see Wyatt 2007: 11–14, 64–65.

parody such beliefs, but also presupposes such a practice. The Rephaim of 14.9 correspond to the *Rāpi'ūma* of the Ugaritic text KTU 1.161 (see Wyatt 2002: 430–41).[47] The latter are evidently divine, and appear in a number of informative texts. In KTU texts 1.20–22 (all very fragmentary), they travel in chariots to participate in a *kispum* rite, a celebration of solidarity between living and dead.[48] In KTU 1.124 Ditanu, their eponym (and possibly related to the Greek Titans), is invoked as a healing deity. KTU 1.161, which bears a close relationship with Isa. 14.4b-21, is the liturgy for the funeral of Niqmaddu III–IV, the penultimate king of the city. Let us begin with this, for it provides a clear entrée into the topic. The liturgy is structured as follows:

1	title;
2–10	summons of the *Rāpi'ūma* into the atrium of the tomb;
11–12	summons of Ammithtamru and Niqmaddu (II), predecessors of the lately deceased king;
13–17	address to the king's royal furniture, throne, footstool, table;
18–19	invocation of Shapshu (royal psychopomp) who will guide the king into the underworld;
20–25	instruction to the dead king to go down to join his ancestors, kings and *Rāpi'ūma*;
26–30	series of seven offerings;
31–34	blessings on the acceding king, Ammurapi, his house, and the city.

The scene envisaged in Isaiah 14, before the vituperations take over,[49] is a similar evocation of dead kings who come into the threshold of a royal tomb to greet a newly deceased monarch.[50] The text presupposes familiarity with a ritual such as this, and it is most easily explained as belonging to the Jerusalem royal cult, here transferred to the enemy monarchy.[51] If the ritual tradition is so close to the Ugaritian example, it is probable that a similar theology obtained, and we should therefore understand the kings in the drama to be divine (i.e. now underworld deities). In Saul's necromantic evocation of Samuel (1 Sam. 28.13), Samuel is called an *'ĕlōhîm*, and perhaps reflects a royal necromantic tradition, proscribed by the Deuteronomists, in which dead kings

47.   For general treatment of the Rephaim see Schmidt 1994: 71–93, 267–73; del Olmo Lete 1999: 193–207; Rouillard 1999; Nutkowicz 2006: 257–300; Wyatt 2009: ch. 3.

48.   KTU 1.113, which contains a king-list, appears to have been a litany for use at a *kispum* rite, in which each king named was invoked in turn. The *Rāpi'ūma* do not seem to feature in this list. See Wyatt 2002: 399–403 for translation, commentary and bibliography. For KTU 1.20–22 see Wyatt 2002: 314–23; for 1.124, see Wyatt 2002: 423–25; and for 1.161, see Wyatt 2002: 430–41. Further bibliography *ad loc.*

49.   See the layers of tradition envisaged by Smith 2007: 19.

50.   Perhaps their statues were used in the ritual: see the comparative evidence adduced by Schmidt 1996: 15 (Ebla), 110–12 (Ugarit). On the Ugaritian ritual, see the important discussions of Niehr 2006, 2007, which also suggest possibilities for research into Judahite practice.

51.   This incidentally readily explains the much-discussed problem of Helel ben Shahar of Isa. 14.12-15 (see, for example, Heiser 2001) and the associated passages in Ezekiel 28. Athtar (= Helel ben Shahar) is a royal god in Ugarit (see KTU 1.6.i. 43–67 for his enthronement). His descent here is not a deposition, but simply a mythic expression of a king's death. The element of hubris introduced in the biblical versions belongs to the Babylonian (or Tyrian in Ezekiel) context of the prophet's satire, though it may have arisen in response to the demise of the monarchy. The reservations of Schmidt 1996: 269 concerning the active post-mortem divinity of the Rephaim fails to take into account the polemical dimension of the record. They are downplayed and denigrated *because* they are powerful.

advised the living. This may be the allusion of such passages as Lev. 19.31; Deut. 18.11; 2 Kgs 21.6 and Isa. 1.29; 8.19; 65.4.

Some of these passages locate such cultic activities in a 'garden'. These may be allusions to the royal burial garden, which also lay, at least in some periods, within the temple-palace precinct, as with the Ugaritian 'garden' (*gn*). There was evidently a cult of dead kings,[52] analogous to practices elsewhere (Stavrakopoulou 2006), and it is reasonable to locate the Rephaim in such a context. Apart from the possibility of rites like the *kispum* (solidarity and communion with the dead as continuing members of society), the story of Saul and the medium at Endor (1 Samuel 28) may indicate that dead kings were consulted for oracles.

6
Asherah and the Role of the Gĕbîrâ[53]

A feature of kingship in Judah was matrilinearity (Brown 1968: 167–68)[54] and indeed matrilocality (Brown 2003: 124–27); that is, the possession of the throne passed through the female line, and the queen was the embodiment (as incarnation of the goddess) of the genius of the city. In a polygamous context, the chief queen's son was heir, despite him being the youngest. The narrative concerning Solomon's succession reflects this (Wyatt 2005a: 5–9, 13–22, 49–53; contra Ben-Barak 1991: 29, 31). The chief queen or dowager queen was sometimes termed the *gĕbîrâ*, which corresponded to Ugaritic *rabitu*, a title of this office in Ugarit and Amurru, and also of the goddess Athirat (*rbt atrt ym*).[55] There appears to have been a link between the *gĕbîrâ* and the goddess Asherah in Jerusalem,[56] as indicated in Asa's reform, dismissing the *gĕbîrâ* from her office because she made an 'obscenity' for the goddess (1 Kgs 15.13; see Ackerman 2003: 459–61). As in Ugarit (see n. 14), a royal birth appears to have been treated mythically, the heir being born to the goddess,[57] suggested by Pss. 19.2-7 (ET vv. 1–6) and 110.3 (LXX) cited above.[58]

So the king originally held power by marriage to the appropriate female. This might entail marrying his own mother (which need not involve any sexual element: it was

52. Perhaps the *zibḥê mētîm* of Ps. 106.28, at Baal Peor, is an allusion to such cults? Its wilderness setting may be life in 'Canaan' viewed from the present experience of exile. For the Ugaritic evidence see del Olmo Lete 1999: 213–53. On the *kispum* see Tsukimoto 1985 and Jonker 1995: 223–30.

53. See Molin 1954; Donner 1959; Ahlström 1963: 57–88; Andreasen 1983; Ben-Barak 1991; Ackerman 1993, 1998; Day 2000: 42–67; Bowen 2001; Wyatt 2005a: 5–10; Wiggins 2007: 218.

54. See Gen. 35.22; 2 Sam. 3.7; 5.13; 16.22; 20.3; 1 Kgs 5.22. Not to be confused with matri-archy, as apparently by Ben-Barak 1991: 23.

55. See, for example, KTU 1.3.v.40–41.

56. On Asherah, see Olyan 1988; Dietrich and Loretz 1992; Dijkstra 1995; Hadley 2000; LaRocca-Pitts 2001: 187–92; Wiggins 2007.

57. On the *gĕbîrâ* as an embodiment of the goddess see Ahlström 1963: 76; Ackerman 1998: 153–54.

58. See Wyatt 2005a: 109–28 and 1996: 270, respectively. Perhaps it is also hinted at in Ps. 2.7, commonly taken as a rather empty legal formula. This is the language of the 'sacred marriage', which has been given a rough ride by biblical scholars, on the assumption that it involves a 'fertility cult' (see, for example, Smith 2006: 11). This mythic use of the theme of coition is essentially ideological in purpose, reinforcing the divinity of the king by an assertion of his 'divine' blood. (It also distinguishes him from other princes of the blood in a polygynous society. *Only* the king is divine.)

primarily an ideological and legal matter), and evidently did in the case of Abijam of Judah (Wyatt 2005a: 5–6, 58, 240–41). The significance of this was theological rather than merely sociological: it was part of the persona of the king, who shared in both earthly (human) existence and in the divine order. Recent discussions of the *gĕbîrâ* (Ben-Barak 1991; Bowen 2001), which tend to downplay or even deny her importance, make too much of the paucity of evidence. These were the roots of later Christology, which sought to link Christ to both dimensions, and involved the quasi-apotheosis of Mary.

Another oracular tradition may have centred on the Asherah cult, with its icon the stylized tree (*'ăšērâ*, 'asherah'). Trees were a primary locus of oracular messages. Given the tradition of royal oracles, where arboreal procedures survive in the literature we may also discern the oracular function of the *'ăšērâ* (O'Bryhim 1996; Ruiz 2005; Wyatt 2007: 167–92, esp. 190, n. 76). Such an assessment also provides an explanation for the abrupt cessation of the cult of Asherah at the demise of the monarchy in 587–586 BCE.

7
Conclusion

My remarks on eisegesis above (in n. 2) are worth recalling in concluding this discussion. While there has always been a body of scholarship, usually characterized as devotional rather than dispassionate, which saw Christ at every turn in the narrative, but above all in the hymnic and prophetic books of the Hebrew Bible, there has also been a strong current that saw this as essentially eisegetical and thus spurious so far as understanding the 'original' meaning of the tradition was concerned. But at the same time, this more sceptical approach tended rather naïvely to accept the Hebrew Bible's own perspective that kingship was essentially a foreign institution, while striving to evacuate this tradition of all ideological content. My view is that this is nonsensical. The whole point of 'borrowing' such an ideology, if that is what happened – I am myself of the view that this foreignness has been much exaggerated – would surely have been precisely to adopt the ideology. In any event, by careful scrutiny of the text, and openness to analogous and cognate materials in the world outside Judah and in Israel, it seems increasingly likely that we should see the biblical material as organically related to the broader cultural pattern, rather than see the pattern as something alien. This is not to accept the pattern uncritically, as was claimed of the 'myth and ritual' approach of the mid-twentieth century. The case must be made at every juncture, carefully assessing each piece of the jigsaw.

Bibliography

Ackerman, S.
1993 'The Queen Mother and the Cult in Ancient Israel', *JBL* 112: 385–401.
1998 *Warrior, Dancer, Seductress, Queen* (AB Reference Library; New York, NY: Doubleday).
2003 'At Home with the Goddess', in W.G. Dever and S. Gitin (eds), *Symbiosis, Symbolism, and the Power of the Past: Canaan, Ancient Israel, and Their Neighbors from the Late Bronze Age through Roman Palestinia* (Winona Lake, IN: Eisenbrauns), 455–68.

Ahlström, G.W.
1963   *Aspects of Syncretism in Israelite Religion* (HS 5; Lund: Gleerup).

Albright, W.F.
1935   'The Horites in Palestine', in L.G. Leary (ed.) *From the Pyramids to Paul: Festschrift for G.L. Robinson* (New York, NY: Nelson), 9–26.

Andreasen, N.-E.A.
1983   'The Role of the Queen Mother in Israelite Society', *CBQ* 45: 179–94.

Athas, G.
2003   *The Tel Dan Inscription* (JSOTS 360/CIS 12; London and New York, NY: T&T Clark International).

Batto, B.F. and K.L. Roberts (eds)
2004   *David and Zion. Biblical Studies in Honor of J.J.M. Roberts* (Winona Lake, IN: Eisenbrauns).

Ben-Barak, Z.
1991   'The Status and Right of the *Gĕbîrâ*', *JBL* 110: 23–34.

Bowen, N.R.
2001   'The Quest for the Historical Gebira', *CBQ* 63: 597–618.

Brooke, G.J, A.H.W. Curtis and J.F. Healey (eds)
1994   *Ugarit and the Bible* (UBL 11; Münster: Ugarit-Verlag).

Brown, J.P.
1968   'Literary Contexts of the Common Hebrew-Greek Vocabulary', *JSS* 13: 163–91.
2003   *Ancient Israel and Ancient Greece: Religion, Politics and Culture* (Minneapolis, MN: Fortress Press).

Caquot, A.
1990   'Kingship in Ancient Israel', in J.-C. Galey (ed.), *Kingship and the Kings* (Chur: Harwood), 31–55.

Cazelles, H.
1957   'Le titulaire du roi David', in [A. Robert (no named ed.)], *Mélanges Bibliques Rédigés en l'Honneur d'André Robert* (Paris: Bloud & Gay), 131–36.

Cooke, G.
1961   'The Israelite King as Son of God', *ZAW* 73: 202–25.

Craigie P.C.
1983   *Ugarit and the Old Testament* (Grand Rapids, MI: Eerdmans).

Dalley, S.
1990   'Yahweh in Hamath in the 8th Century BC: Cuneiform Material and Historical Deductions', *VT* 40: 21–32.

Davila, J.R.
2001   *Descenders to the Chariot: The People behind the Hekhalot Literature* (SJSJ 70; Leiden: Brill).

Day, J.
1998   'The Canaanite Inheritance in the Israelite Monarchy', in J. Day (ed.), *King and Messiah in Israel and the Ancient Near East* (JSOTS 270; Sheffield: Sheffield Academic Press), 72–90.
2000   *Yahweh and the Gods and Goddesses of Canaan* (JSOTS 265; Sheffield: Sheffield Academic Press).

Day, J. (ed.)
1998   *King and Messiah in Israel and the Ancient Near East* (JSOTS 270; Sheffield: Sheffield Academic Press).

Dietrich, M. and O. Loretz
1992   *Jahwe und seine Aschera* (UBL 9; Münster: Ugarit-Verlag).

Dijkstra, M.
1991   'The Weather-God on Two Mountains', *UF* 23: 127–40.
1995   'El, Yahweh and their Asherah', in M. Dietrich and O. Loretz (eds), *Ugarit: ein Ostmediterranes Kulturzentrum im Alten Orient* (ALASP 7 i; Münster: Ugarit-Verlag), 43–73.

Donner, H.
1959   'Art und Herkunft des Amtes der Königinmutter im Alten Testament', in R. von Kienle, *et al.* (eds), *Festschrift Johannes Friedrich* (Heidelberg: Winter), 105–45.

Dozeman, T.B.
2000   'Masking Moses and Mosaic Authority in the Pentateuch', *JBL* 119: 21–43.

Durand, J.-M.
1993   'Le mythologème du combat entre le dieu de l'orage et la mer en Mésopotamie', *MARI* 7: 41–61.

Emerton, J.A.
1965   'Ugaritic Notes', *JTS* 16: 438–43.

Geyer, J.B.
2007   'Where and What?', in W.G.E. Watson (ed.), *'He Unfurrowed his Brow and Laughed': Essays in Honour of Professor Nicolas Wyatt* (AOAT 299; Münster: Ugarit-Verlag), 95–111.

Gillingham, S.E.
1998   'The Messiah in the Psalms: A Question of Reception History and the Psalter', in J. Day (ed.), *King and Messiah in Israel and the Ancient Near East* (JSOTS 270; Sheffield: Sheffield Academic Press), 209–37.

Gnuse, R.
2002–3 Review of M.S. Smith, *The Origins of Biblical Monotheism*, *JHS* 4. Online: http://www.arts.ualberta.ca/JHS/reviews/031.htm (accessed 9 January 2009).

Grabbe, L.L.
2007   *Ancient Israel: What Do We Know, and How Do We Know It?* (London: T&T Clark International).

Hadley, J.M.
2000   *The Cult of Asherah in Ancient Israel and Judah* (UCOP 57; Cambridge: Cambridge University Press).

Hamilton, M.W.
2005   *The Body Royal: The Social Poetics of Kingship in Ancient Israel* (BIS 78; Leiden: Brill).

Heiser, M.
2001   'The Mythological Provenance of Isa. XIV 12–15: A Reconsideration of the Ugaritic Material', *VT* 51: 354–69.

Johnson, A.R.
1955   *Sacral Kingship in Ancient Israel* (Cardiff: University of Wales Press).

Jonker, G.
1995   *The Topography of Remembrance: The Dead, Tradition and Collective Memory in Mesopotamia* (SHR 68; Leiden: Brill).

Kantorowicz, E.H.
1957   *The King's Two Bodies* (Princeton, NJ: Princeton University Press).

Kapelrud, A.S.
1963   *The Ras Shamra Discoveries and the Old Testament* (Oxford: Blackwell).

Keel, O. and C. Uehlinger
1998   *Gods, Goddesses and Images of God in Ancient Israel* (trans. T.H. Trapp; Edinburgh: T&T Clark International).

Knoppers, G.N.
1997   'The Vanishing Monarchy: The Disappearance of the United Monarchy from Recent Histories of Ancient Israel', *JBL* 116: 19–44.

LaRocca-Pitts, E.C.
2001   *'Of Wood and Stone': The Significance of Israelite Cultic Terms in the Bible and Its Earlier Interpreters* (HSM 61; Winona Lake, IN: Eisenbrauns).

Launderville, D.
2003   *Piety and Politics* (Grand Rapids, MI: Eerdmans).

Mithen, S.
2005   *The Singing Neanderthals* (London: Weidenfeld and Nicolson).

Molin, G.F.
1954   'Die Stellung der Gebira im Staate Juda', *TZ* 10: 161–75.

Moran, W.L.
1992   *The Amarna Letters* (Baltimore, MD: The Johns Hopkins University Press).

Murtonen, A.
1952   *A Philological and Literary Treatise on the Old Testament Divine Names 'El, 'Elôah, 'Elohîm, and Yhwh* (Studia Orientalia 18.1; Helsinki: Societas Orientalis Fennica).

Niehr, H.
2006   'The royal funeral in ancient Syria: a comparative view on the tombs in the palaces of Qatna, Kumidi and Ugarit', *JNSL* 32: 1–24.
2007   'The Topography of Death in the Royal Palace of Ugarit: Preliminary Thoughts on the Basis of Archaeological and Textual Data', in J.-M. Michaud (ed.), *Le royaume d'Ougarit de la Crète à l'Euphrate. Nouveaux axes de recherche* (POLO II; Sherbrooke, QC: Éditions GGC), 219–42.

Nutkowicz, H.
2006   *L'Homme Face à la Mort au Royaume de Juda* (Patrimoines Judaïsme; Paris: Cerf).

O'Bryhim, S.
1996   'A New Interpretation of Hesiod, "Theogony" 35', *Hermes* 124: 131–39.

O'Callaghan, R.T.
1948   *Aram Naharaim* (AnOr 26; Rome: Pontifical Biblical Institute).

Olmo Lete, G. del
1999   *Canaanite Religion according to the Liturgical Texts of Ugarit* (trans. W.G.E. Watson; Bethesda, MD: CDL Press).

Olyan, S.M.
1988   *Asherah and the Cult of Yahweh in Israel* (SBLMS 34; Atlanta: Society of Biblical Literature).

Pardee, D.
2000   *Les Textes Rituels* (2 fascicles. RSO 12; Paris: ERC).
2002   *Ritual and Cult at Ugarit* (SBLWAW 10; Atlanta: Society of Biblical Literature).

Porter, B.N.
2003   *Trees, Kings, and Politics* (OBO 197; Fribourg: Universitätsverlag; Göttingen: Vandenhoek and Ruprecht).

Propp, W.H.
1987   'The Skin of Moses' Face – Disfigured or Transfigured?' *CBQ* 49: 375–86.

von Rad, G.
1965   'The Royal Ritual in Judah', in *The Problem of the Hexateuch and Other Essays* (trans. N.W. Porteous; Edinburgh: Oliver and Boyd), 222–31.

Rouillard, H.
1999   'Rephaim', *DDD*, 692–700.
2005   'L'énigme des refa'îm bibliques résolue grâce aux rapa'uma d'Ougarit?', in J.-M.

Michaud (ed.), *La Bible et l'Héritage d'Ougarit* (POLO I; Sherbrooke, QU: Éditions GGC), 145–82.

Ruiz, C. López
2005   'El Dicho del Árbol y la Piedra. Sabiduria ancestral y árboles sagrados en Grecia arcaica y el Levante', in R. Olmos, P. Cabrera and S. Montero (eds), *Paraiso Cerrado, Jardín Abierto. El Reino Vegetal en el Imaginario Religioso del Mediterráneo* (Madrid: Polifemo), 103–24.

Sanders, S.L.
2002   'Old Light on Moses' Shining Face', *VT* 42: 400–6.
2002–3 Review of M.S. Smith, *The Early History of God*, *JHS* 4. Online: http://www.arts.ualberta.ca/JHS/reviews/119.htm (accessed 9 January 2009).

Schmidt, B.B.
1994   *Israel's Beneficent Dead: Ancestor Cult and Necromancy in Ancient Israelite Religion and Tradition* (FAT 11; Tübingen: J.C.B. Mohr; repr. Winona Lake, IN: Eisenbrauns, 1996).

Schmidt, B.B. (ed.)
2007   *The Quest for the Historical Israel: Debating Archaeology and the History of Early Israel* (I. Finkelstein and A. Mazar; ABS, Atlanta, GA: Society of Biblical Literature).

Shipp, R.M.
2002   *Of Dead Kings and Dirges* (Atlanta, GA: Society of Biblical Literature).

Smith, M.S.
2001   *The Origins of Biblical Monotheism* (Oxford: Oxford University Press).
2002   *The Early History of God: Yahweh and Other Deities in Ancient Israel* (2nd edn; Grand Rapids, MI: Eerdmans).
2006   *The Rituals and Myths of the Feast of the Goodly Gods of KTU/CAT 1.23: Royal Constructions of Opposition, Intersection, Integration and Domination* (RBS 51; Atlanta, GA: Society of Biblical Literature).
2007   'Recent Study of Israelite Religion in the Light of the Ugaritic Texts', in K. Lawson Younger (ed.), *Ugarit at Seventy-Five* (Winona Lake, IN: Eisenbrauns), 1–25.

Speiser, E.A.
1953   'The Hurrian Participation in the Civilization of Mesopotamia, Syria and Palestine', *CHM* 1/2: 311–27, reprinted in *Oriental and Biblical Studies* (Philadelphia, PA: University of Pennsylvania Press). First published in *AASOR* 13 (1931–32).

Stavrakopoulou, F.
2004   *King Manasseh and Child Sacrifice: Biblical Distortions of Historical Realities* (BZAW 338; Berlin and New York, NY: de Gruyter).
2006   'Exploring the Garden of Uzza: Death, Burial and Ideologies of Kingship', *Biblica* 87: 1–21.

Tatlock, J.R.
2006   'How in Ancient Times They Sacrificed People', PhD thesis, University of Michigan: UMI 3224761.

Thompson, T.L.
2006   *The Messiah Myth: The Near Eastern Roots of Jesus and David* (London: Jonathan Cape).

Trapp, T.H.
2002–3 Review of M.S. Smith, *The Origins of Biblical Monotheism*, *JHS* 4. Online: http://www.arts.ualberta.ca/JHS/reviews/105.htm (accessed 9 January 2009).

Tsukimoto, A.
1985   *Untersuchungen zur Totenpflege (*kispum*) im Alten Mesopotamien* (AOAT 216; Neukirchen-Vluyn: Neukirchener Verlag; Kevelaer: Verlag Butzon and Bercker).

Ussishkin, D.
2003   'Jerusalem as a Royal and Cultic Center', in W.G. Dever and S. Gitin (eds), *Symbiosis,*

Symbolism, and the Power of the Past: Canaan, Ancient Israel, and Their Neighbors from the Late Bronze Age through Roman Palestinia (Winona Lake, IN: Eisenbrauns), 529–38.

Vanderhooft, D. and W. Horowitz
2002   'The Cuneiform Inscription from Tell en-Nasbeh: The Demise of an Unknown King', *TA* 29: 318–27.

Van Seters, J.
1972   'The Terms "Amorite" and "Hittite" in the Old Testament', *VT* 22: 64–81.

Vaux, R. de
1961   *Ancient Israel* (London: Darton, Longman and Todd).

Widengren, G.
1950   *The Ascension of the Apostle and the Heavenly Book* (UUÅ 1950.7; Uppsala: Lundequistska).
1951   *The King and the Tree of Life in Ancient Near Eastern Religion* (UUÅ 1951.4; Uppsala: Lundequistska).

Wiggins, S.A.
2007   *A Reassessment of Asherah* (2nd edn; GUS 2; Piscataway, NJ: Gorgias).

Wyatt, N.
1989   'Near Eastern Echoes of Āryan Tradition', *SMSR* 55 (NS 13): 5–29.
1996   *Myths of Power* (UBL 13; Münster: Ugarit-Verlag).
2001   *Space and Time in the Religious Life of the 'Ancient' Near East* (BS 85; Sheffield: Sheffield Academic Press).
2002   *Religious Texts from Ugarit* (2nd edn; BS 53; London: Continuum).
2005a   *'There's Such Divinity Doth Hedge a King': Selected Essays of Nicolas Wyatt on Royal Ideology in Ugaritic and Old Testament Literature* (SOTS Monograph Series; London: Ashgate).
2005b   *The Mythic Mind: Essays on Cosmology and Religion in Ugaritic and Old Testament Literature* (BibleWorld; London: Equinox).
2005c   'The Religious Role of the King in Ugarit', *UF* 37: 695–727.
2005d   'Epic in Ugaritic Literature', in J.M. Foley (ed.), *Blackwell Companion to Ancient Epic* (Oxford: Blackwell), 246–54.
2007   *Word of Tree and Whisper of Stone, and Other Papers on Ugaritian Thought* (GUS 1; Piscataway, NJ: Gorgias).
2008   'Grasping the Griffin: Identifying and Characterizing the Griffin in Egypt and the West Semitic Tradition', *JAEI* 1: 29–39.
2009   *The Archaeology of Myth: Papers on Old Testament Tradition* (BibleWorld; London: Equinox).

Chapter 6

Cultic Sites and Complexes beyond the Jerusalem Temple

Diana Edelman

During the time of the kingdoms of Israel (c. 975–721 BCE; Iron IIA–B) and Judah (c. 960–586 BCE; Iron IIA–C), a range of cultic sites existed throughout both kingdoms, some built and maintained by royal decree from local taxes-in-kind and others built and maintained by local townspeople or privately, by families or clans. Evidence for the existence of both categories is provided in various texts in the Hebrew Bible as well as by artefactual remains uncovered during archaeological excavations. I will examine the evidence primarily for the former in this chapter, though I will include some examples of the latter.

The biblical texts relate stories and events that are set in a chronological framework that extends from creation and the patriarchal age through the Exodus, the wilderness wanderings, the occupation of the land, the era of the judges, the united monarchies, the kingdoms of Israel and Judah, the exile, and the post-exilic period. For modern historians, the texts reflect the worldviews of the time when they were written, though they might preserve some earlier views if their authors drew on source material. While the dates of composition of most texts remain debated, most scholars argue for dates during the Judahite monarchy or during the period it existed as Yehud, a province of Neo-Babylonia (586–538 BCE) and then Persia (538–333 BCE), or as Judaea, a province that passed back and forth between the Ptolemaic and Seleucid Empires during the Hellenistic period (333–52 BCE). The texts are thought to have been composed by scribes from Judah/Yehud/Judaea or members of the Jewish diaspora who had ties to Jerusalem; little input is assigned to scribes of Israel and its successor province, Samerina, although what appears to be northern source material is used and the present-day Samaritan community holds the first five books to be their sacred canon. Their predecessors likely contributed to the creation of these books.

1
Temples and Cultic Sites in the Hebrew Bible

Other temple or cultic sites are mentioned besides Jerusalem in the collective texts of the Hebrew Bible. However, they tend to be sidelined or portrayed negatively in the texts. This is likely due to the eventual successful implementation of the call for a single site that Yahweh would choose to 'place his name' (perhaps with the additional sense, 'to dwell/remain') that is reiterated often in the book of Deuteronomy (12.5, 11, 14, 18, 21, 26; 14.23-25; 15.20; 16.6, 11, 16; 26.2). The texts reflect the hindsight practice of a single central temple and wish to present that as a norm throughout the monarchic period, and earlier. But this has created some misleading impressions about the location and function of cultic complexes in ancient Israel and Judah in the Iron Age.

1.1 'The Patriarchal Age' (Genesis)

There was no need to avoid mentioning the building of altars by the patriarchs in the 'Promised Land' in the book of Genesis because they represent what was acceptable in the distant past under human initiative, before God announced he would choose a single temple site once the people entered the land. On this assumption, it is possible to suggest that sacred sites with some sort of official set-up for the enactment of cult and ritual had once existed at the sites named in Genesis as places of religious activity of the forefathers: Shechem (Gen. 12.6-7; 33.18-20; 35.4), Bethel (Gen. 12.8; 28.8-20; 35.6-7, 9-15), Hebron (Gen. 13.18), Beersheba (Gen. 21.33; 26.25), Salem (Gen. 14.17-20) and possibly at Peniel on the Jabbok River in Transjordan (Gen. 32.22-32). It can be noted, however, that there is never an explicit account of a sacrifice being offered on any of these altars; instead, we have the dedication of the altar at Bethel to Yahweh via an act of 'invocation of the name' (*qārā' bĕšem yhwh*), while at Beersheba, Abraham plants a tamarisk tree and there 'invokes the name' of Yahweh El-'Olam and later, Isaac builds an altar there as well, invoking the name of Yahweh. The altars at Shechem and Hebron are built in response to a theophany and an audition, respectively. At Salem, Abram seemingly shares a meatless meal of bread and wine with the priest/king Melchizedek before El-Elyon, though bread can designate 'food' more widely. Yet, are we to assume that the altars were not intended for the offering of animal sacrifice? Why build an altar at all, then, and not simply set up a memorial of some sort dedicated to a deity?

The invocation of the name of Yahweh at the altars at Bethel and Beersheba would have been part of the process of identifying the deity for whom the altar was established; the reverse process is detailed in Deut. 12.3. The Israelites are instructed to demolish completely all the places (*mĕqōmôt*) where the nations in Canaan that are about to be dispossessed have served their gods. Specifically, they are to break down their altars as part of the process of 'destroying/making perish their names from that place'. Thus, it seems as though the ancestors are depicted as having built altars that they dedicated to the worship of various forms of Yahweh through a process of identifying a given site as belonging to Yahweh. Implicitly, they offered sacrifices on these altars, but the failure to state that explicitly might be a deliberate tactic on the part of the author of the book to reinforce in his readers a respect for the pre-eminence in their day of a single site chosen directly by the deity, where animal sacrifice was to take place exclusively (see Deut. 12.5-7).

It might be relevant to note here that when the temple for Yau (Yahweh) was rebuilt in the military fortress on the island of Elephantine in the Nile sometime c. 405 BCE, it was to be an 'altar house' but one where animal sacrifice was no longer to be offered. The altar(s) was/were to be used to offer incense and meal offerings only. When the Jews in the colony had failed to get permission from the Persians to rebuild their temple that had been destroyed by the local priests of the god Khnum c. 410 BCE, they had sought a patron with clout in Jerusalem and subsequently in Samerina to support their cause and gain the sought-after permission. Drafts of their letter specified use of the altar house in the past for animal sacrifice in addition to the offering of incense and meal offerings and anticipated its use for all three purposes after rebuilding (*AP*

30.21, 31.21; Cowley 1923). The memorandum that records the official response sent back eventually from representatives from Samerina and Jerusalem jointly gives support for the building of an altar house but specifies it is to be used for incense and meal offerings only (*AP* 32).

It could be argued that the patriarchal altars in Genesis were modelling this new attitude that had emerged by the end of the fifth century BCE; the offerings/meal Abram shares at Salem are/is arguably meatless. On the other hand, the altar at Salem was not built by Abraham or explicitly dedicated to a form of Yahweh, so the absence of meat explicitly brought out by the priest might reflect other concerns. Nevertheless, Elephantine shows us that altars need not have been intended for animal sacrifice exclusively (see also Joshua 22). Thus, the actions and attitudes of the patriarchs in Genesis can be seen either to be an example of discontinuity, where implicit practices of animal sacrifice and multiple altars used in the past no longer hold in the time of the reader, or an example of attitudes and practices in force at the time of the reader that have been set into the past to give an impression of continuity in spite of actual discontinuity.

1.2 'The Occupation of the Land' (Joshua) and 'the Period of the Judges' (Judges–1 Samuel 12)

The books that describe the actions of the 12 tribes during the occupation of the land and before the rise of the monarchy, during the time of the so-called Judges (Joshua; Judges; 1 Samuel 1–12), tend to depict the ark's dwelling at a series of sites in succession, as though there had been a rotating central sanctuary: Shechem (Joshua 24), Gilgal (1 Sam. 7.15; 11.14-15), Shiloh (Judg. 18.31; 1 Sam. 1.3, 24; 3.23; 4.3-4), Mizpah (Judg. 20.1-2; 1 Sam. 7.5, 15; 10.17-27), Bethel (Judg. 21.2-3; 1 Sam. 7.15; 10.3), Kiriath-Jearim (1 Sam. 7.1-2), Ramah (1 Sam. 7.15), and Gibeath-elohim (1 Sam. 10.5-6). In addition, in texts dealing with the period of the occupation and judges, there is mention of an altar for Baal and Asherah in Ophrah of the Abiezerites that was replaced by an altar for Yahweh (Judges 6), a temple to Baal Berit/El Berit in Shechem (Judg. 9.4, 46) and an apparent sacred site to Yahweh in Mizpah in Transjordanian Gilead (Judg. 11.12). The tribe of Dan had a temple (Judg. 18.27-31), while Micah is said to have had a private shrine somewhere in the hill country of Ephraim (Judges 18).

1.3 'The Era of the United Monarchy' (1 Samuel 13–1 Kings 11) and 'the Era of the Kingdoms of Israel and Judah' (1 Kings 12–2 Kings 25)

From the monarchic era there are sacred complexes with altars, buildings and personnel mentioned in various books. Their locations include Gilgal (1 Sam. 15.12-15; 2 Kgs 4.38-44; Hos. 4.15; 12.11; Amos 4.4; 5.5), Bethlehem (1 Sam. 16.2; 20.6) Nob (1 Sam. 21.1-6; 22.1-12, 20-23), Hebron (2 Sam. 5.1-5), Gibeon (2 Sam. 21.6), Dan (1 Kgs 12.30; Amos 8.14), Bethel (1 Kgs 12.30-33; 13; 17.27-28; Hosea 10 [Beth-Aven]; Amos 4.4; 5.5; 7.13), Mount Carmel (1 Kings 18), Samaria (2 Kings 10; Hosea 10; Mic. 1.7), Mizpah (Hos. 5.1); Shiloh (Jer. 7.12, 14; 26.6, 9) and Beersheba (Amos 5.5; 8.14). Not all were dedicated to Yahweh. Samaria housed a temple of Baal but probably also one or more dedicated to Yahweh.

Of these named sites, Bethel, Hebron and Beersheba, three of the four 'patriarchal era' sites, appear again. Shechem, the remaining patriarchal site, is mentioned in the period of the judges but not in the monarchic eras as explicitly housing a temple, although it could be surmised the intended coronation of Rehoboam in Shechem was to have taken place in a temple (1 Kgs 12.1) and that we are to understand that Jeroboam was crowned in a temple in Shechem instead (v. 20). There are five sites that appear in the narratives describing the periods of the occupation and judges and again in those narrating events in the periods of the united and divided monarchies: Mizpah, Gilgal, Shiloh, Bethel and Dan. The focus on sites located in the northern kingdom of Israel or in the territory of Benjamin, a border area between Israel and Judah that changed hands over time, is probably due in part to the nature of the source material underlying the book of Judges. It is widely thought that the core stories gathered in this book are derived from a northern venue (see, for example, Mayes 1985: 20–27), though even in its present form, there is only one 'judge' from Judah/the south: Othniel. His story, along with that of his successor Ehud from Benjamin, a region that was part of the kingdom of Israel but became part of Judah or the province of Yehud at some point, illustrate the pattern of ideal judgeship. They are the only two judges to fulfil their commissions without incident, showing this form of leadership could work. The negative portrayal of the tribes living north of Judah, who form the focus of the book, represents 'those who did not know Yahweh nor what he had done for Israel (Judg. 2.10), failing to drive out from their lands the Canaanites, who subsequently 'became a snare to Israel' (2.3). In this way, the book seems designed to prepare the reader/hearer for the account of the period of the 'united' and 'divided monarchies', told in Samuel and Kings, when Israel breaks from Yahweh's chosen royal line and fails to keep to Yahweh's paths (Amit 1999: 149–50).

Nevertheless, since one reads the biblical texts through the canonical 'glasses' supplied by the present order of the books, the impact of the references to the many cultic sites that existed in addition to the temple in Jerusalem during the monarchic era is minimized; the reader often accepts the idea planted solidly in the book of Deuteronomy that there was to be a primary, central temple site (chs 12, 13, 14, 24 and 26) with no use of trees or sacred pillars next to the altar to Yahweh (16.21) and accepts the account of the building and dedication of the temple in Jerusalem by David and Solomon in 1 Kings 3–9 as the fulfilment of the divine plan enunciated in Deuteronomy. As a result, there is an understandable tendency to depict in the mind's eye the other holy sites and complexes mentioned as being contemporaneous with the temple in Jerusalem as minor, insignificant outlying institutions of dubious pedigree. This view is reinforced by the account of cultic reform and implied centralization undertaken by the exemplary monarch Hezekiah (2 Kgs 18.3-6, 22), reversed by his successor Manasseh (2 Kgs 21.3-9) and the subsequent reforms and centralization undertaken by the equally exemplary King Josiah (2 Kgs 23.4-20). The effusive account of the temple's building by Solomon in Chronicles as well as the story of its rebuilding in the Persian period after 'the end of the exile' in Ezra 1–6 help foster and reinforce the centrality of Jerusalem as Yahweh's chosen temple site in 'the Promised Land.'

It is interesting to note, however, that the account of Josiah's cultic reform and centralization never refers to the explicit closing down of Yahwistic places of worship – only to the removal of the 'high places' or cultic complexes (*bāmôt*) in the walled settlements of Judah and around Jerusalem from Geba to Beersheba and in the gates of Jerusalem (2 Kgs 23.5, 8), as well as the firing of their cultic personnel, the *kĕmārîm* (v. 5) and the more standard *kōhănîm* (v. 8). By implication, the closed places of worship included the royally endorsed and supported installations that

Manasseh had created (2 Kgs 21.3-9). The characterization of the *bāmôt* by B. Long as 'illegitimate shrines outside the Jerusalem temple's authority' and his understanding of those closed by Josiah as being rural shrines in the northern territories 'presumably left in use after the demise of Israel' illustrates well the effect of reading with canonical glasses (1991: 195).

The *kĕmārîm* were cultic specialists of some sort or rank; this is the common designation for a cultic functionary in Aramaic (*kûmrā'*) and Phoenician (*kmr*) and is the equivalent of the more usual Hebrew term *kōhănîm* (Görg 1985). The term only occurs in two other biblical passages (Zeph. 1.4; Hos. 10.5). As a result, it is hard to grasp what distinction is being drawn in 2 Kgs 23.5 and 8 between the *kĕmārîm* and the *kōhănîm*. But in Zeph. 1.4, the *kĕmārîm* are one of a number of categories of inhabitants of Judah and Jerusalem who have turned back from following Yahweh or have not sought him, along with those who are 'the remnant of the Baal', those who worship the host of heaven on the roofs, and those who swear by Yahweh and also by 'their King'. This list is very reminiscent of the list of those cut off by Josiah in 2 Kings 23. Yahweh says he will stretch out his hand against 'the name of the *kĕmārîm*', which could mean the deity ('the name') they worship, which by implication would be a god other than Yahweh, or could refer to their general reputation, which will now be sullied. The ensuing phrase, 'with the *kōhănîm*', is lacking in Greek and is probably a secondary gloss. In Hos. 10.5, the *kĕmārîm* are priests who attend the calf image of Yahweh in the sanctuary at Bethel, which is being denigrated as a 'house of iniquity' (*bêt-'āwen*) by the author of Hosea in a play on the place-name. They and its people will mourn for it when it is carried to Assyria.

The very limited use of this term makes it impossible to grasp the reason for the specification in 2 Kgs 23.5 that the *kĕmārîm* appointed by the kings of Judah to offer sacrifices by fire (Edelman 1985) in *bāmôt* complexes in the walled settlements and the areas surrounding Jerusalem were deposed; they seem to be identical with the *kōhănîm* who also had been making offerings by fire in *bāmôt* in the walled settlements of Judah from Geba to Beersheba, who were removed from the walled settlements in v. 8. The suggestion of H.-D. Hoffmann that the former officiated for deities other than Yahweh while the *kōhănîm* officiated for Yahweh is contradicted by Hos. 10.5, unless one wants to claim that the cult of Yahweh in Samaria is being classed as 'foreign' or 'other' because it involved a different manifestation of Yahweh from the one prominent in Judah, Yahweh Sebaot; he does not make this explicit distinction, however (1980: 214–15). The common rendering of the term *kĕmārîm* as 'idolatrous priest' in the NRSV and other Bibles is guesswork based on the three uses and the assumption that this type of cultic functionary served gods other than Yahweh represented in statue form in the cult; its application to those tending the calf representing Yahweh of Samaria is tendentious and demonstrates that *kĕmārîm* could officiate before Yahweh in whatever form he was made manifest.

It would be possible to deduce from the standard translation of the comment in 2 Kgs 23.9 about the *kōhănîm* from the closed *bāmôt* not being allowed to serve immediately at the altar in the temple in Jerusalem that these complexes had been used to worship Yahweh, perhaps alongside other deities. Here, we would need to assume that these cultic personnel had been associated in some capacity with Yahweh but were deemed 'contaminated' by their postings in the *bāmôt* of dubious legal status or which also honoured other deities in addition so they were being excluded from a right to serve in Jerusalem – a right they otherwise would have been entitled to exercise (assuming they were Levites: Deut. 18.6-8). Yet, it would be equally possible to deduce that, like the cultic paraphernalia associated with gods other than Yahweh, both 'Canaanite'/autochthonous (2 Kgs 23.4, 6) and 'foreign' (23.13-14), which was removed from the temple in Jerusalem and from locations around Jerusalem, these *kōhănîm* of the de-activated high places were officiating for gods other than Yahweh or in addition to Yahweh and so were excluded from serving Yahweh in Jerusalem.

W. Boyd Barrick has noted, however, that the syntax of v. 9 has the first verb in the imperfect and the verb after *kî 'im* in the perfect. On the basis of comparative biblical use, this verse must be translated, 'But the *bāmôt*-priests would/could not go up to the altar of Yahweh in Jerusalem *unless/until* they had eaten unleavened bread with their brothers' (Barrick 2002: 189–96). It does not permanently preclude their officiating in Jerusalem; rather, it temporarily bars them from serving at the main altar until some sort of 're-ordination ritual' (Barrick 2002: 192) or means of integrating them into the existing priestly rotations could be accomplished. Even so, the reader is left with an impression that there was some sort of problem with these priests that had to be set right before they could serve 'properly' or 'legitimately', which takes us back to the same impressions discussed in the preceding paragraph.

The 'cultic reforms' of Hezekiah and Josiah are contrasted by the approach each king is said to have used to deal with the unwanted worship complexes. Hezekiah broke down or physically removed (*hēsîr*) the *bāmôt*, implementing the ancient commandments (*miṣwōt*) that Yahweh had commanded Moses either with full knowledge of them or instinctively, because of his 'holding fast' to Yahweh (2 Kgs 18.4-6). The choice of verb suggests an intention to eliminate them permanently by physically removing the buildings that constituted the *bāmôt* complexes. While many uses of the hiphil of the root *swr* denote the 'removal' of more abstract things like judgments, reproach, prayer, violence or oppression, a few uses refer to the removal of a physical object, like a head (2 Sam. 16.9), alloy (Isa. 1.25), clothes (Gen. 38.9), a veil (Gen. 38.19), and mediums and wizards (1 Sam. 28.3). By contrast, Josiah defiles (verb *timmē'*) those rebuilt by Manasseh and existing into his time in Judah in direct response to the '(re)discovery' of 'the book of the law' (2 Kgs 22.8; 23; for this literary topos, see Römer 1997: 7–9), elsewhere described as 'the book of the covenant' (2 Kgs 23.2, 21). He is said to have acted according to the 'teaching of Moses' (*tôrat mōšeh*), not the commands (*miṣwōt*) of Moses, as Hezekiah had done (2 Kgs 23.25). However, he is portrayed to have physically destroyed (*hēsîr*) the *bāmôt* in Samaria (23.19-20).

Debate continues over whether this book is meant to be part of Deuteronomy (for ch. 32, see Lundbom 1976; for chs 12–26 see Fritz 2003: 408), Deuteronomy in its present form or in an earlier form (for a summary of those who espouse this view, see Nicholson 1967: 1–22; Gerbrandt 1986: 195–200), the five books of Moses (Genesis, Exodus, Leviticus, Numbers and Deuteronomy) (for example, Gordon 1962: 292–93), or the Hexateuch and Kings (Barrick 2002: 113–14). In spite of this uncertainty, it has been noted that no texts exist in the current books forming the Pentateuch that specify the destruction of objectionable cultic places by ritual pollution using human bones, so it does not appear that the claim that Josiah acted according to the 'teaching of Moses' in 2 Kgs 23.5 should be taken literally; this appears to be meant to be understood as his particular solution to dealing with a more general call to destroy such facilities.

While defilement is a serious condition, it is ritually reversible, as seen, for example, by the cleansing and rededication of the temple in Jerusalem to the exclusive worship of Yahweh by the Maccabees after its pollution by Antiochus IV (1 Maccabees 1; 4.36-58; for a general discussion of pollution, see Wright 1987). The demolition of a building is also reversible, as seen in the action attributed to Manasseh of rebuilding these same *bāmôt* (2 Kgs 21.3); however, it takes much more time, effort, and resources to construct a physical structure than to purify an existing one. Thus, by comparison with Hezekiah's policy, Josiah was not as thorough in his dealing with the permanent obliteration of the *bāmôt* (Östreicher 1923: 48–49; Hollenstein 1977: 332; Barrick 2002: 183–84; contra Hoffmann 1980: 229; Lowery 1991: 160–61; Eynikel 1996: 234; Cohen 2000: 157–58).

The assigning of this less effective strategy to Josiah may have been an attempt by the author of the book of Kings or a subsequent pious scribe to explain why this king met a dishonourable death by execution at the hand of Pharaoh Necho rather than the peaceful, natural death Yahweh announces awaits Josiah as a reward for his penitence and recognition of the disobedience of his and the people's ancestors (2 Kgs 22.11-20). Since he did not choose the most effective, permanent policy to eliminate the recurring problem of the *bāmôt* complexes and worship of gods in addition to Yahweh, even though he was allowed a long reign that showed he had gained much divine favour, he was implicitly punished by Yahweh in the end by dying violently instead of peacefully.

If one reflects on the anomaly of the failure to mention the explicit closing down of Yahwistic places of worship in either the reform of Hezekiah or Josiah, one is left with an unsatisfactory plethora of Yahwistic cultic places outside of Jerusalem that, using logic consistent with the 'canonical reading glasses' so often employed, must be seen to be human initiatives that are permitted to exist alongside the divinely chosen (central) site because they differ in some important respect (for example, they do not contain 'the name' whose presence has been permanently established at the deity's direction in the temple in Jerusalem). Otherwise, one would have to assume they were all dedicated to 'Canaanite'/autochthonous deities and so should not have existed but exemplified the problem of the people not being able to carry out or remain loyal to the divine command to destroy all such sites in Deut. 12.2-4. A quick review eliminates this latter understanding, however. Dan, Bethel and Gilgal are associated with the worship of Yahweh – of Israel, not of Judah, accounting for the negative attitude expressed toward all three.

The account of Hezekiah's reforms does not mention the location of the *bāmôt*, pillars or 'sacred poles' he rejected in the summary of the actions in 2 Kgs 18.3-6. It is only in v. 22, in the context of the eve of the Assyrian siege of Jerusalem, where we learn from an Assyrian official that it was Yahweh's altars and *bāmôt* that Hezekiah removed to establish Jerusalem as the sole site of worship. Are we, the reading audience, to accept this statement as reliable in the narrative world, or should we assume this 'foreigner' has misunderstood the situation? In the former case, we gain a sense of relief while wearing our 'canonical reading glasses' that we cannot get if we assume the latter. However, this same relief is not supplied by the subsequent story about Josiah's reforms, unless we assume, on analogy, that Manasseh's rebuilt *bāmôt* were for the worship of Yahweh (but not necessarily for him alone). By implication, Josiah would have been destroying Yahwistic cultic complexes located outside of Jerusalem that the forefathers should never have built according to Deuteronomy, but places where the people may have simultaneously worshipped Yahweh and other gods.

1.4 Section Summary and Conclusion

The theological concern to limit the sacrificial cult of Yahweh to a single temple site expressed in Deuteronomy has created some misleading impressions about where cultic complexes existed in ancient Israel and Judah in the Iron Age and subsequently, and in how religion was practised in the southern Levant more generally. The biblical texts allow some general observations to be made: cultic sites could be located on natural heights (Deut. 12.2; 1 Kgs 14.23; 18; 2 Kgs 16.4; 17.10; 2 Chron. 28.4; Jer. 2.20; 3.6; 13.27; 17.2; Ezek. 6.3, 13; 20.28; Hos. 4.13; Mic. 4.1) or associated with landmark trees (e.g. Gen. 21.33; Deut. 12.2; 1 Kgs 14.23; 2 Kgs 16.4; 17.10; 2 Chron. 28.4; Isa. 57.5; Jer. 2.20; 3.6, 13; 17.2; Ezek. 6.13; 20.28; Hos. 4.13). Cultic action could be performed in complexes known variously as the temple (*hêkāl*; *bayit*) or the 'high place' (*bāmâ*), both of which contained some sort of buildings, an altar, and dedicated personnel (1 Kings 5–9; 1 Sam. 9.11-25). It was customary in the Iron Age to plant a tree beside an altar and to have a standing stone as well (Deut. 12.3; 16.21). Sacrifices and libations were offered (Leviticus); sacred meals were held (1 Sam. 9.11-25), and annual religious festivals took place in such complexes (Exod. 23.14-17; Leviticus 23; Deuteronomy 16). City gates could contain *bāmôt* (2 Kgs 23.8; Ezek. 8.3, 5). Some complexes were royal initiatives, like Dan, Bethel and Jerusalem (1 Kings 4–9; 12.26-29); privately sponsored complexes also existed, like Micah's building (Judges 17) and the open-air altar in Ophrah of the Abiezerites under an oak tree (Judg. 6.24). Temples could serve as treasuries and storehouses (2 Kgs 14.14; 16.8; Neh. 12.44).[1]

2
Artefactual Remains

Setting aside the biblical texts, what can we infer from material cultural remains in the inland region east of the coastal plain and west of the Jordan River in the southern Levant from strata (str.) that date from c. 975 BCE (the Iron IIA period and likely time of the beginning of the Israelite and Judahite monarchies) to c. 333 BCE (the end of the Persian period)? How does one confidently identify a building or built complex where acts of worship and ritual took place from excavated remains alone? Considering that the primary term that is translated 'temple' is the common word for 'house' and context alone determines which value the word is assigned, how does a god's house differ from a human dwelling?

Temples were routinely looted by invading armies since they contained dedicatory gifts and storehouses; archaeologists are unlikely to find much original splendour still intact or *in situ*. Nevertheless, the presence of small or miniature vessels that would have been votive gifts to a deity, places with many benches where offerings could be deposited, one or more wall niches or alcoves for the display of deity statues, the presence of a large built altar for the offering of sacrifices and many animal bones and ash deposits signalling sacrificial activity, receptacles for liquid offerings poured as libations built into the ground, large basins of water to be used for ablutions, remains of cultic stands, kernoi (ceramic rings used in making libations), chalices, masks, items that would have been votive gifts, and items marked with symbols commonly

---

1. For a useful discussion of these functions, see Stevens 2006, though caution must be exercised in her uncritical dating of the texts; some practices may only have emerged after the monarchy.

associated with a particular male or female deity are all taken as indicators of cultic space (see, for example, Aldhouse-Green 1978; Renfrew 1985; Rutkowski 1986; Coogan 1987; Holladay 1987; Burdajewicz 1990; Bergquist 1993; Wasilewska 1994; Blomquist 1999: 23–46; Jones 1999; Smith and Brookes 2001). Favissae, which are pits in which altars and figurines and assorted vessels have been discarded, most after having been broken, perhaps to render them powerless, are another indication that a cult site was located somewhere in the vicinity. These pits for the burial of ritual objects are not routinely located in sanctuary complexes, however, so they do not allow us to identify a sacred precinct directly.

Before turning to excavated cultic structures in the southern Levant, a caution against arguing from silence or from limited data is in order. Few sacred complexes, buildings, or altars have been identified so far; this should not be taken as an indication that few existed. A very limited number of sites have been excavated, and usually less than 20 per cent of a site is dug systematically and then, not always to bedrock. Excavation is a costly and time-consuming enterprise and logistically it is not always possible to reach bedrock because the artificially created walls of archaeological squares (balks) deteriorate and erode over time and threaten physical collapse. Thus, even a site that has been excavated may well contain cultic areas and complexes that have failed to come to light because they lie in areas that were not selected for systematic excavation. For example, the Hebrew Bible refers to a temple at Shiloh (Judg. 18.31; 1 Sam. 1.3, 24; 3.23; 4.3-4; Jer. 7.12, 14; 26.6, 9) and one at Bethel (Gen. 12.8; 28.8-20; 35.6-7, 9-15; Judg. 21.2-3; 1 Sam. 7.15; 10.3; 1 Kgs 12.30-33; 13; 17.27-28; Hosea 10 [Beth-Aven]; Amos 4.4; 5.5; 7.13); both sites have been excavated in a very limited area of exposure and neither has yet yielded an identifiable cultic complex (for Bethel, see Kelso 1968; for Shiloh, see Finkelstein, Bunimovitz and Lederman 1985). Yet, it is virtually certain that were the entire site to be exposed in either case, such a complex would be uncovered.

It is likely that any settlement the size of a village and upwards would have contained a cultic complex of some sort, which should be identifiable from its remains, were that part of the site to be excavated. While Jer. 11.13 certainly has an element of exaggeration for effect, its claim that 'your gods equal the number of your walled settlements, O Judah; and the altars you have set up . . . to make offerings to the Baal equal the number of the alleyways of Jerusalem' suggests that cultic sites were widespread, with towns having multiple sites, not just a single one.

Turning now to the evidence that has been uncovered, it is possible to identify a range of cultic spaces. I will discuss them under four headings: intramural local shrines/temples in cities and towns; shrines in city gates; cultic complexes in forts; and shrines associated with trade. Biblical texts will be included where they relate to the specific type of cultic complex under investigation; in theory, the archaeological remains have been labelled 'cultic' on the basis of the characteristic finds listed above, though in some instances it is likely the excavators also were influenced by biblical descriptions.

2.1 Intramural Local Shrines/Temples in Cities and Towns

Excavated examples of intramural local temples, shrines, or cultic enclosures are surprisingly few from the Iron II and Persian periods in the geographical area under investigation, in spite of the biblical references to their existence at Gilgal, Bethlehem, Nob, Hebron, Gibeon, Dan, Bethel, Samaria, Mizpah, Shiloh and Beersheba. In addition to the passage cited above in Jer. 11.13, Ezek. 16.24, 31 expresses similar sentiments in its claim that 'you built for yourself a platform (*gab*) and made for yourself an 'elevated area/podium' (*rāmâ*) in every broad space', 'building your platform at the head of every street and making your elevated area/podium in every broad space'. While T. Blomquist has suggested that the latter passages from Ezekiel may refer to gate shrines because gates were the only assured broad places for gatherings in cities and towns (1999: 174–81), this is not necessarily the case, as will be seen in the example from Tel Rehov. However, 'the elevated area' might well be illustrated by the cultic installations in the eastern gate at et-Tell to be discussed in the ensuing section on gate shrines, so Ezekiel may be describing two types of local cultic spaces that were located in or associated with various parts of walled settlements.

One example of an intramural cultic space or shrine comes from Tel Rehov in the Jordan Valley, 6 km west of the Jordan River, 3 km east of the Gilboa ridge, and 5 km south of Beth She'an. In Area E, in the northwest corner of the mound, a likely *bāmâ* complex or local shrine dating to the Iron IIA period has been uncovered (str. V–IV; c. 950–830 BCE). No determination of the deity, deities or (perhaps) deified ancestors to whom it was dedicated can be made from the material remains *in situ* at its final destruction c. 830 BCE.

The complex included a courtyard area bounded on the north by an enclosing wall. Circular bins made of unbaked mud brick, ovens and benches lay at the northern end of the open space. South of these was a low square platform built of mud bricks, measuring 3 × 3.55 m, and rising 0.4 m above the original courtyard surface. On top of it was a smaller stone platform, measuring 1 × 1 m, in which were embedded three small, unworked upright stones, which probably were *maṣṣēbôt*. When the courtyard surface had built up to the height of the original platform, the stone one might have been added to allow activities to continue. A large flat stone supported on five smaller stones positioned just north of the brick platform may have been used as an offering table. Pieces of a ceramic altar with two rows of triangular windows were found near this platform, as was an elaborately decorated, imported Phoenician jar. The horn of a mountain goat and bones from this species were found associated with the platform as well (Mazar 1999: 23–28).

The platform was built up against the north-eastern corner of the 'western' building, in a recessed area of the courtyard created because a northern room of the building extended out into the open space immediately to the west. The building had a main hall apparently accessed from a path beside the western side of the platform; it ran the full breadth of the building and was the largest of the three rooms. Its mud-plastered walls had been impressed with designs that included volutes and alternating lotus flowers and buds. This space had a small storage area marked off by a thin curtain wall in its easternmost part, directly south of the exterior cultic installation. Inside this area, part of an inscribed storage jar was found; it began with the letters *my* and ended with *ym*. From the entry hall, a broad room running the full breadth of the building, like the main hall, could be accessed to the south through a doorway almost straight ahead from the entry. From the western end of the entry hall, a smaller northern room could be accessed; it covered only half the breadth of the building; the brick platform with stone platform and *maṣṣēbôt* occupied the remaining exterior space to the east.

Opposite this building, across a wide passageway or lane, was the 'eastern' building containing plastered storage compartments, probably for foodstuffs, and a room where many pottery vessels and chalices were housed at the time of destruction in str. IV, c. 830 (?) BCE. It was entered from the alleyway, on the western side of the building. Built up against the northern face of this building was another square-shaped building whose entry lay in its northern wall, in the northwestern corner; its southern wall abutted the northern wall of the eastern building with a gap of only a few centimetres. The result was a recessed courtyard area immediately west of the square building and north of the 'eastern' building, paralleling the one in front of the 'western' building. It, however, contained no comparable platform. It appears that the western building and probably also the eastern building were used in connection with the platforms and stone *maṣṣēbôt*, forming what could be called a *bāmâ* complex (Mazar 2008: 2016–18).

What is uncertain is whether the complex was unifunctional or multifunctional and whether it was used to petition various divinities or perhaps (deified?) ancestors. In the present context, the *maṣṣēbôt* might represent dead ancestors, deities or the living who want to be represented or remembered before the gods (Mazar 2008: 2018; for the range of uses and symbolism of such standing stones, see Avner 1993; Mettinger 1995; van der Toorn 1997).

Another intramural cultic complex likely existed at Beersheba in the Iron II period, though its location has not been established. Stone blocks that had once been part of a large worked, horned altar, however, which would have been used within the complex, have been found reused in three secondary contexts at Beersheba (Tel Beersheva). Parts of the altar were used to repair a segment of wall belonging to the str. II pillared storehouse complex (Aharoni 1974: 3), while six stones were found sealed in the fill underlying the stratum II glacis. One of the latter was reported as being part of a str. III retaining wall within the rampart (Aharoni 1975b: 154; Herzog, Rainey and Moshkovitz 1977: 57–8). Another altar block was found in the wall of a building west of the gate; no stratigraphic details were given (Aharoni 1975b: 154).

The altar blocks indicate that a cultic complex of some sort had once functioned somewhere on site, whose altar was disassembled perhaps in str. IV or an even earlier stratum, but definitely by some point in str. III, when some of the blocks were used to build the retaining wall in the rampart. No temple or shrine complex has yet been excavated, however, and the dates of its use remain unknown (Edelman 2008: 418–21).

Other possible examples of intramural shrines, *bāmôt* or temples in cities or towns dating from the Iron II and Persian periods include Tel Dan, I str. IV, tenth century BCE and str. III, ninth-eighth centuries BCE (Zevit 2001: 180–91); Hazor, str. XI, the first half of the tenth century BCE (Zevit 2001: 202–5), 'cult corner' 2081 and 'cult room or temple' 340 in building 338 at Megiddo, both belonging to str. V, tenth century BCE (Zevit 2001: 219–31; Edelman 2008: 413–14), cult room 49 at Lachish from str. V, destroyed in the second half of the tenth century BCE (Zevit 2001: 213–17; Edelman 2008: 421–24), and the solar shrine at Lachish (Persian period, fifth century BCE (Tufnell, *et al.* 1953: 141–45; Aharoni 1968a, 1975a). One of some 1,000 ostraca that have been illegally dug and sold in antiquities markets mentions a temple to Yahweh in a boundary description (#283). It is a fixed point or landmark associated with a land allotment: 'The hillock/ruin that is under the house of 'Uzza, and the field/vine terrace of the house of Yaho, the fallow land/bad land of Zabi, the terrace of the terebinth, the devastated terrain of Saʿad/ru, the tomb/village of Gilgul, the fish pool of the house of Nabu, the tomb/village of Yonqom' (Lemaire 2002: 149–56). The ostraca mention storehouses in Makkedah and Idnah and so probably were found at one of these two sites; they bear recorded dates from 363–31 BCE, thus spanning the transition from Persian to Hellenistic rule (Eph'al and Naveh 1996; Lemaire 2002). The specific locations of the Bet Yahweh and the Bet Nabu have not been pinpointed or excavated.

2.2 Gate Shrines

Biblical texts mention the existence of gate shrines (2 Kgs 23.8; Ezek. 8.3, 5). The first is best understood to refer to an installation located in the open space between an outer and inner city gate of Jerusalem (Emerton 1994; Blomquist 1999: 151–63) while the second, also localized in Jerusalem, could refer to an altar in an open area between an inner and outer city-gate complex on the north side of Jerusalem (Blomquist 1999: 169) or to one located in a plaza inside the city, but outside an inner gate that gave entry to the temple complex from the north. The use of the term 'inner and outer city gate' can be ambiguous; it can designate a gate complex that had an outer gate that opened into a walled, protected plaza before entering through an inner gate with one to three chambers on either side into the city proper, into an inner plaza. Such an arrangement can be seen at et-Tell (Beth Saida), or at Lachish, for example, with a bent-access entry. Or, it could refer to an arrangement where the outer city gate opened into a plaza, which had on its opposite side a gate to the walled acropolis area within the city. In Ezekiel, it is not clear that either of these arrangements is being assumed, however; it could be depicting a plaza inside a city before a gate to the acropolis that was not aligned with an outer city gate.

2.2.1 Et-Tell (Beth Saida)

One clear example of a gate shrine has been excavated at et-Tell (Beth Saida), c. 2.3 km north of the Sea of Galilee and 1 km east of the Jordan River. Access to the acropolis area in str. II in the Iron IIB period, dating from the mid-ninth to the last half of the eighth century BCE, was probably via a bent-access, inner and outer gate system located on the eastern side of the area. In Area A, in the courtyard inside the postulated outer gate, immediately to the right side of the gate that was attached to the city wall and which gave access to the city proper via four-chambers comprising the gate area, a stepped podium was built into an L-shaped recess in the wall. A stone platform measuring $1.5 \, m^2$ sat at the top of two steps; inset into it was a rectangular shallow basalt basin, in which were found three tripod cups whose upper bodies were perforated. A well-shaped, 1.15 m high stele with rounded top bearing the image of a horned bull deity wearing a sword carved in relief lay face down, broken into four pieces, at the foot of the podium. It is assumed that it had once stood behind the basin on top of the podium.

Three other uninscribed stelae were found in this intra-gate courtyard; two flanked the recesses in the city wall immediately before the gate opening while a third stood in the northeastern quadrant. Benches lined the face of the city wall segment that ran north within the courtyard area and possibly also the wall recess to the left of the main gate, along the northern face of the L-shaped recess in the city wall that ran south from the inner gate opposite the podium. On the other side of the wall from the podium (chamber 4), a number of bowls, plates, juglets and tripod cups were found. Among them was a jug with the inscription, '*lsm* + *ankh* sign'. This vessel appears to have been used to make a libation 'in the name of' a life-giving deity or 'for the sake' of such a deity (Blomquist 1999: 49–57; Zevit 2001: 148–53).

2.2.2 Tell el-Qadi (Tel Dan)

A second strong candidate is located at Tel Dan (Tell el-Qadi) at the foot of Mount Hermon in the Upper Galilee, next to one of the springs that serve as a source for the Jordan River. The main entrance to the city in str. III (ninth to eighth centuries BCE) included a bent-access, double-gate system with a large, protected courtyard/plaza area between the gates. In str. II, the outer gate was no longer used, leaving the inner, four-chambered gate to serve as the exterior city gate; a new inner gate was built to give access to the citadel from the main road ascending in the city from the main gate.

In str. III, the large plaza contained two sets of *maṣṣēbôt* alongside the eastern wall (loci 5181 and 5122), one of which was in an inner courtyard with benches and a stepped podium made of cut stone ashlars with pomegranate-shaped bases for pillars at its corners. The podium was located immediately to the right of the inner gate entrance, with a stele to its left, at the corner of the gate, as at et-Tell. In str. II, the gate to the citadel had a group of *maṣṣēbôt* in the inner courtyard and a small room built into the outer courtyard that housed an ashlar podium of some sort (Blomquist 1999: 57–67).

2.2.3 Other Examples

Other possible examples of gate shrines from the Iron II period include Kinneret str. II, Megiddo str. VA–IVB, Lachish str. III, Beersheba str. V–IV, Tell el-Farah North str. VIIb and d, Timnaʿ site 30, and Yotvata (Blomquist 1999).

2.3 Cultic Complexes in Forts

Examples of cultic complexes located in forts have been excavated at Arad and Horvat ʿUza and probably also at Horvat Radum.

2.3.1 Arad

An assumed Yahwistic cultic complex has been uncovered inside the fortress of Arad on the northern side of the Arad-Beersheba valleys. According to the recently revised stratigraphy, the sanctuary complex was first built in str. X, which is to be dated to the mid-eighth century BCE on the basis of the pottery finds. It was repaired after fire damage at the beginning of str. IX, and then was eliminated from use, perhaps sometime before the end of str. IX (Herzog 2002: 49–67) but more likely during alterations made by the occupiers of the fort in str. VIII when they rebuilt in wake of the capture of the str. IX fort (Edelman 2008: 407–10).

The complex was located in the northwestern quadrant of the fort and was walled; one entered an open courtyard from the south originally, which contained an altar built of unhewn stones with a step in front. It was built against the northern courtyard wall into a corner formed by an adjacent small storage room immediately to the west. The western end of the courtyard had steps by which one mounted into the sanctuary proper, which contained the *děbîr* or holy of holies in a recess built into the western wall of the sanctuary opposite the entry into the sanctuary from the courtyard. Access to a broad room lying north of the courtyard and running its length was gained on the western side of the small storage room adjacent to the altar, to the right as one approached the steps to the holy of holies. Remains of benches were found built into the northwestern corner of the courtyard, against the eastern wall of the sanctuary, to the right of the entrance, and inside the sanctuary immediately to the right after entry as well as all along the southern wall and the southern stretch of the eastern wall to the right of the stepped entrance into the holy of holies (Herzog 2002: 11–12, 32–33).

Inside the holy of holies proper, the floor was paved with two layers of stones. It has been suggested that a *maṣṣēbâ* that was found built into the back wall of the niche might have been set up inside the str. X holy of holies (Herzog 2002: 57) and perhaps was decommissioned and placed inside the wall during the rebuilding phase of str. IX or placed in its current location by those who closed down the complex in str. VIII and reconfigured the space. In str. IX, a stone platform was built into the northwest corner of the niche (Herzog 2002: 63) and it is likely that two *maṣṣēbôt* had been set up within or near the platform. Two were reportedly found covered with plaster and 'leaning against the [north] wall' (Aharoni 1968b: 18–20); however, Herzog reports that one of these was lying outstretched instead next to the platform and had traces of red paint on it (2002: 63). If the third was placed in the wall by the builders of str. VIII, there could have been three *maṣṣēbôt* in the str. IX sanctuary (Ahlström 1993: 524). Two incense altars with lumps of plaster adhering to them were used secondarily within a wall constructed above the former steps into the sanctuary; it has been suggested that they once would have stood inside the sanctuary against walls just before the entrance to the holy of holies in str. IX (Herzog 2002: 35, 64). It is equally possible they had been used in str. X originally.

In str. IX, certain changes were introduced, allegedly after fire damage to the area. The courtyard area was reduced in its dimensions due to the expansion of storage facilities that encroached on the eastern half of the former open space. A new entrance to the complex was made from the east, adjacent to the new storage building, in a corridor that measured 1.5 m wide and 5 m long (Herzog 2002: 59, 62). The courtyard floor was raised in height by 1.2 m, which would have required the walls and roofs of all the adjoining buildings of the complex to have been raised to have been accessible. The original floor of the sanctuary was raised 0.3 m, but steps were now introduced to allow one to descend to it from the new higher, courtyard. The altar was rebuilt on the new courtyard surface in its previous location; however, the small storage room to the west was eliminated; only the eastern wall was left intact because the altar was rebuilt against it, as before (Herzog 2002: 59). A sunken, stone-lined square bin measuring 2.60 × 2.60 m with a central, elliptical depression measuring 1.40 × 0.70 m was embedded in the new courtyard surface c. 2 m south of the altar. Cereal grains were found inside it, so at the time of the destruction of the str. IX fort at least, it was being used for grain storage (Herzog 2002: 37–38, 60–61). It is uncertain if this had been its primary function at the time of its creation.

2.3.2 Horvat 'Uza

At Horvat 'Uza, located about 8 km south of Tel Arad above the Nahal Qina, alongside the road known as 'the way of Edom', an altar measuring 1.5 × 1 × 1 m, built of unhewn stones, was found in a courtyard area southeast of the entrance gate to the fortress. It is assigned to str. IVA, which represents the second occupational phase in the seventh century BCE. A small settlement covering seven dunams lay outside the walls of the fort, built on terraces that stepped down the steep wadi slope.

A thick accumulation of animal bones and ash lay to the east of the altar on the opposite side of a narrow wall. Room 366 lay immediately to its north; the altar lies in its entrance, creating a space similar to that of the main hall of the 'western' building in the cultic complex at Tel Rehov. Room 370 lay across the courtyard, to the south, in a configuration similar to the eastern building at Rehov (Blomquist 1999: 98–100).

An inventory of finds from both spaces awaits final publication so it is difficult to say much more.

2.3.3 Horvat Radum

A third likely example of cultic complex in a fort is a raised podium uncovered inside the fort of Horvat Radum, located about 2 km south of Horvat 'Uza and 9 km south-west of Arad, also overlooking the Nahal Qina. This facility was built in the late seventh century BCE. Immediately inside the gate lies a stone podium built against the eastern wall of the fortress, accessed by three steps; a bench lies at its eastern edge, in line with the right-hand side of the gate; another flanks the left-hand side of the gate (Blomquist 1999: 85–86).

2.3.4 Other Examples

The Elephantine papyri indicate that a temple (*egora*) or 'altar house' (*byt mdh*, AP 32.3) had existed in the fort at Yeb in the Neo-Babylonian and Persian periods. It is mentioned as a landmark in a house conveyance document, a deed of renunciation of claim on a house, and also was the subject of a series of letters and a memorandum (*AP* 13.14; 25.6, 30; 31, 33.8; Cowley 1923). As noted above in the first section, it had contained an altar for animal sacrifice and had been a place where grain offerings and incense had been offered as well until its destruction c. 410 BCE at the instigation of the priests of the temple of the local deity Khnum, which was located next door. It was rebuilt c. 405 BCE, but apparently without a sacrificial altar. The structure itself has not been definitively excavated, or if it has, was not detailed in the German excavation report for political reasons. Unsurprisingly, it is not marked or mentioned on any map or explanation given by the Egyptian government for tourists who visit the site today.

2.4 Shrines Associated with Trade

Three examples of shrines located along trade routes that appear to have been fre-quented by caravanners include Kuntillet 'Ajrud (Horvat Teman), Qitmit and Mesad Haseva str. IV. All are facilities that lie outside the confines of walled settlements.

2.4.1 Kuntillet 'Ajrud

Kuntillet 'Ajrud is located close to a crossroads on the road from Gaza to Elat in the northern Sinai; it is at the Wadi Quraya, about 50 km south of the oasis of Qadesh Barnea. It appears to have been a single-period site, dating perhaps to the second half of the eighth century BCE (Singer-Avitz 2006; Freud 2008; Finkelstein and Piasetsky 2008). It contains a complex of buildings set on top of a steep plateau. The function of the site has been variously interpreted: a fortress/look-out complex, a caravanserai (Hadley 1993), and a shrine/temple complex (Meshel 1978; Zevit 2001; Na'aman and Lissovsky 2008).

The main building, 'A', measured 25 × 15 m with corner towers. The bent-access entrance to building 'A' featured a small open-air vestibule lined with benches as well as two chambers flanking the main double-door entryway into the building proper. These also were lined with benches.

The one on the northern side of the entry contained pithos A with its drawings of two crowned man-lion figures arm in arm and a woman playing a lyre, a cow suckling a calf, and a stylized tree from which ibexes feed on either side. A blessing is written on the jar's shoulder that refers probably to 'Yahweh of Samaria and his Asherah' (Zevit 2001: 382). This bench room also contained two wall plaster fragments invoking the blessings of Yahweh, Baal and Asherah and two inscribed stone basins. The adjoining tower room contained bowls, juglets, jugs, flasks and lamps and several stone vessels. An *in situ* plaster inscription was found on the northern doorjamb of the inner doorway that led into the building's interior courtyard (Meshel 1978; Hadley 1993; Blomquist 1999: 94–100).

Inside the building, fragments of wall paintings and other inscriptions were found, along with an inscribed basin, and pithos B with graffiti and a drawing of five individuals facing left with arms bent in a position of worship or petition. In addition, this jar contains a drawing of an ibex, an unfinished mother cow, an unfinished bull, the beginnings of a lion, and the upper torso on an archer (Zevit 2001: 383). There were ovens and two long storerooms, one at the western end of the building opposite the entryway, and one along the southern wall with two staircases near either end that appear to have given access to an upper floor above the store-room. Fragments of textiles were found in this room and elsewhere, and the presence of loom weights, flax fibres, yarn, and twisted thread indicate weaving was conducted in the complex (Zevit 2001: 375–76). According to the Hebrew Bible, weaving was an economic activity associated with the worship of Asherah in the temple complex in Jerusalem (2 Kgs 23.8). Two installations were positioned across the interior courtyard along the northern wall of the building.

A small part of an eastern building was also excavated, with some sort of cluster of structures located south and southwest of it. Neutron activation analysis has confirmed that most of the large pithoi at the site were made from clay that originated from the region of Jerusalem, suggesting this complex was supported and supplied by the Judahite monarchy (Zevit 2001: 379), whatever its function(s).

2.4.2 Horvat Qitmit
A one-period, open-air religious complex was located at Horvat Qitmit atop a hill about 10 km southwest of Arad. The site sat beside a road that cut southwest from the Beersheba Valley to intersect the main north-south road through the Negev highlands at Tel Aroer. No water or wells are there; the closest water source was 5 km northwest at Tel Malhata. It is dated to the late seventh or early sixth century BCE on the basis of the Transjordanian and Judahite shapes of the pottery forms found there. Neutron activation analysis has demonstrated that most of the 'Edomite'-shaped vessels and some of the cultic ones were made from local clay sourced in the Beersheba Valley (Gunneweg and Mommsen 1990). Thus, one or more potters had settled locally and were producing pots they had learned to make while resident in Transjordan.

There were two main buildings some 20 m apart, with various associated enclosures and structures. Complex A, to the south, had three rooms, all opening to the south, toward two nearby stone enclosures; one U-shaped and the other circular. Benches lined the east wall of each room, and a platform was located in each as well, within the centre of the room or on the west side. Steps led into the central chamber; a small circular stone installation lay a few metres in front of them. The U-shaped enclosure contained a square platform or altar made of stone measuring 1 × 1.25 × 0.30 m. On a plastered surface in front of it over 85 clay vessels, stands with human and animal features, figurines, daggers and models of malformed limbs and the head of a three-horned female deity were found. The circular enclosure included a large stone, a basin and a pit. Northwest of Complex A lay a large circular 'pen'.

Complex B, 15 m north of Complex A, was an L-shaped building measuring 8 × 8.5 m. Its layout is not fully known, but it appears to have had two rooms in its western 'wing' and one or two possibly in its northern 'wing'. Each wing faced a courtyard with a bin or installation, a possible *maṣṣēbâ*, and thin stone wall/windbreak on the eastern side (Beit Arieh 1991, 1995; Zevit 2001: 142–49).

This site is isolated; even though it lay close to a subsidiary road in the Negev highlands, it is not associated with a local, nearby settlement. Tel Malhata was the closest, some 5 km away. The presence of many 'Edomite'-shaped vessels and Edomite cooking pots that have sand originating in the region of Edom as temper used to help prevent cracking under heat (Beit Arieh 1995: 225) suggests it may well have been used by Edomite traders traversing the Arad and Beersheba valleys en route to Gaza. There is evidence of a lot of Edomite influence in the region at the end of the Judahite monarchy, and scholars continue to debate whether the Edomites gained physical control over the region after 586 BCE or were allowed to establish shrines on foreign soil to petition their gods to protect their caravans (Beit Arieh 1991, 1995; Finkelstein 1992: 156–66; 1995: 139–53; Singer-Avitz 1999; Bienkowski and van der Steen 2001).

2.4.3 'En Haseva

'En Haseva housed the largest spring in the western Arabah, making it a logical stopping point for travellers and caravans. Two buildings were built near the spring: a fort or administrative centre, and a rectangular building that probably was a U-shaped shrine, built some 45 metres' distance from the northern façade of the other building. Nearby the cultic building, a favissa contained deliberately broken cultic vessels that had probably been used in the shrine: human-shaped stands representing worshippers (similar to those found at Qitmit), stands, incense burners, chalices, tripod cups, limestone altars and a shaped limestone slab containing a possible libation bowl (Beck 1996; Blomquist 1999: 100–5). Lying outside the walls of a nearby settlement, this shrine, like the one at Qitmit, may have been used by traders passing by rather than by locals stationed in the fort or administrative centre. It is not certain the two were even contemporary. An intramural shrine or cultic complex may lie buried, awaiting excavation.

3
Conclusion

The Hebrew Bible assumes, on the one hand, that a range of cultic complexes existed during the existence of the kingdoms of Israel (c. 985–721 BCE) and Judah (970–586 BCE), dedicated to the worship and supplication of Yahweh and of other deities, especially Asherah, Astarte/Ishtar and Baal, other members of the host of heaven, and also perhaps to deified ancestors. Some were royally sponsored and others were locally and privately sponsored. The texts assume, on the other hand, that the only legitimate place to worship Yahweh after entry into the Promised Land was in Jerusalem, in the main royal temple complex, and that no other gods should have been worshipped besides him.

On the basis of comparative studies, and in spite of the limited area that is able to be excavated at a site due to various mitigating factors, examples of cultic spaces that range from a *maṣṣēbâ* (standing stone) with a basin nearby to an altar, with or without accompanying *maṣṣēbôt*, to complexes containing an altar and accompanying buildings with benches and one or more cultic niches have been identified as cultic sites. Some are considered more likely examples than others. Some sites demonstrate the sacred nature of a space continued to be recognized for centuries, whether or not the same deity or deities were honoured and petitioned there over time; without texts and iconographic evidence, we cannot be certain. Other sites indicate that a sacred complex could have a short life-span, which could be ended when the site or the protection of its deity was no longer needed and simply abandoned, or could be terminated and converted to ordinary land on which new, non-religious structures could be erected. The archaeological evidence, even in its limited state, confirms that cultic sites of various size and sponsorship were widespread in the inland southern Levant in the Iron II period and were significantly less numerous in the Persian era. However, the current data pool is too limited and the means of dating by pottery forms is too broad to allow a historian to pinpoint when cult centralization was first introduced, if it was reversed and then re-implemented, or when it was successfully introduced and implemented.

Bibliography

Aharoni, Y.
1968a 'Trial Excavation in the "Solar Shrine" at Lachish: Preliminary Report', *IEJ* 18: 157–69.
1968b 'Arad: Its Inscriptions and Temple', *BA* 31: 2–32.
1974 'The Horned Altar of Beer-sheba', *BA* 37: 2–6.
1975a *Investigations at Lachish: The Sanctuary and Residency (Lachish V)* (Publications of the Institute of Archaeology, Tel Aviv University, 4; Tel Aviv: Gateway Publishers).
1975b 'Excavations at Tel Beer-sheba: Preliminary Report of the Fifth and Sixth Seasons, 1973–1974', *TA* 2: 146–68.

Ahlström, G.W.
1993 *The History of Ancient Palestine from the Palaeolithic Period to Alexander's Conquest* (JSOTS 146; Sheffield: Sheffield Academic Press).

Aldhouse-Green, M.
1978 *Small Cult Objects from the Military Areas of Roman Britain: Roman Cult Objects* (British Archaeological Reports British Series 52; Oxford: British Archaeological Reports).

Amit, Y.
1999 *The Book of Judges: The Art of Editing* (BibInt Series 38; Leiden: Brill).

Avner, U.
1993 'Mazzebot Sites in the Negev and Sinai and their Significance', in A. Biran and J. Aviram (eds), *Biblical Archaeology Today: Proceedings of the Second International Congress on Biblical Archaeology, June–July 1990* (Jerusalem: Israel Exploration Society), 66–181.

Barrick, W.B.
2002 *The King and the Cemeteries: Toward a New Understanding of Josiah's Reform* (VTS 88; Leiden: Brill).

Beck, P.
1996 'Horvat Qitmit Revisited via 'En Hazeva', *TA* 9: 3–68.

Beit Arieh, I.
1991 'The Edomite Shrine at Horvat Qitmit in the Judaean Desert', *TA* 18: 93–116.

1995   *Horvat Qitmit: An Edomite Shrine in the Biblical Negev* (Tel Aviv: Institute of Archaeology, Tel Aviv University).

Beit-Arieh, I. and P. Beck
1987   *Edomite Shrine: Discoveries from Qitmit in the Negev* (Jerusalem: The Israel Museum).

Bergquist, B.
1993   'Bronze Age Sacrificial Koine in the Eastern Mediterranean', in J. Quaegebeur (ed.), *Ritual and Sacrifice in the Ancient Near East* (OLA 55; Leuven: Peeters), 11–14.

Bienkowski, P. and E. van der Steen
2001   'Tribes, Trade, and Towns: A New Framework for the Late Iron Age in Southern Jordan and the Negev', *BASOR* 323: 21–47.

Blomquist, T.H.
1999   *Gates and Gods: Cults in the City Gates of Iron Age Palestine – An Investigation of the Archaeological and Biblical Sources* (ConBOT 46; Stockholm: Almqvist & Wiksell International).

Burdajewicz, M.
1990   *The Aegean Sea Peoples and Religious Architecture in the Eastern Mediterranean at the Close of the Bronze Age* (BAR International Series 558; Oxford: BAR).

Cohen, R.L.
2000   *2 Kings* (Berit Olam; Collegeville, MN: The Liturgical Press).

Coogan, M.D.
1987   'Of Cults and Cultures: Reflections on the Interpretation of Archaeological Evidence', *PEQ* 119: 1–8.

Cowley, A.E.
1923   *Aramaic Papyri of the Fifth Century B.C.* (Oxford: Clarendon).

Edelman, D.V.
1985   'The Meaning of *qiṭṭer*', *VT* 35: 395–404.
2008   'Hezekiah's Alleged Cultic Centralization', *JSOT* 32: 395–434.

Emerton, J.
1994   '"The High Places of the Gates" in 2 Kings XXIII 8', *VT* 44: 455–67.

Eph'al, I. and J. Naveh
1996   *Aramaic Ostraca of the Fourth Century BC from Idumaea* (Jerusalem: Israel Exploration Society).

Eynikel, E.
1996   *The Reform of King Josiah & the Composition of the Deuteronomistic History* (OTS 33; Leiden: Brill).

Finkelstein, I.
1992   'Horvat Qitmit and the Southern Trade in the Late Iron II', *ZDPV* 108: 156–70.
1995   *Living on the Fringe: The Archaeology and History of the Negev, Sinai and Neighboring Regions in the Bronze and Iron Ages* (Monographs in Mediterranean Archaeology 6; Sheffield: Sheffield Academic Press).

Finkelstein, I. and E. Piasetsky
2008   'The Date of Kuntillet 'Ajrud: The 14C Perspective', *TA* 35: 175–85.

Finkelstein, I., S. Bunimovitz and Z. Lederman
1985   'Excavations at Shiloh 1981–1984: Preliminary Report', *TA* 12/2: 123–80; plates 13–20.

Freud, L.
2008   'The Date of Kuntillet 'Ajrud: A Reply to Singer-Avitz', *TA* 35: 169–74.

Fritz, V.
2003   *1 & 2 Kings: A Continental Commentary* (trans. A. Hagedorn; Minneapolis, MN: Fortress Press).

Gerbrandt, G.
1986   *Kingship according to the Deuteronomistic History* (SBLDS 87; Atlanta, GA: Scholars Press).

Gordon, C.H.
1962   *Before the Bible: the Common Background of Greek and Hebrew Civilizations* (London: Collins).

Görg, M.
1985   'Die Priestertitel *kmr* und *khn*', *BN* 39: 7–14.

Gunneweg, J. and H. Mommsen
1990   'Instrumental Neutron Activation Analysis and the Origin of Some Cultic Objects and Edomite Vessels from the Horvat Qitmit Shrine', *Archaeometry* 39: 7–18.

Hadley, J.
1993   'Kuntillet 'Ajrud: Religious Centre or Desert Way Station?', *PEQ* 125: 115–24.

Herzog, Z.
2002   'The Fortress at Tel Arad: An Interim Report', *TA* 29.1: 3–109.

Herzog, Z., A.F. Rainey and Sh. Moshkovitz
1977   'The Stratigraphy at Beer-sheba and the Location of the Sanctuary', *BASOR* 225: 49–58.

Hoffmann, H.-D.
1980   *Reform und Reformen: Untersuchungen zu einem Grundthema der deuteronmistischen Geschichsschreibung* (AThANT 66; Zurich: Theologischer Verlag).

Holladay, J.S.
1987   'Religion in Israel and Judah under the Monarchy: An Explicitly Archaeological Approach', in P.D. Miller, P.D. Hanson and S.D. McBride (eds), *Ancient Israelite Religion: Essays in Honor of Frank Moore Cross* (Philadelphia, PA: Fortress Press), 249–99.

Hollenstein, H.
1977   'Literarkritische Erwlagungen zum Bericht über die Refomassnahmen Josias 2 Kön. XXIII 4 ff.', *VT* 27: 321–36.

Jones, D.W.
1999   *Peak Sanctuaries and Sacred Caves in Minoan Crete: A Comparison of Artefacts* (Studies in Mediterranean Archaeology and Literature Pocket-book 156; Jonsered: P. Åstrom).

Kelso, J.L.
1968   *The Excavation of Bethel (1934–1960)* (AASOR 39; Cambridge, MA: ASOR).

Lemaire, A.
2002   *Nouvelles inscriptions araméenns d'Idumée, II* (Supplement a Transeuphratene 9; Paris: Gabalda).

Lohfink, N.
1987   'The Cult Reform of Josiah of Judah: 2 Kings 22–23 as a Source for the History of Israelite Religion', in P.D. Hanson, P.D. Miller and S.D. McBride (eds), *Ancient Israelite Religion: Essays in Honor of Frank Moore Cross* (Philadelphia, PA: Fortress Press), 459–75.

Long, B.O.
1991   *2 Kings* (FOTL 10; Grand Rapids, MI: Eerdmans).

Lowery, R.H.
1991   *The Reforming Kings: Cults and Society in First Temple Judah* (JSOTS 120; Sheffield: JSOT Press).

Lundbom, J.R.
1976   'The Lawbook of the Josianic Reform', *CBQ* 38: 293–302.

Mayes, A.D.H.
1985   *Judges* (Old Testament Guides (Sheffield: JSOT Press).

Mazar, A.
1999   'The 1997–1998 Excavations at Tel Rehov: Preliminary Report', *IEJ* 49: 1–42.
2008   'Rehov, Tel', *NEAEHL* 5.2013–18.

Meshel, Z.
1978   *Kuntillet 'Ajrud: A Religious Centre from the Time of the Judaean Monarchy on the Border of Egypt* (Israel Museum Catalogue 175; Jerusalem: Israel Museum).

Mettinger, T.N.D.
1995   *No Graven Image? Israelite Aniconism in its Ancient Near Eastern Context* (ConBOT 42; Stockhom: Almqvist).

Na'aman, N.
1991   'The Kingdom of Judah under Josiah', *TA* 18: 3–71.

Na'aman, N. and N. Lissovsky
2008   'Kuntillet 'Ajrud, Sacred Trees and the Asherah', *TA* 35: 186–208.

Nicholson, E.W.
1967   *Deuteronomy and Tradition* (Philadelphia, PA: Fortress Press).

Östreicher, Th.
1923   *Das deuteronomische Grundgesetz* (BFChTh 27/4; Gutersloh: C. Bertelsmann).

Renfrew, C.
1985   *The Archaeology of Cult: The Sanctuary at Philakopi* (British School of Archaeology at Athens, Suppl. vol. 18; London: British School of Archaeology at Athens).

Römer, T.C.
1997   'Transformations in Deuteronomistic and Biblical Historiography: On "Book-Finding" and other Literary Strategies', *ZAW* 109: 1–11.

Rutkowski, B.
1986   *The Cult Places of the Aegean* (New Haven, CT, and London: Yale University Press).

Singer-Avitz, L.
1999   'Beer-sheba – A Gateway Community in Southern Arabian Long-Distance Trade in the Eighth Century B.C.E.', *Tel Aviv* 26: 3–75.
2006   'The Date of Kuntillet 'Ajrud', *TA* 33: 196–228.

Smith, A.T. and A. Brookes
2001   *Holy Ground: Theoretical Issues Relating to the Landscape and Material Culture of Ritual Space Objects* (British Archaeological Reports International Series 956; Oxford: Archaeopress).

Stevens, M.E.
2006   *Temples, Tithes, and Taxes: the Temple and the Economic Life of Ancient Israel* (Peabody, MA: Hendrickson).

Toorn, K. van der
1997   'Worshipping Stones: On the Deification of Cult Symbols', *JNSL* 23: 1–14.

Tufnell, O., *et al.*
1953   *Lachish III –Tell ed-Duweir: The Iron Age* (London: Oxford University Press).

Wasilewska, E.
1994   'The Search for the Impossible: The Archaeology of Religion of Prehistoric Societies as an Anthropological Discipline', *Journal of Prehistoric Religion* 8: 62–75.

Weinberg, S.S.
1978   'A Moabite Shrine Group', *Muse* 12: 30–48.

Wiseman, D.J.
1993   *1–2 Kings: Introduction and Commentary* (TOTC 9; Leicester: Inter-Varsity Press).

Wright, D.P.
1987   *The Disposal of Impurity: Elimination Rites in the Bible and in Hittite and Mesopotamian Literatures* (SBLDS 101; Atlanta, GA: Scholars Press).

Würthwein, E.

1976   'Die josianische Reform und das Deuteronomium', *Zeitschrift für Theologie und Kirche* 73: 395–423.

Zevit, Z.

2001   *The Religions of Ancient Israel: A Synthesis of Parallactic Approaches* (London: Continuum).

Chapter 7

URBAN RELIGION AND RURAL RELIGION

Philip Davies

Much research has been done on ancient Near Eastern urbanism and urban religion in general,[1] and on Greco-Roman urbanism as a factor in the spread of early Christianity (e.g. Meeks 1983; Stark 2006), but relatively little attention has been paid to urban and rural religion in ancient Israel and Judah.[2] But before considering religion in particular, we must understand the relationship of city and countryside in ancient Israel and Judah.

Biblical Hebrew recognizes various levels of human settlements. The words *'îr* and (less commonly) *qiryâ*, are rendered in English as 'city' or 'town'; such places would be walled. Three more terms are normally translated as 'village': *ḥāṣēr* (literally 'court[yard]'), more rarely *kĕpar*, and (in the plural) *ḥawwōt*. Finally, there is *pĕrāzôt* (again, plural only), which the NRSV (problematically) translates as 'unwalled villages': perhaps 'hamlet' would be better, since many 'villages' might be without walls. Next, *nāveh* and *śādeh* (singular or plural) are usually translated respectively as 'pasture' and 'field'. The former seems to refer to land seasonally used for animals, while the latter means land permanently grazed, sown or planted and close to a city, town or village. In Deut. 22.22–27, then, a betrothed woman suspected of sexual misconduct is acquitted if the act occurred 'in the *śādeh*', where cries for help might not be heard. Again, Esau is a 'man of the *śādeh*' while Jacob lives 'in tents' (Gen. 25.27). In Gen. 34.28, 'field' is again contrasted explicitly with 'city' (in this case, Shechem). Finally, *midbār* ('wilderness') denotes uncultivated territory devoid of regular human presence. The spectrum of human settlement throughout the first millennium BCE is also revealed through archaeology: cities/towns have been excavated and smaller settlements traced in surveys. However, we must reckon with herders who seasonally moved with their flocks but would at times settle temporarily close to, or in, villages or cities. Such tent-dwellers leave little or no direct trace of their presence.

Based on biblical and archaeological evidence, the two major studies of human settlement by Fritz (1995) and de Geus (2003) distinguish three categories of settlement cluster: capital city, city (Fritz) or town (de Geus), and village. Fritz further subdivides

---

1.   Collected studies include those edited by Kraeling 1960; Lapidus 1969; Ucko, Tringham and Dimbleby 1974; Aerts 1990; Aufrecht, Mirau and Gauley 1997 and Matsushima 1993; see also the discussions by Adams 1966; Lampl 1968; Whitehouse 1997; Gates 2003. On Babylonian cities specifically, see Van de Mieroop 1997, and on Greco-Roman Palestine, Sperber 1998; Richardson 2002.

2.   No discussion is found, for example, in the standard treatments of religion by Dearman 1992, Albertz 1994, Zevit 2001 or Kessler 2008. On urbanism and prophecy, see the studies collected in Grabbe and Haak 2001, which contains a critique by Grabbe 2001 of the concept of 'urbanism' as applied in biblical studies.

the village into three kinds: 'ring' (with a central open space – the *ḥāṣēr* – used, for example, for animals), agglomerated (collections of individual houses with the land surrounding) and the individual 'house', the farmstead. The last of these probably should be a category of its own. But where does the boundary between 'urban' and 'rural' lie – specifically in cultural respects like religion? The answer involves defining 'city' not in terms of size or population density but function. For while ancient cities are generally regarded as having developed either as the result of population pressure or as a by-product of state formation,[3] a city is not simply – nor even necessarily – defined by a high concentration of population, or even by having walls and gates. Moreover, cities can predate states. The essential feature of a city is that it is not economically autonomous but parasitic on (or perhaps symbiotic with) a rural hinterland. Unlike villages and towns, which are more or less self-sustaining units, a city does not provide its inhabitants with their basic resources, especially food, but relies on the surrounding countryside to deliver food and other animal or vegetable derivatives such as wool, leather and oil. In turn, cities provide their inhabitants with potential for human activity beyond subsistence, and this capacity is the basis for an 'urban' lifestyle ('civilization', from Latin *civitas*, 'city'). The city also provides facilities for its associated rural population, such as protection from attack, a dedicated body of troops for defence and deterrence, a large, central marketplace and more reliable, cheaper and varied services and manufactured goods. As Falconer and Savage put it (1995: 37), an 'urbanized' society comprises 'city centers differentiated from, but integrated with, their rural peripheries'. In Joshua 15–23 several of the 'cities' listed are named along with their own 'villages'; elsewhere such places are referred to as the city's 'daughters' (Judg. 11.26).

The ancient Palestinian city, then, is not another autonomous human settlement, but the nucleus of a wider system, the kernel ('central place' in the language of anthropological theory) of an economic and political unit in which staple resources are transferred from the rural to the urban population, since a proportion of which was agriculturally unproductive, while the city in other ways served its rural hinterland. This exchange, however, required a degree of administration that was located within the city and typically required a ruler, a patron, who would exact surplus (effectively taxation) in return for benefits that he bestowed from 'his' city. Urbanization, monarchy and state formation are therefore related, but not necessarily by a strict causal chain. The bond between city and ruler is dramatically shown in Gen. 34.1, cited earlier, where the name of the city, Shechem, is bestowed on the 'prince (*nāśî*)' of the land ('*āreṣ*)' that comprises both 'city' and its 'fields'.

The economic activity within the city and the development within it of a formal political structure stratified the urban population by income and status, while specialization also created vertical divisions that could cut across traditional kinship relations. The city ruler's power was sustained less by consent or custom or kinship (as was the case with a village head) than through a 'retainer class' – an immediate set of clients such as soldiery, scribes and priests. Rulers enhanced their status within cities through monumental urban architecture, especially palaces and temples, but also walls and gates. The surplus wealth that became available was also spent on luxury

---

3.   Among most influential proposals on the origins of cities are those of Childe 1950 and Adams 1966. For a discussion of the wide range of proposals and classification methods, see Wheatley 1972.

goods and leisure (banqueting affords an instance of both). Additional wealth was acquired through 'royal' initiatives like predatory warfare and trade – in the broadest sense, including production, infrastructure and tolls.

These developments promoted a distinct urban culture, at the base of which was the profile of the city as a place of wealth and power reflected in its ruler, a profile maintained to a very large extent through religion, for the king's authority was projected as divinely appointed, his authority an extension of divine authority, which, while extending beyond the city walls, was symbolized mostly within them.

Urbanization in Israel and Judah

The early books of the Bible might appear to depict the ancient Israelites as originally and essentially 'rural'. The Genesis narratives describe semi-nomadic lifestyles, while those of Exodus to Deuteronomy portray a nation wandering in the wilderness. This 'rural' impression has been translated into biblical scholarship, too. Albrecht Alt (1966 [1925]), for instance, proposed that the Israelites were originally semi-nomads who gradually came to settle on lands they had previously used for seasonal farming and from there later developed urban forms of life; Norman Gottwald (1979) more dramatically portrayed Israelites as withdrawing to the highlands to form an egalitarian alternative to the urban systems of Canaan. More recently, systematic surveys of the central Palestinian highlands (see Finkelstein 1988) have identified newly created agricultural settlements in which lived the core population of what would become the kingdoms of Israel and Judah. This discovery has tended to support the view that 'Israel' began as farmers who became 'urbanized' over time. The 'urbanization' of this society is thus usually associated with state formation, and until recently with the 'united monarchy' of David and Solomon. Thus, Fritz (1995: 13–14) gives four reasons for the rise of cities in Israel and Judah: to reflect the new self-confidence of the state; to enable the country to be defended against external enemies; to administer the kingdom by institutions that could best function from cities; and to accommodate population growth. As remarked by Dever (1997), however, the development of cities normally precedes the development of a state, and he therefore argues that the population of Israel was already large enough in the twelfth century BCE to make urbanization possible, and thus open the way for monarchy. Like Fritz, Dever consequently accepts the existence of a 'united monarchy' in the tenth century BCE, but while Fritz sees urbanization as the result of deliberate royal policy, Dever sees monarchy as outcome of urbanization.

There are some problems with either view. In the period before the highland settlements appeared, namely in the Late Bronze Age (c. 1550–1250 BCE), Palestine had been urbanized, with several of the political and economic 'city' systems described earlier. Many of the fourteenth century BCE Amarna letters were exchanged between the Pharaoh and city-rulers of Palestine such as Shechem and Jerusalem, both in the central highlands. This system partially collapsed at the end of the Late Bronze Age, and the new villages were one outcome of the urban decline (for a detailed description of the process, see Liverani 2005: 32–76). But several cities survived, and it is likely that some of the new villages interacted with them. It is, of course, difficult either to deny or confirm such interaction archaeologically, but such had been the pattern previously and was to be the pattern again in the urbanized kingdoms of Israel and Judah.

There was undoubtedly a rebalancing of the urban–rural population and economy, but not a political, economic or social revolution. Urbanization was a constant feature, even affecting the highlands.

It is important to bear in mind also that Judah and Israel probably developed separately, at different rates and in different ways (Herzog and Singer-Avitz 2004). The 'united monarchy' of David and Solomon, if it existed at all, can only have been a transient episode. In the view of Finkelstein (conveniently summarized in Finkelstein and Silberman 2001: 169–95), the kingdom of Israel properly began in the ninth century BCE with Omri, who built his capital at Samaria (the kingdom was regularly referred to by the Assyrians as the 'house of Omri'). This kingdom emerged, Finkelstein argues, from the destruction of the major cities by the Pharaoh Sheshonq (biblical Shishak) in the late tenth century BCE (Finkelstein 2003). Whether or not he is correct, cities were playing a major role in the politics and economy of Palestine as the two kingdoms were being formed (though Judah, on Finkelstein's theory, became an independent, monarchic state only in the eighth century).

The kingdoms of Israel and Judah were therefore formed with populations that included both farmers and city-dwellers. The urbanization of Israel and Judah certainly increased under their monarchies, but some of their cities were inherited. Fritz (1995: 76) lists cities including Dan, Hazor, Lachish, Megiddo, Gezer and Beth-Shemesh as being rebuilt or redeveloped on existing city sites, with others (many fewer) such as Kinneret or Beersheba located on the site of previous villages. The impression given in Joshua that the cities of Canaan were conquered and destroyed is now known to be wrong (and contradicted by the lists of 'cities' in the tribal allotments of Joshua 15–21): more realistic is the view in Deut. 6.10:

> (When) Yhwh your God has brought you into the land that he swore to your ancestors, to Abraham, to Isaac, and to Jacob, to give you – a land with fine, large cities that you did not build.

Of course, this text reflects a later period, as does Numbers 35, where Moses is commanded to build cities for Levites and to designate six cities for refuge. But this chapter also points us to the fact that different types of city came into existence in Israel and Judah. Apart from the royal capital and the regular 'residential city' (see Fritz 1995: 117–35) were those with specialized inhabitants, such as palace cities, created largely for the benefit of the king and his entourage ('disembodied capitals'), or administrative or garrison cities, or temple-cities inhabited largely by priests. Excavations suggest, for example, that Jezreel was a garrison city and royal palace; Ramat Rahel, just outside Jerusalem, a residential/palace city; and Lachish an administrative city (as well as an important fortress), while the biblical narratives portray Shiloh and Bethel as temple cities – like Gerizim which was, according to recent excavation results, built in the late fifth century BCE. Many cities (Jerusalem especially) combined several such functions. In a territorial state, such as Israel or Judah – as in the later imperial provinces – the individual city and its hinterland was no longer the political and economic unit but part of a larger entity – though the use of the name 'Samaria' for the Assyrian province shows how the terminology of the city-state persisted, while at the end of Hezekiah's reign Judah consisted of little more than Jerusalem and its immediate environs (and even today it is common to find 'London' or 'Washington' used as labels for national governments).

Urban and Rural Religion in Israel and Judah

We can now turn to the religious aspects of urbanism. How should we expect urban and rural religion to differ? Some aspects, of course, were shared by both, including elements of so-called 'popular' and 'official' religion (on which see Chapter 4 in this volume). But how did urban and rural populations differ in their religious life? There is, of course, no question of speaking simply of 'urban religion' as if it were either single or monolithic. Major new elements that urbanism specifically brought to religion were the cults of the ruling dynasty and of the city, but these did not monopolize: the city also brought into close juxtaposition the different cultic spheres of its inhabitants – the court, merchants, soldiers, farmers, artisans, and other foreign residents, so that alongside the city temple or temples were numerous smaller shrines and alongside the great festivals were everyday rites. We know (see Chapter 6 in this volume) of city shrines, for example, at gates and crossroads, as well as altars within households. There was an urban religion of the home, the street, the gate and the market as well as the more public religion of the temples.

Reconstructing the urban religion of Jerusalem or of Samaria – or of other major cities of the two kingdoms – encounters one huge difficulty, and that difficulty itself is actually a by-product of urbanism. Both biblical texts and archaeology tell us more about urban than rural religion, for it is in cities that the material traces of cultic activity are most easily discernible, while the written sources – almost entirely biblical – are themselves the products of urban centres. Professional scribes were essential to the maintenance of a kingdom and, of course, resided mainly in the cities, particularly the capitals and administrative centres. Within some of these (and certainly in the capital) archives, scribal schools and libraries would have come to be attached to one or both of the great monarchic institutions, palace and temple. Without cities, then, there would be no Hebrew Bible, and the biblical texts convey an overwhelmingly urban perspective. The role of the scribal class in creating as well as reflecting and inscribing religious belief and behaviour can be seen, for example, in the drafting of law codes, the development of mythology, the composition of liturgy and the creation of narratives about the past that fashioned social identity.

Unfortunately, this does not mean that we have a reliable biblical portrait of urban religion during the monarchies. Although we are told more about urban conditions than rural conditions, this does not mean it is easy to reconstruct urban religion. The biblical books, whatever earlier sources they use, come to us from Judah, which, after the cessation of its monarchy, was an imperial province under the Neo-Babylonians, Persians, Ptolemies and Seleucids. These writings were mostly composed, copied and canonized in Jerusalem, which dominated the province of Yehud not only as its political capital but through a temple that imposed itself as an exclusive cult (see Ben Zvi 1997). It would be accurate to regard Jerusalem at this time as a temple-city, especially if it provided the inspiration for the exaggerated description of the temple administration in Chronicles (see Wright 2007), whose authors, attached to the temple, retrojected the contemporary scene into the time of David and Solomon (as perhaps also the authors of Kings, though with less exaggeration). How far the biblical portrait of Judah's religion is historically reliable constitutes perhaps the single most important and hotly debated issue in current biblical scholarship. Its portrayal of the religion of its neighbour Israel/Samaria is perhaps even less reliable. The religion of post-monarchic Jerusalem was certainly quite different from that of the cities of monarchic Israel and

Judah. For one thing, its cult of the high god Yahweh Elohim was monotheistic (in a qualified sense), aniconic and ultimately confined to a single sanctuary. None of these features is demonstrable for the monarchic period in either Israel or Judah, though many scholars continue to write as if some Judahite kings sought to impose this later Yahwistic 'orthodoxy' on their subjects while others blatantly departed from it. Some doubts must be expressed over the biblical presentation of 'rural' religion, though in fact its descriptions of 'Canaanite' religion are not too far removed from the reality of common Israelite and Judahite practice. The descriptions that follow, then, inevitably contain a good deal of inference and deduction, and, rather than a systematic account, form a set of discrete topics.

The Urban God

As noted, the urbanizing process generated both diversity of population and also physical concentration. The population of a city is more diverse than in the village, and less organic. Village society is maintained through kinship and well-entrenched custom, and each village also has its own customs as well as those shared with other villages: in the city a greater degree of more formal means are employed to regulate social relations, and such mechanisms are typically a function of monarchic rule. Hence the city contains a greater variety of religious customs than any single village, as well as being more directly affected than the countryside in royal and national cults. Alongside the diversity of urban practice the city and royal cults promoted a degree of unity or solidarity, even character, on the city.

In particular, urbanization characterizes the divine realm as urban too. For the urban dweller, the great gods are like kings and live in cities; they sit on thrones, dwell in palace-temples, hold court and have a multitude of servants (both heavenly and earthly) ministering to them, representing them, and mediating their power to their subjects. Like kings, gods issue laws and go to war, threatening their enemies all the while. They take pride in the city that is their home, and in return for proper care of their residence, they protect that city. Yahweh's protection of Zion is a constant theme in the Psalms (how often is he said to protect other cities or villages?). For gods are not farmers: agriculture is a role they have bequeathed to humans (see Genesis 2!), even if some of them (including Yahweh) claimed control of the vital rainfall. The special intimacy of the earthly king and the heavenly king is part of royal ideology (see Ps. 2.7). The splendour of the city (especially palace and temple) was a reflection of both royal and divine glory and this glory set apart the city from the countryside and its towns and villages as a place of prestige, power and divine presence.

Heaven on Earth

In view of this privileged status, an ancient city might itself be personified. The imagery of a city as the wife of the deity who lived in it is ancient (Ezekiel 16). As a divine wife, its inhabitants might be symbolized as her children (Isa. 66.7–16). The city itself could also be mythologized as a reflection of the celestial realm. The idea of the temple city as a gateway, a link to heaven, even a replica of heaven is ancient. The name Babylon = Babel means 'gate of god'; the 'tower of Babel' is a route to heaven. During the Second

Temple era, however, Jerusalem came to monopolize these forms of characterization. In Lamentations we find Zion as both the wife and the daughter of Yahweh, while in the New Testament book of Revelation we find the emphatic expression of the city as the replica of a heavenly counterpart: 'And I saw the holy city, the new Jerusalem, coming down out of heaven from God, prepared as a bride adorned for her husband' (Rev. 21.2). In Ezekiel 40–44 and in both the Qumran Temple Scroll and the 'New Jerusalem' texts, we find such idealized conceptions of Jerusalem. Because of its obsession with Jerusalem's pre-eminence, the Bible tells us little about other cities, though the royal Israelite temple-city of Bethel was almost certainly conceived as a gateway to heaven, for as Jacob is made to exclaim when he 'founds' the sanctuary: 'This is none other than the house of God, and this is the gate of heaven' (Gen. 28.17).

Nissinen (2001) describes how the Mesopotamian city of Arbela, the dwelling of the goddess Ishtar, was apparently deified, as attested by personal names that include 'Arbela' as a theophoric element. There is little evidence that any of the Israelite or Judahite cities, even Jerusalem, was itself deified, but Jerusalem was presented as an extension of the celestial sphere and, as we have seen, as Yahweh's 'bride', the 'mother' of his Judahite children. The description of the future Jerusalem in Ezekiel 47, with its four streams flowing from the temple suggests a comparison with the divine garden, the paradise 'east of Eden' in Genesis 2. Indeed, the second of the rivers in Genesis 2 is called Gihon, the name of a spring on the east side of the city (1 Kgs 1.33, 38). The divine garden depicted in Ezekiel 28 in an oracle against the king of Tyre may be an ironic depiction of that city as a divine estate ('paradise' is literally a royal park), borrowing from a similar Jerusalem tradition (note especially 'the guardian cherub drove you out', v. 16, cf. Gen. 3.23–24). Undoubtedly Jerusalem's temple, and by extension the city itself could be conceived as not only a part of earth, but also a part of heaven. These images were cultically as well as textually expressed. The statue of the city's protective deity, for example, would be taken from the temple, outside the city and brought back in, all in a ceremonial procession. Such a ritual is well-attested in Babylon, for instance, and many scholars have suggested that such a celebration lies behind Psalm 24, while Psalm 132 (and indeed 2 Samuel 6) suggests that the story of David's bringing of the ark to Jerusalem may have been linked to this festival. When the High Priest entered the Holy of Holies on the Day of Atonement he was, by virtue of stepping into the divine presence, stepping into the heavenly world. In all such rituals earthly and heavenly movements coincided, and the city itself assumed both an earthly and a heavenly context for the divine procession and the divine presence that was its ultimate affirmation. Studies of ancient temples have also demonstrated how this celestial aspect was conveyed architecturally (e.g. Hurowitz 1992).

Agriculture and Fertility

Fertility is closely associated with rural activity and concerns, and here we can also consider the way in which the countryside is projected in certain biblical texts – especially Deuteronomistic – as a place of religious apostasy. Cities, of course, also rely upon agriculture: their inhabitants depend on the fertility of animals and crops. If many city-dwellers had little direct involvement with agriculture, others would have owned or worked fields. All over the ancient Near East, of course, we encounter gods and goddesses of fertility (human as well as animal and vegetable), along with myths that describe the seasonal cycle of dry and wet, sowing and reaping in terms of conflict between forces of life and death. But this evidence comes, of course, also from texts preserved in urban sites. In the mythological tablets from Ugarit, for example, the god of rain/storm, Baal, encounters an opponent called Mot ('death') who is associated with dryness. This clearly reflects the agricultural perspective. Elsewhere in the texts, however his enemy is Yamm, representing a different urban interest: seafaring trade.

'Fertility' religions are dealt with elsewhere in this volume (see Chapters 4, 8 and 9) and there is no need for a detailed description here. We need only note that both feminine and masculine deities need to be present, and that ancient Israel and Judah were no exception. Just as we encounter Inanna/Ishtar, Isis, Astarte and Persephone in the fertility cults of other religions, the most common religious artefact encountered in archaeological excavations in Palestine is a female figurine. Additionally, inscriptions have also been found at Kuntillet 'Ajrud (in the Sinai desert) and Khirbet el-Qom (20 km west of Hebron) that associate Yahweh with a consort, Asherah. In the Hebrew Bible Asherah is a name for both the goddess and her symbol. But several texts locate such a symbol in the Jerusalem temple (1 Kgs 15.13; 2 Kgs 21.7; 23.4–7, 14) and according to Jeremiah 44 the cult of the 'Queen of Heaven' had been prevalent from the very beginning 'in the cities/towns of Judah and in the streets of Jerusalem' (v. 17). This was neither a purely 'popular' nor rural cult; Asherah 'lived' with Yahweh in Jerusalem (see Chapter 4 in this volume).

The biblical perspective on fertility cults and on Asherah is of course negative. In Hosea, the 'Baals' are symbolized as Israel's 'lovers': 'I will go after my lovers; they give me my bread and my water, my wool and my flax, my oil and my drink' (Hos. 2.7 [ET v. 5]). It is Yahweh, not Baal, who is Israel's 'husband' (one of the meanings of *ba'al*) – and perhaps the role of Israel as his 'wife' in the book underlines the absence of a heavenly consort, and implicitly makes fertility a matter of cooperation between the Israelites and their god, not between god and goddess. In Hosea, Yahweh provides rain and crops, but he is no fertility god himself: he is the head of the household in which the wife (Israel) plays a secondary role.

In the biblical use of fertility imagery we might detect something of an urbanizing process. According to several texts the cult of Baal was conducted at numerous places called *bāmôt*, 'high places', cult sites located in 2 Kgs 16.4 'on the hills and under every leafy tree' (cf. Deut. 12.2). Indeed, the Deuteronomistic literature as a whole implies that fertility cults had their stronghold in the countryside. The rural represents a place of illicit religious practice, and the figure of Baal, bringer of rain and thus of fertility, sometimes approximates to a divine opponent of Yahweh (as mostly in Kings, for example in 1 Kings 18), while at other times is pluralized into 'the baalim' (for example in Hosea, Jeremiah or Chronicles). This 'idolatrous' portrait of the countryside also seems to be used to justify the doctrine of (urban) cult centralization (see below). Baal, the agricultural god, is worshipped in many sites over the countryside: Yahweh, who is a single god, belongs only in one city! Even so, the books of Kings admit that the worship of Baal 'infected' the Israelite court of Ahab, and that most of the Judahite kings also permitted the worship of Baal (see, for example, 2 Kgs 3.2; 21.3).

The opposition of Yahweh and Baal is not historically a matter of urban versus rural, but it is an aspect of the Deuteronomistic ideology of Jerusalem, which stems most probably from the Second Temple. Most scholars still accept that some 'Yahwistic orthodoxy' was promoted in Jerusalem by the exceptional 'righteous' kings, but the whole issue of what 'Yahwistic orthodoxy' was historically under the monarchies is disputed. The description of the cults of both Judah and Israel in the biblical texts reflects a concern to contrast the population of post-monarchic Yehud as the true Israel with a Samaria that was no longer regarded as 'Israel' at all, as well as to compare a largely idolatrous past in both kingdoms with an 'orthodox' present in Judah/Yehud. Such propaganda does not make for reliable historical description, but tells us a lot about Yehud's urban religion.

Cult Centralization

Political and social centralization is certainly one of the by-products of urbanization, and many biblical books give the clear impression that Jerusalem was always supposed to be the central, even exclusive, temple of Yahweh in both Israel and Judah. But Israel and Judah were not a unified state or unified society (Davies 2007), and neither the kingdom of Israel nor the province of Samaria ever acknowledged such a status for Jerusalem. There may have been economic or political reasons for some religious centralization: collection of royal revenue through temple offerings would be facilitated by imposing a single centre for their collection, while the power of priesthoods of various temples and cults may have needed now and then to be curtailed. But it makes little sense for a king to require his subjects to adhere to a single cult or a single temple. This would prove impossible to impose, and would weaken royal authority and social stability. The adoption of Yahweh as the dynastic, national god and/or city god (and as the 'god of Israel' in the kingdom of Israel) was surely sufficient to ensure royal control over religious behaviour. The cult centralizations of Hezekiah and Josiah, for example, are either fictitious or exaggerated retrojections from a later, post-monarchic period when the political role of the temple was different. To all this it should be added that the cult of 'Yahweh of Hosts' was identified with Jerusalem rather than Judah. No 'god of Judah' is ever mentioned in the Bible – in contrast with the title 'god of Israel', originally the deity of the national cult in Israel, perhaps centred on Bethel, from where it came into Judah along with the city itself (Davies 2007).

The Urbanizing of Festivals

It was probably during the post-monarchic period that the major Judahite agricultural seasons and their religious festivals became fully 'urbanized' in Jerusalem. But the process may have begun earlier. From a city's point of view, harvest celebrations represent income in the form of taxes to the king and tithes or first-fruit offerings to the urban temple. These 'offerings' are therefore the city's (i.e. its temple's and its king's) financial 'harvest'. The Jewish liturgical year contains three great festivals, all of them coinciding with agricultural moments: Passover at the birthing of lambs, Weeks (Pentecost) at the cereal harvest, Booths at the fruit harvest. Some of the agricultural features have been retained, but all have been linked with events in an invented national history. The agricultural festivals, at home in the fields, became pilgrimage festivals to the city, and commemorated Yahweh's deliverance from slavery in Egypt (Passover), the Sinai lawgiving (Weeks/Pentecost) and the wilderness wandering (Booths/Tabernacles). As urban festivals, they constituted part of the larger economic transfer of wealth from village to city and also represent the imposition of urban onto rural culture.

Prophecy

Urbanizing can also be observed in the case of prophecy and other forms of divination. There is clearly a large contrast between the circles of itinerant 'holy men' depicted in the stories of Elijah and Elisha and the Levitical 'prophets' of Chronicles embedded in the Jerusalem temple. Such a contrast has suggested separate roles of 'central' and 'peripheral' prophets (Petersen 1981), while Amos, for example, is often presented in modern commentaries as a 'rural' figure railing against primarily 'urban' abuses. But the biblical presentation of 'prophecy' cannot be translated so simply into historical or sociological realities. Most of the major prophetic figures (including Elijah and Elisha) deal with monarchs, while Jeremiah, Ezekiel and perhaps also Isaiah were themselves priests, and others, such as Huldah, Haggai and Zechariah seem to have been closely allied with the urban priesthood and temple. Of course there were historically holy men in the countryside, who would, like Elijah or Elisha, be praying for rain, curing illness, miracle-working, divining, or performing magic (and these no doubt also occurred in the city); but the biblical 'prophets' are drawn into national politics. Partly this is because biblical prophecy is an idealized institution representing the key channel of covenant mediation, but historically much prophecy was urban, where temple and court afford opportunity for engagement and the square (just inside the city gate) provided an audience. Certainly, any form of written prophecy points to the urban scribe and his textual archive.

Warfare

In the catalogue of divinely sent disasters, Amos 4.6–11 mentions famine (v. 6), lack of rainfall at crucial times (vv. 7–8) and several kinds of pest or plant disease (v. 9), asserting Yahweh's control of natural processes. But the passage goes on to mention military defeats and the destruction of cities (vv. 10–11). If fertility is the major concern of rural life, that of the fortified city is security, especially from military attack. The warlike aspect of Yahweh may have been part of the ideology of a warrior king, of course, and emphasized by Israelite and Judahite soldiers posted in the major cities of the land – and beyond, such as those at the colony in Elephantine or in numerous other foreign military settlements during the Second Temple period. Indeed, the royal and civic cult of Jerusalem worshipped *yhwh ṣĕbā'ôt*, 'Yhwh of armies' who was seated, apparently, over the ark within the monarchic Jerusalem temple. In Numbers 35, too, Yahweh is apparently carried, with the ark, into warfare.

While rural populations also feared military attack, of course, they also required other forms of divine security. Undoubtedly travellers had their own deities and practices and wayside shrines. The formula *yhwh smrwn* on the Kuntillet 'Ajrud graffito is usually rendered 'Yhwh of Samaria', but it is also possible to translate 'Yhwh the guardian'. Psalm 121, in both its wordplay on *šmr* ('keep', 'protect', 'guard') and its various images of protection – not from invaders, but from more mythological adversaries – including the protection of travellers (like those passing through Kuntillet 'Ajrud), suggest that *šmrn* might have been a title of Yhwh (= 'protector': see Davies 1998). Perhaps the city of Samaria was named, not after the previous owner of the site (as 1 Kgs 16.24) but after the epithet of the tutelary god who became identified with the 'Yahweh god of Israel'. For travellers, of course, city gods were not particularly helpful, until they can believe in a universal and omnipotent creator deity (compare Jonah with his fellow travellers!).

Urban Images of the Countryside

Where rural contexts are described in the Hebrew Bible, they are often modified from an urban perspective or disapproved as places where numerous cultic sites fostered idolatry. The story of Samuel's parents going up to Shiloh for an occasional festival (1 Samuel 1–2) may suggest to some readers that, apart from cities, there were local shrines to which villagers would resort regularly. But the presence of the ark and the dynastic priesthood represent Shiloh as a forerunner of Jerusalem and not as a 'local' sanctuary of dubious status; we have an 'urbanized' image. The story of the capture of women in Judges 21, by contrast, hints at a different kind of festival at Shiloh during the grape harvest and is suggestive of some kind of fertility celebration. The stories of Gideon's attack on the Baal temple (Judges 6), the retreat of Jephthah's daughter (Judges 11), the Song of Songs and the book of Ruth also have rural contexts, but give us little more than the occasional glimpse of rural religion. It has also been speculated that in the Song of Songs lie some possible relics of a rural fertility myth. But if so, the presence of King Solomon, the 'daughters of Jerusalem', and the interludes in the city itself again underline the extent to which urban has been superimposed on rural. Just as modern urban life has its own images of the 'countryside', from a place of boredom and dreariness to an Elysian paradise, so the biblical texts can be understood as conveying less a true picture of country life than an urbanite's view of country life, both positive and negative. The same, of course, can be said of the third kind of terrain, the 'wilderness': this has also both good and bad connotations, from a place of 'honeymoon' (Hosea) to a derelict wasteland, the fate of the doomed city (Isa. 64.10). It would be interesting to explore the biblical, urban notions of the 'sacred spaces' of countryside and wilderness, but for the biblical texts, on the whole the only legitimate 'sacred space' was urban, and more precisely, Jerusalem.

Summary

This chapter has tried to show that while differences between 'urban' and 'rural' religion in ancient Israel and Judah can be detected and sometimes inferred, the distinctions are partly cultural but also partly theological and indeed idealized. City and country were in reality symbiotic, and the land occupied by the kingdoms of Israel and Judah was urbanized before these kingdoms emerged. Most importantly of all, since high literacy itself is an urban phenomenon, the Hebrew Bible represents an urban perspective on almost everything. The result is that we cannot easily gain an objective view of rural Israel and Judah, nor – since the urban perspective largely reflects one city, Jerusalem – do we know much about the realities of urban and rural religion. But in realizing the urban nature of the biblical texts and their ideology we can resist the false impression of some biblical scholarship of the past that traditional Israelite religion was somehow essentially 'rural', or that the Hebrew Bible is a reliable source for the religious life of either the countryside or the cities – especially those other than Jerusalem.

Bibliography

Adams, R. McC.
1966   *The Evolution of Urban Society* (Chicago, IL: Aldine Press).

Aerts, E. (ed.)
1990   *The Town as Regional Economic Centre in the Ancient Near East: Session B-16: Proceedings, Tenth International Economic History Congress, Leuven, August 1990* (Leuven: Leuven University Press).

Albertz, R.
1994   *A History of Israelite Religion in the Old Testament Period* (2 vols; trans. J. Bowden. OTL; London: SCM Press).

Alt, A.
1966 [1925]   'The Settlement of the Israelites in Palestine', in *Essays on Old Testament History and Religion* (Oxford: Blackwell), 133–69.

Aufrecht, W.E., N.A. Mirau and S.W. Gauley (eds)
1997   *Urbanism in Antiquity* (Sheffield: Sheffield Academic Press).

Ben Zvi, E.
1997   'The Urban Center of Jerusalem', in W.E. Aufrecht, N.A. Mirau and S.W. Gauley (eds), *Urbanism in Antiquity* (Sheffield: Sheffield Academic Press), 194–209.

Childe, V.G.
1950   'The Urban Revolution', *Town Planning Review* 21: 9–16.

Davies, P.R.
1998   'Yahweh as Minder', *Old Testament Essays* 11: 427–37.
2007   *The Origins of Biblical Israel* (LHBOTS 485; New York, NY, and London: T&T Clark).

Dearman, J.A.
1992   *Religion and Culture in Ancient Israel* (Peabody, MA: Hendrikson).

de Geus, C.H.J.
2003   *Towns in Ancient Israel and in the Southern Levant* (Leuven: Peeters).

Dever, W.G.
1997   'Archaeology, Urbanism and the Rise of the Israelite State', in W.E. Aufrecht, N.A. Mirau and S.W. Gauley (eds), *Urbanism in Antiquity* (Sheffield: Sheffield Academic Press), 172–93.

Falconer, S.E. and S.H. Savage
1995   'Heartlands and Hinterlands: Alternative Trajectories of Early Urbanization in Mesopotamia and the Southern Levant', *American Antiquity* 60: 37–58.

Finkelstein, I.
1988   *The Archaeology of the Israelite Settlement* (Jerusalem: Israel Exploration Society).
2003   'From Canaanites to Israelites: When, How and Why', in M. Liverani (ed.), *Convegno Internazionale: Recenti tendenze nella ricostruzione della storia antica d'Israele* (Rome: Accademia Nazionale dei Lincei), 11–27.

Finkelstein, I. and N.A. Silberman
2001   *The Bible Unearthed: Archaeology's New Vision of Ancient Israel and the Origin of its Sacred Texts* (New York, NY: Free Press).
2006   *David and Solomon: In Search of the Bible's Sacred Kings and the Roots of the Western Tradition* (New York, NY: Free Press).

Fritz, V.
1995   *The City in Ancient Israel* (BS 29; Sheffield: Sheffield Academic Press).

Garr, W.R.
1987   'A Population Estimate of Ancient Ugarit', *BASOR* 266: 31–43.

Gates, C.
2003   *Ancient Cities: Introduction to the Archaeology of the Ancient Near East and Egypt, Greece and Rome* (London: Routledge).

Gottwald, N.K.
1979   *The Tribes of Yahweh* (Maryknoll: Orbis) (2nd edn; Sheffield: Sheffield Academic Press, 1999).

Grabbe, L.L.
2001   'Sup-Urbs or Only Hyp-urbs? Prophets and Populations in Ancient Israel and Socio-Historical Method', in L.L. Grabbe and R.D. Haak (eds), *Every City Shall be Forsaken: Urbanism and Prophecy in Ancient Israel and the Near East* (JSOTS 330; Sheffield: Sheffield Academic Press), 95–123.

Grabbe, L.L. and R.D. Haak (eds)
2001   *Every City Shall Be Forsaken: Urbanism and Prophecy in Ancient Israel and the Near East* (JSOTS 330; Sheffield: Sheffield Academic Press).

Herzog, Z. and L. Singer-Avitz
2004   'Redefining the Centre: The Emergence of State in Judah', *TA* 31: 209–44.

Hudson, M. and B.A. Levine (eds)
1999   *Urbanization and Land Ownership in the Ancient New East* (Cambridge, MA: Peabody Museum of Archaeology and Ethnology).

Hurowitz, V.
1992   *I Have Built You an Exalted House: Temple Building in the Bible in Light of Mesopotamian and Northwest Semitic Writings* (JSOT/ASORMS 5; Sheffield: JSOT Press).

Jones, S.
1997   *The Archaeology of Ethnicity: Constructing Identities in the Past and Present* (London and New York, NY: Routledge).

Kessler, R.
2008   *The Social History of Ancient Israel: An Introduction* (Philadelphia, PA: Fortress Press).

Killebrew, A.
2005   *Biblical Peoples and Ethnicity: An Archaeological Study of Egyptians, Canaanites, Philistines, and Early Israel 1300–1100 BCE* (Atlanta, GA: Society of Biblical Literature).

Kraeling, C.H. (ed.)
1960   *City Invincible: A Symposium on Urbanization and Cultural Development in the Ancient Near East* (University of Chicago, IL: Oriental Institute).

Lampl, P.
1968   *Cities and Planning in the Ancient Near East* (London: Studio Vista).

Lapidus, I.M. (ed.)
1969   *Middle Eastern Cities: A Symposium on Ancient, Islamic and Contemporary Middle Eastern Urbanism* (Berkeley, CA: University of California Press).

Liverani, M.
2005   *Israel's History and the History of Israel* (trans. C. Peri and P.R. Davies; London: Equinox).

Matsushima, E. (ed.)
1993   *Official Cult and Popular Religion in the Ancient Near East: 1st Colloquium on the Ancient Near East – The City and Its Life* (Heidelberg: Universitatsverlag).

Meeks, W.A.
1983   *The First Urban Christians* (New Haven, CT: Yale University Press).

Nissinen, M.
2001   'City as Lofty as Heaven: Arbela and Other Cities in Neo-Assyrian Prophecy', in L.L. Grabbe and R.D. Haak (eds), *Every City Shall be Forsaken. Urbanism and Prophecy*

in Ancient Israel and the Near East (JSOTS 330; Sheffield: Sheffield Academic Press), 172–209.

Petersen, D.L.
1981   *The Roles of Israel's Prophets* (JSOTS 17; Sheffield: JSOT Press).

Richardson, P.
2002   *City and Sanctuary: Religion and Architecture in the Roman Near East* (London: SCM Press).

Sperber, D.
1998   *The City in Roman Palestine* (New York, NY: Oxford University Press).

Stark, R.
2006   *Cities of God: The Real Story of How Christianity Became an Urban Movement and Conquered Rome* (San Francisco, CA: HarperSanFrancisco).

Ucko, P.J., R. Tringham and G.W. Dimbleby (eds)
1974   *Men, Settlement and Urbanism* (London: Duckworth).

Van de Mieroop, M.
1997   *The Ancient Mesopotamian City* (Oxford: Clarendon Press).

Wheatley, P.
1972   'The Concept of Urbanism' in P.J. Ucko, R. Tringham and G.W. Dimbleby (eds), *Men, Settlement and Urbanism* (London: Duckworth), 601–37.

Whitehouse, R.
1997   *The First Cities* (Oxford: Phaidon).

Wright, J.
2007   '"Those Doing the Work for the Service in the House of the Lord": 1 Chronicles 23:6–24:31 and the Sociohistorical Context of the Temple of Yahweh in Jerusalem in the Late Persian/Early Hellenistic Period', in O. Lipschits, G.N. Knoppers and R. Albertz (eds), *Judah and the Judeans in the Fourth Century BCE* (Winona Lake, IN: Eisenbrauns), 361–84.

Zevit, Z.
2001   *The Religions of Ancient Israel: A Synthesis of Parallactic Approaches* (London and New York, NY: Continuum).

Chapter 8

HOUSEHOLD RELIGION
Carol Meyers

1
Introduction

Even the casual reader of the Hebrew Bible will have noticed the considerable attention given to Israel's central shrines – the wilderness shrine or Tabernacle (Exodus 25–40)[1] and the Jerusalem temple (1 Kings 6–8; 2 Chronicles 3–4) – and to their sacrifices and maintenance (much of Leviticus and Numbers). In contrast, there are no specific biblical guidelines for religious practices carried out in the homes of average Israelites.[2] Are we to assume that there were no such practices, and that the religious lives of all Israelites were linked to practices at the Tabernacle or temple? Does the paucity of biblical evidence mean the non-existence of household religious practices?

A priori, it is unimaginable that the answer to these questions might be *yes*. That is, it is inconceivable that the religious lives of any people would be limited to and dependent upon their participation in activities at a single locale, especially if that locale were many travel-days distant from where they lived. Virtually no society lacks some kind of religion, and people's religious lives hardly consist solely of what they or their professional representatives (priests) carry out at community shrines. The dearth of biblical information about what people did in their homes is probably a consequence of the Hebrew Bible's general focus on Israel's 'national' existence and its corporate or royal cults. It is thus unremarkable that it lacks detailed descriptions of other forms of religious life.

If the central shrine was inaccessible on a regular basis to most Israelites, what were the other options? Various biblical passages indicate that Israelites had other shrines

1.   The description of the Tabernacle in Exodus may reflect the Second Temple built in Jerusalem after the exile. However, the existence of a more modest portable shrine cannot be ruled out; see Friedman 1992 and Meyers 2005a: 219–20.

2.   The term 'Israel' – used variously in the Hebrew Bible to denote a person, a nation, a people, or the northern kingdom – and its gentilic 'Israelite' are used in a general cultural, rather than a specific political, sense in this chapter. Except for the historicized form of some of the practices to be discussed, most of the religious activities considered Israelite were probably not limited to a particular time period or segment of the population (although the deities invoked may have differed). Indeed, the similarity of some of these practices to ones discernable in the textual and archaeological records from other parts of the ancient Syria-Canaan (as reported in Bodel and Olyan 2008a) indicates that many Israelite religious responses to the conditions and challenges of household life were common to the wider world of the Hebrew Bible. Also, activities taking place in the central shrine, according to Deuteronomic or priestly sources, may well have originated in local shrines or even households.

at major population centres,[3] and also in rural or village settings, in addition to the national one.[4] Moreover, religious practices were carried out in domestic contexts. But the biblical evidence for the religious practices of Israelites in their own homes is more tenuous. There are occasional allusions and indirect references; but for the most part the Hebrew Bible is, understandably (given its 'national' focus), an inadequate source.

The absence of explicit biblical attention to household[5] religion does not mean that it was unimportant, nor does it mean a total lack of information. Thus this chapter will first describe Israelite households and the resources for investigating household religious practices. Then it will examine specific areas of household religion: regular (daily and seasonal) activities; life-cycle events; and several other practices.

2
The Israelite Household and Sources for Its Religious Life

2.1 The Israelite Household

Biblical scholars have long recognized that Israelite society comprises three socio-political levels below the national one – tribe, village (or clan or region), and household – and that religion was a part of each. These levels correspond, although not entirely consistently, to biblical terms and concepts (e.g. Josh. 7.14-18) as well as to the structure of pre-modern agrarian societies as analysed by social anthropologists.[6] They are conceptually linked in the biblical genealogies, which may be constructed to a certain extent yet present an over-arching kinship dimension to Israelite society. This kinship dimension situated people in larger social structures, which in turn lent stability to social and political interactions.[7]

Because of the Hebrew Bible's focus on religion at the national or macro level, the household level has received less scholarly attention; indeed, only in the last decade and a half, since the publication of Albertz's monumental study of Israelite religion (1994), have scholars begun to give serious attention to religious practices at the micro level.[8] This attention is long overdue, for the household was arguably the foundational component of Israelite society. Although the smallest unit, the household was the most numerous; and it dominated the lives of most people. People were surely aware of the larger structures in which the household was embedded[9] but their daily lives took place in this primary social unit.

---

3.   As at Beersheba, Beth-aven, Bethel, Dan, Gilgal, Samaria and Shiloh. See 1 Kgs 12.28-29; Ps. 78.60; Hos. 4.15; Amos 4.4-5; 5.4-5; 8.14.

4.   Their legitimacy is challenged in many biblical texts (e.g. Deut. 12.2-4; 1 Kgs 14.22-23). See Chapters 6 and 7 in this volume.

5.   The use of 'household' rather than 'family' is intentional and will be explained below.

6.   See McNutt 1999 for a general introduction to Israelite social structure, Gottwald 1979 for an extensive examination of pre-monarchic society, Bendor 1996 for an overall view, and Stager 1985 and van der Toorn 1996: 183–205 for useful summaries.

7.   Wilson 1992 describes biblical genealogies and their function in Israelite society.

8.   For example, van der Toorn 1996; Meyers 2005b; Bodel and Olyan 2008a. Note too the attention to 'Religious practices of the individual and family' in Johnston 2004.

9.   This was especially so to the degree that patrimonialism was a symbolic as well as social reality for Israelite society as Schloen contends (2001: 50–53 and *passim*).

The household was also the basic economic unit for the Israelites, most of whom – as many as 90 per cent – lived in agricultural settlements.[10] Survival depended upon the ability to raise crops and animals and to convert them into edible and wearable forms. A family's land holdings were thus integral to its survival, as were the family members, children as well as adults, who carried out the necessary productive and maintenance activities. Because the term 'household' acknowledges the material as well as human components of Israel's basic unit, it is more useful and perhaps more socially accurate to label the micro level of Israelite society as the 'household', or 'family household'. A household in ancient Israel was not simply a family or a domestic abode. Rather it was a socio-economic unit consisting of persons (family members and sometimes unrelated servants or sojourners), their material culture (their living quarters and all its associated installations and artefacts, including its lands and animals), and their activities (Rapoport 1994: 461). Those activities could take place in community spaces or structures as well as within the household domain.

The biblical term for the household, *bêt 'āb* or 'house of the father', which usually denotes a compound or extended family or even a lineage rather than a nuclear family, indicates the patrilineality of Israelite society. The material aspects of a household were transmitted across generations via the male line. With survival dependent upon the household's productivity, the holdings of a family – its 'inheritance' (*naḥălâ*), or patrimonial allotment – were central to the household's identity. Maintaining the ancestral inheritance and family continuity, considered God-given in the Hebrew Bible (as in Num. 33.54; Joshua 13–19; cf. Judg. 21.24), was of great significance as the story of Naboth's vineyard attests (1 Kings 21); and a major responsibility of the senior male member of the household was to preserve the family's patrimony (see Westbrook 1991: 12–18) and ensure the presence of heirs.

Israelites were so interdependent in a variety of social, economic and religious ways that they were not really viable as individuals and would not have understood the pronounced individualism of today. People were 'deeply embedded, or engaged' in their social context and 'enmeshed in the obligations of kinship' (Di Vito 1999: 221, 223; also, van der Toorn 1996: 3). This collective identity means that ancient Israel could be characterized as 'an aggregate of groups rather than a collection of individuals' (Rogerson 1989: 5). Thus the household religious practices considered here served the unit to which people belonged as much as the religious needs of people as individuals.

Because the materiality of a household was necessary for the survival of its members, because its land (inheritance) was an integral part of family identity, and because individual identity was subsumed into the collective household group, the term 'household religion' seems more appropriate than 'family religion'.[11] 'Household religion' helps convey the way religious activities were integral to and reflected in social and economic

---

10.   The word 'city' in English translations of the Bible is misleading, for the Hebrew term (*'îr*) usually designates walled towns that lacked truly urban functions and features. See Lenski 1984: 199–200; Frick 1997; Levine 1999; and Chapter 7 in this volume.

11.   For example, Albertz 1994 uses 'family religion', 'religious elements of early small family groups', 'family piety', 'subsidiary cult in the family', and 'personal piety'; he also uses 'domestic cult' (Albertz 2008: 97). Van der Toorn has recently admitted that 'household religion' might be a useful compromise, avoiding the limitations of 'domestic' or 'family' religion (van der Toorn 2004: 20); cf. Bodel and Olyan 2008b: 2–3 and Olyan 2008.

aspects of the Israelite household – agriculture, connection to ancestors, progeny to work and inherit the land, collective identity. Because divine powers were understood to affect both human and agricultural fertility, religious activities directed to the household's god(s) were considered essential for household viability and continuity.

Just who was the deity or deities involved in Israelite household religion? Tracing the history of Israelite beliefs is a major scholarly concern (e.g. Gnuse 1997; M.S. Smith 2002, 2004) but will not be part of this discussion, which instead will focus on the activities directed towards the supernatural realm and the compelling reasons for those activities. Belief in divine powers would hardly have existed apart from actions directed toward them, for religion involves not only belief in one or more supernatural beings but also a set of practices or rituals often meant to influence them (cf. Cavanagh 1978: 116–19; Zevit 2001: 11–17; Stowers 2008: 8–10). Focusing on beliefs or doctrinal systems, following the model of Christianity, is inadequate for the study of many ancient peoples, the Israelites included (van der Toorn 2004), just as the focus on national practices reveals little of the religious lives of most people in their own households. Religious practices tend to be very conservative; and it is likely that the activities described here would have changed little, even as the god(s) to whom they were directed changed.[12]

2.2 Sources of Information about Household Religion

The materiality of many religious activities means that some of them leave traces in the archaeological record. Archaeological data are thus a rich resource for studying household religion, although interpreting them is not always a straightforward enterprise. Texts from neighbouring cultures are also important resources, as are anthropological data and models.[13] Finally, the Hebrew Bible itself does provide information.

Archaeological data are not as plentiful as might be expected, given the enormous amount of fieldwork that has been carried out in the lands mentioned in the Hebrew Bible. The Hebrew Bible focuses on national matters; and the agenda of the text has often set the agenda of expeditions, which tend to excavate the cities and larger towns rather than the small agricultural settlements in which most people lived. Moreover, although hundreds of rural sites have been identified in the past two decades, archaeologists have been more concerned with dating them than with systematically excavating individual domestic units. But the picture isn't entirely bleak. Archaeologists rarely dig *only* for monumental structures and so have also recovered domestic buildings; and a number of field projects have endeavoured to excavate small agricultural settlements of the period of the Hebrew Bible.[14]

Thus various artefacts that can be associated with household religious practices have been discovered although identifying them as such is not a straightforward task. For example, some – such as lamps and vessels for offerings – are the same as those with

---

12.   This does not preclude the existence of individual variations among households within a shared framework of common practices.

13.   Anthropological models and ethnographic analogues are key to the interpretative process and are mentioned below.

14.   That is, the Iron Age (c. 1200–587 BCE), Persian period (587–332 BCE) and early Hellenistic period (332–141 BCE). Most materials mentioned in this chapter date to the periods identified with pre-monarchic times (1200–1000 BCE) and the Israelite and Judahite monarchies (c. 1000–587 BCE), which correspond to the Iron I and Iron II periods, respectively.

'secular' functions.[15] Even items such as incense burners, usually considered cultic[16] because they are found in identifiable religious shrines, were also used for mundane, odour-dispelling purposes.[17] However, certain items (figurines, amulets, ceramic stands, model shrines, anthropomorphic and zoomorphic vessels, and probably chalices and miniature vessels) are generally considered cultic wherever they are found. Often it is an assemblage or cluster of artefacts that would not normally be found together, especially if some of them are specifically cultic, that suggests religious activities. These activities are linked to the nature of the artefacts – providing food offerings, pouring libations, burning incense, and lighting lamps.[18] Yet the specific occasion for using this array of activities in household religion cannot readily be determined; and it is likely that they were used together on many occasions.[19]

Areas in household settings dedicated exclusively to religious activities are rare. Rooms with raised benches – as at Ai, Lachish, and Megiddo (Zevit 2001: 153–56, 212–17, 227–50) – perhaps served cultic functions. However, it is not certain that the putative cult rooms at Ai and Lachish were in domestic structures, and the one at Megiddo is probably a small temple. More promising are so-called 'cult corners', areas of rooms or courtyards in which cultic artefacts were found. The relatively small Iron Age domiciles associated with Israelites rarely had areas used solely for one purpose; rather, the use of household space shifted during the course of the day or from season to season depending on the tasks to be performed or activities to be carried out. The discovery of cultic items along with the artefacts of food processing or consumption, for example, indicates the multipurpose character of a given household space. An excellent example is a room in an Iron II dwelling at Tell Halif, where artefacts of food preparation, food consumption and ritual/religious activity were found in close proximity (Hardin forthcoming). Note that Judges 17, which indicates the presence of cultic objects in a household shrine, represents a well-to-do family (Ackerman 2008: 135–36) and should not be taken to indicate that there was dedicated cultic space in all households.

Another important resource is the corpus of texts from the Canaanite city of Ugarit (Ras Shamra), located on the Mediterranean coast in Syria and prominent especially in the Late Bronze Age (1550–1200 BCE), the period immediately preceding the emergence of ancient Israel. Because much of Israelite culture seems to have developed from Canaanite culture, information from Ugaritic texts plays a significant role in biblical scholarship.[20] For this chapter, information in Ugaritic texts about mortuary practices is especially relevant.

15.   On identifying cultic artefacts, see Holladay 1987: 251, 275 and Zevit 2001: 81, 267.

16.   'Cult' and 'cultic' designate religious practice and observance, or more widely, the entire religious culture of a people. (This differs from the contemporary use of the terms to refer to religious groups considered out of the mainstream and usually viewed negatively.)

17.   An exception may be the 'four-horned altar', arguably a specifically ritual object and thus a reliable marker of sacred space (Gitin 2002).

18.   As suggested by the assemblage found at Tell Jawa (Daviau 2001: 221–23).

19.   Note that these activities are the same as those performed at the national shrine, conceptually YHWH's domicile, and probably constitute a basic ritual pattern in the ancient Near East whereby providing for the deity secured divine presence and the accompanying benefits; see Meyers 2005a: 220–23, 231–32, 248–49. Indeed, temple praxis may, to a certain extent, be family praxis writ large (Stowers 2008: 12).

20.   The striking connections between Israelite and Canaanite culture suggests that at least

Anthropological resources are helpful in several ways. For one thing, archaeologists are heavily dependent on ethnography for interpreting and understanding material remains. Especially useful is ethnoarchaeology, which studies living traditional communities in order to learn how excavated artefacts and structures might be used (Carter 1997). Ethnography also provides information about the range of religious activities in households of traditional cultures. For example, if it is typical for agrarian people to have household rituals and festivals related to their agricultural calendar, it becomes possible to posit such activities for the Israelites in addition to ones that entailed national celebrations. Just as important is the contemporary anthropological perspective on religion, which acknowledges that religion and magic – the latter often viewed as deviant or even anti-religious – were not necessarily oppositional categories in the ancient world.[21] Thus many household religious practices considered magical should be recognized as significant aspects of Israelite religious culture.

Finally, although the Hebrew Bible does not provide specific guidelines for household religion, it is hardly devoid of relevant information. In fact, biblical texts are virtually the only source of information about many of the religious phenomena to be discussed. It is important to remember, however, that because biblical texts come from a wide time-span, a given verse may not reflect practices or beliefs that existed throughout the biblical period. Similarly, biblical texts may reflect the activities of some Israelites but not necessarily all of them. Thus the extent in time and space to which the household religious practices described here existed in ancient Israel remains uncertain. Nevertheless, they may well have been part of household life for much of the biblical period because, as already noted, religious practices (apart from the associated beliefs) tend to be conservative.

3
Household Religious Practices

The importance of certain activities, perhaps better termed *rituals*, in household religion cannot be overstated. Although perhaps inflated, the claim that ritual acts are not only universal aspects of religion but constitute 'the single most important characteristic of any living religiousness' (Pilgrim 1978: 64) has merit. Religious activities constitute the lived religious experience of the sacred. In addition, traditional religious behaviours provide essential psychological and social functions for their practitioners, linking them to the divine power(s) believed to affect their lives and also stabilizing and solidifying the collective identity of the group to which they belong.[22]

Household religious practice can be examined according to several types: 1) regular religious activities geared to the natural season or calendar; 2) recurring activities related to the human life cycle; and 3) activities that occur sporadically and might be considered crisis or interventional acts. All were part of Israel's central (and probably

some of the Israelites were originally Canaanites; see, for example, Dever 1993, Finkelstein 2007 and Chapter 3 in this volume.

21.   To avoid the pejorative term 'magic', some instead use 'ritual power' to designate methods to influence suprahuman powers or acquire suprahuman knowledge (e.g. Meyer and Mirecki 1995).

22.   See, *inter alia*, Bell's discussion (1997: 3–60) of the origins and function of ritual.

regional) shrines and 'national' or group religious life. However, the household setting is arguably where most people would have experienced them most of the time.

3.1 Regular Religious Activities (Seasonal, Weekly, Daily)[23]

Like virtually all agricultural peoples, ancient Israel had festivals and ceremonies associated with cycles of harvesting and of raising herd animals. Biblical tradition historicizes these events; for example, the Passover links memories of the Exodus with spring agricultural festivals.[24] Yet the core agricultural processes clearly determined the place of Israel's three major festivals – the feasts of Passover, Weeks and Booths (e.g. Deut. 16.1-17; cf. Exod. 23.14-17; Lev. 23.4-25) – in the annual calendar. Although Leviticus and especially Deuteronomy depict these events as pilgrim festivals, with all people enjoined to bring the appropriate offerings to the central (Jerusalem) shrine,[25] these festivals not only originated in household celebrations, but also probably continued to be celebrated by households even after their possible centralization late in the Iron Age and their subsequent historicization.

That Passover originated as a household celebration can be deduced from Exodus 12, which mentions individual households joining together if they are too small to consume in one evening the entire lamb to be sacrificed for this occasion (vv. 1–4) and to be eaten inside one's dwelling (v. 46). Pragmatic reasons – the impossibility of all Israelites leaving their homes for over a week and of one city accommodating such an influx – as well as the household setting for Passover celebrations in post-biblical times, suggest that Passover was a household festival throughout the biblical period. Similar information about household origins is not available for the other two pilgrim feasts (but see Neh 8.16), yet their analogous connection to key points in the farming calendar suggests that they too were ancient agricultural celebrations that became linked to the Hebrew Bible's master narrative of deliverance from servitude, wilderness sojourn and Sinai covenant.

These annual festivals entailed sacrifices, and sacrificial altars were readily constructed wherever needed. A multiplicity of legitimate sacrificial altars, convenient to any and every household, are mentioned in Exod. 20.24. Genesis portrays the ancestors as offerants at altars that they construct on their land wherever they settle (Gen. 13.3-4, 18; 26.25; 33.19-20; 35.1). Similarly, Samson's parents present an animal and grain offering on a rock, presumably in a field that was part of their household (Judg. 13.19-23).

---

23.   Although not considered here, the seventh-year Sabbatical (with farm lands lying fallow) and especially the fiftieth-year Jubilee (with the restoration of any land a household may have sold), if historical, had a sacral dimension as well as socio-economic functions that benefited household patrimonies; see Leviticus 25 and Milgrom 2001: *ad loc.*

24.   The paschal (Passover) lamb likely originates in the transfer of herd animals to their summer pastures and the unleavened bread (matzoh) in the sprouting of the first grains (Meyers 2005a: 95–104).

25.   Wives – but not daughters, female servants and widows – seem to be omitted from the Deuteronomic directives (Deut. 16.11, 14); and Deut. 16.16 requires only males to participate in the pilgrimage festivals. Yet women are not forbidden to attend; and the directives addressed to the senior male in a household probably include the wife as part of a conjugal pair (Meyers 2008). In Deut. 31.10-12 all the people, including women, are enjoined to attend the Booths festival in the seventh year. Overall, it is significant that these festivals are still depicted as celebrations by household groups, even if at a remove from their domiciles.

The biblical emphasis on sacrifice along with information from ethnographic data and Canaanite texts suggests that the activities associated with the major festivals centred on animal (bloody) sacrifice. Sacrifices meant feasting. Only one of the sacrifices mentioned in the Hebrew Bible was fully burnt; the rest provided a special meal for the offerants.[26] The slaughter of an animal for food was not an ordinary event, and eating meat at the time of elation over crop or animal yields increased its emotional value. A sacrifice also conceptually meant the sharing of a meal with the deity. This religious dimension of a meat-eating household event, whether held at a communal shrine or on household property, would be all the more significant as an expression of thanksgiving for crops and animals. Whenever and wherever the historicized aspect of these three festivals became operant, celebrating them took on the added dimension of commemorating Israel's *Heilsgeschichte*, instilling in their participants a sense of belonging to a common past, and so promulgating social solidarity and a sense of community.[27]

Other household feasts likely took place monthly. The new moon, which was fundamental to the reckoning of time in the ancient Near East, marked the miraculous re-emergence of the moon after weeks of gradual disappearance; it is no wonder that lunar celebrations are widely attested (Hallo 1977: 4–9). The new moon celebration, apparently a popular Israelite festival heralded by trumpet blasts (Num. 10.10; Ps. 81.4 [ET v. 3]), involved sacrifices at the Jerusalem temple (2 Chron. 8.12-13) and was widely celebrated along with festivals and Sabbaths (Hos. 2.13 [ET v. 11]; Amos 8.5). Just as the major festivals and Sabbath (see below) were rooted in household observance, so too the new moon observance was surely a household festival (Levine 2000: 405). Indeed, the priestly regulations in Num. 28.11-15, unlike those for the three major festivals, do not call the new moon observance a 'sanctuary convocation', a designation for events requiring the community to gather at the central shrine. A family feast in the royal household at the new moon is anticipated by Jonathan and David, but David instead celebrates with his own family in Bethlehem (1 Sam. 20.5-29). The new moon sacrificial offerings at the temple likely echo regional clan and local household offerings and concomitant feasting, perhaps to honour deceased ancestors (see below) as well as to celebrate the new moon.

Weekly celebrations are not found elsewhere in the ancient Near East; and most scholars consider the Sabbath an Israelite innovation, perhaps out of humanitarian concern for those engaged in the arduous work of agrarians (Meyers 2005a: 132–33). Although priestly texts mention Sabbath offerings at the central shrine (Num. 28.9-10), the directives in the Decalogue (Exod. 20.8-11; Deut. 5.12-15) and elsewhere (e.g. Exod. 23.12; Lev. 23.2-3) assume household observation of the Sabbath. Again, as for the festivals and new moon, festal meals in the household were likely the counterpart of (or model for?) sacrifices at the shrine. The manna narrative in Exodus 16 centres upon the availability of food for the Sabbath; and, with work ceasing even in the labour-intensive period of planting and harvesting (Exod. 34.21), a special family meal was likely. The Sabbath is linked to God's rescue of Israel from Egypt (Deut. 5.15) and to God's creation of the world (Exod. 20.11), and one or both of those commemorative

---

26. Sacrifices made at a shrine having priestly personnel also involved providing meat for the officiants (priests).

27. Hayden 2001 explores the functions of feasting, and Dietler and Hayden 2001 provide ethnographic examples. See also MacDonald 2008b.

conceptions likely enhanced the religious meaning of household Sabbath observance. In addition, the Sabbath meal (like those at annual or monthly festivals) likely entailed the consumption of special foods, perhaps even prestige items such as meat, thus heightening the celebratory nature of the household meal.[28]

Another type of regular household observance is related to the fact that the festivals, new moons and Sabbath all entailed sacrifices and correlate festal meals in the household. That is, food consumption probably had religious meaning on a daily basis too. As for all peoples, foodways were part of Israelite identity; and choices of what to eat and what to avoid became part of the dietary regulations of Leviticus and Deuteronomy by the late Iron Age or Persian period. Thus, even though they originated much earlier as part of a complex set of features of the political economy (see Hesse and Wapnish 1997 and Finkelstein 1997: 227–30), the foodways of at least some segment of the Israelite population were imbued with religious meaning. Dietary patterns reflect deep forms of human culture according to the views of anthropological modernism (noted by Hendel 2008), and the mundane act of food consumption can encode cultural values and be considered part of lived religion. In her consideration of culinary meanings, Mary Douglas puts it this way: 'a very strong analogy between table and altar stares us in the face' (1999: 241). Similarly, Jonathan Z. Smith describes ways in which ordinary meals 'are routinely "marked" as religious' (2004: 327).

Thus a hierarchy can be identified in the meals of Israelite households – triannual festivals, monthly new moons, weekly Sabbaths, and daily food consumption. No doubt the most emotion-laden and heightened in terms of religious experience lay at the top of the hierarchy, but all activities surrounding the preparation and consumption of food were theoretically imbued with religious values that embodied both cosmic order and social identity.

3.2 Recurring Activities Related to the Human Life Cycle

Just as peoples everywhere mark seasonal and lunar cycles with religious practices, so too do they mark passages or transitions in the life cycle. For the Israelites, the beginning and end of a person's life were especially significant. Although religious ceremonies are part of marriage as a life-cycle event in many cultures, such appears not to have been the case for ancient Near Eastern peoples, the Israelites included; and so it is not considered here.[29] Puberty rituals are also common across cultures, but the typical *rite de passage* of circumcision was part of Israelite birth rituals, perhaps uniquely so, and thus will be mentioned in relation to reproductive religious practices.

Having children, unlike in present-day Western cultures, was not a matter of choice for the Israelites. Children were essential for the agricultural work upon which survival depended. They were also needed to care for elderly parents. And, as already indicated, (male) offspring were required to inherit their household's patrimony. Yet reproduction in the biblical world was fraught with difficulties. Infertility, infant mortality,

---

28.   Meat-eating was rare in the pre-monarchic period and toward the end of the monarchy, and the somewhat greater incidence of meat-eating in the interim centuries was probably restricted to urban elites (MacDonald 2008a: 75, 78–79).

29.   Marriage as a specifically religious institution in Judeo-Christian culture probably begins in the medieval period (Yalom 2001: 45–55). However, the apparent absence of explicitly religious marriage rites in the ancient Near East does not preclude the possibility that matrimony was experienced religiously (van der Toorn 1994: 59–60).

childbirth complications causing maternal death, and lactation problems all threatened the vitality of the household. Divine power was believed to help with conception, safe pregnancy and birth, and successful care of newborns. Religious activities thus were surely part of each stage of the childbearing process. In this ancient context, religious reproductive behaviours can be considered strategies, like the preventative and restorative medical procedures of the modern world, to achieve reproductive success (Meyers 2005b: 17). Although the actual details of these practices are not always clear, archaeological and ethnographic data as well as ancient Near Eastern magico-medical texts indicate a rich assortment of religious behaviours, carried out mainly by women, meant to gain the benevolent and protective presence of divine power and avert malevolent and destructive demonic forces.

Reproductive rituals included the use of sacrifice at a shrine or offerings in the domicile, along with prayer, to achieve conception (Gen. 25.21; Judg. 13.2-24; 1 Sam. 1.1-20).[30] The small terracotta pillar figurines showing a nude woman holding her breasts and found in many Iron Age households (and tombs, see below) were likely votive figurines used in household rituals to assure successful reproduction (Meyers 2007). Amulets depicting the Egyptian dwarf god Bes or the eye of the god Horus and frequently found at Iron Age sites probably represent Israelite appropriation of well-known powerful symbols thought to be especially protective of pregnant women and newborns. Red threads, mentioned in Gen. 38.28 and known from Mesopotamian texts and ethnographic data, similarly were considered protective, as was shiny jewellery. Lamplight too was thought to keep away the demonic powers associated with darkness and believed to threaten mothers and infants; this may be one reason that lamps are frequently part of household cultic assemblages. Metal blades found in households served utilitarian functions and also, as indicated by ethnographic and iconographic data, were wielded outside birthing rooms to scare away dangerous forces. Newborns were washed, smeared with ointment, and swaddled (Ezek. 16.4), all protective procedures considered religious and persisting into the twentieth century among Christian, Jewish and Muslim women in the Middle East. That naming of children was also a religious event is indicated by the theophoric component of so many Israelite names (Albertz 2006 and Chapter 9 in this volume).

The apotropaic character of many of the religious practices surrounding reproduction is likely a feature of circumcision, performed on male infants on the eighth day (Gen. 17.12; Lev. 12.3), presented in the Hebrew Bible as a distinguishing mark of membership in the covenant community (Gen. 17.9-14; cf. Josh. 5.1–8). However, the enigmatic episode recounted in Exod. 4.24-26, in which Moses' wife Zipporah circumcises her son and uses the bloody foreskin to avert mortal danger, may reflect a hoary protective aspect of this procedure (Meyers 2005a: 62–67). The mass circumcision of Joshua 5 mentions no shrine, and the emphasis in Genesis 17 (cf. Exod. 12.43-49) on the circumcision of all male household members suggests it was a household rite.

End-of-life household practices, none of which were performed at a shrine, have drawn considerable attention. Scholars have used archaeological remains, Ugaritic texts, and biblical verses to examine funerary customs and beliefs about the existence of the deceased.[31] Like all peoples, the Israelites had a variety of mourning and

---

30.   See Meyers 2005b for details about these and other reproductive rituals mentioned.

31.   See Lewis 1989, 2002; Bloch-Smith 1992; and Olyan 2004 for references to the extensive literature on this subject and to relevant biblical texts.

burial customs, which may have differed over time and among different sectors of the population. The biblical prohibitions against certain mourning customs, such as shaving the head or gashing the body (e.g. Lev. 21.5; Deut. 14.1; but cf. Isa. 15.2-3; Mic. 1.16), reflect practices acceptable to some but not to others. Yet some mourning customs – the rending of garments, the donning of mourners' garb, and perhaps fasting (2 Sam. 1.11-12; 3.31) – were probably found in all households for the week of intense mourning (Gen. 50.10). Rolling in ashes may also have been common (Jer. 6.26) as was the singing of laments, usually by women (Jer. 9.17-20).[32]

Rapid interment in the family tomb was *de rigueur* (Olyan 2005). Many Israelites in the Iron II period – perhaps only those who could afford them – were buried in rock-cut or cave tombs that were re-used for generations (Bloch-Smith 1992: *passim*). These tombs may be reflected in the Genesis 23 narrative about Abraham acquiring a tomb-cave along with considerable land and in biblical language referring to death as being gathered to one's people (Gen. 25.8; 35.29; 49.33). The family tomb was an integral part of the concept of the household's inheritance, or landholdings; and connection with deceased forebears was instrumental for maintaining the patrimonial claim to property (Brichto 1973; Stager 1985: 22; van der Toorn 1996: 233–35; Stavrakopoulou forthcoming). Israelite views about what happens to the deceased have been much debated, but most scholars now recognize that dead ancestors were believed to exist in some shadowy state (as 1 Sam. 28.3-25).[33] Tomb goods typically include an assortment of vessels for food and drink offerings, which were part of the burial rite and may also have served as provisions for the deceased, perhaps offered monthly at the new moon celebration mentioned above (van der Toorn 1996: 218). Providing for the dead, viewed unfavourably in Deut. 26.14, indicates the conception that the dead not only survived, but also could be of assistance to the living, perhaps to aid in reproductive matters, judging from the presence of pillar-figurines in tombs, and to help restore health to ill descendants. The latter function is possible because the dead are sometimes called Rephaim (e.g. Ps. 88.11 [ET v. 10]), which can mean 'healers' rather than NRSV 'shades' (van der Toorn 1996: 231–32).[34]

Household practices focusing on deceased ancestors are sometimes called a 'cult of the dead'. This designation does not mean that the ancestors were considered deities in their own right and venerated as such. The term *ʾĕlōhîm*, which often denotes the God of Israel, can also designate an ancestor as a preternatural being (1 Sam. 28.13; Isa. 8.19) but not a fully fledged deity (Lewis 1989: 49–51, 115–16). Also, the household *tĕrāpîm* of Gen. 31.19, 34-35 (NRSV 'gods') and 1 Sam. 19.16 (NRSV 'idol') may well have been representations of departed ancestors who had important roles in maintaining intergenerational connections and household property rights but were not the same as deities (van der Toorn 1990).

---

32.   A funerary feast to console mourners may have been held at a community *bêt marzēaḥ* or 'house of mourning' (Jer. 16.5-9; cf. Amos 6.7 [NRSV 'revelry']). The nature of this custom is a matter of considerable debate; see, for example, McLaughlin 2001, who perhaps is overly cautious in concluding that it lacked explicit funerary connections.

33.   The partial vitality of the dead is related to the potential for bodily resurrection, an idea reflected in a number of biblical texts (Levenson 2006).

34.   In Ugaritic texts (and perhaps in some biblical verses), the Rephaim enable the birth of progeny (Liwak 2004). On the Rephaim, see Chapter 5 in this volume.

3.3 Occasional Activities: Crisis or Interventional Acts

In addition to seasonal and life-cycle events, some religious activities were ad hoc practices, carried out in relation to biological processes, contaminations, disease and other issues of immediate concern. Because biblical references, mainly in priestly texts, constitute the major source for these procedures, it is impossible to ascertain when and how widely they were practised.

A number of procedures deal with the impurity, considered a crisis in priestly perspective, associated with uncontrollable situations: infections, bodily discharges and contact with unclean items including corpses.[35] The 'infection' of a house with fungus growths, which were considered ominous portents for its occupants, was perhaps the only circumstance in which a priest visited a household.[36] The summoned priest carried out or supervised elaborate procedures, from quarantine to demolition, and purification rites (Lev. 14.34-53). Another set of purification procedures dealt with impurities related to sexuality (Lev. 12.2-8; 15). Normal female and male genital discharges necessitated purificatory measures – washing bodies and laundering clothes and other items – for affected persons and any who had contact with them; these procedures were carried out in the household. Abnormal genital discharges and lochia required similar household procedures and also sacrifices at the shrine. Interventions for people or household items that touched 'unclean animals' required only appropriate washing in the household (Lev. 11.24-40; cf. 22.5-9). Finally, impurity caused by contact with corpses was resolved in the household after seven days by bathing and laundering and by sprinkling corpse-contaminated persons and objects with water containing ashes from a burnt offering (Numbers 19; see Levine 1993: 457–79).

Various kinds of distress (including illness and infertility) impelled people to seek relief in several ways (see Meyers 1999). Some used magico-medicinal substances (2 Kgs 20.7 = Isa. 38.21) and perhaps the service of professional healers or prophets (1 Kgs 17.17-24; 2 Kgs 4.32-37). These magico-religious modes served functions handled in the modern world by medicine (which doesn't preclude the use of prayer). Appealing to deceased ancestors as healers (mentioned above) was also a way to seek relief from distress. Another way was to make binding vows, which were conditional promises to the deity that would be fulfilled when and if the deity granted the accompanying request for the alleviation of a problem (Cartledge 1992: 12). The Hebrew Bible is replete with references to vow-making, suggesting it was widespread among Israelites as among other ancient Near Eastern peoples. Vows were made in households if the distress – problems such as illness or human or agricultural infertility – was experienced there (Albertz 2008: 100). Vowed items were typically offered at community shrines (e.g. Deut. 12.6; Ps. 66.13-14); but the location is often unspecified (e.g. Prov. 7.14) and may at times have been at household shrines (see Jer. 19.13; 44.17-19, 25 and Ackerman 2000). Closely related to vows were oaths – blessings or curses – made with positive or negative intent. In either case, appeal was made to the deity to take some desired action against or for another. Because these oaths were considered efficacious, they served as a warning or a good omen to an implicated person (see Judg. 17.2-3). Distress was also the motivation for petitionary practices resembling

35.   Milgrom 1991: *ad loc.* and Appendix F explains the impurity system and rituals mentioned here.

36.   Purificatory rites for infected people or items meant taking them to the shrine (Lev. 13.2–14.32; cf. Num. 5.1-2).

mourning rites (Olyan 2004: 21–27, 62–110). They could occur on a 'national' level, typically at a shrine (e.g. Ezra 9.1–10.1); but petitionary mourning occurred in households or wherever people experienced difficulties, as when Hezekiah turns his face to the wall and petitions YHWH for healing from a mortal affliction (2 Kgs 20.1-3).

Procedures for dealing with impurity were performed on individuals (and houses and household items); and vows, oaths, and petitionary mourning were made by individuals and may be considered acts of personal piety. Yet all these practices concerned issues that affected, directly or indirectly, the well-being and stability of the households of which the individuals, structures and items were part and thus are within the realm of household religion.

4
Summary

The Hebrew Bible presents religious activities from the top down. It provides much information about 'national' practices at the top of the socio-political pyramid but little about the practices of the myriad of households comprising the bottom. Yet practices involving virtually all people took place in the household, which was the fundamental unit of society. Thus examining its religious practices reveals a critically important dimension of life in ancient Israel. Using biblical references, archaeological discoveries, and anthropological (especially ethnographic) data and theory, it is possible to identify a rich sequence of regular religious activities carried out over the course of a year and in a lifetime as well as a variety of procedures performed occasionally as needed.

These activities, many of which involved the hope for, acquisition of and consumption of life-sustaining substances (food and drink), served to define the identity of the participants, establish their place within larger social groups, and bring them into contact with the supernatural power(s) believed to impact natural and human events. Many others helped people deal with physical and emotional distress. Whatever the form or function of these practices, they entailed experiencing the sacred. They can be considered transformative moments through which Israelites make sense of aspects of life that otherwise would have seemed chaotic and beyond their control. The emotional quality of both joyful and sorrowful occasions had psychological and social value. And, to the extent that many of these household activities were celebratory, they provided a major way for Israelites to enjoy the company of kin and the fruits of their not inconsiderable labour.

Bibliography

Ackerman, S.
2000   'Queen of Heaven', in C. Meyers, T. Craven and R. S. Kraemer (eds), *Women in Scripture: A Dictionary of Named and Unnamed Women in the Hebrew Bible, the Apocryphal/Deuterocanonical Books, and the New Testament* (Boston, MA: Houghton Mifflin), 538–39.
2008   'Household Religion, Family Religion, and Women's Religion in Ancient Israel', in J. Bodel and S.M. Olyan (eds), *Household and Family Religion in Antiquity* (Oxford: Blackwell), 127–58.

Albertz, R.
1994   *A History of Israelite Religion in the Old Testament Period* (2 vols; trans. J. Bowden; Louisville, KY: Westminster/John Knox).
2006   'Ritual Setting and Religious Significance of Birth in Ancient Israel', Paper given at the annual meeting of the European Association of Biblical Studies, Piliscaba, Hungary.
2008   'Family Religion in Ancient Israel and its Surroundings', in J. Bodel and S.M. Olyan (eds), *Household and Family Religion in Antiquity* (Oxford: Blackwell), 89–112.

Bell, C.M.
1997   *Ritual: Perspectives and Dimensions* (New York, NY, and Oxford: Oxford University Press). Online: http://www.netlibrary.com/Details.aspx (accessed 30 June 2008).

Bendor, S.
1996   *The Social Structure of Ancient Israel: The Institution of the Family* (beit 'ab) *from the Settlement to the End of the Monarchy* (Jerusalem Biblical Studies 7; Jerusalem: Sinor).

Bloch-Smith, E.
1992   *Judahite Burial Practices and Beliefs about the Dead* (JSOTS 123; Sheffield: JSOT Press).

Bodel, J. and S.M. Olyan (eds)
2008a   *Household and Family Religion in Antiquity* (Oxford: Blackwell).
2008b   'Introduction', in J. Bodel and S. M. Olyan (eds), *Household and Family Religion in Antiquity* (Oxford: Blackwell), 1–19.

Brichto, H.
1973   'Kin, Cult, Land and Afterlife – A Biblical Complex', *HUCA* 44: 1–54.

Carter, C.E.
1997   'Ethnoarchaeology', *OEANE* 2.280–84.

Cartledge, T.W.
1992   *Vows in the Hebrew Bible and the Ancient Near East* (JSOTS 147; Sheffield: JSOT Press).

Cavanagh, R.R.
1978   'The term "religion"', in T.W. Hall (ed.), *Introduction to the Study of Religion* (New York, NY: Harper & Row), 1–19.

Daviau, P.M.M.
2001   'Family Religion: Evidence for the Paraphernalia of the Domestic Cult', in P.M.M. Daviau, J.W. Wevers and M. Weigl (eds), *The World of the Arameans II* (JSOTS 325; Sheffield: Sheffield Academic Press), 199–229.

Dever, W.G.
1993   'Cultural Continuity, Ethnicity in the Archaeological Record, and the Question of Israelite Origins', *ErIsr* 24: 22*–33*.

Dietler, M. and B. Hayden (eds)
2001   *Feasts: Archaeological and Ethnographic Perspectives on Food, Politics, and Power* (Washington, DC: Smithsonian Institution).

Di Vito, R.A.
1999   'Old Testament Anthropology and the Construction of Personal Identity', *CBQ* 61: 217–38.

Douglas, M.
1999   'Deciphering a Meal', in *Implicit Meanings: Selected Essays in Anthropology* (2nd edn; London: Routledge), 231–51; first published in *Daedalus* 101 (1972), 61–81.

Finkelstein, I.
1997   'Pots and People Revisited: Ethnic Boundaries in Iron Age I', in N.A. Silberman and D. Small (eds), *The Archaeology of Israel: Constructing the Past, Interpreting the Present* (JSOTS 237; Sheffield: Sheffield Academic Press), 216–37.
2007   'When and How did the Israelites Emerge?', in I. Finkelstein and A. Mazar, *The Quest*

for the Historical Israel: Debating Archaeology and the History of Israel* (Atlanta, GA: Society of Biblical Literature), 73–83.

Frick, F.S.
1997   'Cities: An Overview', *OEANE* 2.4–19.

Friedman, R.E.
1992   'Tabernacle', *ABD* 6.292–300.

Fritz, V.
1997   'Cities of the Bronze and Iron Ages', *OEANE* 2.19–24.

Gitin, S.
2002   'The Four-Horned Altar and Sacred Space: An Archaeological Perspective', in B.M. Gittlen (ed.), *Sacred Time Sacred Place: Archaeology and the Religion of Israel* (Winona Lake, IN: Eisenbrauns), 95–123.

Gnuse, R.K.
1997   *No Other Gods: Emergent Monotheism in Israel* (Sheffield: Sheffield Academic Press).

Gottwald, N.K.
1979   *The Tribes of Yahweh: A Sociology of the Religion of Liberated Israel, 1250–1050 BCE* (Maryknoll, NY: Orbis).

Hallo, W.W.
1977   'New Moons and Sabbaths', *HUCA* 48: 1–18.

Hardin, J.W.
Forthcoming   *Households and the Use of Domestic Space at Iron II Tell Halif: An Archaeology of Destruction. Reports of the Lahav Research Project Excavations at Tell Halif, Israel,* vol. 2 (Winona Lake, IN: Eisenbrauns).

Hayden, B.
2001   'Fabulous Feasts: A Prolegomenon to the Importance of Feasting', in M. Dietler and B. Hayden (eds), *Feasts: Archaeological and Ethnographic Perspectives on Food, Politics, and Power* (Washington, DC: Smithsonian Institution), 23–64.

Hendel, R.
2008   'Mary Douglas and Anthropological Modernism', *JHS* 8 (8): 1–13. Online: http://www.arts.ualberta.ca/JHS/Articles/article_85.pdf (accessed 30 April 2008).

Hesse, B., and P. Wapnish
1997   'Can Pig Remains Be Used for Ethnic Diagnosis in the Ancient Near East?', in N.A. Silberman and D. Small (eds), *The Archaeology of Israel: Constructing the Past, Interpreting the Present* (JSOTS 237; Sheffield: Sheffield Academic Press), 238–70.

Holladay J.S., Jr.
1987   'Religion in Israel and Judah under the Monarchy: An Explicitly Archaeological Approach', in P.D. Hanson, P.D. Miller and S.D. McBride (eds), *Ancient Israelite Religion: Essays in Honor of Frank Moore Cross* (Philadelphia, PA: Fortress Press), 249–99.

Johnston, S.I. (ed.)
2004   *Religions of the Ancient World – A Guide* (Cambridge, MA: Belknap Press of Harvard University Press).

Lenski, G.
1984   *Power and Privilege: A Theory of Social Stratification* (2nd edn; Chapel Hill, NC: University of North Carolina Press).

Levenson, J.D.
2006   *Resurrection and the Restoration of Israel: The Ultimate Victory of the God of Life* (New Haven, CT: Yale University Press).

Levine, B.A.
1993   *Numbers 1–20: A New Translation with Introduction and Commentary* (AB 4; New York, NY: Doubleday).
1999   'The Biblical "Town" as Reality and Typology: Evaluating Biblical References to Towns

and their Functions', in M. Hudson and B.A. Levine (eds), *Urbanization and Land Ownership in the Ancient Near East, Vol. II* (Cambridge, MA: Peabody Museum of Archaeology and Ethnology, Harvard University), 421–53.

2000 *Numbers 21–36: A New Translation with Introduction and Commentary* (AB 4A; New York, NY: Doubleday).

Lewis, T.J.
1989 *Cults of the Dead in Ancient Israel and Ugarit* (HSM 39; Atlanta, GA: Scholars Press).
2002 'How Far Can Texts Take Us? Evaluating Textual Sources for Reconstructing Israelite Beliefs about the Dead', in B.M. Gittlen (ed.), *Sacred Time, Sacred Place: Archaeology and the Religion of Israel* (Winona Lake, IN: Eisenbrauns), 169–217.

Liwak, R.
2004 'rᵉpā'îm', *TDOT* 13.602–14.

MacDonald, N.
2008a *What Did the Ancient Israelites Eat? Diet in Biblical Times* (Grand Rapids, MI: Eerdmans).
2008b *Not Bread Alone: The Uses of Food in the Old Testament* (Oxford: Oxford University Press).

McLaughlin, J.
2001 The *marzēaḥ* in the Prophetic Literature: References and Allusions in Light of the Extra-Biblical Evidence (VTS 86; Leiden: Brill).

McNutt, P.
1999 *Reconstructing the Society of Ancient Israel* (LAI; Louisville, KY: Westminster John Knox).

Meyer, M. and P. Mirecki
1995 'Introduction', in M. Meyer and P. Mirecki (eds), *Ancient Magic and Ritual Power* (Boston, MA: Brill), 1–8.

Meyers, C.
1999 'Wellness and Holiness in the Bible', in D.L. Freeman and J.Z. Abrams (eds), *Illness and Health in the Jewish Tradition: Writings from the Bible to Today* (Philadelphia, PA: Jewish Publication Society).
2005a *Exodus* (NCBC; New York, NY: Cambridge University Press).
2005b *Households and Holiness: The Religious Culture of Israelite Women* (Facet Series; Minneapolis, MN: Fortress Press).
2007 'Terracottas without Texts: Judean Pillar Figurines in Anthropological Perspective', in R.B. Coote and N.K. Gottwald (eds), *To Break Every Yoke: Essays in Honor of Marvin L. Chaney* (Social World of Biblical Antiquity Second Series 3; Sheffield: Sheffield Phoenix), 115–30.
2008 'Another View [on R'eih, Deut 11:26–16:17]', in T.C. Eskenazi and A.L. Weiss (eds), *The Torah: A Woman's Commentary* (New York, NY: URJ Press), 1134.

Milgrom, J.
1991 *Leviticus 1–16: A New Translation with Introduction and Commentary* (AB 3; New York, NY: Doubleday).
2001 *Leviticus 23–27: A New Translation with Introduction and Commentary* (AB 3B; New York, NY: Doubleday).

Olyan, S.M.
2004 *Biblical Mourning: Ritual and Social Dimensions* (Oxford: Oxford University Press).
2005 'Some Neglected Aspects of Israelite Interment Ideology', *JBL* 124: 601–16.
2008 'Family Religion in Israel and the Wider Levant of the First Millennium BCE', in J. Bodel and S.M. Olyan (eds), *Household and Family Religion in Antiquity* (Oxford: Blackwell), 113–36.

Pilgrim, R.
1978   'Ritual', in T.W. Hall (ed.), *Introduction to the Study of Religion* (New York, NY: Harper& Row), 64–84.

Rapoport, A.
1994   'Spatial Organization and the Built Environment', in T. Ingold (ed.), *Companion Encyclopedia of Archaeology* (London: Routledge), 460–502.

Rogerson, J. W.
1989   'Anthropology of the Old Testament', in R.E. Clements (ed.), *The World of Ancient Israel: Sociological, Anthropological and Political Perspectives* (New York, NY: Cambridge University Press), 17–38.

Schloen, D.
2001   *The House of the Father as Fact and Symbol: Patrimonialism in Ugarit and the Ancient Near East* (Winona Lake, IN: Eisenbrauns).

Smith, J.Z.
2004   *Relating Religion: Essays on the Study of Religion* (Chicago, IL: University of Chicago Press).

Smith, M.S.
2002   *The Early History of God: Yahweh and the Other Deities in Ancient Israel* (2nd edn; Grand Rapids, MI: Eerdmans).
2004   *The Memoirs of God: History, Memory, and the Experience of the Divine in Ancient Israel* (Minneapolis, MN: Fortress Press).

Stager, L.E.
1985   'The Archaeology of the Family in Ancient Israel', *BASOR* 260: 1–35.

Stavrakopoulou, F.
Forthcoming   *Land of Our Fathers: The Roles of Ancestor Veneration in Biblical Land Claims* (New York, NY, and London: T&T Clark International).

Stowers, S.K.
2008   'Theorizing Religion of Ancient Households and Families', in J. Bodel and S.M. Olyan (eds), *Household and Family Religion in Antiquity* (Oxford: Blackwell), 5–19.

Toorn, K. van der
1990   'The Nature of the Biblical Teraphim in Light of the Cuneiform Evidence', *CBQ* 52: 1–54.
1994   *From Her Cradle to Her Grave: The Role of Religion in the Life of the Israelite and Babylonian Woman* (trans. S.J. Denning-Bolle; BS 23; Sheffield: JSOT Press).
1996   *Family Religion in Babylonia, Syria and Israel: Continuity and Change in the Forms of Religious Life* (SHCANE 7; Leiden: Brill).
2004   'Religious Practices of the Individual and Family: Introduction', in S.I. Johnston (ed.), *Religions of the Ancient World – A Guide* (Cambridge, MA: Belknap Press of Harvard University Press), 423–24.

Westbrook, R.
1991   *Property and the Family in Biblical Law* (JSOTS 113; Sheffield: JSOT Press).

Wilson, R.R.
1992   'Genealogy', *ABD* 2.929–32.

Yalom, M.
2001   *The History of the Wife* (New York, NY: Harper Collins).

Zevit, Z.
2001   *The Religions of Ancient Israel: A Synthesis of Parallactic Approaches* (New York, NY: Continuum).

Chapter 9

Personal Piety

Rainer Albertz

In biblical scholarship of the past, personal piety in ancient Israelite religion was often overlooked. In focusing on Israel as a 'sacral community' (von Rad 1962: 1.30, 399, 402) within which the individual was totally embedded, scholars understated or even denied the individual's relationship with the divine. In ancient Israel and Judah, people were not independent 'individuals' in the modern sense. Rather, each person was much more integrated in and dependent upon different social groups, such as the family, the clan, the local community and the 'people' at large. However, this does not negate the probability that people also had their own individual relationships with the divine. More recent investigations (Albertz 1978; van der Toorn 1996; Miller 2000; Gerstenberger 2001) have shown that the personal piety of family members constituted a specific stratum of beliefs and ritual practices within the religion of ancient Israel and Judah. Although interconnected with the broader religious context in many ways, family piety had its own religious and cultic focus (see Chapter 8 in this volume) and clearly differed from those theological concepts and cultic rituals promoted by the courts, central sanctuaries and religious functionaries. The latter represented 'official' religion and claimed to be valid for the people as a whole – that is, for the entirety of Israelite or Judahite society.[1] In Judah, it was not until the seventh century BCE that familial piety began to be increasingly controlled and more closely integrated into 'official' religion. It could be claimed that this kind of religious diversity, which I have called 'internal religious pluralism', is founded in the different basic needs of small (family) and large (people) societal groups; it is much more fundamental than all those diversities stemming from local, political, economical or educational variations and it can be observed in almost every religion, be it ancient or modern.

1
Sources for Personal Piety

One practical reason why familial personal piety has often been overlooked has to do with the sparseness of evidence for it. Most Hebrew Bible texts were written by

---

1.   However, according to Karel van der Toorn (1996: 338–72) personal piety in a stricter sense did not emerge before the destruction of the northern kingdom in the late eighth century BCE, when many clans and families lost their paternal estates and became refugees. He is right that an increasing individualization started from the late eighth century onwards, but this does not negate the probability that the family members had some kind of personal relationship with the divine before this point. Thus the difference is more a question of definition.

religious functionaries and address the needs of the entire people broadly designated 'Israel'. Only where the scribes deal with the life of Israelite families (as in the patriarchal history of Genesis 12–50) or the personal piety of their heroes (as in Judg. 15.18 and 1 Sam. 23.16) do we glimpse elements of personal piety, which may have been typical in the period when the narratives were composed. Given the literary character and educational purpose of most biblical texts, of course, we must be aware that personal piety is reflected here in an idealized form. But some individual ritual practices, which often diverge from the 'official concepts', can be reconstructed from the prophetic polemics against them (e.g. Jer. 2.27; 44.15-19; Ezek. 13.17-23; 14.1-11), and others from the prohibitions of Torah (e.g. Exod. 22.17; 23.14-19).

Unfortunately, there are only a few sources apart from the Hebrew Bible itself that could help us in reconstructing the personal piety of ancient Israel. We must be aware that most private prayers, vows, blessings and curses, magic spells and family rituals were likely never written down. The few that were recorded in writing have nearly all been lost, primarily because Israelites and Judahites tended to use papyrus sheets for their writings and these are rarely preserved given the wet climate in most regions of Palestine. Only a few inscriptions written on pottery or carved in the rock survive; these may represent private blessings (as at Kuntillet 'Ajrud and Khirbet el-Qom). Apart from these rare inscriptions, hundreds of ritual objects such as cult stands, censers, libation juglets and figurines have been found in private houses and graves, which well attest a domestic cult and a care for the dead in ancient Israel and Judah during all periods. More specifically revealing of personal piety are masses of amulets mostly shaped in an Egyptian style. Nonetheless, compared with the findings in ancient Mesopotamia or Egypt, where many kinds of private rituals and spells for birth or healing are recorded, our access to ancient Israelite and Judahite personal piety is very limited.

There are three main sources from the Hebrew Bible and the archaeological findings that offer us limited access to individuals' personal beliefs. The first is the theophoric personal names recorded on seals, bullae and ostraca, or in the Hebrew Bible. Many biblical texts (e.g. Gen. 16.11, 15; 29.31–30.24; 35.17-18; 1 Sam. 1.20) suggest that naming in ancient Israel and Judah was much less a matter of fashion than in modern societies. Rather, it was an expression of personal experience during the long and dangerous processes of pregnancy and birth. Personal names offer scholars direct and untainted access to the positive core of the individual beliefs of the parents, often those of the mother. The second source is constituted by the individual lament and thanksgiving psalms in the Hebrew Bible, including oracles of salvation. Although in their present form they probably reflect later periods and were likely stylized by priests and scribes for ritual use, they often still reflect typical elements of personal piety, as we can see from their correspondence with the theophoric names. The third source can be seen in proverbial material in the Hebrew Bible, which reveals different elements of personal piety from those implied by prayers and personal names. All these sources are focused on the belief system and accentuate its positive elements; the archaeological sources shed only a little light on ritual practices. Thus given the limitations of the sources, both the darker side and the ritual character of personal piety will probably remain underexposed.

2
The Absence of Official Religious Traditions

It has often been noted that the book of Proverbs does not refer to any of the official religious traditions of Israel and Judah: not the Exodus, nor Sinai, Zion or Davidic kingship. It is not so obvious that virtually the same is true of the individual laments in the book of Psalms;[2] in contrast to the collective laments (e.g. Ps. 80.9-19) the psalms normally do not refer to Israel's salvation history. The few cases where they do can be proven to be the result of later editing (Pss. 22.4-6; 143.5)[3] or have to do with the specific catastrophe of exile, in which individuals complain not because of their own needs, but because God's mighty acts in history seem to have disappeared (Psalm 77). Never in individual laments does the (arguably entirely natural) argument appear that God should rescue the individual from hardship, having already liberated the people from Egyptian slavery. Thus, the religious spheres of the individual and of the people as a whole seem to be separated to a certain degree.

This reading is supported by a close investigation of Hebrew personal names. The epigraphical material found thus far from the ninth to sixth centuries BCE contains 675 different Hebrew names, which are attested nearly 3,000 times altogether. The Hebrew Bible contains about 1,000 different Hebrew names across the whole biblical period. Amazingly, no single name from this extensive Hebrew onomasticon commemorates any occasion in the salvation history of 'Israel'. Of course, there are many names describing YHWH as a rescuer, helper and supporter, which sound similar to biblical claims about what YHWH has done for the people as a whole. But the verbs most commonly used in biblical texts to refer to the exodus (*yāṣā'* Hif.: 'to lead out'; cf. Exod. 3.10–12; 20.2; Deut. 6.12; 26.8 – almost 78 times in total) and to the Israelites' immigration into the promised land (*'ālāh* Hif.: 'to lead up') are lacking among Hebrew personal names. It is thus unlikely that the language of 'rescue' in these names reflects Israel's salvation history. Rather, they may refer to the personal religious experience of the parents of the name bearer. In his seminal study on Hebrew names, Martin Noth (1928) essentially characterized personal names as expressions of personal piety. However, he related two names in particular to Israel's salvation history. According to him, the hope for a return from exile was expressed in the name *'Elyāšîb*, which he took to mean 'God may cause a return (of the dispersed Israel)'. He also suggested that the name *Šĕkanyāh*, 'YHWH has taken (his) home', referred to the construction of the Second Temple (Noth 1928: 213). However, both explanations have since been disproven by the epigraphical material. The former name was already attested in the eighth century BCE, long before the exile; and there is evidence of the latter from the seventh century BCE – and, in its northern variant *Šĕkanyau*, even in the ninth century BCE (Kuntillet 'Ajrud) – long before the destruction of the First Temple. Moreover, Stamm (1980: 71) has convincingly shown that *'Elyāšîb* is to be understood as a 'substitution' name: 'God has brought back (a deceased child with a

---

2.   The psalms of thanksgiving are connected with a sacrificial meal which was originally celebrated at the local sanctuary (Pss. 66.13-20), and could therefore be more easily associated later with the pilgrimage festivals in Jerusalem (Pss. 107; 116; 118; 138). On these festivals and their likely links to local and household religion, see Chapter 8 in this volume.

3.   The same is true for the final intercessions for Israel, Zion (Pss. 3.9; 25.22; 28.8-9; 51.20; 53.7 = 14.7), or the king (61.7-8; 63.12).

new infant)'. In my view, the name *Šĕkanyāh* might be more appropriately rendered 'YHWH has become present', and does not refer to any established sanctuary, where the divine presence is accepted as a matter of course, but to the domestic cult, where YHWH's presence, proven by the lucky birth of a child, is noteworthy.

Thus on the basis of the epigraphical evidence there existed no single personal name that referred to an event in the 'national' histories of Israel and Judah. Though one cannot conclude from this that the Exodus or Zion traditions were not known by the members of Israelite and Judahite families, it might be inferred that these traditions were of minor importance in the day-to-day religious life of families. The personal piety evidenced by personal names, individual prayers and proverbs attests to a wealth of religious experience almost independent from the official state and temple religion.

3
The Shape of Personal Piety in Ancient Israel and Judah

Having seen that the personal piety of ancient Israelite and Judahite families constituted a belief system of its own, we can now describe its elements as shown by the main sources. We focus first on the older period, before the Deuteronomic reform in the late seventh century BCE.

3.1 Personal Piety Expressed by Personal Names

Hebrew personal names can be grouped in six categories: names of thanksgiving, names of confession, names of praise, 'equating' names, birthing names and 'secular' names. From the distribution of these groups the following insights can be drawn: first, the overwhelming majority of parents chose theophoric names for their children and thereby made their piety public; only about 15 per cent of all known Hebrew names are 'secular' names, and most of these are comparatively rare. Thus, personal piety is likely common to almost all families in Israel and Judah without any discernable differences between classes or educational levels. Second, names of thanksgiving and confession, which praise a helpful deed by God or celebrate a close personal relationship to the divine, make up about half of all personal names, while names of praise, which generally extol God's greatness, cover only 7 per cent. The vast majority of names, which in some way praise God, therefore refer to a concrete religious experience of the name-giver, rather than to more general theological claims. (Given that names of thanksgiving and names of confession have close correspondences both to individual laments – such as petitions of divine attendance and rescue, and confessions of confidence – and thanksgiving psalms, they will be considered below.) Third, birthing names constitute the second largest group, accounting for nearly 30 per cent. They show that pregnancy and birth, which not only dominated most of a mother's lifetime, but also had great significance for her whole family, were of central importance for personal piety.

Indeed, it is amazing to see what kinds of events in the long process of childbearing are reflected in the personal names in a religious perspective. They include the distress of infertility (*'Asāpyāhû*: 'YHWH has taken away [the stigma of childlessness]'; cf. Gen. 30.23); prayers and vows for a child (*Ten'ēl*: 'Give, oh God!'; *Dĕrašyāhû*: 'YHWH has asked for [the payment of the vow]'); divine birth oracles (*'Amaryāhû*: 'YHWH has spoken'); and confinement (*Pĕtaḥyāh*: YHWH has opened [the womb];

cf. Gen. 29.31). Most interesting is the fact that pregnancy is experienced as a period during which the child is divinely created (Jer. 1.5; Job 10.8-11); this experience is expressed in the large group of creation names (*Sĕbakyāhû*: 'YHWH has woven [the child in the womb]; cf. Ps. 139.13; or more commonly: *Bĕnāyāhû*: 'YHWH has created'), which covers 39 different names altogether. Indeed, it will become clear that the divine creation of humans constitutes the basis of personal piety.

Moreover, the delivery of the child is performed by God himself (*Daltāyāhû*: 'You, oh YHWH, have drawn out [the child]'). YHWH is portrayed as behaving like a midwife (Ps. 22.10); he even cuts the navel-cord (*Gāzā*': '[the deity] has cut [the child from the navel-cord]'; cf. 71.6). Just after birth, God supports the newborn (*Ḥawwîyāhû*: 'YHWH has brought to life'), presents the new life to the family (*'Elnātān*: 'El has given'), and blesses the infant (*Berekyāhû*: 'YHWH has blessed'). Even the circumcision of the baby boy, which seems to become an apotropaic rite for infants in the seventh century BCE, is carried out by God himself (*Malyāhû*: 'YHWH has circumcised'). Of course, not every birth ended happily; the high rate of infant mortality is reflected in the group of 'substitution' names, which render the new child a substitute for a deceased one (*Šelemyāhû*: 'YHWH has replaced [the deceased child]'). Thus there is almost no event in the dangerous and wonderful childbearing process that is not conceived of as divine care for the individual, especially for the mother and her child.

3.2 Personal Piety in the Individual Lament and Thanksgiving Psalms
Personal names not only express the special religious experiences of the birth process, but also reflect a wider spectrum of divine rescue, help and care that has been experienced during the life of the family members. The large group of thanksgiving and confession names correspond to a high degree with individual lament and thanksgiving psalms, which also address a wide range of needs.

When seeking specific traits of piety in these psalms we become aware that they are strongly shaped by the close personal relationship of the individual with the divine. The deity imagined here is a personal god, invoked as 'my god' (e.g. Pss. 3.8; 5.3; 22.2, 11; 18.3; 30.13),[4] or confessed as being 'my help', 'my protection', 'my trust' or 'my hope'.[5] This close relationship of personal trust can be shown to have been established by the divine creation of every individual:

> Ps 22.9   But you are he who drew me from the womb,
>   who instilled confidence into me at my mother's breast.
>   10   Upon you I was cast from the day of my birth;
>   from my mother's womb you have been my god.[6]

Since they are created by the deity, all people stand in a close relationship of personal trust to the god from their birth for as long as they live. Thus in the book of Psalms it

---

4. The epithets *'ēlî* or *'ĕlōhay* occur 29 times in the individual laments and 19 times in the thanksgiving psalms.

5. See, for example, Pss. 18.3; 27.1; 31.4; 38.16; 40.18; 54.6; 59.17-18; 62.3, 7; 71.5-7; 94.22; 140.8.

6. Cf. Pss. 71.5-6 (MT!); 119.73; 138.8; Job 10.3, 8-13; 35.10-11; cf. Ps. 139.13; Isa. 64.7; Jer. 2.27 and the corresponding oracles of salvation already shifted from the individual to the people: Isa. 43.1; 44.2, 21; 49.5; 54.5.

is explicitly shown that divine creation – as also attested by the birthing names – actually constitutes the basis of all personal piety. Within personal piety the individual's close relationship to God was understood to be founded not on history, be it Israel's deliverance from Egypt or Jerusalem's election for YHWH's dwelling, but on natural, physical or even biological grounds. Thus – unlike Israel's relationship to YHWH – it was independent from human decision, unconditional, and not dependent on ritual or ethical behaviour; it was almost indissoluble and indestructible during one's life (Albertz 1978: 23–96). It can be demonstrated that in all these specific features, the symbolic world of personal piety was constructed according to the personal relationships between children and their parents, which are generally unconditional, indissoluble and indestructible in a similar way. Beliefs about confidence, protection and security in relation to the personal god correspond to the ideal experiences of all young children with respect to their parents. Thus, the basic features of personal piety were heavily shaped by the basic relations and experiences within the family group.

In the Psalms it is naturally the national god, YHWH, who is also addressed as the personal god of the individual. But, as far as we can see, this need not have been the case all the time. Even in the late seventh century BCE the prophet Jeremiah accused the Judahites of confessing personal trust in local deities or their images, but crying to YHWH in their collective laments when they encountered national hardship (Jer. 2.27-28). Of the personal names attested in the Hebrew Bible for the early monarchic period (1 Samuel 14–2 Kings 4), only 20 per cent include YHWH as a theophoric element; the same proportion name the god El, and 6 per cent Baal; but the majority (over 30 per cent) employ divinized designations of kinship, such as *'āb* 'father', *'āḥ* 'brother', *'am* 'paternal uncle', and *ḥam* 'father-in-law'. These designations likely refer to family gods or deified ancestors. Personal names attested in the epigraphical material of the eighth to sixth centuries BCE mostly attest to YHWH as a personal god. The same is true for the biblical names of the late monarchic period (reflected in texts including 2 Kings 22–25 and Jeremiah), although some names with different theophoric elements (El, Baal, Shalem, Mot, Gad, Horus, Bes and perhaps Isis) are also attested.

Somewhat surprisingly, the increasing appeal to YHWH, the 'state' deity, in personal names appears not to have prompted any distinctive new theological emphases or changes to Hebrew names. At the level of personal piety, the various gods were divested of the special character ascribed to them in official religions. Instead, they were primarily defined by their functions for individuals and families. And since these functions essentially remained constant over a long period, the differences between the gods were levelled.[7] Thus, it is no wonder that the personal pieties of ancient Israelites and Judahites had much in common with the personal pieties of their Near Eastern neighbours. Shaped by basic social relations and fundamental human needs, the symbolic world of personal piety was more closely aligned with the broader religious environments of Israel and Judah than the symbolic world of official YHWH religion.

There is, however, one phenomenon concerning the implicit polytheism of personal piety, which remains strange. We know from the private blessing formulae attested in Kuntillet 'Ajrud and Khirbet el-Qom (ninth and eighth centuries BCE) that YHWH was

7.   By this, the existence of the group of 'equating' names (e.g. *'Abîyahû*: 'my [divine] father is YHWH') can probably be explained. They aim at making sure that all the divine names and designations used in the sphere of personal piety at least are identical.

conceived to be accompanied by the goddess Asherah (see *HAE* 1.59–64, 202–11), who seems to have functioned as a kind of mediatrix between YHWH and the individual.[8] Thus it would make good sense if Asherah were invoked for private needs.[9] In personal names, however, Asherah is not mentioned at all, and other goddesses are only rarely attested (including, perhaps, Isis).[10] In this way, the Hebrew onomasticon accords with those of the Ammonites, Moabites and Aramaeans, but differs from that of the Phoenicians.

3.3 Personal Piety in Proverbs

Broadly speaking, biblical proverbs do not deal with personal piety as a central topic; they aim instead at providing individuals with counselling, enabling them to make good decisions in the conduct of their everyday lives. Thus, in most cases, the individual's *rationality* rather than *piety* is addressed. Nonetheless, in several instances, Proverbs includes religious arguments reminding individuals of their personal piety.[11] On the one hand, these arguments aim to encourage people who are anxious to act: they should not fear humans, because those who trust in YHWH are sheltered (Prov. 29.25); or they should commit all that they do to YHWH, and their plans will be fulfilled (16.3). Everyone can exercise their eyes and ears (the receiving and analysing tools of their minds) with confidence, because God has created them (20.12). In all these cases, in being reminded of personal piety, the individual is able to engage with that basic confidence which is necessary to make rational decisions.

On the other hand, and more frequently, the arguments which remind the individuals of their relationship with God seek to show the limits of human planning, striving and wisdom and warn of over-estimation. In spite of all the best plans and efforts, the success of human work depends on God's blessing and decision; it is not simply at human disposal (Prov. 10.22; 16.9, 33; 19.21; 21.31). Thus, people are warned of trusting too much in their own wisdom (3.5); knowledge has to be educated by the fear of God (15.33). Everybody should be aware that YHWH will examine their most secret thoughts and deeds (15.3, 11; 17.3; 20.27); God will uncover any self-deception (16.3; 21.2), will not accept any unjust and deceitful cleverness (11.1, 20; 12.22), and will punish evildoers and defend victims (12.2; 15.25; 22.22-23). Thus, in Proverbs, personal piety is penetrated by an ethical orientation. Divine protection is no longer meant for everybody, but reserved for the pious (10.29); close and trusting relationship with God is no longer unconditional, but often connected with one's decision to avoid evil (16.16), greed (28.25), jealousy (23.17) or revenge (20.22; 25.28), and support the needy (19.17; 22.22-23). It is no wonder, then, that in Proverbs even the creation motif, which is central to personal piety, exhibits a notably social dimension. The belief that YHWH has created every individual is used as an argument that no poor person is to be despised; all social stratification has to be limited (14.31; 17.5; 22.2).

---

8.   Lines 2–3 of the grave inscription of Khirbet el-Qom run: 'Blessed was Uriyahu by YHWH. He has rescued him from his enemies by his Asherah' (*HAE* I.208–11).

9.   Explicitly the veneration of a goddess known as the 'Queen of Heaven' is only attested for the late seventh and early sixth centuries BCE (Jer. 7.18; 44.15-19).

10.   See the name *M'S*, which was interpreted as *Me'is*, 'From Isis' (*HAE* 2/2.215, 320), and which is now epigraphically attested six times. This interpretation, however, is uncertain.

11.   I have restricted my investigation mostly to Proverbs 10–29 because this part of the book seems to be older than Proverbs 1–9 and 30–31.

Thus, the piety shown in Proverbs differs considerably from that attested in Psalms and by personal names. In her doctoral thesis Tae-Kyung Kim (2008) has argued that this difference has to do with the different contexts in which the texts belong. The lament psalms in particular, but also the personal names, relate to personal crises, be they illnesses or dangerous births, when social relations are threatened or weakened. Here individuals seek shelter in God like little children who flee into the skirts of their mothers. Thus God's unconditional protection, and the principal indissolubility of the individual's relationship with God, stand in the foreground. In contrast, the proverbs are directed to people conducting their everyday life. Here individuals are addressed as adults, who are responsible for the deeds done in their social networks. In this situation, God cannot only be conceived as creator and supporter of the individual, but also as examiner and judge, because in this case, the relationship with the divine could easily be forgotten. Thus, during the conduct of everyday life, personal piety has to be proven by the individual again and again; it includes a specific sort of social behaviour, which necessarily excludes egoistical alternatives. Understood in this way, the piety shown in Psalms or personal names and in Proverbs can be seen as two different dimensions of the same personal piety – a suggestion that broadens the scope of my earlier descriptions of personal piety, that did not include proverbial material within its focus (Albertz 1978, 2008).

3.4 Archaeological Remains Related to Personal Piety

From the cultic assemblages found in private houses (such as cult stands, censers, zoomorphic bowls and so on) we can probably conclude that prayers, vows and laments were accompanied by incense offerings, meal offerings and libations. The thanksgiving psalms were recited during a sacrificial meal (*zebaḥ hattōdāh*), which was likely celebrated outside the house in local sanctuaries like the 'Bull Site' in the Samarian hill country. The many Judahite pillar figurines depicting a nude woman with prominent breasts probably played an important role in rituals accompanying confinement, pregnancy and delivery. There is nothing to indicate that they were meant to represent a goddess, so their identification with Asherah is improbable. Rather, they likely functioned as mediators, transferring fertility and divine support to suffering women on the one hand, and carrying their prayers and laments to the deity on the other. It is thus unsurprising to find pillar figurines in sanctuaries as votives.[12]

Individuals could protect themselves against demons, sorcery and the evil eye with amulets, which are frequently attested by archaeology (Herrmann 1994).[13] These amulets were heavily influenced by the Egyptian style and take the form of scarabs, seals, anthropomorphic figures portraying Egyptian gods and goddesses (Anat, Isis, Sachmet, Theoris, Bes, Pataeke), objects (Horus-eye, moon, Djed-pillar) and animals (lion, sow, sow with piglets). In the Hebrew Bible these amulets are termed *ḥōtām* 'seal' (an Egyptian loan-word), *lĕḥāšîm* 'conjured amulets' (Isa. 3.20), *śaḥărōnîm* 'little moons', or *šĕbisîm* 'little suns' (3.18). They were denounced by the prophet Ezekiel as *gillûlîm* 'dung pellets' (Ezek. 14.3; 20.7). The apotropaic function of the amulets was based on imitative magic (Schmitt 2004: 182–86; 202–3, nos 30–33), a function taken

---

12.   The mediatory function of a similar figurine is apparent from an Egyptian birth ritual (papyrus Leiden I, 348, lines 369–72 [Borghouts 1971: 29]), in which the healing spell, in which Hathor and Horus promise their help, is spoken over a Bes figurine placed on the brow of the woman.

13.   He counts 232 amulets from Iron Age I, and 525 from Iron Age II Palestine.

on by the blessings inscribed upon the luxury silver amulets from Ketef Hinnom (*HAE* 1.447-56). In serious conflicts individuals could make use of magical experts, often women, who manufactured special amulets and other magic tools (Ezek. 13.17-23), or formulated private incantations against their enemies; the ostracon from the seventh century BCE found in Horvat 'Uza seems to have been such a private incantation (Beit-Arieh 1993). This sort of harmful magic performed by sorceresses appears to have been officially prohibited in Judah in the period following the late eighth century BCE (Exod. 22.17). Thus, the individual's fundamental need for divine protection and defence in the face of life-threatening powers, which is attested in personal names and laments, is likewise apparent in the ritual and magical equipment shown by these archaeological finds.

4
Later Developments of Personal Piety

Up to the eighth century BCE the personal piety of members of family households appears not to have undergone any considerable change. But, as of the seventh century BCE onwards, several major developments can be observed. Only a rough outline of these developments can be sketched here; I have given a more detailed depiction elsewhere (Albertz 1994: 1.210–16; 2.399–411, 507–22, 556–63).

4.1 Personal Piety under the Control of the Deuteronomic Reformers
In the late eighth and early seventh centuries BCE, when Judah had become an Assyrian vassal state, Judahite culture – including personal piety within families – came under the strong influence of the Syro-Babylonian religions. In accordance with their astralized symbolic world, family rituals were now performed on the roofs of houses (Zeph. 1.5-6; Jer. 19.13; 32.29), and the veneration of the 'Queen of Heaven', an Ishtar figure re-imaging the goddess Asherah, became very popular among Judahite families (Jer. 7.18; 44.15-19).

The obvious syncretistic traits of personal piety in the seventh century provoked the Deuteronomic reformers, under King Josiah, to bring it under official control. Consequently, Judahite families' veneration of gods other than YHWH was strictly forbidden and punished with death (Deut. 13.7-12) and familial sacrificial meals came under the control of the central sanctuary in Jerusalem (12.11-19). In addition, official religious traditions, including those of the Exodus and Conquest, were implanted into the symbolic world and rituals of family members (6.21-24; 26.1-11). But in merging these official cults and traditions with family and personal pieties, the reformers also recast Judah's relationship with YHWH in the close emotional terms typical of the relationship between an individual and his or her personal god (6.4-5). Thus, from Josiah's reign onwards, the differences between personal piety and official religion in ancient Judah were lessened.

4.2 The Vicarious Role of Personal Piety during the Exile
During the exile, when most of the official Israelite religious traditions went through a severe crisis, personal piety took over several vicarious functions of official religion, which helped the latter to survive. In being so historically rooted, Exodus-Conquest theology, Zion theology and kingship theology were all heavily questioned by the

course of events. However, the personal piety of those families that survived the political catastrophe remained basically intact – their personal piety was founded not on history, but on creation. Even after the national catastrophe, children were born; even after being deported to Babylonia, Judahite families could experience good fortune and luck. As we can see in the communal laments in the Hebrew Bible, the theologians of the exilic period often borrowed elements from personal piety in order to find a starting-point of creating new hope for the nation (Lamentations 3; Isa. 64.7). The prophet Deutero-Isaiah used the motif of the creation of humans, the very heart of personal piety, in his salvation oracles in order to help mend Israel's damaged relationship with YHWH by encouraging a new sense of confidence (43.1; 44.2, 24; cf. 49.5). Moreover, already existing or newly created family rituals, including the circumcision of infants (Gen. 17.12), food regulations (Leviticus 11), and Sabbath observance (Exod. 31.17), became identity-markers of emergent Judaism. Thus during the exile, every family member became responsible for the survival of Israelite religion.

4.3 Different Personal Theologies in the Post-Exilic Period

Following the collapse of the Babylonian empire and the failed attempt to restore the Judahite state, personal piety and its family contexts became much more closely aligned with the official religions supported by priests, officials and prophets than in pre-exilic times. A mutual influence in both directions can be observed – for example, a promise for Zion in an individual lament (Ps. 102.13-25) and a confession of confidence in a collective complaint (90.1-2).

Personal piety was now much more thought-out and became a kind of personal theology. As a result of the breakdown of Judahite society into different classes in the midst of the Persian period, two different personal theologies emerged: the 'piety of the poor', promulgated by the lower class ('the righteous'), who felt exploited by certain members of the upper class who were only interested in their own material benefits ('the wicked men'); and the 'pious wisdom' of some members of the upper class (also 'the righteous') who still felt responsible for the poor in the social crisis and strongly opposed their antisocial colleagues.

In opposing 'the wicked men', the pious members of the upper class sought to invest personal trust in God with an ethical commitment (Job 4.6). Individuals could not simply claim protection from their creator without having to moderate their behaviour; only those who led an irreproachable life in the fear of God and stood up for the poor (29.12-17; 31.13-27) could safely hope for God's support and reward (29.18-20). The book of Job shows how this ambitious personal theology was subjected to severe testing under the pressure of social crisis: Job lost all his wealth and high social rank in spite of his exemplary piety and charity. Though the author of Job could not supply the pious members of the upper class with an answer to the question of theodicy, he nevertheless suggested the possibility that, after his death, Job would become reconciled with God and his merits would be recognized (14.13-17; 16.18-22; 19.23-27a). Thus, in the face of massive social injustice, the individual's personal relationship with God transcended even the borderline of death.

The question of God's fairness was also fiercely debated in the piety of the poor. Given that the poor were unable to demonstrate their faith in their deeds, they commended in their prayers their own poverty and misery to God, hoping to move God to mercy (Pss. 10.12; 69.30; 70.6; 109.22). Powerless themselves, they put their hopes for vengeance in appeals to YHWH, asking him to demonstrate his great power as a judge of the world (7.8-9; 10.16; 75.3), and to destroy the powerful wicked and their foreign allies, so that the oppressed might once again rejoice before God (9.6, 18; 109.5-10). Thus the piety of the poor included elements of the old temple theology, but converted them to a call for social revolution.

Finally, in the Hellenistic period a new kind of personal theology, 'Torah piety', emerged – probably developed by middle-class professional scribes. It incorporated the basic document of official Jewish religion, the canonized Torah, into the individual's personal relationship with God (Psalms 1; 19; 119). Here the Torah functioned as a very specific mediator: all the confidence, hope and love which were meant for God were now directed to the Torah and its divine promises (119.47, 97, 131). It was no longer general experiences of God, but rather intensive meditation on the scriptures (1.2), which revealed God's merciful presence (119.1-16, 73). Thus, at the end of the Hebrew Bible period, Israelite personal piety or theology was given a distinctively Jewish shape.

Selected Bibliography

Albertz, R.
1978   *Persönliche Frömmigkeit und offizielle Religion: Religionsinterner Pluralismus in Israel und Babylon* (CThM A9; Stuttgart: Calwer; repr. Atlanta, GA: Society of Biblical Literature, 2005).
1994   *A History of Israelite Religion in the Old Testament Period* (2 vols; OTL; Louisville, KY: Westminster/John Knox).
2008   'Household and Family Religion in Antiquity', in J. Bodel and S.M. Olyan (eds), *Household and Family Religion in Antiquity* (Oxford: Blackwell), 89–112.

Beit-Arieh, I.
1993   'A Literary Ostracon from Horvat 'Uza', *TA* 20: 55–65.

Borghouts, J.F.
1971   *The Magical Texts of Papyrus Leiden I 348* (Oudheidkundige Mededelingen 51; Leiden: Rijksmuseum van Oudheden).

Gerstenberger, E.S.
2001   *Theologien im Alten Testament: Pluralität und Synkretismus alttestamentlichen Gottesglaubens* (Stuttgart: Kohlhammer).

Herrmann, C.
1994   *Ägyptische Amulette aus Palästina/Israel* (Fribourg: Universitätsverlag).

Kim, T.-K.
2008   'Frömmigkeit in der Weisheit. Untersuchungen zum religiösen Geschehen zwischen Gott und dem einzelnen Menschen in der Weisheitstradition'. Theological dissertation, Münster.

Miller, P.D.
2000   *The Religion of Ancient Israel* (LAI; Louisville, KY: Westminster John Knox).

Noth, M.
1928   *Die israelitischen Personennamen im Rahmen der gemeinsemitischen Namengebung* (BWANT 46; Stuttgart: Kohlhammer).

Rad, G. von
1962   *Theologie des Alten Testaments* (2 vols; München: Kaiser).

Schmitt, R.
2004   *Magie im Alten Testament* (AOAT 313; Münster: Ugarit-Verlag).

Stamm, J.J.
1980   *Beiträge zur Hebräischen und Altorientalischen Namenkunde* (OBO 30; Fribourg: Universitätsverlag).

Toorn, K. van der
1996   *Family Religion in Babylonia, Syria and Israel: Continuity and Change in the Forms of Religious Life* (SHCANE 7; Leiden: Brill).

PART III

GEOGRAPHICAL DIVERSITIES

Chapter 10

SOUTHERN, NORTHERN AND TRANSJORDANIAN PERSPECTIVES[1]

Jeremy M. Hutton

1
Theoretical Focus: Local versus Regional Expressions of Religion

The historical study of what is loosely termed ancient Israelite religion has always been, and perhaps can only ever be, plagued by difficulties associated with the 'curated' nature of the biblical material, the paucity of clear archaeological and epigraphic evidence, and the varieties of hermeneutical interpretations of that evidence. As one facet of this difficulty, the geographical contingencies of Israelite and Judahite history provide an arena in which can be found a complex, and perhaps ultimately impregnable, matrix of interrelated yet distinct forms of ethnic identification and socio-political affiliation that undoubtedly prohibit any easy systematization of the religious situations of Israel and Judah. In recent biblical studies, which generally assume some degree of variation among the forms of Israelite religion, this geographic variation is normally conceptualized in the broad rubrics of 'northern' (= 'Israelian'), southern (= 'Judahite') and eastern (= 'Transjordanian') religion.[2] The popularity of this schema is most likely due in large part on one hand to the fact that it is easiest to trace religious practices in the Hebrew Bible as they correlate to the two dominant polities in the pre-exilic period, Israel and Judah, and on the other hand to the necessary simplification of what can only have been an incredibly complex religious milieu. This simplification, moreover, has been performed on at least two fronts: 1) by scholars attempting to systematize the structures, styles and expressions of Israelite religion; and 2) by

1.   I am grateful for the work of my research assistant Paul Kurtz, who assisted greatly in the conceptual stages of this project. As will become clearer below (see n. 23), his own work, which originated as a component of this piece but which I am unable to include for considerations of space, has provided me with ample material for consideration, and has helped me to clarify my own thoughts on religious differentiation. Portions of sections 1 and 2.2 are condensed paragraphs to be published in expanded form as part of Hutton forthcoming.
2.   The terms 'Israelian', 'Judahite' and 'Transjordanian' are used here to indicate the inhabitants of the major polities in monarchic Israel in distinction to the term 'Israelite', which will be used as an overarching category distinguishing any Israelian, Judahite or Transjordanian from the surrounding peoples, such as Edomites, Ammonites, etc. Thus, the term 'Transjordanian' here serves as a shorthand for Transjordanian Israelites, as opposed to those people who lived 'across' the Jordan, but who apparently did not self-identify as Israelites. For the differentiation between northern and southern expressions of Israelite religion, see, for example, Albertz 1994: 126–46; Zevit 2001: 439–79; Venter 2003; Christian 2007: 221–26. For the geographic independence of less commonly discussed Transjordanian traditions, see Levine 1985: 338; and Hackett 1987.

the biblical text itself (e.g. Zevit 2001: 447–48). Despite the current chapter's general sympathy with this dominant and schematic tripartite model of religious variation, it is not entirely clear that this simplification should be wholeheartedly adopted without analysis of its assumptions.

The earliest reconstructable social situation of the southern Levant in the Iron Age is not one in which a broad national identity obtains, with its overarching meta-narrative and thoroughgoing statement of submission to a single sovereign deity, as presented in the current shape of the Hebrew Bible (e.g. Joshua and Judges). Instead, the 'biblical Israel' encountered in the historical books is a literary and historiographical construct, the theologized depiction of what was in actuality a congeries of politically independent and ethnically distinct populations in the southern Levantine highlands during the Iron I (e.g. Gottwald 1999 [1979]; Hauser 1979; Killebrew 2005: 149–96, esp. 184–85; Miller 2005; cf. Sparks 1998). Yet for all the nuanced sensitivity with which contemporary scholars have attended to the social situations of emergent Israelite and Judahite groups, the biblical text itself remains stalwart in identifying all these groups as the people 'Israel' and asserting that 'Israel' was in its best days devoted entirely to its sole deity Yahweh. It is precisely this monolithic vision of an early 'Yahwistic Israel' that led earlier commentators to assume the normative unity of Israelite society, especially within the realm of religion. But the historical accuracy of this monolithic vision of Israelite monotheism may be challenged (Mayes 1997:52–57).

The geographic, cultural and ethnic diversity of southern Levantine groups translated into aspects of religious diversity as well. Although it is possible to trace distinctions between the geographically fixed historical traditions found in disparate biblical texts (e.g. Deuteronomy 32; Psalms 29 and 78; Nehemiah 9; see recently Venter 2003: 472–85), this geographically constituted diversity is borne out most fully in the variation among what P.K. McCarter has called the 'local manifestations' of Yahweh (1987: 139–43; see also Emerton 1982: esp. 5). These Yahwistic manifestations included 'Yahweh-in-Hebron' (*YHWH běḥebrôn*; 2 Sam. 15.7), and perhaps also 'Yahweh-in-Zion' (*YHWH běṣîyôn*; Ps. 99.2), as well as the 'Yahweh of Samaria' (*yhwh šmrn*) and 'Yahweh of Teman' (*yhwh tymn/[h]tmn*) known from the Kuntillet 'Ajrud inscriptions. Non-Yahwistic deities or deities identified with Yahweh bear this locally specific nomenclature in biblical texts as well: in the former category we read of a Philistine deity *dāgôn bě'ašdôd* ('Dagan in Ashdod'; 1 Sam. 5.5), and in the latter is found a *ba'al pěrāṣîm* (2 Sam. 5.20), whom McCarter identifies as a 'locally worshiped god, "the lord of [Mount] Perazim," who was subsequently identified with Yahweh' (1987: 140–41). For McCarter, these local manifestations of Yahweh became 'semi-independent, almost as if they were distinct deities' (1987: 142; although cf. Emerton 1982: 11–12). It is therefore most expedient to keep in mind this near ubiquitous local variation in the Levant as the dominant model in which socio-religious groups operated, and from which monarchic Israel and Judah drew much of their own traditional cultic material.

The dominant tripartite model of modern interpreters must then be clarified with the following theoretical proposal, drawn on analogy to climatology: in the same way that large-scale weather patterns over long durations – climates – can be composed of smaller geographically and topologically defined microclimates, the particular form of religious expression peculiar to any one of the significant ethnically defined polities should itself already be thought of as a bundle of local, temporally limited religious expressions. By analogy, these small-scale local religious expressions may be designated 'micro-religions'. These local micro-religions comprise the constituent elements of the larger regionally and politically defined 'macro-religions', which themselves constitute subunits of what might be termed pan-Israelite religion. Because of the paucity of data, and particularly because each datum provides only a snapshot of what is evidently a moving target, it will be virtually impossible to know whether these micro-religions should be seen as local pockets or enclaves of religious heterogeneity isolated within a larger, more homogenous religious environment; or if each macro-religion should be interpreted as a patchwork of micro-religions, in which none of the peculiar religious expressions is particularly prevalent over its contiguous neighbours. This chapter will attempt to survey briefly the two smaller members of this model as they can be traced in the biblical, archaeological and epigraphic records, with the caution that in discussing *regional* variation of religious expression (i.e. macro-religious variation) we are in fact discussing geographic and temporal snapshots of *local* expressions (micro-religions).

2
Epigraphic and Iconographic Evidence for Regional Religious Diversity

In order to minimize the historical relativity imparted by biblical texts, this chapter will treat epigraphic and iconographic evidence as an outside control. This method must not entail archaeological data completely over-riding textual evidence; rather, it can provide a reasoned and sustained alternative to taking biblical texts at face value (e.g. Zevit 2001). Yet while attentiveness to the archaeological situation of the epigraphic material may provide deeper insight into the extent and normativeness of the worship of these manifestations in Israel and Judah, this claim should be tempered with a healthy respect for the degree of interpretation required of the archaeologist and epigrapher in their respective endeavours. In none of the examples presented here or available in longer, more thorough treatments is the information provided in a readily understood package; the data, like literary texts, are always ambiguous, indeterminate, and subject to the imagination of their auditors. This is not to say, however, that all interpretations are equally valid. The most likely synthesis is the one most able to account for all the data adequately, without resorting to over-readings, under-interpretation, or the eschewal of evidence because it does not 'fit the model'. In concordance with the theory outlined above, and, one hopes, in accordance with the caveats offered here, the epigraphic data presented in the following pages point to the regional and local varieties of a single over-arching religious framework, the heterogeneous within the homogeneous.

2.1 Geographic Variation in Cultic Implements
Unfortunately, some archaeological phenomena of the Iron II southern Levant are too circumscribed temporally to serve as indicators of the geographic diversity of religious practice. For example, the context of pillar figurines is limited to Judah in the period between the Assyrian invasion into the southern Levant (c. 720 BCE) and the Babylonian destruction (c. 586 BCE), and thus both temporally and geographically restricted.[3] These factors constrain our ability to include them productively in the

---

3.   For a discussion of these small, stylized female figures, see Hess 2007: 308–11 and bibliography there.

present discussion, and they are perhaps better treated in a discussion of household religions.

On the other hand, there are several such phenomena that may serve as indicators of various religious expressions across a wide geographic area, and through a significant duration. Although the small four-horned altars and terracotta tower-shaped incense stands might also best be treated within the rubric of household religion, there are a few indications that their forms and uses in cultic contexts may be distinguished on the basis of geography as well. Using the data compiled by Gitin (2002), we may present a basic – and undoubtedly oversimplified – distribution of incense altars in the Iron Age II southern Levant. In Philistia, the horned altar form predominates over the hornless form by a count of 18 horned to 4 hornless altars, and an only slightly lower ratio applies in the kingdom of Israel, where 12 horned and 6 hornless altars have been found. In Judah, however, only three such altars have been found, two of which are hornless and found in the context of the more 'official' cultic practice at the Arad sanctuary. It is tempting to conclude that Judahite religion permitted fewer such expressions of domestic piety, and when such implements were utilized, their employment was limited to more official or officializing contexts. But this conclusion is prima facie, and takes into account neither the typology of altars ('shaft' versus 'block'), nor the biblical (e.g. 1 Kgs 2.28) and archaeological (e.g. Herzog 1981) evidence for the use of large horned ashlar altars in monarchic Judah. One wonders furthermore whether the paucity of such altars in Judah may not simply be traced to the contingencies of archaeological excavation. Again, the onus of interpretation of these phenomena falls necessarily on the researcher.

2.2 Kuntillet 'Ajrud and Local Manifestations of Yahweh

Since their discovery in 1976, several elements of the inscriptions of Kuntillet 'Ajrud (Horvat Teman) have furnished evidence for geographic diversity in Yahweh worship. Although there is much debate as to the nature of the site (Meshel and Meyers 1976: 10; Meshel 1978: unnumbered pages; 1979: 34; Zevit 2001: 374; cf. Hadley 1993; Soumeka 2002: 83), it is most expedient to agree with Schmidt's formulation (2002: 103) that there was 'extensive religious use of the site's architectural space', whether or not we believe that space to have been deliberately constructed as such (see also Coogan 1987: 118; and the later and, in my opinion, more developed solution of Hadley 2000: 108–20). As is the case with the inscriptions from Khirbet el-Qom (e.g. Hadley 2000: 84–105; Zevit 2001: 359–70; Wiggins 2007: 190–96), most of the debate surrounding Kuntillet 'Ajrud's inscriptions, dated to c. 800 BCE, has focused on the nature of the phrase 'Yahweh . . . and his Asherah/asherah' (in the last two decades, e.g. Hess 1991: 12–23, 1996, 2007: 283–89; Binger 1997: 94–109; Mayes 1997: 63–64; Schmidt 2002; Smith 2002: 108–47; Wiggins 2007: esp. 197–208). More important in the context of the present discussion is the naming of two local or regional manifestations of Yahweh.

As noted above, the 'DN [= Divine Name] of GN [= Geographic Name]' sequence occurs with two distinct manifestations of Yahweh, localizable to two different regions of monarchic Israel and Judah.[4] First, we find a 'Yahweh of Samaria' (*yhwh šmrn*) in

---

4.   One might compare here as well the Khirbet Beit Lei inscription (*HI* BLei 5) mentioning the 'God of Jerusalem' (*'lhy yršlm*), if the reading of Naveh is followed (1963: 84–85 [see 2 Chron. 32.19]); although the reading is far from certain, and generally not accepted (cf. Cross 1970: 299–302;

one of the inscriptions on pithos A.[5] Second, the manifestation 'Yahweh of Teman' occurs four times in three distinct formulations. The name appears twice in a plaster inscription as *yhwh (h)tymn*;[6] once in one of the pithos B inscriptions as *yhwh tmn*;[7] and once again on pithos B as *yhwh htmn*.[8] The former manifestation, Yahweh of Samaria, was obviously worshipped in that northern, Israelian city. On the other hand, the referent of Teman is more ambiguous; it possibly designates the southern lands generally, but it may also indicate a region of Edom (Emerton 1982: 9, citing de Vaux 1969; see also Hadley 2000: 127–29).[9]

One of the legible plaster inscriptions in the so-called bench-room of Structure A was the ink-on-plaster dedicatory inscription in which 'Yahweh of Teman' is mentioned twice (*HI* KAjr 14). The bench-room thus seems to have been claimed officially for the worship of Yahweh's Temanite manifestation. Each of the other two inscriptions mentioning that manifestation (*HI* KAjr 19; 20) was discovered written in ink on pithos B, which was found in the courtyard of the same structure. However, apart from these inscriptions, the courtyard otherwise shows little evidence of cultic use. Thus, consideration of the entirety of Structure A as specifically dedicated to cultic practice (with, for example, Meshel 1978; Zevit 2001: 374) may overstep the available evidence, although part of the structure was undoubtedly claimed as such (Schmidt 2002). If this delimitation of the sacred space from the secular space is accepted, the distribution of devotional material dedicated to 'Yahweh of Teman' may indicate the porousness of such boundaries: the three inscriptions referring to that manifestation were found in two loci within the complex, one of which is only with difficulty identified as reserved for specifically cultic purposes. Conversely, the blessing by 'Yahweh of Samaria' occurs on pithos A, found in the bench-room along with the aforementioned plaster inscription. Thus, even in a space apparently dedicated to the worship of a specific regional – if not local – manifestation, a 'competing' local manifestation of Yahweh was worshipped. This may suggest that worship of this northern local manifestation was informal and ad hoc, the prayer a dedicatory note left by the author of the inscription as an expression of personal piety in a cultic setting dedicated to a variant manifestation of the same deity (Hutton forthcoming).

2.3 The Samaria Ostraca and Biblical Onomastics

Inasmuch as we may relate onomastic data to religious observance – an issue currently up for debate (e.g. Callaway 1999; Zevit 2001: 608–9; Hess 2007: 269–74) – the Samaria ostraca may provide an important witness to the northern monarchy's

Zevit 2001: 417–27; Dobbs-Allsopp, *et al.* 2005: 128–30).

5. *HI* KAjr 18 = *AHI* 8.017 = *HAE* 1.59-61. Meshel 1978 initially read *šmrn* incorrectly as the 3.m.s. perfect inflection of *šāmar*, with a 1.c.pl. object suffix (*šōměrēnū*, hence, 'our guardian'). But over time, and with comparison to *t(y)mn*, it became clear that 'Samaria' was the correct reading (Meshel 1979: 31; Gilula 1978–79, cited in Emerton 1982: 3).

6. As read by *HI* KAjr 14; cf. *AHI* 8.015 + 8.023 = *HAE* 1.58-59.

7. *HI* KAjr 19.5–7 = *AHI* 8.021 = *HAE* 1.62-63.

8. *HI* KAjr 20.1 = *AHI* 8.016 = *HAE* 1.63-64.

9. Whether the worship of Yahweh of Teman is better classified as a *local* or *regional* expression of religious piety is irrelevant here, since no matter the conclusion of that argument, this southern cultic expression is neither quintessentially northern Israelian – although it seems to have garnered Israelian patrons – nor is it normatively southern Judahite – since Teman is already *at most* a subregion of Judah.

religious differentiation. The Yahwistic theophoric element comprises the most wide-spread divine name in the Samaria corpus, with at least 15 different anthroponyms compounded from the element, found or reasonably reconstructed by my count in 40 different isolated incidents. Five personal names incorporating the theophoric element 'Baal' occur as well in the corpus, totalling 11 actual or reconstructed occurrences. Some interpreters have attributed this unexpectedly high frequency of theophoric names compounded with 'Baal' to the substandard religious practices of the lower classes, whose children tended to bear the Baal-names (e.g. Noth 1928: 120–21; Bright 2000 [1959]: 260; see also Albright 1942: 160). According to this theory, it was the members of the upper class who bestowed Yahweh-names on their own children. This relatively high proportion of Baal-names was also to be contrasted to the anthroponymic repertoire of monotheistic Judah, they argued, where there is very little evidence of such degenerate Baal worship.[10] Jeffrey Tigay has argued that most of what had previously been taken to be anthroponymic indications of polytheistic practice in the southern kingdom may be dismissed as indications of a prolific angelology, and that it is therefore difficult to make a sustained argument that any of the data indicate a syncretistic or polytheistic regional Judahite religion (Tigay 1986: 65–73; 1987: 163–68). Accordingly, it would thus appear that the epigraphic anthroponymic evidence from the northern kingdom (specifically, the Samaria ostraca) displays evidence for polytheistic or non-Yahwistic cultic practice, while that from the southern kingdom does not. However, Tigay's interpretation remains a point of contention within the study of Israelite religion. Not only does it make certain assumptions about the nature of the entities commemorated in these names, it also puts forward a date for the advent of monotheism that is dramatically earlier than most other reconstructions (cf. Hess 2007: 43–80, esp. 69, 71). Moreover, it is readily apparent that Noth, Albright and Bright were all working with data that is now somewhat out of date (the proportion of Baal-names to Yahweh-names has changed as more ostraca have been found), as well as with significant assumptions as to the various positions of the *l*-men in the ostraca (for the history of the discussion, see especially Dobbs-Allsopp, *et al.* 2005: 423–26).

An additional set of considerations comes from the biblical text itself. In MT Samuel, a few of the names that were originally compounded with the element 'Baal' (as can be demonstrated by comparison with the parallel passages in 1 Chronicles and LXX Samuel) were preserved instead with the element *bōšet*,[11] or in one case, with the

---

10.   Indeed, this situation has changed only nominally in the last decades (cf. *'ṣb'l: HI* MHsh 7.1; *yhwb'l*; mentioned in Avigad 1988: 8–9; and *b'lḥnn*: Diringer 1934: 195 no. 36). Two difficulties proceed from these last two artefacts: in the first case, the element *b'l* is in fact the attribute or predicate, and not the theophoric element ('Yahweh is lord'). And, more importantly, our confidence in the authenticity of non-provenanced artefacts such as these last two has been deeply eroded in the years since their publication (that the seal mentioned by Avigad is non-provenanced is my own assumption, based on the omission of any pertinent data, and the exclusion of the seal from Avigad and Sass 1997; for the burgeoning problems of non-provenanced epigraphic materials, see Rollston 2003, 2004).

11.   (a) *yĕrubbaʿal*: e.g. Judg. 6.32; 7:1; cf. *yĕrubbešet* in 2 Sam. 11.21; for discussion see Hamilton 1998: 234; (b) *'iš-bōšet*: MT 2 Samuel 2–4; cf. *'ešbaʿal* in 1 Chron. 8.33; 9.39; cf. also *yōšēb baššebet*: 2 Sam. 23.8, generally assumed to be a corruption of *yišbaʿal* (cf. Ιεβοσθε in LXX, as at 2 Sam. 2.8, for example); (c) *mĕpîbōšet*: 2 Samuel 4; 9; 16; 19; 21.28 (cf. Hutton 2009b); cf. *mĕrîb baʿal* in 1 Chron. 8.34 (twice); 9.40 = *mĕrî-baʿal*: 1 Chron. 9.40. It is not entirely clear that the identification in 2 Samuel of two individuals named Mephibosheth/Merib-baal is due to anything other than confusion occasioned by the complex redactional history of the book.

element *'ēl 'ēlyādā'* [in pause]: 2 Sam. 5.16; cf. *bĕ'elyādā'* [in pause]: 1 Chron. 14.7) (Noth 1928: 119; Tigay 1987: 160). Although the *-bōšet* element has been interpreted as an authentic historical relic of an original element cognate to Akk. *bāštu* ('dignity', 'pride', 'vigour', 'guardian angel', 'patron saint'; Tsevat 1975: 76; Hamilton 1998), most commentators continue to dismiss the overlap between names compounded with 'Baal' and those formed with 'Bosheth' simply as a case of 'dysphemism', in which the latter word, *bōšet* 'shame', was substituted in MT Samuel for the theophoric element *ba'al* (see bibliography in Hamilton 1998: 229 n. 7; and cf. especially Tigay 1987: 160, 181 n. 9). Regardless of the precise divine referent of whichever theophoric element is preferred, it is not at all clear that these names should not be understood as authentically Yahwistic names (wherein the theophoric element was used simply as an epithet, meaning 'lord' or 'master'), in which case they do not constitute evidence of widespread Baal worship in the northern kingdom, especially among those portrayed in the Hebrew Bible as members of Saul's family.[12] Even if the theophoric element were understood as indicating the deity Baal (if limitable to a single deity; cf. Dearman 1993), questions remain regarding the extent of Baalistic practice among the ethnically Israelite population of the northern kingdom (as opposed to any foreign elements living in that polity).

Tigay points out that 'assimilation to foreign culture is typically found among the upper strata' (1987: 162); even this prima facie observation may vitiate the plausibility of Noth's assertion that the Baal-names found their context in the lower classes. Moreover, it may be reasonable to assume that all names found in Israel were names of native, ethnic Israelites, but the Israelite birth of these names' respective bearers is by no means guaranteed (Tigay 1987: 169). Thus, there are several possible explanations for the presence of the Baal-names in the Samaria ostraca, each of which points towards a certain degree of regional religious variation within the northern kingdom, although not necessarily among ethnic Israelites. If *b'l* in Israelite names is understood to refer to the 'Phoenicio-Canaanite' Baal, the diversity among Israelites is patent and unworthy of further discussion. But two more nuanced explanations exist. First, if the names compounded with *b'l* are understood as authentic Yahwistic names, in which the element meaning 'lord', 'master' serves as a metonym for Yahweh, then there would likely have been some degree of religious variation between those who accepted that element as a viable and pious epithet for Yahweh and those who did not.[13] The book of Hosea might suggest that already in eighth century Israel such diversity obtained. It would appear to be precisely the same ambiguity wrapped up with this use of the epithet *b'l* that the prophet addresses in Hos. 2.18 (ET v. 16):[14]

12.   As admitted already by Albright 1942: 160 and Bright 1959: 60–61; see also Tigay 1986: 14–15, 68; 1987: 163; Dearman 1993: 189; Hamilton 1998: 237; Hess 2007: 242–43; cf. for example, Noth 1928: 120–21; Avigad 1987: 197; Day 2000: 227–28; Smith 2002: 44–47.

13.   Presumably, this variation would have been expressed primarily diachronically and geographically. For example, it was in all probability a later Judahite editor of Samuel who sought to shame the Saulide dynasty with the replacement of their proper theophoric elements with *bōšet*, and to exonerate insofar as possible the Davidic family with the insertion of *'ēl* (2 Sam. 5.16; but cf. the apparent alternation of the name Eshbaal/Ishbosheth with the corrupted Yahwistic name Ishvi [*yišwî* < **yiš-yaw* or the like]: 1 Sam. 14.49 [e.g. Dearman 1993: 188–90]).

14.   So too Mays 1969: 48; Anderson and Freedman 1980: 278–79; Tigay 1986: 68; cf. Zevit 2001: 608–9; for the difficulties of dating the book, see Ben Zvi 2005.

On that day, says the Lord, you will call me, 'My husband (*'îšî*)', and no longer will you call me 'My Baal (*ba'lî*)'.

(NRSV)

The second more nuanced explanation would be to find in the use of *b'l* evidence of Tigay's supposed foreign population associated with the Israelite crown. In this understanding, the use of the theophoric element under discussion would have been largely coincident, if not completely coterminous, with the residual immigrant Phoenician population. Again, one could conclude that there existed geographic diversity between Israel and Judah, here simply because of the northern kingdom's closer relations with the kingdoms to its north.

A final caveat to an over-reliance on the anthroponymic data may be adduced. In his study of theophoric toponyms, Ziony Zevit found that toponyms containing the element *b'l* 'indicate a more ubiquitous distribution of Baal worship than might be concluded on the basis of the biblical data alone' (Zevit 2001: 606; see also Hess 2007: 274). Yet here too the interpreter must exercise caution in assigning too consolidated an identity to the 'Baal' represented (Day 1992: 547). In his earlier study of 'Baal' toponyms, J.A. Dearman stressed that 'Most likely, the Ba'al place names reflect a mixture of local and high god cults. A few may be Israelite and even refer to Yahweh with the appellative *ba'al*' (1993: 190). Unfortunately, we are cast back on the same problems occasioned by attempts to interpret the anthroponymic data. Until some diagnostic test is devised whereby the referent of divine epithets-turned-divine names is elucidated, the indeterminacy of the epigraphic and biblical onomastic data precludes solid and irrefutable conclusions.

3

The Deuteronomistic History as Historical Source and Its Portrayal of Jeroboam's Reforms as Indicative of Northern Religion

The challenge to a single, undifferentiated religious identity encompassing the entire population of early Israel proceeds not simply from a culturally and ethnically sensitive survey of the demographic diversity of the southern Levant as demonstrable through study of archaeological and epigraphic evidence from the region roughly coterminous with biblical Israel, but also from an analysis of the preserved biblical historiographic traditions purporting to depict the religion of Israel during the Iron Age (especially Judges, 1 and 2 Samuel, 1 and 2 Kings). This approach occasions three significant cautions concerning the nature of the biblical text.

First, the character of the finalized Deuteronomistic History (DtrH) as a curated document that underwent a long history of development, elaboration and redaction before reaching its final form cannot be overemphasized. As part of that development, the DtrH – and indeed, the entire biblical corpus – has been filtered through a post-exilic, southern, officializing perspective, which therefore dominates the biblical view of pan-Israelite religion (Zevit 2001: 439–79). Second, the constituent sources of the DtrH that might provide some witness to the religious situation of Iron Age Israel (c. 1200–586 BCE) have been collected and edited into a theologically oriented framework by the author(s) of that corpus. For example, Mark Smith has argued that the association of Asherah with Baal (Judg. 3.7; 1 Kgs 18.19; 2 Kgs 23.4) is the product purely of Deuteronomistic invective that attempted to displace the veneration or worship of Asherah from its traditional (and legitimate) position within the mainstream of the Yahwistic cult (Smith 2002: 125–33; although cf. Hess 2007: 287). A third caution, derivative of the preceding two, is to stress that the religious importance assigned to various institutions depends to a large degree on how one reconstructs the redaction history of the biblical witness. For example, Iain Provan argued that the Hezekian reform claimed by the original, Josianic-era author of the DtrH was, in fact, geared towards removing peripheral Yahwistic cultic sites in favour of the Jerusalem temple. It was only with the production of the second, exilic edition that the Deuteronomists began to make the claim that the reforms removed the 'high-places' of foreign, non-Yahwistic deities (Provan 1988: 57–90). However, it is not clear that this is a necessary interpretation of the biblical data, and even studies that basically accept a double-redaction schema disagree on the details of the redactions' respective concerns (e.g. O'Brien 1989: 229–33).

In sum, it is impossible to gain much traction on the Deuteronomistic portrayal(s) of northern (Israelian) and southern (Judahite) religious expression without first coming to grips with several as yet undecided problems in the interpretation of the DtrH as a whole, arbitrating between the various schematic presentations. Such arbitration is clearly beyond the scope of this study, and has been summarized elsewhere (Knoppers 2000; Römer and de Pury 2000; Römer 2005). Yet, because the theologies of the respective Deuteronomistic editors are subject to interpretation, they play a minor role in the following discussion; the discussion requires mention only of the DtrH itself as a whole, and the many relatively minute variations between the reconstructed Deuteronomistic editors may be glossed over in favour of using the assemblage of traditions in the DtrH (Zevit 2001: 439–48, esp. 441) in tandem with the other avenues of research discussed above, epigraphy and archaeology.

The DtrH presents as its central focus the duration of the Davidic Dynasty's control over Judah until that polity's fall to the Babylonians in 586 BCE. As part of that history, the writers were forced to come to grips with what they perceived to be a political and religious schism between the northern and southern polities in the late tenth century BCE. Because of their staunch belief that Yahweh's will had been worked out in history, the Deuteronomists needed to come to grips with the enduring effects wrought by that perceived split, whether it was historical or not. Part of their explanation for this break came in the form of blaming Solomon's syncretistic cultic practices, and adoption of foreign cultic implements and expressions. These cultic offenses comprised primarily the provision of cultic installations for the foreign cults imported from Moab and Ammon, along with Solomon's tacit support for those cults in the form of permitting his wives' royal patronage (1 Kgs 11.7-8). In this manner the Deuteronomists 'explained' Yahweh's tearing of the northern kingdom from Solomon (1 Kgs 11.9-13, 29-39), presaging the destruction of the Davidic dynasty by the Babylonians. With the premise that Yahweh's punishment of Solomon had been worked out in the Israelian rebellion against Judahite hegemony came the concomitant need to explain the destruction of the northern kingdom in 720 BCE. Why, if it was divinely ordained that Israel should secede from Judah, should the northern kingdom be punished as well? For the Deuteronomists, the causes for the Assyrian destruction of the north were easily attributed to the northern kings' promulgation and promotion of what the Deuteronomists held to be non-standard Yahwistic – or even foreign and non-Yahwistic – cultic practices: they worshipped other gods; participated in

Canaanite and other 'indigenous' forms of religious practice; and established cultic sites and expressions that were not sanctioned by the Jerusalem religious establishment (2 Kgs 17.7-12). Jeroboam himself introduced these prohibited religious expressions at the very inception of the northern monarchy (or is at least blamed for having done so), and the Deuteronomists used every available opportunity to remind their audience of that deviancy. Beginning with 1 Kings 12, adherence to the 'sins/way of Jeroboam' (*ḥaṭṭōʾt/derek yārob'ām*), which was tantamount to having done 'evil in Yahweh's sight' (*ʿāśâ hāraʿ bĕʿênê yhwh*) becomes the principle by which northern kings and particularly substandard Judahite kings (here 'the ways of Israel/the House of Ahab'; 2 Kgs 8.18, 27; cf. 21.3) are nearly ubiquitously criticized.[15] However, given our reticence, expressed above, to endorse wholeheartedly the Deuteronomistic evaluation of the northern monarchy's religious expression without critical engagement, it would be wise to ask whether this presentation is a wholly fair one. Zevit has provided a thoroughgoing discussion of the problem, and concluded that 'Many of the elements in Jeroboam's program presented negatively by Dtr were most likely customary northern practices and therefore not innovative. If anything, they were Jeroboam's attempt to restore cultic practices in the north to what they had been prior to the establishment of Jerusalem as the major center of the united monarchy' (Zevit 2001: 449; see also Zevit 1985; Talmon 1958). His synthesis of the problem serves as the basis for the following discussion.

According to 1 Kgs 12.28-33, Jeroboam instituted five significant components of the post-schism Israelite cultus: 1) he set up two golden 'calves' (*ʿeglê zāhāb*) at Bethel and Dan, apparently in an effort to avert losing pilgrimage revenue and prestige to the Judahite sanctuary in Jerusalem (vv. 28–30); 2) he established smaller, local shrines (MT *bêt bāmôt*, emended to *bātê bāmôt*; v. 31a); 3) he promoted non-Levites to cultic leadership positions in the new shrines, and at the Bethel installation (vv. 31b, 32b); 4) he prompted some sort of calendrical change in the festival cycle (vv. 32a, 33a); and, relatedly, 5) Jeroboam himself served as a cultic functionary at the Bethel sanctuary in the newly established festival calendar (vv. 32b, 33b).

Zevit's analysis is a good one, and for the most part the results of that study will not be reproduced in much detail here. The reader is referred to that source (2001: 448–57; see also Talmon 1958), especially for further discussion of the above mentioned cultic calendar (Zevit 2001: 449–51), which according to Zevit had more to do historically with the periodic intercalation of a month in order to bring the Israelite cultus into synchronicity with the natural ecological and meteorological cycles that constrained farming activities in the northern kingdom than with any theological malfeasance on the part of Jeroboam. There are, however, two elements of the Deuteronomists' criticism of Jeroboam's activities to which I may add further observations: namely, the supposed impropriety of the bull iconography, and the promotion of non-Levites to cultic authority.

3.1 Bovine Imagery

As Zevit suggests, the use of the term 'calf' (*ʿēgel*) to describe the cultic images at

---

15.   For this critique of northern kings, see 1 Kgs 15.26, 34; 16.19, 25-26, 30-31; 22.53-54 (ET vv. 52–53); 2 Kgs 3.2-3; 13.2; 10.29, 31; 13.2, 11; 14.24; 15.9, 18, 24, 28. For recent discussions of the Deuteronomistic evaluations of the kings and summaries of earlier works, see Eynikel 1996 and Aurelius 2003.

Bethel and Dan is contrary to what is expected: namely, the bull, the image by which El (with whom Yahweh was identified unproblematically) was most often portrayed in Canaanite religious literature and praxis. Accordingly, the reason that the biblical author called the images 'calves' was because of their small size (Zevit 2001: 448 n. 22). This reading, I would argue, is only partially correct in its particulars. The linkage of El to the image of the bull is fairly well established by reference to the Ugaritic mythological texts, where El is often called by the epithet 'Bull' (*tr. il*; e.g. KTU 1.1.iii.26; 1.3.iv.54; 1.3.v.35; 1.4.iv.47; reconstructed, for example, in 1.4.i.4; 1.4.iv.1). Iconography of the southern Levant confirms that the bovid was an important image there as well, but because the images are rarely, if ever, accompanied by explanatory texts, the symbolism is considerably more difficult. Most scholars extrapolate the identification of the bull image with El from the purely textual indications (e.g. Cross 1973: 44–75, esp. 74; Keel and Uehlinger 1998: 191–95; Day 2000: 34–41); however, the image's symbolism remains ambiguous, and more than one deity could have been called by the epithet 'divine bull' (Fleming 1999; Smith 2002: 83–85 and n. 66).

One wonders, though, whether Zevit's assumption that the term 'calf' was used because the bull images were small holds back too readily from the point that the author of 1 Kgs 12.28-33 sought to convey. Working from cognate Mesopotamian and Anatolian material, Daniel Fleming has shown that bovine imagery in the ancient Near East tends to distinguish deities according to three categories: 'domestication, gender, and age' (Fleming 1999: esp. 23*). Despite the polysemy of the bull image, the pantheon head is invariably represented as such, regardless of whether other deities (such as the storm god in Anatolia) are also likened to that animal. Conversely, 'there is no evidence that the specific young form of the bull is ever attributed to the older, chief of a pantheon' (1999: 25*). If Fleming's observations are correct, the use of the age-specific designation for the cultic images at Bethel and Dan as 'calves' suggests that some derogatory meaning may have been intended. Two conclusions follow: first, the term need not have described merely the diminutive stature of the images themselves, but may have comprised a deprecating swipe at the representation's supposed power and vigour. Second, the description was possibly an intentionally belittling transfer of the deity's assumed identity Yahweh-El to the more blasphemous Baal-Hadad. In this understanding, the historical purpose of the imagery would have been to represent Yahweh in his El-type capacity as a bull, but the Deuteronomistic commentators, unable to make the explicit charge that Jeroboam had instituted Baalism in Israel, nonetheless sought to implicate that 'renegade' king through a campaign of subtle innuendo. The term 'calf' appears in other such intentionally polemic passages directed at the Bethel and Samaria cults,[16] but the cultic image is represented as a bull in texts that portray the cult favourably. Smith notes the petition in Amherst Papyrus 63, col. XI ('Horus-Yaho, our bull, is with us. May the lord of Bethel answer us on the morrow'; Steiner 1997: 318; although cf. translation and philological notes in Zevit 1990: 216–17, 219),[17] as well as a few biblical passages containing the terms

16. Exodus 32; Deut. 9.16, 21; 2 Kgs 10.29; 17.16; 2 Chron. 11.15; 13.8; Neh. 9.18; Ps. 106.19; Hos. 8.5-6; 10.5 ('*eglôt*; notice the insulting use of feminization!); 13.2.

17. If Steiner (1991: 363; 1995: 205) has correctly understood the passage of Amherst Papyrus 63 in which the words *y.š.k*[m] and '.*kryk*[m] occur in proximity to one another as having to do with 'kissing calves (*'āgālîm yiššāqûn*)', Hosea's apparently derogatory description of the rites at Bethel (13.2), then my assertion that the lexeme *'ēgel* was used in a deprecating manner will have to be reformulated.

'*abîr*, 'bull' (Gen. 49.24; Isa. 1.24; 49.26; 60.16; Ps. 132.2, 5; for the maturity of the animal see, for example, Isa. 34.7; Jer. 46.15) and *rě'ēm*, 'wild bull' (Num. 23.22; 24.8; Deut. 33.17). In light of Fleming's observation that the categories of bovine imagery were marked not only for gender and age, but for domestication as well, it is pertinent to note the use of *rě'ēm* in these passages preserving older traditions; one assumes that the undomesticated nature of the *rě'ēm* was an intentional allusive representation of Yahweh's dwelling place in the wilds of the Teman (e.g. Hab. 3.3). Moreover, the epithet of Yahweh as the 'bull of Jacob' ('*ăbîr ya'ăqōb*; Gen. 49.24; Isa. 49.26; 60.16; Ps. 132.2, 5; cf. the appellation '*ăbîr yiśrā'ēl* in Isa. 1.24) might draw our attention to the favourably portrayed cultic foundation narrative wherein that patriarch established the cult at Bethel (Genesis 28). Thus, given the evidence that the Bethel cult established by Jeroboam was securely within the pale of Yahwism, the Deuteronomistic description of Jeroboam's cultic implements as 'calves' may betray the rhetorical belittling of those images underlying the Judahite authors' patent disapproval of the cults' establishment.

3.2 Cultic Personnel

The biblical text claims that Jeroboam 'appointed priests from among all the people, who were not Levites (*way-ya'aś kōhănîm miqṣôt hā'ām'ăšer lō[']-hāyû mibbĕnê lēwî*)' (1 Kgs 12.31; NRSV). Regardless of the date of its composition, the criticism is most often considered as Judahite polemic aimed at discrediting the northern cult in theological retrospect.[18] Zevit takes this notice as an indication that Jeroboam's 'reforms may also have been aimed at regulating and controlling various families of Levites – disowned by Dtr – who competed for power in the northern kingdom after the departure of the Aaronid Levites' (Zevit 2001: 449). There is much to recommend an interpretation along these lines, provided this explanation is clarified and nuanced.

Frank Moore Cross has suggested that the origin of this Deuteronomistic critique is to be traced to the competition between the Aaronid and Mushite priestly families rather than to the profligate institution of unqualified commoners as priests in the shrines (cf. Exod. 32.26-29; Lev. 10.1-7; Numbers 12; and Deut. 33.8-11 contra Numbers 16; 25.6-15; Cross 1973: 195–215). Jeroboam's selection of Dan and Bethel was then in effect a savvy political attempt to infuse both of these priestly houses with some power, thereby stemming the potential internal conflict that might have been occasioned upon Israel's secession from Judah (Cross 1973: 211, 215). Accordingly, Bethel was a religious centre that fell under the purview of the Aaronids at the time of Jeroboam's accession to the throne, and the Deuteronomists' polemical characterization of that competing family as laity (*miqṣôt hā'ām*) asserted Mushite prerogatives over the northern cultic installations.[19]

Developing Cross's theory, Baruch Halpern argued that Jeroboam did not invest the Aaronid priestly family with authority, but rather ousted it from its traditional position at Bethel (2 Chron. 11.13-15; 13.8-11), because of its potential operation

---

18. Compare the various schemas of Campbell 1986: 89–91 (nn. 56, 58), 189 and O'Brien 1989: 186–87 with those of Cross 1973: 199, Nelson 1981: 112 and Zevit 2001: 449 on the one hand, and those of Jepsen 1953: 102–3 and Dietrich 1972: 138 on the other.

19. The Deuteronomistic interest in supporting Levites – especially *northern* Levites – is well accepted, and may be found most recently in the work of, for example, Geoghegan 2003: 217–20, 226; Leuchter 2007; Christian 2007: 219–21.

in favour of Rehoboam's Judah. Jeroboam then installed in its place Mushite Levites with a strong tradition of bull iconography, which encountered its primary opposition from a competing Mushite lineage located in Shiloh, which had previously supported Jeroboam's secession from Judah (1 Kgs 11.29-39), and which favoured cherubim iconography (Halpern 1976: 34-38; 1974).

Inasmuch as these models comport with the same sorts of competition for clients occurring between families of religious personnel found in anthropological analogues, they plausibly describe the probable historical situation in the pre-schism and schismatic monarchic periods (Stager 1985: 27; Hutton 2009a). Yet, it is insufficient simply to dismiss the allegations of the investiture of laity as the product of Levitical sour grapes without further elaboration, because there are several indications that Levitical genealogy was fluid in the early monarchic period, permitting the entry of non-Levites into the ranks of the initiated unproblematically.[20] Cross-cultural comparison with analogous hereditary saintly lineages suggests that it is not unheard of for families who have abrogated their saintly positions to attempt subsequently to re-enter the market of sainthood (Hutton 2009a). In coordination with Halpern's recognition that Jeroboam incurred the displeasure of his Shilonite supporters by instating a non-Shilonite family to the Bethel cultic leadership, it may thus be proposed that the notice of Jeroboam's selection of priests 'from among all the people' (NRSV) was an accurate perception of the pro-Shilonite Deuteronomists, who found objectionable Jeroboam's re-instatement of a Levitical clan that had lost its claim to effective saintly status, and which had formerly been effectively laicized. If correct, this reconstruction would demonstrate that even within the macro-religious expression of the northern kingdom during the divided monarchy, there were a number of locally defined micro-religions, some of which came to ascendency in lieu of others by virtue of real or imagined genealogies, or through certain political affiliations, and which found expression in a variety of iconographic and textual modes.

4
Biblical and Archaeological Evidence for Transjordanian Religion

The religious differentiation of the Israelite-controlled territories east of the Jordan is an under-represented subject of discussion in secondary literature on Israelite religion.[21] This deficiency is perhaps due to the apparent shortage of relevant biblical material: for every *hieros logos* grounding the cultic installation at the Transjordanian Penuel (Gen. 32.31 [ET v. 30]; 33.10), there is a corresponding aetiology for the Cisjordanian ritual city Bethel (Gen. 28.18-22); for every tale concerning Mahanaim (Gen. 32.1-2, 8-11 [ET vv. 2-3, 7-10]), there is another tale instituting Israelite presence

20. For example, Judg. 17.7; the genealogy of the Ephraimite Samuel in 1 Sam. 1.1; 2.18-21; and 3.1 in comparison with his Levitical credentials in 1 Chron. 6.18-23 (ET vv. 33–38); the Gittite origins of Obed-edom in 2 Sam. 6.11-12 and 1 Chron. 13.13-14 in comparison with his implied Levite ancestry in 1 Chron. 15.16-24; for bibliography, see Hutton 2009a.

21. Notice that I provide only the ethnic affiliation here ('Israelite'), and not the political affiliation ('Israelian'). Although Baruch Levine has argued cogently from a historical perspective that 'even during periods of Aramaean hegemony in Transjordan, Gilead was part of the political configuration of the northern kingdom' (1985: 332), the political status of these territories is not the focus of this section.

at Shechem (Genesis 34) or a poetic turn of phrase alluding to Jerusalem's displacement of the northern sanctuary at Shiloh (Gen. 49.10: *lō'-yāsûr šēbeṭ mîhûdâ . . . 'ad kî-yābō' šîlōh*). A complicating factor is experienced in the ostensible statistical over-representation that one archaeological site in particular, Deir 'Alla, has garnered in the consideration of Transjordanian Israelite religion. However, there is every indication that the same sociological and demographic forces that were at work in shaping Israelian religious expressions simultaneously shaped Transjordanian cultic forms as well. Consideration of several biblical traditions demonstrates that any scarcity of biblical material on Transjordan is only perceived, and a proper contextualization of the Balaam text from Deir 'Alla can provide much needed insight into both the points of divergence and the continuities between Transjordanian and Judahite (here ostensibly synonymous with biblical) religion.

4.1 Deir 'Alla as Transjordanian Israelite Centre

The starting point for any modern engagement with the religious traditions of the Transjordan is the study by Jo Ann Hackett, published in 1987. In that piece, Hackett discusses the nature of the epigraphic finds at Deir 'Alla, then surveys three large biblical complexes that deal with Transjordanian religious traditions: 1) the Balaam traditions, found primarily in Numbers 22–24, but represented or recalled also in 31.15-16 and Josh. 13.15-23 (both of which seem to conflate the Balaam tradition with Num. 25.6-18); Deut. 23.4-7; Neh. 13.2; Josh. 24.9-10; Mic. 6.3-5; as well as in early Christian and Rabbinic sources (Hackett 1987: 127–28); 2) the traditions concerning the participation of Reuben and Gad in the Cisjordanian conquest (Numbers 32), and of the related narrative in which a Cisjordanian contingent confronts those Transjordanian tribes for their alleged construction of an altar in non-conformity with Torah law (Joshua 22) (Hackett 1987: 129–30); and 3) the biblical traditions in which child sacrifice seems to be permissible, if not condoned (Judg. 11.34-40; 2 Kgs 3.27; cf. passages treating the practice with opprobrium: e.g. Deut. 12.31; 18.9-14; Ps. 106.37-38; Jer. 7.31-32; Ezek. 20.25-26; Mic. 6.7-8). Both passages expressing the legitimacy of child sacrifice (Judg. 11.34-40; 2 Kgs 3.27) occur across the Jordan (Hackett 1987: 131–33). Hackett argues that careful consideration of the available biblical traditions yields several salient conclusions, all of which seem to point to the biblical authors' attempts to neutralize the centrifugal tendencies of the deviant Transjordanian cult located at Deir 'Alla, or to rehabilitate and reincorporate Yahwistic segments of Transjordanian society into the mainstream (i.e. biblical, conceptualized as primarily Judahite) Yahwistic fold (Hackett 1987: 131, 134). Two of the neutralized tendencies are particularly relevant here:

4.1.1 Šadday

The cultic remains at Deir 'Alla do not indicate any sort of relationship to the specifically Yahwistic cult, which elsewhere serves as a significant marker of pan-Israelite religion, although El does seem to have been the chief deity in the cult represented at the site.[22] The inscription refers also to two groups of minor deities, the *'lhn* ('gods'; I.5), and the *šdyn* ('shaddays'; I.6, reconstructed in I.5), which may be identical. No matter the precise identification of either group, the relationship between the *šaddayîn*

---

22.   See, for example, the description of the vision as *kms' 'l* 'like an oracle of El' (I.2; see also II.6); Hackett 1984: 86; Levine 1985: 333–34.

of Deir 'Alla and the biblical term *šēdîm* (reformulated from an original **šaddayīm*), which designated a class of minor deities in biblical texts excoriating the Israelites' past cultic abuses (Deut. 32.16-17; Ps. 106.37-39), is obvious. The approximation of this appellation to the soubriquet of El, Shadday (e.g. Gen. 17.1; 28.3; 48.3), is patent and could explain why in the biblical text, a literarily reformed Balaam is said to have been a devotee of Shadday (Num. 24.4, 16; Hackett 1984: 85–89).

It is presumably not coincidental that the epithet Shadday is used of the deity worshipped by Jacob at the establishment of Bethel (Gen. 28.3). Jacob's itinerary upon his return to Cisjordan includes a report that he built himself a *bayit* in Sukkoth (Gen. 33.17). Although this is normally translated as 'house' (ASV, RSV, NRSV, JPS), the word also means 'temple' (as in the 'house' of the deity), and may implicitly participate in the larger aetiological project of Genesis 28–33, namely, the grounding of several prominent cultic sites (Bethel in Genesis 28; Mahanaim, Penuel and Sukkoth in Genesis 32–33; Levine 1985: 333). Although the excavator of Deir 'Alla, the late H.J. Franken, repeatedly – and until the time of his death – shunned an identification of the site as Sukkoth (e.g. Aharoni 1979: 442; Levine 1985: 331 [possible]; Weippert 1997: 22; but cf. MacDonald 2000: 143–44; and Franken 1969: 4–8; 1991: 9; 2008: 27), such an identification may serve to explain the apparent continuity between the divine or semi-divine epithets in use at the site (*šdyn*) and in biblical texts incorporating the site into the broader pan-Israelite orthodoxy (Gen. 33.17). Hackett (1987: 129–31; building on Kloppenborg 1981) has proposed that the episode of the confrontation between 'orthodox' Cisjordanian Israelites and allegedly unorthodox Transjordanians in Joshua 22 fulfils a similarly inclusive purpose, countermanding the Priestly eschewal of Transjordan as part of the Promised Land (for which view, see especially Weinfeld 1983): 'The effect of the story as we now have it, however, is to represent the point of view of the Transjordanian tribes over against the Priestly jumping the gun, and . . . to integrate, or reintegrate in this case, the wayward group into the fold of Yahwist Israel' (Hackett 1987: 130–31; see recently Havrelock 2004: 63–70).

4.1.2 Child Sacrifice

Hackett argues (1987: 131–33) that Ps. 106.37-39 provides a chilling corroboration of the supposition that Jephthah's sacrifice of his daughter (if the text of Judg. 11.34-40 may indeed be read to indicate such) and Mesha's immolation of his firstborn son (2 Kgs 3.27) are not simply tangentially related to the stories' respective geographical locations in Transjordan. Instead, the tacit localization of Ps. 106.37-39 in Transjordan (cf. vv. 28–31, which narrate the events at Baal-peor, with no intervening mention of the conquest; and Ezek. 20.25-26) may accordingly confirm the relationship of child sacrifice with this area (for the portrayal of the practice as 'foreign' see recently Stavrakopoulou 2004: 148–79).

This recognition, however, may be taken a step farther, and may be removed from a specifically Transjordanian venue. Although child sacrifice was a practice that some biblical authors portrayed polemically as having derived from Ammonite custom (e.g. 1 Kgs 11.7 in combination with Lev. 18.21; 20.2-5; 2 Kgs 23.10; Isa. 57.9; and esp. Jer. 32.35), Jeremiah's profession of Yahweh's innocence in the people's practice (*lō' ṣiwwîtî wě-lō' 'ālětā 'al-libbî* 'I did not command it – it didn't even enter my mind!') suggests that there was more than mere pride at stake for the Judahite apologists (Smith 2002: 171). In fact, child sacrifice may plausibly be related to certain variations of Mediterranean (Phoenicio-Punic) worship of the Phoenician deity El (in his instantiations as Hellenistic Kronos-Saturn and Punic Baal Hamon; Mosca 1975: 1–27, esp. 4–5, 17–20, 24–25; Olyan 1988: 38–69, esp. 67–68), with whom both Yahweh and the Ammonite high deity (= Milcom?) were likely identified.[23] As Francesca Stavrakopoulou has recently reiterated, the practice of child sacrifice was hardly unknown or even antithetical to the Yahweh cult of Judah (2004: 179–206, 283–99; see also Smith 2002: 171–81). Thus, Jeremiah's outright denunciation of the practice, combined with those texts claiming its foreign (and specifically Transjordanian) origins, may have the effect of strengthening our impression that child sacrifice was in fact a legitimate feature of at least some forms of Judahite, if not pan-Israelite, cultic expression. The available data imply that there existed historically a great deal more continuity between the ('legitimate') El-Yahwism of Cisjordanian Judah and the El-centred religions of Ammon and Moab than the biblical texts admit. Therefore, ironically, the biblical assertions that there obtained a particularly strong link between child sacrifice and the tacitly substandard Transjordanian religion, recognized by Hackett, may unwittingly betray those assertions' own origins as products of mere literary artifice rather than of authentic historical realities, the polemical attempts of the biblical authors to construct the practice as Other.

4.2 Deir 'Alla as Non-Yahwistic Enclave

The precision of Hackett's trenchant analysis notwithstanding, I would offer here further clarification of the socio-religious role played by Deir 'Alla in the monarchic period (c. 700 BCE) through special consideration of the micro-religion expressed at the site. Rather than treating the cultic remnants of Deir 'Alla as representative of the bulk of the Transjordanian Israelite religious environment, it is perhaps preferable to regard the site as at best an enclave of divergent Transjordanian Israelite religious expression during the late monarchic period, if not as an example of Aramaic or Ammonite hegemony in the post-Omride period of political turmoil experienced by the inhabitants of Transjordan (for the region's geopolitical history, see, for example, Lemaire 1991: 36–41). The linguistic affinities to Aramaic displayed by the dialect spoken at Deir 'Alla have led Lemaire (1991) and Wolters (1988: esp. 108–11) to posit the presence there of a group of Aramaean refugees from the Assyrian destruction whose traditions preserved this text in a form of archaic Aramaic. This postulation would supposedly account for the Canaanite features discernable in the text (e.g. the retention of the N-stem and the *waw*-consecutive; Hackett 1984: 123–24; Levine 1985: 329–30) either as features of a hybridized form of Aramaic which assimilated to the Canaanite language(s) of the enclave's surrounding environment, or as relics from a very early stage of Aramaic that still displayed the features (Wolters 1988: 108–11, esp. 110–11; see similarly Lemaire 1991: 50; for the inscriptions as basically Aramaic, see, for example, Hoftijzer and van der Kooij 1976: 300; McCarter 1980:

---

23.   For Yahweh as an El-type figure, see, for example, Cross 1973: 44–75; Olyan 1988: 38–69; Day 2000: 13–17; Smith 2002: 32–43; and, particularly relevant in the present context, Levine 1985: 336–38; for Ammonite worship of El, see Tigay 1986: 19 n. 60; Daviau and Dion 1994; Aufrecht 1999: 158–60. I thank Paul Kurtz for his bibliographic help here. Unfortunately, space limitations preclude study of the manifold textual and historical difficulties in determining the nature of Molech (i.e. sacrifice or deity?) as well as his or its relationship to the Ammonite deity Milcom. Related to this problem is the religious background of the cultic practice of child sacrifice. For the most recent statement on the problem and a comprehensive review of the literature, see Stavrakopoulou 2004.

50–51).[24] However, as McCarter noted subsequent to his original statement on the issue (1991: 91), philologists have increasingly called into question the overly simplistic bifurcation between Aramaic and Canaanite, and more modern schemas have increasingly interpreted the dialect of Deir 'Alla as a language separate from both Aramaic and Hebrew, but which shares certain retentions, as well as innovations, with both language families (McCarter 1991: 97; Huehnergard 1991; cf. the slightly different reconstruction of Pardee 1991: 104–5).

Like Kuntillet 'Ajrud, the sanctuary at Deir 'Alla seems to have been associated somehow with the trade industry, the infrastructural networks of which ran close by the site (Franken 1991: 10–11). Several recent studies have demonstrated that the site controlled a major corridor for trade and transhumant pastoralism leading from the Transjordanian highlands surrounding Amman into the Jordan Valley, across the river at the Adam or Umm Sidre fords, and into the Cisjordanian hill country at Shechem (Franken 1991: 11; Hutton 2006: esp. 172 n. 52, 173–74; van der Steen 2008; for the Cisjordanian portion of the route, see Dorsey 1991: 174–75 [S16]). This trade artery, like that at Kuntillet 'Ajrud, would have been a thoroughfare for travellers and merchants of multiple nationalities and ethnicities, and we should likely expect to find a similar *mélange* of cultural artefacts at the site, no matter the predominant ethnic affiliations held by the bulk of the population.

True to these expectations, Franken uncovered both a stone and a potsherd bearing the quintessentially Aramaic inscriptions *'bn / zy šr''* (respectively, 'rock of/belonging to ŠR'' '; see Franken 2008: 44, fig. 4); both artefacts serve to demonstrate the presence of Aramaeans at the sanctuary during the eighth century. But the presence of Aramaic cultural material does not demand that we understand the site or the language in use there as Aramaean. Hackett argues, appositely, that the 'very fact that the plaster text *does not* look like that Aramaic, that an inscribed stone and potsherd have to be called upon to provide the evidence of real, regular Aramaeans at Deir 'Allā, should logically push us in the direction of looking for some culture *other* than that of Aram-Damascus for the source of the ideas and mythology included in the text' (Hackett 1991: 82–83; see also Levine 1985: 328, 332). McCarter's suggestion (1991: 98) that the language of the inscription be considered a 'local dialect' that need not be derived from the cluster of Aramaic languages moves towards a similar conclusion: the cult evidenced at Deir 'Alla seems to be indigenous, rather than imported.

Despite the widely divergent forms and expressions of religion discussed here and already above, the Judahite, Israelian and Transjordanian micro-religions demonstrate a few theoretical commonalities. As was the case with Kuntillet 'Ajrud, we have at Deir 'Alla evidence of an apparently locally circumscribed official religious establishment with its own dedicated sanctuary and text inscribed in plaster, combined with epigraphic and material indications of the temporary presence of religious devotees whose origins lay outside the immediate locale. Worship at the site may, by analogy, have been simultaneously both regularly practised and ad hoc, depending on the respective backgrounds of the practitioners. Moreover, as was the case with the Baal-based theophoric names above, the indeterminacy of the available data similarly permits our conclusions here concerning the religious variation in Transjordan to be conditionalized. If the cult at Deir 'Alla is understood as representative of a more

---

24. For the *waw*-consecutive in early Aramaic inscriptions, compare both the Tel Dan and Zakkur inscriptions (Muraoka 1995: 19–20).

widespread Transjordanian Israelite religion, the apparently non-Yahwistic (or perhaps only putatively 'substandard' Yahwistic?) shrine at Deir 'Alla provides solid evidence for intra-Israelite differentiation, and the biblical texts adduced above sought to re-incorporate those 'lapsed' Israelites (and presumed Yahwists) back into the covenant community. In this heuristic model, which I take to be the basis of Hackett's formulation (1987; also Levine 1985), the biblical attempt at the religious reintegration of the Transjordanian tribes is actual and personal, if conducted only literarily. It was carried out by a Cisjordanian (and particularly Judahite) intelligentsia whose primary concern was the integrity of the Yahweh-worshipping Israelite community.

However, this construal of the biblical texts is not the only possible interpretation. It seems to me to be equally possible – and, given the geopolitical, historical and linguistic differences, it is perhaps much more plausible – that the population of the Transjordan already early in the Iron Age comprised a multitude of ethnicities, only a few of which could [legitimately] be considered (i.e. would have self-identified as) ethnically 'Israelite', and that the portion of the population represented in the cultic remains at Deir 'Alla derived from one of the remaining demographic segments. Despite its geographic position within the broader boundaries of a political Israel, that enclave may have been ethnically non-Israelite, and either retained its own enigmatic and conservative dialect of Northwest Semitic that was neither a familiar form of Aramaic nor of Canaanite, but which displayed its own innovations, or it preserved a religious text in just such a dialect.[25] (Without corroboration from other inscriptions of varying genres, found in the area and displaying similar linguistic features, it is impossible to know which of these options obtained.) The religious expression exemplified at Deir 'Alla, in which El seems to have been the primary deity (see above; compare also the nearby toponym of Penuel), potentially existed side-by-side with quintessentially Yahwistic manifestations in Transjordan. Compare, for example, Mesha's claim to have removed the [k]ly yhwh 'vessels of Yahweh' from the Israelite sanctuary at Nebo (KAI 181, lines 17–18; also Levine 1985: 334).[26] In this interpretive model, the biblical tradents inherited a number of [early] monarchic traditions that provided cultic aetiologies for several important Israelite (and perhaps non-Israelite or only temporarily Israelite) sanctuaries in Transjordan (i.e. the constituent traditions of Genesis 32–33), and, influenced by the Deuteronomistic camp that considered the Arnon (and not the Jordan) to be the true boundary of the Promised Land (Weinfeld 1983), these editors of the biblical corpora ultimately sought to reclaim these literary traditions as their own, irrespective of whether the inhabitants of the claimed locales displayed any awareness of having been ethnically 'Israelite' at any point. On this understanding, the 'integration' here is perhaps one not of saving souls but of 'saving soles'. That is to say, the issue is one of the literary appropriation of sacred geography, and particularly the appropriation or reclamation of the very physical – and simultaneously the

25.　　Compare the well-known example of Pella to the north of Deir 'Alla. The city was evidently never considered 'Israelite', but lay well within the classically construed Israelite boundaries. A modern analogue to what I am suggesting here may be found in Native American reservations in the US. Geographically, the reservations fall within the political boundaries of the US but retain some degree of political autonomy and an independent ethnic identity.

26.　　One wonders whether the notice in Deut. 34.6 that Moses' burial site remained unknown in the days of the narrator was itself a Deuteronomistic attempt to suppress the authority and legitimacy of a well-known Transjordanian Israelite religious centre whose cultic personnel claimed to know *precisely* where Moses was buried (e.g. Dijkstra 2006: esp. 19–22)!

metaphysical, transfigurative – pilgrimage paths along which the covenant community of the biblical Israel purportedly received its identity: as Levine notes (1985: 333), Israel's eponymous ancestor received his new, El-based theophoric name in the Jabbok River Valley just upstream from Deir 'Alla at Penuel (see Hutton 2006). The editors sought retrospectively to extend 'biblical' Israel's literary control over the region as far as possible, even if political control and ethnic uniformity were unattainable for the leadership of historical Judah. The prominence in the developing 'canon' of Israel's historico-literary traditions and the importance in Israelian and Judahite communal memory of Jacob's travels would have required that literary measures be taken to claim the Valley of Sukkoth (Ps. 60.8 [ET v. 6]) as Israelite, whether or not the literature matched the ethnic and geopolitical situation at the time of the text's formation.

5

A Preliminary Synthesis

The complexity of the preceding argument, compounded by the indeterminacy of much of the available data, suggests that any closing remarks should be brief, and must be considered only preliminary. I have every anticipation that the argument laid out here will be both challenged by contemporaries and superseded with the discovery of new data and the concomitant recognition of new connections between old texts.

The thesis defended here is that the bewildering variety of biblical, epigraphic and archaeological evidence points to an unfathomably complex religious environment in the southern Levant that can only schematically be represented as 'Southern, Northern, and Transjordanian approaches' to Israelite religion. Evidence from Kuntillet 'Ajrud attests to the worship of various local manifestations of Yahweh. This worship was conducted in a variety of manners: the locally indigenous worship of Yahweh of Teman occurred in what appears to have been 'officially' sanctioned devotional spaces, while the worship of Yahweh of Samaria seems to have occurred in an ad hoc manner within and between those spaces. A survey of biblical and epigraphic onomastics attests to religious variation in the northern kingdom, if only coterminous with ethnic differences in that region. Critical analysis of the Deuteronomistic critique of the northern kingdom's regional macro-religion, purportedly instituted by Jeroboam after the schism, yields a fuller understanding of the Deuteronomists' rhetorical and polemical attempts to emphasize the Otherness of that cultic expression, and to suppress the extent of the commonalities shared by both regional macro-religions. Similar analysis of passages concerning Transjordanian expressions of Israelite religion, along with consideration of the ambiguity of the position of Deir 'Alla in that region's macro-religion, again throws any attempts at easy schematization into disarray. The cultus itself appears to be indigenous, but it is not clear whether its primary practitioners were ethnically Israelite (perhaps specifically Gileadite), or would have self-identified as a non-Israelite ethnic enclave. No matter the exact position held by the group, the presence of an El-based religious expression alongside the distinctively Israelite Yahwistic cult attested at Nebo demands that we again admit to something like a patchwork of micro-religions.

We may end with a repetition and broadening of a conclusion already reached schematically above: the constituent micro-religions of pan-Israelite religion found expression in a number of different modes, and were adapted to divergent uses by different constituencies among the biblical authors. They remained in tension with one another, and resisted assimilation, even in the literary realm. But when bundled together through literary and editorial devices, these various micro-religions were portrayed as constituent elements of their respective regional macro-religions, and hence of pan-Israelite religion. What is more, only through a long process of theological refinement and textual composition and elaboration did this *pan-Israelite* religion eventually become *biblical* religion.

Bibliography

Aharoni, Y.
1979   *The Land of the Bible: A Historical Geography* (2nd edn; trans. A. Rainey. Philadelphia, PA: Westminster Press).

Albertz, R.
1994   *A History of Israelite Religion in the Old Testament Period* (2 vols; trans. J. Bowden. OTL; Louisville, KY: Westminster John Knox).

Albright, W.F.
1942   *Archaeology and the Religion of Israel* (OTL; Louisville, KY: Westminster John Knox; repr. of 2nd edn [1969], 2006).

Anderson, F.I. and D.N. Freedman
1980   *Hosea: A New Translation with Introduction and Commentary* (AB 24; New York, NY: Doubleday).

Aufrecht, W.E.
1999   'The Religion of the Ammonites', in B. MacDonald and R.W. Younker (eds), *Ancient Ammon* (SHCANE 17; Leiden: Brill), 152–62.

Aurelius, E.
2003   *Zukunft jenseits des Gerichts: Eine redaktionsgeschichtliche Studie zum Enneateuch* (BZAW 319; Berlin and New York, NY: de Gruyter).

Avigad, N.
1966   'Two Phoenician Votive Seals', *IEJ* 16: 243–51, plate 26.
1987   'The Contribution of Hebrew Seals to an Understanding of Israelite Religion and Society', in P.D. Miller, P.D. Hanson and S.D. McBride (eds), *Ancient Israelite Religion: Essays in Honor of Frank Moore Cross* (Philadelphia, PA: Fortress Press), 195–208.
1988   'Hebrew Seals and Sealings and Their Significance for Biblical Research', in J.A. Emerton (ed.), *Congress Volume: Jerusalem, 1986* (VTS 40; Leiden: Brill), 7–16.

Avigad, N. and B. Sass
1997   *Corpus of West Semitic Stamp Seals* (Jerusalem: Israel Exploration Society).

Ben Zvi, E.
2005   *Hosea* (FOTL 21A/1; Grand Rapids, MI: Eerdmans).

Binger, T.
1997   *Asherah: Goddesses in Ugarit, Israel and the Old Testament* (JSOTS 232/CIS 2; Sheffield: Sheffield Academic Press).

Bright, J.
2000 [1959] *A History of Israel* (4th edn, with an Introduction and Appendix by W.P. Brown; Louisville, KY: Westminster John Knox).

Callaway, R.
1999   'The Name Game: Onomastic Evidence and Archaeological Reflections on Religion in Late Judah', *Jian Dao* 11: 15–36.

Campbell, A.F.
1986 *Of Prophets and Kings: A Late Ninth-Century Document (1 Sam 1–2 Kings 10)* (CBQMS 14; Washington, DC: Catholic Biblical Association of America).

Christian, M.A.
2007 'Revisiting Levitical Authorship: What Would Moses Think?', *ZAR* 13: 194–236.

Coogan, M.D.
1987 'Canaanite Origins and Lineage: Reflections on the Religion of Ancient Israel', in P.D. Miller, P.D. Hanson and S.D. McBride (eds), *Ancient Israelite Religion: Essays in Honor of Frank Moore Cross* (Philadelphia, PA: Fortress Press), 115–24.

Cross, F.M.
1970 'The Cave Inscription from Khirbet Beit Lei', in J.A. Sanders (ed.), *Near Eastern Archaeology in the Twentieth Century: Essays in Honor of Nelson Glueck* (Garden City, NY: Doubleday), 299–306.
1973 *Canaanite Myth and Hebrew Epic: Essays in the History of the Religion of Israel* (Cambridge, MA: Harvard University Press).

Daviau, P.M.M. and P.-E. Dion
1994 'El, the God of the Ammonites? The Atef-Crowned Head from *Tell Jawa*, Jordan', *ZDPV* 110: 158–67.

Day, J.
1992 'Baal (Deity)', *ABD* 1.545–49.
2000 *Yahweh and the Gods and Goddesses of Canaan* (JSOTS 265; Sheffield: Sheffield Academic Press).

Dearman, J.A.
1993 'Baal in Israel: The Contribution of Some Place Names and Personal Names to an Understanding of Early Israelite Religion', in M.P. Graham, W.P. Brown and J.K. Kuan (eds), *History and Interpretation: Essays in Honour of John H. Hayes* (JSOTS 173; Sheffield: Sheffield Academic Press), 173–91.

Dietrich, W.
1972 *Prophetie und Geschichte: Eine redaktionsgeschichtliche Untersuchung zum deuteronomistischen Geschichtswerk* (FRLANT 108; Göttingen: Vandenhoeck & Ruprecht).

Dijkstra, M.
2006 'Moses, the Man of God', in R. Roukema (ed.), *The Interpretation of Exodus: Studies in Honour of Cornelis Houtman* (CBET 44; Leuven: Peeters), 17–36.

Diringer, D.
1934 *Le iscrizioni antico-ebraiche palestinesi* (Florence: Felice le Monnier).

Dobbs-Allsopp, F.W., J.J.M. Roberts, C.L. Seow and R.E. Whitaker
2005 *Hebrew Inscriptions: Texts from the Biblical Period of the Monarchy with Concordance* (New Haven, CT: Yale University Press).

Dorsey, D.A.
1991 *The Roads and Highways of Ancient Israel* (Baltimore, MD: The Johns Hopkins University Press).

Emerton, J.A.
1982. 'New Light on Israelite Religion: The Implications of the Inscriptions from Kuntillet 'Ajrud', *ZAW* 94: 2–20.

Eynikel, E.
1996 *The Reform of King Josiah and the Composition of the Deuteronomistic History* (OTS 33; Leiden: Brill).

Fleming, D.E.
1999 'If El Is a Bull, Who Is a Calf? Reflections on Religion in Second-Millennium Syria-Palestine', *ErIsr* 26: 23*–27*.

Franken, H.J.
1969   *Excavations at Tell Deir 'Alla I* (Leiden: Brill).
1991   'Deir 'Allā Re-Visited', in J. Hoftijzer and G. van der Kooij (eds), *The Balaam Text from Deir 'Allā Re-Evaluated: Proceedings of the International Symposium Held at Leiden 21–24 August 1989* (Leiden: Brill), 3–15.
2008   'Deir 'Allā and Its Religion', in M.L. Steiner and E.J. van der Steen (eds), *Sacred and Sweet: Studies on the Material Culture of Tell Deir 'Alla and Tell Abu Sarbut* (Leuven: Peeters), 25–52.

Geoghegan, J.C.
2003   '"Until This Day" and the Preexilic Redaction of the Deuteronomistic History', *JBL* 122: 201–27.

Gilula, M.
1978–79 'To Yahweh Shomron and his Ashera', *Shnaton* 3: 129–37 (Hebrew; English summary, xv–xvi).

Gitin, S.
2002   'The Four-Horned Altar and Sacred Space: An Archaeological Perspective', in B.M. Gittlen (ed.), *Sacred Time, Sacred Place: Archaeology and the Religion of Israel* (Winona Lake, IN: Eisenbrauns), 95–123.

Gottwald, N.K.
1999 [1979] *The Tribes of Yahweh: A Sociology of the Religion of Liberated Israel, 1250–1050 BCE* (The Biblical Seminar 66; Sheffield: Sheffield Academic Press).

Hackett, J.A.
1984   *The Balaam Text from Deir 'Allā* (HSM 31; Chico, CA: Scholars Press).
1987   'Religious Traditions in Israelite Transjordan', in P.D. Miller, P.D. Hanson and S.D. McBride (eds), *Ancient Israelite Religion: Essays in Honor of Frank Moore Cross* (Philadelphia, PA: Fortress Press), 125–36.
1991   'Response to Baruch Levine and André Lemaire', in J. Hoftijzer and G. van der Kooij (eds), *The Balaam Text from Deir 'Allā Re-Evaluated: Proceedings of the International Symposium Held at Leiden 21–24 August 1989* (Leiden: Brill), 73–84.

Hadley, J.M.
1993   'Kuntillet 'Ajrud: Religious Centre or Desert Way Station?', *PEQ* 125: 115–24.
2000   *The Cult of Asherah in Ancient Israel and Judah: Evidence for a Hebrew Goddess* (UCOP 57; Cambridge: Cambridge University Press).

Halpern, B.
1974   'Sectionalism and the Schism', *JBL* 93: 519–32.
1976   'Levitic Participation in the Reform Cult of Jeroboam I', *JBL* 95: 31–42.

Hamilton, G.J.
1998   'New Evidence for the Authenticity of *bšt* in Hebrew Personal Names and for Its Use as a Divine Epithet in Biblical Texts', *CBQ* 60: 228–50.

Hauser, A.J.
1979   'Unity and Diversity in Early Israel before Samuel', *JETS* 22: 289–303.

Havrelock, R.S.
2004   'The Jordan River: Crossing a Biblical Boundary', PhD dissertation. University of California, Berkeley.

Hertzog, Z.
1981   'Israelite Sanctuaries at Arad and Beersheba: Synopsis of Lecture', in A. Biran (ed.), *Temples and High Places in Biblical Times: Proceedings of the Colloquium in Honor of the Centennial of Hebrew Union College-Jewish Institute of Religion* (Jerusalem: Hebrew Union College and the Jewish Institute of Religion), 120–23.

Hess, R.S.
1991   'Yahweh and His Asherah? Religious Pluralism in the Old Testament World', in A.D.

Clarke and B.W. Winter (eds), *One God, One Lord in a World of Religious Pluralism* (Cambridge: Tyndale House), 5–33.

1996 'Asherah or Asherata?', *Orientalia* 65: 209–19.

2007 *Israelite Religions: An Archaeological and Biblical Survey* (Grand Rapids, MI: Baker).

Hoftijzer, J. and G. van der Kooij (eds)
1976 *Aramaic Texts from Deir 'Alla* (Leiden: Brill).

Huehnergard, J.
1991 'Remarks on the Classification of the Northwest Semitic Languages', in J. Hoftijzer and G. van der Kooij (eds), *The Balaam Text from Deir 'Alla Re-Evaluated: Proceedings of the International Symposium Held at Leiden 21–24 August 1989* (Leiden: Brill), 282–93.

Hutton, J.M.
2006 'Mahanaim, Penuel and Transhumance Routes: Observations on Genesis 32–33 and Judges 8', *JNES* 65: 161–78.

2009a 'The Levitical Diaspora (I): A Sociological Comparison with Morocco's Ahansal', in D. Schloen (ed.), *Exploring the* Longue Durée: *Essays in Honor of Lawrence E. Stager* (Winona Lake, IN: Eisenbrauns), 223–34.

2009b *The Transjordanian Palimpsest: The Overwritten Texts of Personal Exile and Transformation in the Deuteronomistic History* (BZAW 396; Berlin and New York, NY: de Gruyter).

Forthcoming 'Local Manifestations of Yahweh and Worship in the Interstices: A Note on Kuntillet 'Ajrud', *JANER*.

Jepsen, A.
1953 *Die Quellen des Königsbuches* (Halle: Niemeyer).

Keel, O. and C. Uehlinger
1998 *Gods, Goddesses, and Images of God in Ancient Israel* (trans. T.H. Trapp; Minneapolis, MN: Fortress Press).

Killebrew, A.E.
2005 *Biblical Peoples and Ethnicity: An Archaeological Study of Egyptians, Canaanites, Philistines, and Early Israel, 1300–1100 BCE* (SBLABS 9; Atlanta, GA: Society of Biblical Literature).

Kloppenborg, J.S.
1981 'Joshua 22: The Priestly Editing of an Ancient Tradition', *Biblica* 62: 347–71.

Knoppers, G.N.
2000 'Introduction', in G.N. Knoppers and J.G. McConville (eds), *Reconsidering Israel and Judah: Recent Studies on the Deuteronomistic History* (Winona Lake, IN: Eisenbrauns), 1–18.

Lemaire, A.
1991 'Les inscriptions sur plâtre de Deir 'Alla et leur signification histoirique et culturelle', in J. Hoftijzer and G. van der Kooij (eds), *The Balaam Text from Deir 'Alla Re-Evaluated: Proceedings of the International Symposium Held at Leiden 21–24 August 1989* (Leiden: Brill), 33–57.

Leuchter, M.
2007 'Why Is the Song of Moses in the Book of Deuteronomy?', *VT* 57: 295–317.

Levine, B.A.
1985 'The Balaam Inscription from Deir 'Alla: Historical Aspects', in *Biblical Archaeology Today: Proceedings of the International Congress on Biblical Archaeology, Jerusalem, April 1984* (Jerusalem: Israel Exploration Society), 326–39.

MacDonald, B.
2000 *'East of the Jordan': Territories and Sites of the Hebrew Scriptures* (ASOR Books 6; Boston, MA: ASOR).

Mayes, A.D.H.
1997   'Kuntillet 'Ajrud and the History of Israelite Religion', J.R. Bartlett (ed.), *Archaeology and Biblical Interpretation* (London: Routledge), 51–66.

Mays, J.L.
1969   *Hosea: A Commentary* (OTL; London: SCM Press).

McCarter, P.K.
1980   'The Balaam Texts from Deir 'Allā: The First Combination', *BASOR* 222: 49–60.
1987   'Aspects of the Religion of the Israelite Monarchy: Biblical and Epigraphic Data', in P.D. Miller, P.D. Hanson and S.D. McBride (eds), *Ancient Israelite Religion: Essays in Honor of Frank Moore Cross* (Philadelphia, PA: Fortress Press), 137–55.
1991   'The Dialect of the Deir 'Alla Texts', in J. Hoftijzer and G. van der Kooij (eds), *The Balaam Text from Deir 'Alla Re-Evaluated: Proceedings of the International Symposium Held at Leiden 21–24 August 1989* (Leiden: Brill), 87–99.

Meshel, Z.
1978   *Kuntillet 'Ajrud: A Religious Centre from the Time of the Judaean Monarchy on the Border of Sinai* (Jerusalem: Israel Museum).
1979   'Did Yahweh Have a Consort?', *BAR* 5.2: 24–35.

Meshel, Z. and C. Meyers
1976   'The Name of God in the Wilderness of Zin', *BA* 39: 6–10.

Miller, R.D., II.
2005   *Chieftains of the Highland Clans: A History of Israel in the 12th and 11th Centuries BC* (Grand Rapids, MI: Eerdmans).

Mosca, P.G.
1975   'Child Sacrifice in Canaanite and Israelite Religion'. PhD dissertation. Harvard University.

Muraoka, T.
1995   'Linguistic Notes on the Aramaic Inscription from Tel Dan', *IEJ* 45: 19–21.

Na'aman, N.
2005   'The Danite Campaign Northward (Judges xvii-xviii) and the Migration of the Phocaeans to Massalia (Strabo iv 1, 4)', *VT* 55: 47–60.

Naveh, J.
1963   'Old Hebrew Inscriptions in a Burial Cave', *IEJ* 13: 74–92.

Nelson, R.D.
1981   *The Double Redaction of the Deuteronomistic History* (JSOTS 18; Sheffield: JSOT Press).

Noth, M.
1928   *Die israelitischen Personennamen im Rahmen der gemeinsemitischen Namengebung* (BWANT 3/10; Stuttgart: Kohlhammer).

O'Brien, M.A.
1989   *The Deuteronomistic History Hypothesis: A Reassessment* (OBO 92; Fribourg: University Press; Göttingen: Vandenhoeck & Ruprecht).

Olyan, S.M.
1988   *Asherah and the Cult of Yahweh in Israel* (SBLMS 34; Atlanta, GA: Scholars Press).

Pardee, D.
1991   'The Linguistic Classification of the Deir 'Alla Text Written on Plaster', in J. Hoftijzer and G. van der Kooij (eds), *The Balaam Text from Deir 'Alla Re-Evaluated: Proceedings of the International Symposium Held at Leiden 21–24 August 1989* (Leiden: Brill), 100–5.

Provan, I.W.
1988   *Hezekiah and the Books of Kings: A Contribution to the Debate about the Composition of the Deuteronomistic History* (BZAW 172; Berlin: de Gruyter).

Rollston, C.
2003   'Non-Provenanced Epigraphs I: Pillaged Antiquities, Northwest Semitic Forgeries, and Protocols for Laboratory Tests', *Maarav* 10: 135–93.
2004   'Non-Provenanced Epigraphs II: The Status of Non-Provenanced Epigraphs within the Broader Corpus of Northwest Semitic', *Maarav* 11: 57–79.

Römer, T.
2005   *The So-called Deuteronomistic History: A Sociological, Historical and Literary Introduction* (London and New York, NY: T&T Clark International).

Römer, T. and A. de Pury
2000   'Deuteronomistic Historiography (DH): History of Research and Debated Issues', in A. de Pury, T. Römer and J.-D. Macchi (eds), *Israel Constructs Its Identity: Deuteronomistic Historiography in Recent Research* (JSOTS 306; Sheffield: Sheffield Academic Press, 2000), 24–141.

Schmidt, B.B.
2002   'The Iron Age Pithoi Drawings from Horvat Teman or Kuntillet 'Ajrud: Some New Proposals', *JANER* 2: 91–125.

Smith, M.S.
2002   *The Early History of God: Yahweh and the Other Deities in Ancient Israel* (2nd edn; Grand Rapids, MI: Eerdmans).

Soumeka, A.
2002   'The Significance of Kuntillet 'Ajrud for the Study of Early Judahite History and Religion', *BBS* 20.2: 80–98.

Sparks, K.L.
1998   *Ethnicity and Identity in Ancient Israel: Prolegomena to the Study of Ethnic Sentiments and Their Expression in the Hebrew Bible* (Winona Lake, IN: Eisenbrauns).

Stager, L.E.
1985   'The Archaeology of the Family in Ancient Israel', *BASOR* 260: 1–35.

Stavrakopoulou, F.
2004   *King Manasseh and Child Sacrifice: Biblical Distortions of Historical Realities* (BZAW 338; Berlin and New York, NY: de Gruyter).

Steen, E. van der
2008   'A Walk through the Wadi Zerqa', in M.L. Steiner and E.J. van der Steen (ed.), *Sacred and Sweet: Studies on the Material Culture of Tell Deir 'Alla and Tell Abu Sarbut* (Leuven: Peeters), 109–33.

Steiner, R.C.
1991   'The Aramaic Text in Demotic Script: The Liturgy of a New Year's Festival Imported from Bethel to Syene by Exiles from Rash', *JAOS* 111: 362–3.
1995   'Papyrus Amherst 63: A New Source for the Language, Literature, Religion, and History of the Aramaeans', in M.J. Geller, J.C. Greenfield and M. P. Weitzman (eds), *Studia Aramaica: New Sources and New Approaches* (Oxford: Oxford University Press), 199–207.
1997   'The Aramaic Text in Demotic Script', *COS* 1: 309–27.

Talmon, S.
1958   'Divergences in Calendar Reckoning in Ephraim and Judah', *VT* 8: 48–74.

Tigay, J.H.
1986   *You Shall Have No Other Gods: Israelite Religion in the Light of Hebrew Inscriptions* (HSS 31; Atlanta, GA: Scholars Press).
1987   'Israelite Religion: The Onomastic and Epigraphic Evidence', in P.D. Miller, P.D. Hanson and S.D. McBride (eds), *Ancient Israelite Religion: Essays in Honor of Frank Moore Cross* (Philadelphia, PA: Fortress Press), 157–94.

Tsevat, M.
1975   'Ishbosheth and Congeners: The Names and Their Study', *HUCA* 46: 71–87.

Vaux, R. de
1969   'Téman, ville ou region d'Édom?', *RB* 76: 379–85.

Venter, P.M.
2003   'Northern Traditions in Second Century BCE Literature', *OTE* 16: 464–88.

Weinfeld, M.
1983   'The Extent of the Promised Land – The Status of Transjordan', in G. Strecker (ed.), *Das Land Israel in biblischer Zeit* (Göttingen: Vandenhoeck & Ruprecht), 59–75.

Weippert, M.
1997   'Israélites, Araméens et Assyriens dans la Transjordanie septentrionale', *ZDPV* 113: 19–38.

Wiggins, S.A.
2007   *A Reassessment of Asherah: With Further Considerations of the Goddess* (GUS 2; Piscataway, NJ: Gorgias Press).

Wolters, A.
1988   'The Balaamites of Deir 'Allā as Aramean Deportees', *HUCA* 59: 101–13.

Zevit, Z.
1985   'Deuteronomistic Historiography in 1 Kings 12–2 Kings 17 and the Reinvestiture of the Israelite Cult', *JSOT* 32: 57–73.
1990   'The Common Origin of the Aramaicized Prayer to Horus and of Psalm 20', *JAOS* 110: 213–28.
2001   *The Religions of Ancient Israel: A Synthesis of Parallactic Approaches* (London: Continuum).

Chapter 11

'MANY NATIONS WILL BE JOINED TO YHWH IN THAT DAY': THE QUESTION OF YHWH OUTSIDE JUDAH

Lester L. Grabbe

The single most characteristic name of the God of Israel was Yhwh.[1] This fact is often opaque to general readers because translations tended to use terms like *kurios* in Greek and 'Lord' in English. In the polytheistic ancient Near East a variety of divine names was known, and even though any particular society would have several different divine names in reasonably common use, certain names tended to be associated with particular peoples. According to 1 Kgs 11.33, Ashtoret (Astarte) is associated with the Phoenicians, Chemosh with the Moabites, and Milcom with the Ammonites. Names and other sources make Qos/Qaus the national god of the Edomites (later known as the Idumaeans).

The concern of the present study is twofold: a) to what extent was Yhwh worshipped by non-Israelites and non-Judahites; and b) to what extent did Israelites and Judahites export their worship of Yhwh to their diaspora settlements?

1
Yhwh Outside Israel/Judah?

The theophoric element *yhwh* begins to appear in Israelite personal names in the Moses tradition of the Hebrew Bible.[2] No name is compounded with Yhwh before the narrative of Moses (though it is not certain whether the name of Moses' mother Jochebed was Yahwistic). The earliest name is Joshua (whose name was actually changed from Hoshea [Num. 13.16]). None of the Genesis genealogies contain names with Yhwh, and none of Moses' contemporaries are said to have such names. The name Yhwh appears in names in the biblical texts only during the later life of Moses. Furthermore, the text of Exodus suggests that Yhwh's name was first revealed to Moses and not before his time. In Exod. 3.6 (usually assigned to the E source according to the Documentary Hypothesis) the god who appears to Moses identifies himself with the ancestral god of Abraham, Isaac and Jacob. Exodus 6.3 (usually assigned to the

---

1.   The form Yhwh will normally be the form used in this chapter. Although several sources suggest that the name might have been pronounced something like 'Yahweh', the exact vocalization is unknown. As is well known, the vowels associated with the name in the Masoretic text belong either to *'ădōnāy* or, occasionally, to *'ĕlōhîm*.

2.   The divine name Yhwh appears in a number of forms in theophoric names (names with a divine element): Yaho-, Yo, Jeho-, Jo-, -yahu, -yah, -iah, -jah.

P source) states that God appeared to Abraham, Isaac and Jacob under the name of El Shadday but was not known to them by his name Yhwh. Thus, if these passages have any weight, they suggest that the name of Yhwh was not known in Israel before the time of Moses.

Exactly what this means for the scholar is no doubt complicated. There is the whole question of Moses' existence and the relationship of the biblical traditions to the actual emergence of the Israelite people in the land. It does broadly conform with most of the extra-biblical data, however, and suggests memory of a time when Yhwh was not known to the Israelites but was introduced to them for the first time. For a writer to dream up a period when Yhwh was not known would be very surprising indeed, if everyone assumed that Yhwh had been in Israelite possession from the beginning.[3] Thus, to the best of our current knowledge, Yhwh originated in Palestine and his worship was confined to the peoples of Palestine. Yet, regardless of when the biblical traditions are ultimately to be dated, some scholars have proposed that Yhwh existed at various points in the ancient Near East long before the origins of Israel. Most recently something of a flurry was created by the Ebla texts, but even before this others had thought they had found versions of Yhwh outside of Israel and Judah, especially in the Mari and the Ugaritic texts.

Ebla

In the mid-1970s it was proposed by Giovanni Pettinato that the name Yhwh was found among the Tell Mardikh tablets (which by that time had been associated with ancient Ebla in the latter part of the third millennium BCE). This was based on the identification of several names with the divine name -il- that seemed to have a counterpart in similar names with -ia- (e.g. the name Mi-kà-il alongside Mi-kà-ia). If correctly read, this would correspond to the Hebrew Michael, with the meaning 'who is like El?' One proposal was that Mi-kà-ia meant, 'who is like Yah?', parallel to Hebrew Mikayahu 'who is like Yahu?' This might suggest the earlier use of the name Yhwh (in shortened form), long before the biblical usage and much further north.[4] Yet as a number of other scholars argued at the time, this seems unlikely, for several reasons.

- The reading -ia- is based on the Sumerogram NI. In some names, Pettinato read it as -ya- or, as here, -ia-. As Alfonso Archi argued, the logogram can be read as -ni, -ia, or lí.[5] This affects the reading of the various names in the texts.
- There is also the question of whether the ending is anything more than a hypocoristicon, a universal element often added to names as a diminutive or

---

3.   It was long ago suggested that the name Yhwh is to be associated with the place name *Yhw3* known from some Egyptian texts and was borrowed by the Israelites from the Midianites-Kenites. This interpretation has had considerable support over the decades, though some have opposed it. See most recently Blenkinsopp 2008 for a discussion and thorough bibliography.

4.   This was suggested by Giovanni Pettinato, first apparently in the *Biblical Archaeologist* and later in his first Italian edition on Elba (Pettinato 1976: 48; 1979: 269–70). A somewhat different interpretation appeared in the English edition of his book (1981: 179–80): 'However, *Il* and *Ya* in the Eblaite onomastica indicate not the gods Il or Ya with their individual characteristics but rather an absolute or divine god. . . . we may at least conclude that the Eblaites had quite an advanced concept of the divine and were very near to henotheism.'

5.   Archi 1981: 145–46, 153; cf. 1980: 42; 1987: 10–11; for a fuller discussion of the entire question, see Müller 1981a: 73–80.

affectionate ending. This was the argument given by Anson Rainey[6] and initially accepted by Archi (1979: 556–57).

- A significant argument is that the logogram NI should be read as *ilī* (the personal divinity) or the divine name Ilu(m). In both cases, the word might be translated generically as 'god' (Müller 1981a: 83; cf. 1981b). Hans-Peter Müller accepts that a god Ya is possibly attested, but this would have be demonstrated from only four names (*su-mi-a-ù, i-a-be, i-a-du-ud* and *en-nu-i-a*). But since no god Ya is attested apart from personal names, it seems that a god Ya at Ebla is unlikely (Müller 1981a: 89). Archi makes a similar point: 'It [-*ya*] could be substituted for other deities as well as for El: for example *iš-ra-ià* could theoretically correspond to *iš-ra*-BE . . . "Dagan (BE = Dagan) fights/is right"' (1979: 559; cf. 1987: 10–11). This may mean that the supposed two names of 'Mi-ka-il' and 'Mi-ka-ya (Mi-ka-NI)' are actually two ways of spelling 'Mi-ka-il' (Müller 1981a: 88–89, 91; cf. Archi 1979: 557–59).
- Finally, it seems likely that in at least some instances, NI is a way of writing the first person singular pronominal suffix (Müller 1981a: 77–79; cf. Archi 1981: 153).

The general view of specialists seems to be that no attestation of Yhwh is to be found among the Ebla tablets.

Mari

In the Mari texts of the early second millennium BCE, a number of names have been interpreted as having a version of Yhwh. It is generally agreed that these are Amorite names and represent the Amorite culture rather than Akkadian. The names include:

Ya-aḫ-wi-AN
Ya-wi-AN
Ya-wi-ᵈIM
Ya-wi-ᵈDa-gan

The problem is that these are written in cuneiform which does not always clearly distinguish between *ḥ* and *ḫ(ẖ)*. Thus, it is debatable whether these names come from a root *ḥwy* 'to be' or *ḥwy* 'to live' (cf. Huffmon 1965: 71–73, 159–60, 191–92; 1971: 283–84).

In either case, though, the names are best analysed as a divine name (e.g. Dagan) and a verb form (*Ya-wi-, Ya-aḫ-wi-*). The name Yhwh is generally analysed as a form of the Hebrew verb *ḥwy* 'to be' (as Exod. 3.14 indicates); thus, there is potentially a relationship with the Amorite names. But none of the Amorite names yet known

---

6.   According to Rainey,

The supposed evidence for Yahweh names at Ebla is highly questionable . . . It is pointed out by several of us that the -*ya* endings on personal names are simply shorted forms (hypocoristic) usually used for endearment and then becoming common usage. The names like *Mika-il* which become *Mika-ya* have nothing to do with Yahwism. The -*ya* element is simply a replacement for the Divine Name element. The same phenomenon is known in many languages of the world . . . Note for example, Richard/Ricky, William/Willie, Peter/Petie, etc. . . . Therefore, it should be stressed that there is really no evidence in these Personal Names for the presence of Yahwism at Ebla.

(Rainey 1977: 38)

appears to be like Yhwh in form and function (cf. Huffmon 1971: 289). Mari has so far not provided an example of Yhwh earlier than its attestation among the Israelites and Judahites.

Ugarit

It has long been known that in KTU 1.1.iv.14 a speech is placed in the mouth of the god Ilu, 'the name of my son (is) *Yw*' (*šm bny yw*). In the context, this individual seems to be identified with the god Yammu. This raised the question of whether a version of Yhwh was known to the inhabitants of Ugarit.[7] This interpretation has generally been rejected, but Johannes de Moor has recently noted that Yammu and Yhwh have many points in common (1997: 166–68). He suggests that the people of Ugarit may have known of Yhwh as a foreign god worshipped by a part of the Sea Peoples and are depicting Yhwh in negative terms by identifying him with Yammu. This is an interesting hypothesis but stands or falls on whether Israel was constituted as a people already this early or, alternatively, another Yhwh-worshipping group was in existence and known to the people of Ugarit. Since the first attestation of an 'Israel' is at least a century or more after this text and we presently have no evidence of Yhwh-worshipping groups among the Sea Peoples, there is necessarily a lot of uncertainty. Other explanations are possible; in any case, it places a great deal of weight on a single name in a broken context.

The argument might be bolstered by an appeal to Sanchuniathon, allegedly an ancient writer in the area of Phoenicia. Philo of Byblos claims to have translated Sanchuniathon's account of early Phoenician history into Greek. Although Philo's account has also been lost, portions of it were quoted by the patristic writer Eusebius in his *Preparation for the Gospel* (*Praeperatio Evangelica* 1.9.19–10.55).[8] Some of those quoted by Eusebius state that Sanchuniathon lived at the time of or even before the Trojan War. This has led some modern scholars to take the view that Sanchuniathon is to be dated to the age of Ugarit and that he gives us important information on that age. This is possible, but Philo's account has nevertheless been clearly influenced by the Greek literary tradition (Barr 1974–75; Baumgarten 1981: 267), showing that whatever ancient material might have been used, it was recast in a Greek literary form.

According to Philo of Byblos, Sanchuniathon took his information from Hierombalos, a priest of the deity Ieuo (*Praep. Ev.* 1.9.21). It is difficult to know how to evaluate Philo's account. One cannot rule out some sort of assimilation of the Phoenician and Israelite traditions. On the other hand, Ieuo does not necessarily represent Yhwh and could be a purely Phoenician deity. It might, for example, be simply an error for Yammu (Eissfeldt 1952). Finally, whether it has anything to do with the *Yw* of the Ugaritic text is a matter of speculation. All in all, the argument for Yhwh at Ugarit seems rather tenuous in the light of present knowledge.

Yhwh in Northern Syria?

Ebla apart, Syria has still been the site for other evidence of Yhwh worship, though in this case it is much later – during the Assyrian period. This conclusion has recently arisen because of a text from Hamath, which refers to an Azriyau (*ᵐAz-ri-a-u/ᵐAz-ri-ia-*

---

7.   For references, see *DULAT* 2.997; de Moor 1997: 164–71; Smith 1994: 151–52.

8.   The text is conveniently available in Attridge and Oden 1981. See also the commentary of Baumgarten 1981.

a-ú: Dalley 1990; cf. Tadmor 1994: 58–59, 62–63). This text has long been known, but interpretation was hampered by another text (especially discussed by Tadmor 1961; cf. Tadmor 1994: 273–74). Recent study has removed the name of Azriyau's country, though it seems to have been in northern Syria or southern Anatolia. In addition, there was a leader from Hamath named Yau-bi'di (ᵈ*ia-ú-bi-i'-di*, ᵈ*ia-bi-i'-di* [Hawkins 1980]) who led an anti-Assyrian coalition in 720 BCE at the beginning of Sargon II's reign. His name also seems to have a form of Yhwh as an element within it. This has led Stephanie Dalley to assume that Yhwh was being worshipped in Hamath and the region in the mid-eighth century BCE (Dalley 1990: 28).[9]

Assuming that this name contains a form of Yhwh, Dalley offers several explanations as to how it occurred in northern Syria, such a long way from Palestine. She rejects the suggestion that these were 'Israelite adventurers' (perhaps charioteers) who seized power temporarily (Dalley 1990: 28–29). One possibility put forward is that some of the groups bringing Yhwh worship from southern Palestine did not stop at Israel but continued on north. Another is that a special connection was established between Israel and Hamath under Jeroboam II, though she finds this unlikely.

Ziony Zevit (1991) has considered further the question of how figures in northern Syria seemed to have Israelite names. He points to the fact that the northern Israelite territories came under Aramaean control several times. Of particular interest is the 30-year period (c. 885–855 BCE) when 'Reuben, Gad, Eastern Manasseh, Naphtali and Dan' (Zevit 1991: 365) were under the hegemony of Damascus. It was at this time that Yhwh worship might have penetrated Aramaic culture and become accepted 'as the cult of a minority group' (1991: 365).

Based on these occurrences, it has even been suggested that Yhwh was not unique to Israel/Judah but rather a deity common to a large part of Syria-Palestine (Thompson 1995: 119 n. 13). The references seem to be certain, but there is no supporting evidence that Yhwh was part of general worship over the region. The existence of two Yhwh names of rulers around Hamath in the eighth century BCE suggest an isolated situation, not a dynasty or continuing tradition. Thus, the suggestion that Yhwh worship had been transplanted from Palestine in some way and had only a temporary impact or remained isolated or confined to a minority seems to be correct. In all the inscriptions and linguistic data from the surrounding region, there is nothing so far to indicate that Yhwh was worshipped generally over the entire region.

2
Yhwh in Diaspora Communities

Yhwh in Mesopotamian Jewish Communities
Certain Neo-Babylonian tablets (ration lists) are generally believed to mention the Yhwh-bearing name Jehoiachin (Weidner 1939; *DOTT*, 84–86):

---

9.   Dalley also mentions Joram of Hamath who was sent to David's court (2 Sam. 8.10). The LXX of 2 Sam. (2 Reigns) 8.10 (*Ieddouran*) and 1 Chron. 18.10 both have Hadoram (i.e. with Hadad rather than Yo- = Yhwh). First Chronicles also has the names Meribaal (8.34; 9.40) and Eshbaal (8.33; 9.39), with the divine element Baal, in comparison with the altered forms in 2 Samuel of Mephibosheth (2 Sam. 4, 9, 16, 19, 21) and Ishbosheth (2 Samuel 2–4). This suggests that the name with Hadad has been altered in the MT of 1 Sam. 8.10 by the substitution of the shortened form of Yhwh.

(a) To Ya'u-kīn, king [of the land of Yaudu].

(b) ½ (PI) for Ya'u kīnu, king of the land of Ya[hu-du]

2½ *sila* for the fi[ve]sons of the king of the land of Yahudu

4 *sila* for eight men, Judaeans [each] ½ [sila]

(c) ½ (PI) for Ya'u [-kīnu]

2½ *sila* for the five sons . . . .

½ (PI) for Yakū-kinu, son of the king of the land of Yakudu

2½ *sila* for the five sons of the king of Yakundu by the hand of Kanama.

(d) . . . Ya]'u-kīnu, king of he land of Yahudu

[. . . the five sons of the king] of the land of Yahudu by the hand of Kanama.

It is generally accepted that this is a reference to the Judahite king Jehoiachin who had been taken captive to Babylonia (2 Kgs 24.8-16).

A bit later, in the early Persian period, we find some references to Jews in Babylonia in three tablets published by Francis Joannès and André Lemaire (Joannès and Lemaire 1999). One tablet has 12 Hebrew names and claims to have been written in the 'city of Judah' (URU *ia-a-ḫu-du*) about 498 BCE. This does not appear to be Jerusalem but a place in Babylonia, though several sites in Mesopotamia are known to have been named after sites in the homeland of the exiles who lived there. It is also reported that another 90 texts in a private collection awaiting publication (Pearce 2006) relate to exiled Jews in the sixth century. The tablets range in date from Nebuchadnezzar, year 33 (c. 572 BCE) to Xerxes, year 13 (c. 473 BCE). They also contain references to the 'city of Judah' (URU*ia-a-ḫa-du* and variants) or 'city of the Jews/Judahites' (URU *šá* LÚ *ia-a-ḫu-du-a-a*). Apparently, of some 500 different names, approximately 80 contain a form of Yhwh. Of 600 or so individuals in the texts, about 120 have Yhwh theophoric names.

One other source seems to mention some Jews specifically. This is the Murašu archive from Nippur, with tablets ranging from c. 454–404 BCE.[10] The Murašu house was a business and financial establishment that made loans and managed estates for absentee landlords, employing a number of servants and agents. It has been argued that some of these servants and agents were Jewish; unfortunately, there is an inevitable circularity in the argument, since the ethnic identification is based on the form of the names. Several of the names have a form of Yhwh (Coogan 1976: 119). Genealogical relations indicate, however, that Jews did not necessarily take 'Jewish' names, and there may be many more named individuals who were Jews than it is possible to recognize now, as seems to be the case generally with Jews in the Persian period.

All of these individuals in Mesopotamia are exiled Judahites, often taken there involuntarily, whether king or commoner. That is, the Yhwh theophoric names all seem to be indications of connections with Judah, not non-Jewish worship.

The Temple of Yhw at Elephantine

From Persian period texts, we know of a Jewish military colony on the island of Elephantine in the Nile, though it may have been established before the fall of Jerusalem (cf. *TAD* A4.7.13-14//A4.8.12-13; *AP* 30.13-14//31.12-13). This colony had its own temple to God. The normal term for God among the Elephantine papyri is *Yhw*. Yet a list of contributors to the cult names the recipients Eshem-Bethel and

---

10. On these texts, see Cardascia 1951; Coogan 1976; Stolper 1985, 1992; van Driel 1989.

Anat-Bethel (*TAD* C3.15.127–28 = *AP* 22.124–25). In another text, a man swears by Anat-Yahu (*TAD* B7.3.3 = *AP* 44.3). Bethel was once a separate deity but may have been identified with Yhw by the Jews of Elephantine (cf. van der Toorn 1992: 94, 97). As far as Anat-Bethel and Anat-Yahu are concerned, they originated no doubt as goddess figures (cf. van der Toorn 1992: 95–97), but it has been suggested that these were actually only 'hypostases' of Yhw by this time (Porten 1968: 179; cf. Niehr 1990: 48). Yet all references to deities as such in the Elephantine texts relating to the Jewish community are to Yhw, and the temple is the 'temple of Yhw'.

After the local priests of the Egyptian cult Khnum destroyed the temple, the Jewish colony mounted a campaign to have it rebuilt. Following is one of the letters (in two copies, which allow a number of the lacunae to be filled), appealing to the Persian authorities for permission to rebuild (*TAD* A4.7//A4.8 = *AP* 30//31):

> Now your servant Jedaniah and his colleagues say thus: . . . If it please our lord, take thought of that Temple to (re)build (it) since they do not let us (re)build it. Regard your obligees and your friends who are here in Egypt. Let a letter be sent from you to them about the temple of YHW the God to (re)build it in Elephantine the fortress just as it was formerly built. And they will offer the meal-offering and the incense, and the holocaust on the altar of YHW the God in your name and we shall pray for you at all times – we and our wives and our children and the Jews, all (of them) who are here. If they do thus until the Temple be (re)built, you will have a merit before YHW the God of Heaven more than a person who offers him holocaust and sacrifices worth silver, one thousand talents.

Another document in the archive offers payment for the expenses if the temple is allowed to be rebuilt (*TAD* A4.10 = *AP* 33):

> Your servants:
> Jedaniah son of Gem[ariah] by name 1
> Mauzi son of Nathan by name [1],
> Shemaiah son of Haggai by name 1
> Hosea son of Jathom by name 1
> Hosea son of Nattun by name 1: total 5 men,
> Syenians, who are heredi[tary property-hold]ers in Yeb the fortress say thus: If our lord [. . .] and the Temple of Yhw our God be rebuilt in Yeb the fortress as it was former[ly bu]ilt, and sheep, ox, and goat will [n]ot be offered there but incense (and) cereal offerings [will be offered there.] (If) our lord gives an order [. . .] we shall give to the house of our lord si[lver . . . and] a thousa[nd] ardabs of barley.

These letters amply demonstrate the importance of the 'temple of Yhw' to this Jewish community. Many individuals (such as Jedaniah in these letters) have Yhwh names. Yet it is clear that this is a colony of Judahites, originating from the country of Judah. The Yhw that they worship is a version of the traditional 'Jewish' worship in Judah itself.

Yhwh in the Samaritan Texts in the Persian and Greek Periods
It might seem strange to include Samaria in this survey. Samaria was originally an Israelite area: why should there not be Yhwh worship attested there? Yet according to 2 Kings 17, the Israelites were all taken away and other peoples settled in their place.

This picture is to be doubted (cf. Grabbe 2007: 149–50), but we need to look for evidence one way or the other. Also, through much of their history Judah and Israel were separate, and our emphasis has been on the existence of Yhwh outside Judah.

Insights into the situation in Samaria is mainly from later sources, but the Samaritan papyri and the bullae from Wadi Daliyeh provide direct information on the situation in the late Persian period, usually dated to the time of the Greek conquest (Grabbe 2004: 55–58). Many of the names are Yahwistic: Hananiah (*WDSP* 7.17), Joshua (*WDSP* 11r.13), Aqabiah (*WDSP* 5.14); also Jehohanan, Yehonur, Delaiah, Yehopadani, Nehemiah, Yehoshuvah, Isaiah and Mikaiah. To this can be added the names found on coins: Bedeiah, Delaiah, Hananiah and Yehoanah (Meshorer and Qedar 1991: 13–17; 1999: 20–28). Unfortunately, some names are abbreviated and uncertain.

Going to an earlier time in the Persian period, it has recently been argued that a Samaritan temple had been built on Mount Gerizim about the middle of the fifth century BCE. Many inscriptions associated with this temple over a period of time have now been published (Magen, Misgav and Tsfania 2004). In them are found a number of Yahwistic names: Elijah? (Inscription 7), Delaiah (147), Honiah (58, 59), Jonathan (16, 20, 28, 29, 170), Jehohanan (33, 47), Joseph (20, 52, 53, 148, 203) and Shemaiah (40). In addition, a number of other names known from the Hebrew Bible occur. All in all, the data are compatible with the assumption that those producing these inscriptions, coins, papyri and so on were descended from the people of Israel.

The 'House of Yhw' in Idumaea
In addition to the temples to Yhw(h) long known (such as in Elephantine and Samaria), another one has recently been attested in ostraca supposedly originating in the area of Idumaea in the fourth century:[11]

1. The hill/ruin which is below the House of 'Z'
2. and the parcel (of land) of the House of Yhw,
3. the ground of Zby, the terrace of the terebinth,
4. the waste ground of S'd/rw, the tomb of Gilgul,
5. the pool of the house of Nabu(?),
6. the tomb of Ynqm.

This appears to be a list of properties that had not paid contributions, for whatever reason. According to André Lemaire's interpretation, at least three of the names are references to temples of deities ('house of D[ivine]N[ame]'). This suggests that there was a shrine of some sort to Yhwh at this time in Idumaea (which fits with the Yhwh names among those in the ostraca). This adds another Yhwh temple to those known to be in existence in the Persian period.

'Iraq al-Amir[12]
In the Hebrew Bible, Tobiah, designated an enemy of Nehemiah, had his base in the

---

11.   Lemaire 2002: 149–56 (my translation follows Lemaire's reading and interpretation for the most part). Unfortunately, the ostraca were obtained on the antiquities market, and the find area is partly a matter of rumour and speculation.

12.   Information and bibliography on this section can be found in Grabbe 2008: esp. 41–42, 75–78, 293–97.

area of 'Ammon' (Neh. 2.10). Judging from the extant Jewish texts, the Tobiad family had a long history, much of it associated with the Transjordan region. The Zenon papyri place another Tobias in the same region (*CJP* #1). According to Josephus' account, Hyrcanus Tobiad built a palace on the other side of the Jordan (*Ant.* 12.4.11 §230–33). This ancestral home of the Tobiads is now usually identified with 'Iraq al-Amir, though there is evidence of building long before the time of Hyrcanus. There has been a considerable debate about the function of the building known as the Qaṣr al-'Abd. Among other suggestions are that it was a temple.

While Paul Lapp (*NEAEHL* 2.648) and others definitely think it a temple (cf. Arav 1989: 107–10; see also Chapter 6 in this volume), this view has not commanded a consensus among archaeologists. One problem with determining its function is that it was never finished. The Qaṣr al-'Abd is a *bit-ḥilani*-style monumental building with pillars topped by Corinthian capitals and life-motif decorations. It has two stories, the second story apparently meant as residential quarters. If it was a temple, it would have been a temple to Yhwh, since the Tobiads were Yhwh worshippers. However, the most recent excavations and interpretations seem to go against the temple idea; rather, it is seen as most likely a residential building (Will 1982: 199–200; Zayadine 1997: 178–80; Lapp 1983: 151–53). Thus, in the light of present scholarly opinion this is probably not an example of another Yhwh temple.

The Temple at Leontopolis in Egypt[13]

According to Josephus, a breakaway temple and cult arose out of events preceding the Maccabean revolt (*War* 7.10.2-4 §§423–36; *Ant.* 12.5.1 §§237–38; 12.9.7 §387–88; 13.3.1-3 §§62–73), though strangely this is not mentioned in 1 or 2 Maccabees. Giving two contradictory accounts, Josephus states that Onias III, the high priest deposed by Jason, fled from Jerusalem to Leontopolis in Egypt where he built a temple. Or so his earlier account (*War* 7.10.2 §423) states, but it was actually his son Onias IV according to the *Antiquities* (12.9.7 §387–88). This site is often identified with Tell el-Yehudieh and some of the remains there, though the archaeology is perhaps less than clear-cut (cf. Holladay 2001: 529; Horbury and Noy 1992: xvi–xix; Schürer: 3.146 n. 33). According to *Antiquities* (13.3.2 §70) there was already a ruined temple on the site which Onias was allowed to cleanse and rebuild (though the passage in the *War* is silent on this). This temple was similar to that in Jerusalem, according to one passage (*Ant.* 13.3.3 §72). Elsewhere, however, it is said to be unlike the Jerusalem temple but instead in the form of a tower (*War* 7.10.3 §427).

A number of inscriptions have been found in the area of Leontopolis, mostly tomb epitaphs. Nearly 80 have been published (Horbury and Noy 1992), but there are apparently a few more (Capponi 2007 [not available to me], according to the review of Noy 2008). These inscriptions are all in Greek, and the name Yhwh does not occur as such. Yet a number of Jewish names are found in these inscriptions (including Abram/Abraham [#39: *Abramos*], Judah [#54: *Ioudas*] and Jacob [#56, 81: *Iakoubos*]). Important for our purposes, however, are three names compounded with Yhwh (i.e. the Greek version of names compounded with Yhwh): Joshua (#34: *Iēsous*), Barachiah (#43: *Barchias*] and Johanan (#57: *Ioanē*). From all the reports available to us, this was a temple dedicated to the God of the Jews.

---

13.   For general information on the Leontopolis temple, see Delcor 1968; Hayward 1982.

3
Conclusions

This study has looked at two aspects of the name Yhwh. First, it asked whether the name Yhwh was known outside Israel and Judah. This has been proposed at various times by scholars. No definitive answer can be given because new discoveries might change the situation, but so far no clear evidence of Yhwh worship independent of that in Israel and Judah has emerged. This includes the ancient kingdoms of Ebla, Mari and Ugarit, where the alleged evidence for the existence of a divinity Ya has not been clear or convincing. More interesting is the presence of a couple of rulers' names that are probably theophoric compounds with Yhwh associated with Hamath. These are probably to be explained by some connection with Palestine, since they seem to be isolated in time (eighth century BCE) and place (near Hamath).

The second part of the study surveyed the evidence for Yhwh in various places in the ancient Near East that were the result of Jewish diaspora communities. This included temples at Elephantine and Leontopolis in Egypt and the evidence of Jews with Yahwistic names in Mesopotamia during Neo-Babylonian and Persian times. It also included temples of Yhwh in Edom and on Mount Gerizim in the Persian period, as well as other evidence of Yahwistic names. It seems unlikely, however, that the building at 'Iraq al-Amir in the region of Transjordan was a temple.

There are still good arguments for the theory that Yhwh originated in southern Palestine, though not everyone is convinced of this. Yet, regardless of where or how Yhwh worship began, the evidence so far available supports the view that the Yhwh deity and Yhwh cults were unique to Israel and Judah.

Bibliography

Arav, R.
1989   *Hellenistic Palestine: Settlement Patterns and City Planning, 337–31 B.C.E.* (British Archaeological Reports International Series 485; Oxford: BAR).

Archi, A.
1979   'The Epigraphic Evidence from Ebla and the Old Testament', *Biblica* 60: 556–60.
1980   'Archi Responds to Pettinato', *BAR* 6.6: 42–43.
1981   'Further Concerning Ebla and the Bible', *BA* 44: 145–54; ET of 'Ancora su Ebla e la Bibbia', *Studi Eblaiti* 2 (1980), 17–40.
1987   'Ebla and Eblaite', in C.H. Gordon, G. Rendsburg and N.H. Winter (eds), *Eblaitica: Essays on the Ebla Archives and Eblaite Language* (Publications of the Center for Ebla Research at New York University; Winona Lake, IN: Eisenbrauns), 1.7–17.

Attridge, H.W. and R.A. Oden
1981   *Philo of Byblos: Phoenician History: Introduction, Critical Text, Translation, Notes* (CBQM 9: Washington, DC: Catholic Biblical Association).

Barr, J.
1974–75 'Philo of Byblos and His "Phoenician History"', *BJRL* 57: 17–68.

Baumgarten, A.I.
1981   *The* Phoenician History *of Philo of Byblos: A Commentary* (EPROER 89; Leiden: Brill).

Blenkinsopp, J.
2008   'The Midianite-Kenite Hypothesis Revisited and the Origins of Judah', *JSOT* 33: 131–53.

Capponi, L.
2007   *Il tempio di Leontopoliin Egitto: Identità politica e religiosa dei Giudei di Onia (c. 150 a.C-71 d.C.)* (Pubblicazioni della Facoltà di Lettere e Filosofia dell' Università di Pavia 118; Pisa: Edizioni ETS).

Cardascia, G.
1951   *Les archives des Murašû* (Paris: Imprimerie Nationale).

Coogan, M.D.
1976   *West Semitic Personal Names in the Murašu Documents* (HSM 7; Atlanta, GA: Scholars Press).

Dalley, S.
1990   'Yahweh in Hamath in the 8th Century BC: Cuneiform Material and Historical Deductions', *VT* 40: 21–32.

Delcor, M.
1968   'Le temple d'Onias en Egypte', *RB* 75: 188–205; repr. in *Etudes bibliques et orientales de religions comparées* (Leiden: Brill, 1979), 328–45.

Driel, G. van
1989   'The Murašûs in Context', *JESHO* 32: 203–27.

Eissfeldt, O.
1952   *Sanchuniathon von Beirat and Ilimilku von Ugarit* (Beiträge zur Religionsgeschichte des Altertums 5; Halle: Max Niemeyer).

Grabbe, L.L.
2004   *A History of the Jews and Judaism in the Second Temple Period 1: Yehud: A History of the Persian Province of Judah* (LSTS 47; London and New York, NY: T&T Clark International).
2007   *Ancient Israel: What Do We Know and How Do We Know It?* (London and New York, NY: T&T Clark International).
2008   *A History of the Jews and Judaism in the Second Temple Period 2: The Coming of the Greeks: The Early Hellenistic Period (335–175 BCE)* (LSTS 68; London and New York, NY: T&T Clark International).

Hawkins, J.D.
1980   'Jau-bi'di', *RdA* 5: 272–73.

Hayward, C.T.R.
1982   'The Jewish Temple at Leontopolis: A Reconsideration', *JJS* 33: 429–43.

Holladay, J.S., Jr.
2001   'Yahudiyya, Tell el-', in D.B. Redford (ed.), *Oxford Encyclopedia of Ancient Egypt* (Oxford University Press), 3.527–29.

Horbury, W. and D. Noy
1992   *Jewish Inscriptions of Graeco-Roman Egypt* (Cambridge: Cambridge University Press).

Huffmon, H.B.
1965   *Amorite Personal Names in the Mari Texts: A Structural and Lexical Study* (Baltimore, MD: Johns Hopkins).
1971   'Yahweh and Mari', in Hans Goedicke (ed.), *Near Eastern Studies in Honor of William Foxwell Albright* (Baltimore, MD: Johns Hopkins), 283–89.

Joannès, F. and A. Lemaire
1999   'Trois tablettes cunéiforme à onomastique ouest-sémitique (collection Sh. Moussaïeff)', *Trans* 17: 17–34.

Lapp, N.L. (ed.)
1983   *The Excavations at Araq el-Emir, Vol. 1* (AASOR 47; Winona Lake, IN: Eisenbrauns).

Lemaire, A.
2002   *Nouvelles inscriptions araméennes d'Idumée, Tome II Collections Moussaïeff, Jeselsohn, Welch et divers* (Suppl. no. 9 à *Transeuphratène*; Paris: Gabalda).

Lemche, N.P.
1991   'The Development of the Israelite Religion in the Light of Recent Studies on the Early History of Israel', in J.A. Emerton (ed.), *Congress Volume: Leuven, 1989* (VTS 43; Leiden: Brill), 97–115.

Magen, Y., H. Misgav and L. Tsfania
2004   *Mount Gerizim Excavations: Volume I The Aramaic, Hebrew and Samaritan Inscriptions* (Judea and Samaria Publications 2; Jerusalem: Israel Antiquities Authority).

Meshorer, Y.and S. Qedar
1991   *The Coinage of Samaria in the Fourth Century* BCE (Jerusalem: Numismatic Fine Arts International).
1999   *Samarian Coinage* (Numismatic Studies and Researches 9; Jerusalem: Israel Numismatic Society).

Moor, J.C. de
1997   *The Rise of Yahwism: The Roots of Israelite Monotheism* (2nd edn; BETL 91; Leuven: Peeters/University Press).

Müller, H.-P.
1981a   'Gab es in Ebla einen Gottesnamen Ja?' *ZA* 70: 70–92.
1981b   'Der Jahwename und seine Deutung Ex 3, 14 im Licht der Textpublikationen aus Ebla', *Bib* 62: 305–27.

Niehr, H.
1990   *Der höchste Gott: Alttestamentlicher JHWH-Glaube im Kontext syrisch-kanaanäischer Religion des 1. Jahrtausends v. Chr.* (BZAW 190; Berlin and New York, NY: de Gruyter).

Noy, D.
2008   Review of L. Capponi, *Il tempio di Leontopoliin Egitto, Bryn Mawr Classical Review* 37.

Pearce, L.E.
2006   'New Evidence for Judeans in Babylonia', in O. Lipschits and M. Oeming (eds), *Judah and the Judeans in the Persian Period* (Winona Lake, IN: Eisenbrauns), 399–411.

Pettinato, G.
1976   'The Royal Archives of Tell Mardikh-Ebla', *BA* 39: 44–52.
1979   *Ebla: Un impero inciso nell'argilla* (Milan: Arnold Mondadori).
1980   'Ebla and the Bible', *BA* 43: 203–16; ET of 'Ebla e la Bibbia', *Oriens Antiquus* 19 (1980), 49–72.
1991   *Ebla: A New Look at History* (trans. C. Faith Richardson; Baltimore, MD: Johns Hopkins).

Porten, B.
1968   *Archives from Elephantine: The Life of an Ancient Jewish Military Colony* (Berkeley, CA, and Los Angeles, CA: University of California).

Rainey, A.
1977   Letter to the editor, *BAR* 3.1: 38.

Schürer, E.
1973–87 *The History of the Jewish People in the Age of Jesus Christ (175 B.C.–A.D. 135* (3 vols in 4; English version revised and edited by G. Vermes, F. Millar and M. Goodman; Edinburgh: T&T Clark).

Smith, M.S.
1994   *The Ugartic Baal Cycle: Volume 1 Introduction with Text, Translation and Commentary of KTU 1.1–1 .2* (VTS 55; Leiden: Brill).

Steckoll, S.H.
1967–9 'The Qumran Sect in Relation to the Temple of Leontopolis', *RQum* 6: 55–69.

Stolper, M.W.
1985   *Entrepeneurs and Empire: The Murašû Archive, the Murašû Firm, and Persian Rule in Babylonia* (Uitgaven van het Nederlands Historisch-Archaeologisch Instituut te Istanbul 54; Leiden: Nederlands Historisch-Archaeologisch Instituut te Istanbul).
1992   'Murashû, Archive of', *ABD* 4.927–28.

Tadmor, H.
1961   'Azriyau of Yaudi', in C. Rabin (ed.), *Studies in the Bible* (Scripta Hierosolymitana 8; Jerusalem: Magnes Press), 232–71.
1994   *The Inscriptions of Tiglath-Pileser III King of Assyria: Critical Edition, with Introductions, Translations and Commentary* (Jerusalem: Israel Academy of Sciences and Humanities).

Thompson, T. L.
1995   'The Intellectual Matrix of Early Biblical Narrative: Inclusive Monotheism in Persian Period Palestine', in D.V. Edelman (ed.), *The Triumph of Elohim: From Yahwisms to Judaisms* (CBET 13; Kampen: Kok Pharos; Grand Rapids, MI: Eerdmans), 107–24.

Toorn, K. van der
1992   'Anat-Yahu, Some Other Deities, and the Jews of Elephantine', *Numen* 39: 80–101.

Weidner, E. F.
1939   'Jojachin, König von Juda, in babylonischen Keilschrifttexten', in *Mélanges Syriens offerts a Monsieur Rene Dussaud par ses amis et ses élèves* (Paris: Geuthner), 2.923–35.

Will, E.
1982   'Un Monument Hellénistique de Jordanie: Le Qasr el 'abd d''Iraq al Amir', *SHAJ* 1: 197–200.

Zayadine, F.
1997   "Iraq el-Amir', *OEANE* 3.177–81.

Zevit, Z.
1991   'Yahweh Worship and Worshippers in 8th-Century Syria', *VT* 41: 363–66.

PART IV

POSTSCRIPT

Chapter 12

REFLECTING ON RELIGIOUS DIVERSITY
John Barton

The Hebrew Bible presents the religion of a people called Israel as a monolith. It followed a complicated and highly ordered form, and its basis was the exclusive worship of YHWH, the one God, at a single sanctuary, the temple in Jerusalem. Any variation on this pattern was apostasy, a descent into the heathenism practised by the native inhabitants of the land, the Canaanites. Israel was monotheistic from the days of the patriarchs, and though at many times it fell away into polytheistic worship and practised 'abominations', there was never any doubt what should be its true religion.

The Hebrew Bible itself recognizes that there were changes within the national religion. The patriarchs worshipped at a variety of sanctuaries, apparently blamelessly. The name YHWH was not known, according to some passages in the books of Genesis and Exodus, until the time of Moses. During the age of the kings, apostasy to other gods became so prevalent that it almost eclipsed the true religion. After the return from Exile, the contemporaries of Ezra and Nehemiah followed a heathenized form of worship and practice until these reformers put them back on the straight path.

But there is never any doubt in the Hebrew Bible as we have it that there was a 'correct' form of religion in Israel throughout its existence, a religion continuous with later Judaism. In challenging this picture so strongly, this book may appear to some to be highly iconoclastic. For the contributors have tried to show that in many different ways the religion of 'Israel' was a highly varied set of practices that cannot be reduced to a single formula. There was geographical variation as between Israel in the historical sense (the northern kingdom) and Judah; variation between different socio-religious groups; a religion of the household and of the individual alongside the temple cults; and variation between those who claimed direct experience of the divine, and those who simply practised the outward forms of religion. What is more, none of these contrasts is simply bipolar: all form part of a spectrum, with infinite grades of variety. More than once the 'Deuteronomists' (whoever exactly they were) are blamed for trying to mask the rich profusion of Israelite and Judahite religious practices, and the reader may well feel that for the authors Deuteronomistic thinking is a Bad Thing.

We are not, however, exactly a group of 'young Turks' (some of us are not so very young, in any case). The kind of challenge to the Hebrew Bible's own monolithic presentation of the religious past goes back at least to Julius Wellhausen. With painstaking labour, and without the advantage of the many ancient Near Eastern texts discovered or published in the twentieth century to back up his work, he showed just how far the religion of 'ancient' (i.e. pre-exilic) Israel differed from the system of orthodox Judaism that eventually prevailed in post-exilic times. Pre-exilic 'Yahwism' (or 'Jehovism' as he called it) was a religion much like that of most of Israel's neighbours, and lacked almost all the defining marks of later Judaism, including monotheism. The drive to monotheism began, certainly, before the Exile, but it was only through the work of the prophets, most of all Deutero-Isaiah, that it became normative. For Wellhausen, the eventual triumph of monotheism was an advance in religious thought and practice. But much else in the post-exilic age marked rather a decline, from the spontaneity of early Israelite religion into the wooden rigidity of a priestly system. The contributors to this volume do not necessarily share Wellhausen's value-judgements (positive or negative), but they are his heirs so far as the facts on the ground are concerned, and they agree with him in seeing an official, monotheistic, centrally organized, non-syncretistic religious system as a late arrival, replacing (so far as it ever did actually replace) the varied tapestry of practices that had earlier constituted the religious life of Israel and Judah, just as it did that of so many of their neighbours. Since Wellhausen's day many biblical scholars have become more 'orthodox' in accepting the Hebrew Bible's own evaluation and reconstruction of early Israelite religion. But the historian should not accept the Bible's testimony at face value, but should seek to get below the surface – the historian's job, after all, is always to 'torture' the evidence, not to absorb it passively. And below the surface of the Hebrew Bible there is ample testimony to the rich, varied, and often surprising or even, to some, shocking reality that was the religion of ancient Israel and Judah.

Two big questions remain unaddressed. First, given the variety of practice in early times, implying the recognition of many divine powers, how did monotheism ever arise? For however far the religion of the Israelites and Judahites was from later Jewish monotheism, later Jewish monotheism did eventually develop, and carried all before it. Was this a purely post-exilic movement of thought, owing something to contacts with a religion such as Zoroastrianism or even with currents of thought in the classical world (the pre-Socratics, for example), or is it an indigenous development? If the latter, which is probably what most biblical scholars think, then what hints are there in early material of what would eventually become this innovative and strikingly distinctive religious position? Perhaps a number of the cultures around Israel and Judah were already tending to 'monolatry' in early times: certainly each had its chief god, as Israel and Judah had YHWH. But nowhere else did there emerge the insistence that there is only one God (rightly spelt with a capital G) who ruled over all nations and must be worshipped in only one, official way. Much work (not surveyed in this book) has been done on this subject in recent years, but the matter cannot be said to be settled.

Secondly, why did Judaism, the heir of all these ancient Israelite and Judahite religious practices, become a religion of the book? There are already signs of this happening in Deuteronomy and the Deuteronomistic corpus. In later Judaism the Book replaces the images of the gods as a focus for the worship of YHWH, but hedged around with rules to make sure that it is not treated as a cult object in itself. And after the destruction of the Second Temple by the Romans, Judaism settled into being one of the most book-centred religions the world had known, at least until the rise of Islam. This is a strange phenomenon that could not at all be predicted from the evidence for religious pluriformity surveyed in the present book. Why did *words* become so important for the heirs of ancient Israel and Judah? The question demands a book in itself.

A final point. In this book we have examined religious practice, touching only lightly on what was believed about the divine realm. Often this cannot be reconstructed: we have evidence of what people did, but not of what they thought. We can, as Queen Elizabeth I famously said, 'make no windows into men's souls'. Yet one of the most obvious features of the Hebrew Bible (perhaps linked to the issue just broached about the bookishness of Judaism) is its talkativeness: it emphatically does not tell us only what is done or to be done, but what is to be believed and thought about. The Hebrew Bible, that is, is a theological as well as a religious document. Even in the earlier stages of its development, in the words of the prophets and the writings of historians (assuming that at least some of these are indeed early), there is evidence of religious thought as well as religious practice. It still makes sense to reflect on theological themes and trains of thought in the Hebrew Bible, and even beneath its surface, even if the quest for *the* theology of the Old Testament is nowadays looking decidedly dubious. Sometimes – for example in Rainer Albertz's reflections on personal piety – the theme of belief has been raised even in the present book, but mostly it has yielded to the study of practice. There is a venerable tradition of saying that later Judaism too is focused on practice rather than on belief, on 'orthopraxy' rather than 'orthodoxy'. But it is a truism that is only partly true: Judaism has produced a huge body of reflective literature thinking rigorously about the being of God and human response to him, and Judaism's forebears, the authors of the Hebrew Bible, were already in the business of thinking about YHWH as well as worshipping him. The varied thoughts they had are also part of the religious diversity in ancient Israel and Judah.

INDEX OF AUTHORS

Abu-'Assaf, A. 32, 33
Ackerman, S. 2, 7, 11, 22, 40,
 41, 42, 43, 45, 48, 49, 50,
 75, 76, 122, 129, 130
Adams, R.McC. 104, 105, 115
Aerts, E. 104, 115
Aharoni, Y. 92, 95, 99, 163,
 168
Ahlström, G.W. 25, 26, 33,
 40, 51, 67, 75, 77, 95, 99
Albertz, R. 2, 5, 7, 40, 43, 48,
 51, 55, 104, 115, 117, 119,
 120, 127, 129, 131, 135,
 140, 142, 143, 145, 149,
 168, 193
Albright, W.F. 23, 24, 33, 38,
 39, 51, 68, 77, 154, 155,
 168
Aldhouse-Green, M. 90, 99
Alt, A. 23, 33, 106, 115
Amit, Y. 85, 99
Anderson, F.I. 155, 168
Andreasen, N-E.A. 75, 77
Arav, R. 183, 184
Archi, A. 176, 177, 184
Assmann, J. 26, 33, 49, 51
Athas, G. 62, 63, 77
Attridge, H.W. 178, 184
Aufrecht, W.E. 104, 115, 164,
 168
Aurelius, E. 158, 168
Avigad, N. 154, 155, 168
Avner, U. 92, 99

Bach, A. 42, 51
Barkay, G. 46, 51
Barley, N. 46, 51
Barr, J. 178, 184
Barrick, W.B. 87, 88, 99
Barton, J. 6, 7, 39, 51
Baumgarten, A.I. 178, 184
Beck, P. 98, 99, 100
Becking, B. 1, 8, 31, 32, 33, 55
Beckman, G.M. 2, 7, 56
Beit Arieh, I. 98, 99, 100, 143,
 145
Bell, C.M. 123, 131
Ben Zvi, E. 108, 115, 155, 168
Ben-Barak, Z. 75, 76, 77
Bendor, S. 119, 131
Bennett, G. 47, 51
Bennett, K.M. 47, 51
Bergquist, B. 90, 100

Berlinerblau, J. 40, 41, 43, 49,
 51, 56
Bienkowski, P. 98, 100
Binger, T. 152, 168
Bird, P. 41, 42, 51
Blenkinsopp, J. 45, 51, 176,
 185
Bloch-Smith, E. 45, 52, 56,
 127, 128, 131
Blomquist, T.H. 90, 91, 93,
 94, 95, 96, 97, 98, 100
Bodel, J. 2, 7, 50, 51, 53, 55,
 57, 118, 119, 120, 130, 131,
 133, 134, 145
Borghouts, J.F. 142, 145
Bourdieu, P. 39, 52
Bowen, N.R. 75, 76, 77
Brakke, D. 12, 22
Brichto, H. 128, 131
Bright, J. 38, 44, 52, 154, 155,
 168
Brooke, G.J. 64, 77
Brookes, A. 90, 102
Brown, J.P. 75, 77
Brown, P. 11, 22
Büchner, D. 41, 43, 52
Bunimovitz, S. 90, 100
Burdajewicz, M. 90, 100
Busink, T. 32, 33
Byrne, R. 43, 52

Callaway, R. 153, 168
Campbell, A.F. 160, 169
Capponi, L. 183, 185
Caquot, A. 62, 70, 71, 77
Cardascia, G. 180, 185
Carroll R., M.D. 40, 41, 42,
 52
Carter, C.E. 123, 131
Cartledge, T.W. 129, 131
Cavanagh, R.R. 121, 131
Cazelles, H. 73, 77
Childe, V.G. 105, 115
Christian, M.A. 149, 160, 169
Cohen, R.L. 88, 100
Coogan, M.D. 27, 28, 33, 52,
 90, 100, 152, 169, 180, 185
Cook, S.L. 39, 52
Cooke, G. 72, 77
Cornelius, I. 28, 33
Cowley, A.E. 84, 96, 100
Cox, J.L. 44, 52
Craigie, P.C. 64, 77

Cross, F.M. 24, 33, 152, 159,
 160, 164, 169
Curtis, A.H.W. 64, 77

Dalley, S. 68, 77, 179, 185
Daviau, P.M.M. 122, 131,
 164, 169
Davies, D.J. 47, 52
Davies, P.R. 4, 38, 50, 52,
 112, 113, 115
Davila, J.R. 71, 77
Davis, N.Z. 37, 52
Day, J. 39, 52, 61, 62, 64, 66,
 67, 71, 72, 73, 75, 77, 155,
 156, 159, 164, 169
Dearman, J.A. 104, 115, 155,
 156, 169
Delcor, M. 183, 185
Dever, W.G. 40, 42, 43, 44,
 52, 106, 115, 123, 131
Di Vito, R.A. 120, 131
Dietler, M. 125, 131
Dietrich, M. 75, 77, 78
Dietrich, W. 2, 7, 23, 31, 33,
 160, 169
Dijkstra, M. 33, 71, 75, 78,
 166, 169
Dimbleby, G.W. 104, 117
Dion, P.-E. 164, 169
Diringer, D. 154, 169
Dobbs-Allsopp, F.W. 153, 154,
 169
Donner, H. 75, 78
Dorsey, D.A. 165, 169
Douglas, M. 126, 131
Dozeman, T.B. 72, 78
Driel, G. van 180, 185
Durand, J.-M. 69, 78

Ebach, J.H. 46, 53
Ebertz, M.N. 39, 53
Edelman, D.V. 1, 2, 4, 7, 35,
 52, 86, 92, 94, 100, 187
Eissfeldt, O. 178, 185
Emerton, J.A. 71, 78, 93, 100,
 150, 153, 169
Eph'al, I. 93, 100
Eynikel, E. 88, 100, 158, 169

Falconer, S.E. 105, 115
Finkelstein, I. 25, 33, 62, 80,
 90, 96, 98, 100, 106, 107,
 115, 123, 126, 131

Fitzgerald, T. 39, 53
Fleming, D.E. 46, 53, 159, 160, 169
Foley, J.M. 13, 22, 81
Foltyn, J.L. 46, 47, 53
Francis, D. 47, 53
Franken, H.J. 163, 165, 170
Frazer, J.G. 44, 47, 53
Freedman, D.N. 155, 168
Freud, L. 96, 100
Friedman, R.E. 118, 132
Fritz, V. 87, 100, 104, 106, 107, 115, 132

Gates, C. 104, 116
Geertz, A.W. 44, 53
Geertz, C. 41, 53
Geoghegan, J.C. 160, 170
Gerbrandt, G. 87, 101
Gerstenberger, E.S. 40, 53, 135, 145
Geus, C.H.J. de 104, 115
Geyer, J.B. 69, 78
Gibson, J.C.L. 31, 33
Gillingham, S.E. 61, 78
Gilula, M. 153, 170
Gitin, S. 122, 132, 152, 170
Gittlen, B.M. 2, 7, 53, 55, 56, 132, 133, 170
Gnuse, R. 67, 78, 121, 132
Gomes, J. 39, 43, 53
Goody, J. 39, 53
Görg, M. 25, 34, 54, 86, 101
Goss, R. 47, 54
Gottwald, N.K. 106, 116, 119, 132, 150, 170
Grabbe, L.L. 6, 11, 22, 28, 34, 38, 53, 62, 78, 104, 116, 182, 185
Greenberg, M. 40, 53
Gunneweg, J. 97, 101

Haak, R.D. 104, 116
Hackett, J.A. 149, 162, 163, 164, 165, 166, 170
Hadley, J.M. 24, 31, 32, 34, 75, 78, 96, 97, 101, 152, 153, 170
Hall, E. 27, 34
Hall, J.M. 27, 34
Hall, S. 39, 54
Hall, T.W. 131, 134
Hallo, W.W. 125, 132
Halpern, B. 25, 34, 45, 54, 160, 161, 170
Hamilton, G.J. 154, 155, 170
Handy, L.K. 28, 31, 34
Hasel, M.G. 25, 34
Hauser, A.J. 150, 170
Havrelock, R.S. 163, 170
Hayden, B. 125, 131, 132
Hayward, C.T.R. 183, 185
Healey, J.F. 64, 77
Heiser, M. 74, 78
Hendel, R. 126, 132
Herrmann, C. 142, 145

Hertzog, Z. 92, 94, 95, 101, 107, 116, 152, 170
Hess, R.S. 1, 7, 39, 54, 151, 152, 153, 154, 155, 156, 157, 170
Hesse, B. 126, 132
Hillers, D.R. 23, 24, 34
Hockey, J. 47, 54
Hoffmann, H.-D. 86, 88, 101
Hoftijzer, J. 164, 171
Holladay, J.S. 90, 101, 122, 132, 183, 185
Hollenstein, H. 88, 101
Horbury, W. 183, 185
Horowitz, W. 68, 81
Horst, P.W. van der 1, 8
Huehnergard, J. 165, 171
Huffmon, H.B. 177, 178, 185
Hurowitz, V. 110, 116
Hutter, M. 40, 54
Hutton, J.M. 6, 149, 153, 154, 161, 165, 167, 171

Ikeda, Y. 42, 54
Isaac, B.H. 27, 34

Jay, N. 2, 7, 41, 54
Jepsen, A. 160, 171
Joannès, F. 180, 185
Johnston, P.S. 45, 46, 47, 54
Johnston, S.I. 28, 34, 119, 132, 134
Jolly, K.L. 39, 54
Jonker, G. 75, 78
Jones, D.W. 90, 101
Jones, S. 116

Kapelrud, A.S. 64, 78
Katz, J. 53
Katz, S.T. 12, 13, 22
Keel, O. 2, 7, 34, 64, 67, 78, 159, 171
Kellaher, L. 47, 53
Kelso, J.L. 90, 101
Kessler, R. 104, 116
Killebrew, A.E. 116, 150, 171
Kim, T.-K. 142, 145
King, P.J. 45, 54
Klass, D. 46, 47, 54
Klingbeil, M. 30, 34
Klopfenstein, M.A. 2, 7, 31, 33
Kloppenborg, J.S. 163, 171
Knoppers, G.N. 62, 79, 157, 171
Köckert, M. 32, 34
Kooij, K. van der 164, 171
Korpel, M.C.A. 33
Kraeling, C.H. 104, 116
Krebernik, M. 31, 34

Labuschagne, C.J. 38, 42, 54
Lampl, P. 104, 116
Lang, B. 40, 54
Lapidus, I.M. 104, 116
Lapp, N.L. 183, 186

Lapp, P. 183
LaRocca-Pitts, E.C. 75, 79
Lederman, Z. 90, 100
Lemaire, A. 92, 93, 101, 164, 171, 180, 182, 185, 186
Lemche, N.P. 24, 25, 26, 34, 38, 55, 186
Lenski, G. 120, 132
Leuchter, M. 160, 171
Levenson, J.D. 128, 132
Levine, B.A. 116, 120, 125, 129, 132, 149, 161, 162, 163, 164, 165, 166, 167, 171
Lewis, T.J. 2, 7, 43, 44, 45, 46, 48, 55, 56, 127, 128, 133
Lightstone, J.N. 46, 55
Lissovsky, N. 96, 102
Liverani, M. 24, 25, 35, 38, 55, 106, 115, 116
Liwak, R. 128, 133
Long, O.B. 86, 101
Lowery, R.H. 88, 101
Lundbom, J.R. 87, 101

MacDonald, B. 163, 171
MacDonald, N. 125, 126, 133
Magen, Y. 182, 186
Marsman, H.J. 41, 55
Matsushima, E. 104, 116
Mayes, A.D.H. 85, 101, 152, 172
Mays, J.L. 155, 172
Mazar, A. 62, 67, 91, 92, 102
McCarter, P.K. 150, 164, 165, 172
McLaughlin, J. 128, 133
McNutt, P. 38, 40, 55, 119, 133
Meeks, W.A. 104, 116
Mendenhall, G.E. 45, 47, 55
Meshel, Z. 96, 97, 102, 152, 153, 172
Meshorer, Y. 182, 186
Mettinger, T.N.D. 92, 102
Meyers, C. 2, 5, 7, 41, 55, 118, 119, 122, 124, 125, 127, 129, 130, 133, 152, 172
Milgrom, J. 45, 47, 55, 124, 129, 133
Miller, P.D. 38, 40, 55, 135, 145
Miller, R.D. 150, 172
Mirau, N.A. 104, 115
Mirecki, P. 123, 133
Misgav, H. 182, 186
Mithen, S. 70, 79
Molin, G.E. 75, 79
Momigliano, A.D. 11, 22
Mommsen, U. 97, 101
Moor, J.C. de 178, 186
Moran, W.L. 63, 79
Mosca, P.G. 164, 172
Moshkovitz, S. 92, 101
Müller, H.-P. 176, 177, 186

Muraoka, T, 165, 172
Murtonen, A. 68, 79

Na'aman, N. 25, 26, 35, 96, 102, 172
Naveh, J. 93, 100, 152, 172
Nelson, R.D. 160, 172
Neophytou, G. 47, 53
Nicholson, E.W. 87, 102
Nickman, J. 47, 54
Niditch, S. 2, 3, 7, 13, 18, 19, 21, 22
Niehr, H. 3, 28, 31, 32, 33, 35, 46, 55, 74, 79, 181, 186
Nissinen, M. 110, 116
Noth, M. 137, 145, 154, 155, 172
Noy, D. 183, 185, 186
Nutkowicz, H. 74, 79

Obeyesekere, G. 12, 22
O'Brien, M.A. 157, 160, 172
O'Bryhim, S. 76, 79
O'Callaghan, R.T. 68, 79
Oden, R.A. 178, 184
Oeming, M. 31, 35, 186
Oldenburg, U. 23, 35
Olmo Lete, G. del 2, 7, 28, 35, 64, 73, 74, 75, 79
Olyan, S.M. 2, 7, 12, 22, 40, 43, 46, 48, 50, 51, 53, 55, 57, 75, 79, 118, 119, 120, 127, 128, 130, 131, 133, 134, 145, 164, 172
Oorschot, J. van 31, 34
Östreicher, T. 88, 102
Otto, R. 11, 22

Pardee, D. 64, 65, 79, 165, 172
Paton, L.B. 44, 47, 56
Parker Pearson, M. 46, 55
Pearce, L.E. 180, 186
Petersen, D.L. 113, 117
Pettinato, G. 176, 186
Piasetsky, E. 96, 100
Pilgrim, R. 123, 134
Pitard, W.T. 45, 56
Porten, B. 181, 186
Prendergast, D. 47, 56
Propp, W.H. 72, 79
Provan, I.W. 157, 172
Pury, A. de 157, 173

Qedar, S. 182, 186

Rad, G. von 71, 79, 135, 145
Rainey, A.F. 25, 35, 92, 101, 177, 186
Rapoport, A. 120, 134
Renfrew, C. 90, 102
Richardson, P. 104, 117
Robben, A.C.G.M. 47, 56
Rogerson, J.W. 40, 45, 56, 120, 134
Rollston, C. 154, 173

Römer, T. 87, 102, 157, 173
Rose, M. 40, 56
Rouillard, H. 74, 79
Routledge, C. 41, 56
Ruiz, C.L. 76, 80
Rutkowski, B. 90, 102

Saler, B. 39, 48, 56
Sanders, S.L. 67, 72
Sass, B. 154, 168
Satlow, M.L. 12, 22
Savage, S.H. 105, 115
Schloen, D. 119, 134
Schmid, K. 25, 31, 35
Schmidt, B.B. 45, 46, 47, 56, 62, 74, 80, 152, 153, 173
Schmitt, G. 23, 26, 35
Schmitt, R. 142, 145
Schniedewind, W.M. 40, 56
Schultheis, F. 39, 53
Schürer, E. 183, 186
Schwemer, D. 28, 35
Segal, J.B. 38, 44, 56
Sharot, S. 39, 40, 41, 56
Silberman, N.A. 107, 115
Silverman, P. 46, 54
Singer-Avitz, L. 96, 98, 102, 107, 116
Smart, N. 11, 22
Smith, A.T. 90, 102
Smith, J.Z. 39, 56, 126, 134
Smith, M.S. 2, 8, 24, 28, 36, 38, 45, 56, 64, 66, 67, 74, 75, 78, 80, 121, 134, 152, 155, 156, 157, 159, 163, 164, 173, 178, 187
Soumeka, A. 152, 173
Sparks, K.L. 150, 173
Speiser, E.A. 68, 80
Spronk, K. 45, 57
Sperber, D. 104, 117
Stager, L.E. 45, 48, 54, 57, 119, 128, 134, 161, 173
Stamm, J.J. 137, 146
Stark, R. 104, 117
Stavrakopoulou, F. 3, 46, 57, 63, 75, 80, 128, 134, 163, 164, 173
Steen, E. van der 98, 100, 165, 170, 173
Steiner, R.C. 159, 173
Stern, E. 39, 43, 57
Stevens, M.E. 89, 102
Stolper, M.W. 180, 187
Stowers, S.K. 121, 122

Tadmor, H. 179, 187
Talmon, S. 158, 173
Tammuz, O. 25, 36
Thompson, T.L. 80, 179, 187
Tigay, J.H. 154, 155, 156, 164, 173
Toorn, K. van der 1, 2, 8, 28, 30, 35, 36, 39, 40, 41, 42, 43, 45, 46, 48, 49, 50, 57, 92, 102, 119, 120, 121, 126,

128, 134, 135, 146, 181, 187
Trapp, T.H. 67, 80
Tringham, R. 104, 117
Tromp, N.J. 47, 57
Tsfania, L. 182, 186
Tsukimoto, A. 75, 80
Tsumura, D.T. 40, 57
Tufnell, O. 92, 102
Tur-Sinai, 66

Ucko, P.J. 104, 117
Uehlinger, C. 2, 7, 23, 25, 34, 36, 64, 67, 78, 159, 171
Ussishkin, D. 62, 80

Valentine, C. 47, 57
Van de Mieroop, M. 104, 117
Van Seters, J. 68, 81
Vanderhooft, D. 68, 81
Vaux, R. de 70, 81, 153, 174
Venter, P.M. 149, 150, 174
Vorländer, H. 38, 57
Vriezen, K.J.H. 33
Vrijhof, P.H. 37, 39, 50, 57

Waardenburg, J. 37, 50, 57
Wagenaar, J.A. 32, 36
Wapnish, P. 126, 132
Wasilewska, E. 90, 102
Weidner, E.F. 179, 187
Weinfeld, M. 40, 58, 163, 166, 174
Weippert, M. 25, 36, 163, 174
Weitzman, M.P. 173
Weitzman, S. 12, 22
Wellhausen, J. 191, 192
Wenning, R. 45, 58
Westbrook, R. 120, 134
Wheatley, P. 105, 117
Whitehouse, R. 104, 117
Whitelam, K.W. 23, 36
Widengren, G. 71, 81
Wiggins, S.A. 75, 81
Will, E. 183, 187
Williams, P.W. 37, 50, 58
Wilson, R.R. 15, 17, 22, 119, 134
Wolters, A. 164, 174
Wright, D.P. 88, 102
Wright, J. 108, 117
Wyatt, N. 4, 61, 63, 64, 65, 66, 67, 68, 69, 70, 71, 72, 73, 74, 75, 76, 81

Xella, P. 28, 36, 45, 58

Yalom, M. 126, 134

Zayadine, F. 183, 187
Zevit, Z. 1, 2, 8, 38, 45, 46, 47–49, 58, 92, 93, 96, 97, 98, 103, 104, 117, 121, 122, 134, 149, 150, 151, 152, 153, 155, 156, 157, 158, 159, 160, 174, 179, 187

Index of Ancient Sources

Hebrew Bible
Genesis
2 109, 110
2.13 71
3.23-24 110
4 67
6.1 73
6.2 73
10.19 25
12 67
12-36 25
12-50 136
12.6-7 83
12.8 83, 90
13.3-4 124
13.18 83, 124
14 62
14.12 13
14.17-20 83
15 67
16.11 136
16.15 136
17 67
17.1 163
17.9-14 127
17.12 127, 144
21.33 83, 89
23 128
24.3-4 26
24.37 26
25.21 127
25.27 104
26.25 83, 124
26.34-35 26
27.46-25.5 26
28 160
28.3 163
28.6-9 26
28.8-20 83, 90
28.12 13
28.17 110
28.18-22 161
29.31 139
29.31-30.24 136
30.23 138
31.19 128
31.34-35 128
32-33 163, 166
32.1-2 161
32.8-11 161
32.22-32 83
32.31 161
33.10 161
33.17 163

33.19-20 124
34 162
34.1 105
34.6 166
34.28 104
35.1 124
35.4 83
35.6-7 83, 90
35.9-15 83, 90
35.17-18 136
35.22 75
35.29 128
37 25
38.9 87
38.19 87
38.28 127
46.2 13
48.3 163
49.10 162
49.24 160
49.33 128
50.10 128

Exodus
1 15
1-12 25
3 67
3.6 175
3.10-12 137
3.14 177
4.24-26 127
6 67
6.3 175
12 124
12.1-4 124
12.43-49 127
12.46 124
15 15
16 125
18 66
19 70
20 70
24 70
20.2 137
20.3-5 32
20.5 30
20.8-11 125
20.11 125
20.24 124
22.17 136, 143
23.12 125
23.14-17 89, 124
23.14-19 136
23.23-24 26

23.28-33 26
24 15, 16, 17
24.9 15
24.9-11 15
24.10 15
24.11 15
24.12 49
25-40 118
29.20-21 70
31.17 144
32 159
32.26-29 160
33.2 26
34.11-16 26
34.13 32
34.13-15 26
34.21 125
34.29 72

Leviticus
10.1-7 160
11 144
11.24-40 129
12.2-8 129
12.3 127
13.2-14.32 129
14.34-53 129
15 129
18 26
18.21 163
19.28 45
19.31 45, 75
20.2-5 163
20.6 21
20.27 21
21.5 128
22.5-9 129
23 89
23.2-3 125
23.4-25 124
25 124

Numbers
5.1-2 129
10.10 125
12 160
12.6-8 14
13.16 175
16 160
19 129
20.14 63
21.33 63
22-24 162
22.4 63

23.22 30, 66, 160
24.4 163
24.8 66, 160
24.16 163
25.6-15 160
25.6-18 162
28.9-10 125
28.22-15 125
31.15-16 162
32 162
33.51-56 26
33.54 120
34.2-12 25
35 107, 113

Deuteronomy
1.7 25
4.16-19 32
4.23-26 32
5.7 30
5.7-9 32
5.12-15 125
5.15 125
6.4 31
6.4-5 143
6.10 107
6.12 137
6.21-24 143
7.1-5 26, 40
7.1-6 26
7.3 26
7.17-26 26
9 71
9.16 159
9.21 159
10 71
12 26, 85
12.2 89, 111
12.2-4 119
12.3 89
12.2-4 88
12.3 83, 89
12.5 82
12.5-7 83
12.6 129
12.11 82
12.11-19 143
12.14 82
12.18 82
12.21 82
12.26 82
12.31 162
13 85
13.2 14

13.4 14
13.6 14
13.7-12 143
14 85
14.1 45, 128
14.23-25 82
15.20 82
16 89
16.1-17 124
16.6 82
16.11 82, 124
16.14 124
16.16 82, 124
16.21 85, 89
18.6-8 87
18.9-12 46
18.9-14 21, 162
18.11 54, 75
20.16-17 26
20.16-18 26
22.22-27 104
23.4-7 162
24 85
26 85
26.1-11 143
26.2 82
26.8 137
26.12-15 21
26.14 45, 46
31.10-12 124
32 87, 150
32.16-17 163
33.8-11 160
33.17 160
33.26 30

Joshua
1-12 26
2.3 63
5.1-8 127
7.13-14 48
7.14-18 119
8.23 63
12.9-24 63
13-19 120
13.15-23 162
15-21 107
15-23 105
21 84
22 162, 163
24 84
24.9-10 162

Judges
1 26
2.1-5 26
2.3 85
2.10 85
2.20-23 26
3.1-6 26
3.7 156
4-5 26, 30
5.4-5 30
6 84, 114
6.24 89
6.32 154

7.1 154
9.4 84
9.46 84
11.12 84
11.26 105
11.34-40 160,
    163
13.2-24 127
13.19-23 124
15.18 136
17 89, 122
17.2-3 129
17.7 161
18 84
18.27-31 84
18.31 84, 90
19.10-11 68
20.1-2 84
21 114
21.2-3 84, 90
21.14 120

1 Samuel
1-2 114
1-12 84
1.1 161
1.1-20 127
1.3 84, 90
1.20 136
1.24 84, 90
2.18-21 161
3.1 161
3.23 84, 90
4.3-4 84, 90
5.5 150
7.5 84
7.15 84, 90
8.1-22 62
8.5 63
9.9 15
9.11-25 89
9.14-10.16 70
9.15-10.16 62
10.3 84, 90
10.5-6 84
10.8 66
10.17-27 84
10.17-11.15 62
11.14-15 84
13.7-15 66
13.9 65
14.49 155
15.12-15 84
16.1-13 62, 70
16.2 84
16.13 70
16.14-23 70
19.16 128
20.5-29 125
20.6 84
21.1-6 84
22.1-12 84
22.20-23 84
23.16 136
28 21, 75
28.3 87

28.3-25 40, 46, 128
28.13 74, 128

2 Samuel
1.4 62
1.11-12 128
1.14 70
2-4 154, 179
2.1-4 67
2.8 154
3.7 75
3.12-19 62
3.31 128
4 154, 179
5.1-3 62
5.1-5 84
5.1-10 68
5.3 70
5.11 63
5.13 75
5.16 155
5.20 150
6 110
6.11-12 161
6.13 65
6.17-18 65
7.1-17 69
8.10 179
9 154, 179
11.21 154
14.2 40
15.7 150
16 154, 179
16.9 87
16.22 75
19 154, 179
19.11 70
20.3 75
21 179
21.6 84
21.9-14 46
21.18 154
23.8 154
24 67
24.16 67
24.18 68
24.23 67
24.25 65

1 Kings
1.9 71
1.33 110
1.38-39 71
1.39 70
1.45 65
2.28 152
3-9 85
3.4 65
3.15 65
4-9 89
5-9 89
5.17-9.14 69
5.22 75
6-8 31, 118
6.2 69
7.1-12 69

7.2 69
7.21 71
8.5 65
8.62-64 65, 66
9.25 65
10.17 69
11.7 163
11.7-8 157
11.9-13 157
11.29-39 157, 161
11.33 175
12 158
12.1 85
12.20 85
12.26-27 66
12.26-29 89
12.26-33 66
12.28-29 119
12.28-30 30, 158
12.28-33 158, 159
12.30-33 84, 90
12.31 158, 160
12.32 158
12.33 65, 158
13 84, 90
13.1-2 65
14.22-23 119
14.23 85
15.13 42, 75, 111
15.26 158
15.34 158
16.19 158
16.24 113
16.25-26 158
16.30-31 158
16.31 66
17.17-24 129
17.27-28 84, 90
18 30, 84, 85, 111
18.19 42, 156
21 120
22 14, 16, 17
22.19-22 31
22.19-23 14, 15
22.53-54 158

2 Kings
3.2 111
3.2-3 158
3.27 162, 163
4.32-37 129
4.38-44 84
8.18 158
8.27 158
9.1-10 70
10 84
10.29 158, 159
10.31 158
11.12 70, 71
13.2 158
13.11 158
14.14 89
14.24 158
15.9 158
15.18 158
15.24 158

15.28 158
16.4 65, 89, 111
16.8 89
16.12-15 65
17 181
17.7-12 158
17.10 89
17.16 159
17.32 40
18.1-22 85
18.3-6 85, 88
18.4-6 87
18.22 88
20.1-3 130
20.7 129
21.2-8 40
21.3 88, 111, 158
21.3-9 85, 86
21.6 21, 75
21.7 42, 111
22-23 49, 140
22.3-10 70
22.8 87
22.11-20 88
23 32, 86, 87
23.2 87
23.4 42, 87, 156
23.4-7 111
23.4-20 85
23.5 85, 86, 87
23.6 87
23.6-7 42
23.8 85, 86, 97
23.9 86, 87
23.10 163
23.13-14 87
23.14 111
23.19-20 87
23.21 87
23.25 87
23.30 70
24. 8-16 180

Isaiah
1.24 160
1.25 87
1.29 75
3.18 142
3.20 142
6 14, 16, 17, 18, 31
8.19 75, 128
8.19-20 45, 46
14 70, 73, 74
14.4 73
14.4-21 74
14.9 74
14.9-11 20
14.12-15 74
14.13-14 31
14.15 20
15.2-3 128
19.1 30
22.8 69
26.19 21
29.4 46
34.7 160

38.21 129
40.12-26 31
40.18-20 32
41.6-7 32
41.21-29 31
42.8 31
43.1 139, 144
43.8-16 31
44.2 139, 144
44.6-7 31
44.9-20 32
44.21 139
44.24 144
45.5-7 31
45.18 31
46.1-7 32
46.9-10 31
49.5 139, 144
49.26 160
54.5 139
56.5 46
57.3-13 21, 45
57.5 89
57.9 163
60.16 160
64.7 139, 144
64.10 114
65.1-5 45
65.4 75
66.7-16 109

Jeremiah
1.5 139
1.11-12 18
2.20 89
2.27 136, 139
2.27-28 140
3.6 89
3.13 89
6.26 128
7 42
7.12 84, 90
7.14 84, 90
7.16-18 42
7.16-20 39
7.18 141, 143
7.31-32 162
8.1-3 46
9.17-20 128
10.13 30
11.3 90, 91
11.12-13 40
13.27 89
14.22 30
16.5-9 128
17.2 89
19.13 129, 143
23.16 14
24 18
26.6 84, 90
26.9 84, 90
27.9 14
29 49
29.8 14
31.12 30
32.29 143

32.35 163
44 42, 110
44.15-19 39, 42,
    136, 141, 143
44.17 110
44.17-19 129
44.18 42
44.24-25 42
44.25 39, 129
46.15 160
51.16 30

Ezekiel
1-3 14, 18, 19
1.1 16
1.1-3 17
1.3 16
1.4 17
1.4-28 16
1.5 17
1.16 17
1.18 16
1.24 16
1.26 16
1.28 16
2.1-7 16
2.2 16
2.8-3.1-3 16
3.12 17
3. 12-14 16
3.14 16, 17
6.3 89
6.13 89
8.3 89, 93
8.5 89, 93
13.2 14
13.6 14
13.7 14
13.17 14
13.17-23 136, 143
14.1-11 136
14.3 142
16 109
16.3 32
16.4 127
16.24 91
16.29 32
16.31 91
17.4 32
20.7 142
20.25-26 162, 163
20.28 89
28 74, 110
28.2-11 70
28.12-18 74
28.16 110
40-44 110
43.7-9 46
47 110

Hosea
2.7 111
2.10 30
2.13 125
2.18 155
4.15 119

8.5-6 159
8.6 66
4.13 89
4.15 84
5.1 84
10 84, 90
10.5 86, 159
12.11 84
13.2 159

Amos
4.4 84, 90
4.4-5 119
4.6 113
4.6-11 113
4.7-8 113
4.9 113
4.10-11 113
5.4-5 119
5.5 84, 90
6.7 128
7.7-9 18
7.13 84, 90
8.1-3 18
8.2 18
8.5 125
8.13 18
8.14 84, 119

Micah
1.7 84
1.16 128
4.1 89
6.3-5 162
6.7-8 162

Habakkuk
3.3 30, 160

Zephaniah
1.4 86
1.5-6 143

Haggai
1.2-12 30
2.15-19 30

Zechariah
1-8 18
6 18
6.1 18
6.1-8 18
7.15 19
7.28 19
8.9-12 30
8.26 19
8.27 19
10.1 30

Psalms
1 145
1.2 145
2.7 72, 75, 109
3.8 139
3.9 137
5.3 139

7.8-9   145
8   70
8.5   72
9.6   145
9.18   145
10.12   144
10.16   145
14.7   137
16.3-4   46
18.3   139
18.8-16   30
18.10-11   30
19   70, 73, 145
19.2-7   70, 75
19.8-11   70
19.12-15   70
21.9-13   30
22.4-6   137
22.8-16   30
22.9-10   139
22.10   139
22.11   139
24   110
25.22   137
27.1   139
28.8-9   137
29   30, 145
29.1   73
29.3-9   30
30.13   139
31.4   139
38.16   139
40.18   139
45.7   72
46.7-12   30
48.3   31
51.20   137
53.7   137
54.6   139
59.17-18   139
60.8   167
61.7-8   137
62.3   139
62.7   139
63.12   137
65.10-14   30
66.13-14   129
66.13-20   137
68.5   30
68.5-34   30
69.30   144
70.6   144
71.5-6   139
71.5-7   139
71.6   139
72.8   69
75.3   145
77   137
78   150
78.60   119
80.9-19   137
81.4   125
82   31, 73
83.14-18   30
88.11   128
89   31

89.7   73
89.26   69
90.1-2   144
94.22   139
99.2   150
102.13-25   144
104   30
106.19   159
106.19-22   66
106.28   46, 75
106.28-31   163
106.37-38   162
106.37-39   163
107   137
109.5-10   145
109.22   144
110   62
110.1   71, 72
110.3   65, 75
110.5   73
115.17   21
116   137
118   137
119   145
119.1-16   145
119.47   145
119.73   139, 145
119.97   145
119.131   145
121   113
132   110
132.2   160
132.5   160
132.17   72
138   137
138.8   139
139.13   139
140.8   139
143.5   137
144.5-8   30

Job
1   31
2.1   73
3.15-19   20
4.6   144
10.3   139
10.8-11   139
10.8-13   139
10.22   20
10.26   20
14.13-17   144
16.18-22   144
19.23-27   144
26.7   31
29.12-17   144
29.18-20   144
31.13-27   144
33.18   20
35.10-11   139
37.22   31
38.7   73

Proverbs
1-9   141
3.5   141

7.14   129
10-29   141
10.22   141
11.1   141
11.20   141
12.2   141
12.22   141
14.31   141
15.3   141
15.11   141
15.25   141
15.33   141
16.3   141
16.9   141
16.16   141
16.33   141
17.3   141
17.5   141
19.17   141
19.21   141
20.12   141
20.22   141
20.27   141
21.31   141
22.2   141
22.22-23   141
23.17   141
25.28   141
28.25   141
29.25   141
30-31   141

Lamentations
3   144

Daniel
7   14, 18, 19
7.9   19
8   18
12.2   21

Ezra
1-6   85
9.1-10.1   130

Nehemiah
2.10   183
8   49
8.16   124
9   150
9.18   159
12.44   89
13.2   162

1 Chronicles
6.18-23   161
8.33   154, 179
8.34   154, 179
9.39   154, 179
9.40   154, 179
13.13-14   161
14.7   155
15.16-24   161
18.10   179
28.5   71
29.23   71

2 Chronicles
3-4   118
8.12-13   125
9.16   69
11.13-15   160
11.15   159
13.8   159
13.8-11   160
28.4   89
32.19   152

Apocryphal Literature
Tobit
4.17   46

Sirach
30.18   46

1 Maccabees
1   88
4.36-58   88

New Testament
Revelation
21.2   110

Classical Authors
Eusebius
Praep. Ev.
1.9.19-10.55   178
1.9.21   178

Hesiod
Theogony   73

Josephus
Against Apion
1.18   66

Antiquities
12.5.1   183
12.9.7   183
13.3.1-3   183
13.3.2   183
13.3.3   183

War
7.10.2-4   183
7.10.3   183

Ugarit Texts
KTU
1.1.iv.12-20   73
1.1.iv.14   68, 178
1.3.v.40-41   75
1.6.i.43-65   71
1.6.i.43-67   74
1.14.ii.9-26   71
1.14.iii.52   71
1.14.iv.8   71
1.15.ii.26-28   65
1.20-22   74
1.23   65, 72, 73
1.41   65
1.124   74
1.161   74

Index of Subjects

Aaron 15, 72, 160
Abihu 15
Abijam 76
abomination 3, 19, 23, 24
Abraham 13, 83, 84, 107,
  128, 175, 176, 183
Adad *see* deities
Adonijah 71n.36
agrarianism 1, 41, 43, 119,
  123, 125
agriculture 5, 105, 106, 109,
  110–12, 120, 121, 123, 124,
  126; *see also* farmstead
Ahab 15, 16, 66, 111, 138
Ai 63
'Ain Dara 32
altar *see* cult
Amarna 25, 63, 68, 69, 106
Amman 165
Ammonites 5, 27, 62, 141,
  149n.2, 157, 163, 164, 175,
  183
Amorites 63, 177
amulet 6, 37, 46, 122, 127,
  136, 142, 143; *see also*
  jewellery
Amun *see* deities
Anat 15, 142
Anat-Bethel 30, 181
Anat-Yahu 30, 181
Anatolia 159, 179
ancestor 1, 3, 29, 42n.4, 44,
  45, 46, 47, 65, 74, 83, 88,
  91, 98, 107, 121, 124, 125,
  128, 129, 140, 167; *see also*
  death
angel *see* messenger gods
aniconism 4, 11, 109
animals 13, 28, 29, 83, 84, 89,
  95, 96, 97, 104, 105, 110,
  124, 125, 129, 142, 159,
  160
  bird 13, 30
  bull 6, 30, 66, 93, 97, 142,
    158, 159, 160, 161
  calf 6, 66, 96, 158, 159,
    160
  cow 96, 97
  falcon 65n.16
  goat 91, 181
  ibex 96, 97
  lamb 112, 124
  lion 96, 97, 142
  piglet 142

sheep 30, 181
sow 142
anointing 62, 69, 70, 71, 72
anthropology 37n.1, 40, 44,
  48, 50, 105, 119, 121, 122,
  123, 126, 130, 161
anthropomorphism 16, 122,
  142
Antiochus IV 88
apostasy 4, 6, 66, 110, 191
Aqhat 64
Arad 63, 94, 95, 96, 97, 98,
  152
Aram 15, 27, 30, 56, 141,
  164, 165, 179
Araunah 67
Arbela 110
archaeology 2, 3, 4, 5, 6, 24,
  37, 45, 47, 48, 82, 89, 90,
  99, 104, 106, 108, 111,
  118n.2, 121, 123, 127, 130,
  136, 142, 143, 149, 151,
  152, 156, 157, 161, 162,
  183
architecture 16, 69, 71, 105,
  110, 152
Ark of the Covenant 84, 110,
  113, 114
army *see* warfare
artisan gods *see* deities
ash 89, 95, 128, 129
Asherah *see* deities
Ashtoret 175
Assyria 13, 25, 64, 86, 88,
  107, 143, 151, 164, 179
Astarte *see* deities
astralization 143
Athirat *see* deities
Athtar *see* deities
Atonement, Day of 110

Baal *see* deities
Baal Hamon *see* deities
Babel 109
Babylonia 17, 18, 23, 32, 61,
  69n.32, 73, 74n.51, 82, 96,
  104n.1, 108, 109, 110, 144,
  151, 157, 179, 180, 184
Balaam 162, 163
bāmôt see cult
Bashan 63
Bathsheba 68
Beersheba 83, 84, 85, 86, 90,
  92, 94, 97, 98, 107, 119n.3

Benjamin 85
Bes *see* deities
Beth-Shemesh 107
Bethel 30, 32, 66, 83, 84, 85,
  86, 88, 89, 90, 107, 110,
  112, 119n.3, 158, 159, 160,
  161, 163; *see also* deities
Bethlehem 84, 90, 125
birth 6, 29, 30, 32, 65, 70, 73,
  75, 112, 126, 127, 128n.34,
  136, 138, 139, 140, 142,
  144, 155
blessing 5, 24, 29, 46, 74, 96,
  97, 129, 136, 139, 140, 141,
  143, 153
blood 44, 75n.58, 125, 127
Boaz 71
body 70, 128
  breast 6, 65n.15, 127, 139,
    142
  brow 142n.12
  ear 141
  eye 16, 127, 141, 142
  face 14, 16, 72, 126, 130
  feet 15, 16
  foreskin 127
  genitals 129
  hair 12, 19
  head 17, 87, 97, 128
  limb 97
  mouth 16, 178
  navel-cord 139
  womb 73n.43, 138, 139
book *see* religion; writing
bread *see* food
bride 110; *see also* marriage
burial *see* death
Byblos 25, 178

calendar 32, 123, 124, 158;
  see also sacred time
Canaanites 3, 19, 23–32, 38,
  39, 45, 64, 83, 85, 87, 88,
  106, 107, 109, 122, 125,
  155, 158, 159, 164, 165,
  166, 191
cannibalism 27
canon *see* writing
Carmel 30, 84
chaos 15, 130
children 29, 30, 41, 42, 109,
  110, 120, 126–8, 137–9,
  140, 142, 144, 154, 181; *see
  also* birth; family

children (*continued*)
  baby 127, 139
  infant 126, 127, 138, 139,
    144
Christ *see* deities
Christianity 3, 39, 47, 48,
  61n.2, 76, 104, 121,
  126n.29, 127, 162
circumcision 126, 127, 139,
  144
clan 48, 63, 82, 119, 125, 135,
  161
clothing 16, 21, 29, 87, 97,
  128, 129; *see also* crown
  laundering 129
coins 182
conception 6, 127; *see also*
  fertility
conquest 72n.40, 143, 162,
  163, 182
corpse *see* death
covenant 87, 113, 124, 127,
  166, 167
creation 15, 31, 82, 114, 125,
  139, 140, 141, 144
crown 71, 73n.44, 85, 96,
  156; *see also* clothing
cult
  location
    bāmôt 4, 32, 38, 85, 86,
      87, 88, 89, 91, 92, 111,
      157, 158
    cult corner 91, 92, 122
    gate 29, 37, 85, 89, 90,
      91, 93–4, 96, 108,
      109–10, 113
    holy of holies 94, 95, 110
    house *see* home; religion
    sanctuary 4, 5, 15, 26,
      29, 30, 32, 45, 46, 48,
      69, 71, 72, 84, 86, 90,
      94, 95, 109, 110, 1114,
      125, 135, 137n.2, 138,
      142, 143, 152, 158,
      162, 165, 166, 191
    shrine 4, 5, 6, 69,
      71n.35, 84, 86, 90,
      91, 92, 93, 94, 96, 98,
      108, 113, 114, 118,
      122, 124, 125, 127,
      129, 130, 158, 160,
      166, 182
    temple 1, 4, 16, 29, 31,
      32, 38, 40, 42, 43, 46,
      48n.6, 66, 67, 69, 70,
      71, 72, 75, 82, 83, 84,
      85, 86, 87, 88, 89, 90,
      92, 93, 96, 97, 98, 105,
      107, 108, 109, 110,
      111, 112, 113, 114,
      118, 122, 125, 137,
      138, 145, 157, 163,
      180, 181, 182, 183,
      184, 191
    tree 76, 83, 85, 89, 96,
      111

threshing floor 67
tomb *see* death
object
  altar 6, 71n.35, 83, 84,
    85, 86, 87, 88, 89, 90,
    91, 92, 93, 94, 95,
    96, 97, 98, 99, 108,
    122n.17, 124, 126,
    152, 162, 181
  basin 89, 93, 97, 99
  chalice 89, 92, 98, 122
  figurine *see* image
  lamp 72, 97, 121, 122,
    127
  mask 72n.38, 89
  models 29, 122
  pillar *see* standing stone
  sacred pole 88; *see also*
    Asherah
  statue *see* image
  table 15, 91, 74, 126
  throne 12, 15, 16, 17,
    19, 20, 31, 32, 65, 69,
    70, 71, 72, 73, 74, 75,
    109, 160
  vessels 89, 90, 92, 93,
    97, 98, 121, 122, 128,
    166
  personnel 84, 85, 86,
    89, 125n.26, 160, 161,
    166n.26, 65, 86, 109,
    135, 136, 158; *see also*
    priests
cult of the dead *see* death
curse 46, 129, 136

Dagan *see* deities
Damascus 165, 179
Dan 30, 66, 84, 85, 88, 89, 90,
  107, 119, 158, 159, 160, 179
David 62, 63, 64, 65, 66, 67,
  68, 69, 70, 72, 85, 106,
  107, 108, 110, 125, 137,
  155n.13, 157, 179n.9
Day of Atonement 110
death 3, 14, 15, 20, 21, 29,
  30, 38, 44, 45, 46, 47,
  74n.51, 88, 111, 127,
  128, 143, 144; *see also*
  underworld
  burial 3, 20, 44, 45, 75,
    128, 166n.26
  corpse 47n.5, 129
  cult of the dead 4, 29, 44,
    45, 46, 47, 73, 74, 75,
    128, 136
  dead, the 3, 4, 5, 11,
    12, 20, 21, 28, 29, 44,
    45, 46, 47, 73, 74, 75,
    92, 128, 136; *see also*
    ancestor
  funerary rites 4, 127,
    128n.32
  ghost 20, 21, 44
  grave 45, 47, 136, 141n.8;
    see also tomb

memorial 46
mortuary practices 44, 45,
  46, 47, 74, 122, 127,
  128n.32
Mot *see* deities
mourning 5, 44, 127, 128,
  130
resurrection 128n.33
shade 20, 128
tomb 1, 4, 20, 37, 45, 46,
  48n.6, 74, 92, 127, 128,
  182, 183; *see also* grave
dedication 66, 69, 83, 84, 85,
  88, 89, 91, 98, 122, 153,
  165, 183
deification 42n.4, 73n.44, 91,
  92, 98, 110, 140; *see also*
  divinization
Deir 'Alla 6, 162, 163, 164,
  165, 166, 167
deities 1, 3, 6, 12, 13, 14, 15,
  16, 19, 23, 24, 28, 29, 31,
  32, 38, 42, 44, 66, 67n.20,
  68, 69, 72n.38, 73, 74, 83,
  86, 88, 89, 90, 91, 92, 93,
  96, 97, 98, 99, 109, 110,
  111, 112, 113, 114, 118,
  121, 122n.19, 125, 128,
  129, 139, 140, 142, 150,
  153, 155, 157, 159, 162,
  163, 164, 166, 177, 178,
  179, 181, 182, 184
  Adad 69
  Amun 73n.44
  Anat 15, 142
  Anat-Bethel 30, 181
  Anat-Yahu 30, 181
  artisan gods 1, 28, 29, 31
  Asherah 1, 5, 24, 28, 30,
    31, 42, 43, 44, 75, 76,
    84, 97, 98, 111, 141,
    142, 143, 152, 156,
    157
  Ashtoret 175
  Astarte 98, 111, 175
  Athirat 75, 65, 73n.43
  Athtar 74.51
  Baal 1, 6, 15, 23, 28, 30,
    64, 84, 86, 90, 97, 98,
    111, 114, 140, 150, 154,
    155, 156, 159, 164, 165,
    179
  Baal Hamon 164
  Bes 127, 140, 142
  Bethel 181
  Chemosh 175
  Christ 76
  Dagan 28, 150, 177
  Ditanu 74
  El 19, 23, 65, 66, 68, 140,
    159, 160, 162n.22, 163,
    164n.23, 166, 167, 176,
    177
  ĕlōhîm 31, 68n.30, 72, 73,
    74, 109, 128, 175n.1
  Gad 140

God 3, 5, 6, 11, 13, 14, 15,
    16, 17, 18, 19, 20, 21,
    31, 83, 107, 110, 120,
    125, 128, 137, 138, 139,
    140, 141, 142, 144, 145,
    176, 180, 181, 191, 192,
    193
god 3, 4, 5, 14, 21, 23, 28,
    29, 30, 31, 65, 66, 68,
    69, 71, 72, 73, 83, 86,
    87, 88, 89, 90, 92, 98,
    109, 110, 111, 112, 113,
    121, 127, 128, 139, 140,
    142, 143, 150, 156, 157,
    159, 162, 175, 177, 178,
    191, 192
goddess 3, 5, 23, 24, 28,
    30, 39, 42–3, 44, 63, 65,
    71n.35, 73n.43, 75, 110,
    111, 141, 142, 143, 181
Hadad 30, 159, 179n.9
Hapat 28
Ḥeba 63
Horus 73n.44, 127, 140,
    142, 159
Horus-Yaho 159
host of heaven 86, 98
Ieuo 178
Inanna 111
Ishtar 23, 98, 110, 111,
    143
Isis 111, 140, 141, 142
Khnum 83, 96, 181
Kronos 164
Marduk 23
Mary 76
messenger gods 12, 18, 28,
    29, 31, 73, 154, 155
Milcom 164, 175
Molech 164n.23
Mot 30, 111, 140
Pataeke 142
Persephone 111
Ptah 73n.44
Qos/Qaus 175
Queen of Heaven 39, 42,
    111, 141n.9, 143
Rahmay 65, 73n.43
Rashpu 28
Rephaim 64, 74, 75, 128
Sachmet 142
Saturn 164
Seth 26, 73n.44
Shadday 163, 176
shadday gods 6, 162
Shala 28
Shalem 140
Shapshu 65, 73n.43, 74
Tiamat 69
Titans 74
Theoris 142
Yamm 111, 178
Yhwh 1, 3, 4, 5, 6, 23, 24,
    28, 30, 31, 32, 38, 39,
    40, 42, 45, 46, 50, 61n.1,
    66, 67, 68, 69, 70, 71,

72, 73, 82, 83, 84, 85,
    86, 87, 88, 89, 92, 93,
    97, 98, 107, 109, 110,
    111, 112, 113, 122n.19,
    130, 137, 138, 139, 140,
    141, 143, 144, 150, 152,
    153, 154, 155, 156, 157,
    158, 159, 160, 163, 164,
    166, 167, 175, 176, 177,
    178, 179, 180, 181, 182,
    183, 184, 191, 192, 193
demons 29, 127, 142
desacralization 65
Deuteronomic 21, 70, 118,
    124, 138, 143
Deuteronomistic 4, 6, 23, 62,
    63, 64, 66, 74, 110, 111,
    156–61, 166, 167, 191, 192
diaspora 6, 82, 175, 179–83;
    see also exile
Ditanu *see* deities
divination 13, 15, 17, 18, 19,
    21, 30, 113
divine council 14–17, 18, 19,
    20, 21, 31
divinization 29, 72, 140; *see
    also* deification
dream 3, 13–14, 16, 18, 19,
    20, 21; *see also* vision

Ebla 6, 23, 68n.25, 74n.50,
    176–7, 178, 184
ecstasy 70
Eden 71, 110 *see also* garden;
    paradise
Edom 27, 63, 95, 97, 98,
    149n.2, 153, 175, 184
Egypt 6, 13, 15, 25, 26, 64,
    65n.16, 66, 71, 73, 96, 112,
    125, 127, 136, 137, 140,
    142, 181, 183, 184
Ehud 85
El *see* deities
Elat 96
elders 15, 65, 126
Elephantine 30, 83, 84, 96,
    113, 180–1, 184
Elijah 30, 113, 182
Elisha 113
Emar 23
emotion 11, 12, 13, 16, 17,
    19, 125, 126, 130, 143
'En Haseva 98
Endor 3, 21, 75
Enmeduranki 71
Enoch 71n.35
equinox 29
Esau 104
eschatology 61
Eshmunazar 66
et-Tell 91, 93, 94
Ethbaal 66
ethics 140, 141
ethnicity 6, 26, 27n.8, 149,
    150, 155, 156, 161n.21,
    165, 166, 167, 180

evil 141, 142, 158
evil eye 142
exile 6, 17, 19, 26, 32, 75n.52,
    82, 85, 118n.1, 137, 143–4,
    157, 180, 191, 192; *see also*
    diaspora
exodus 5, 25, 26, 67, 72n.40,
    82, 124, 137, 138, 143
experiential 14, 15, 16, 19,
    20, 21
eye *see* body

face *see* body
family 13, 29, 40, 43, 44, 46,
    48, 49, 62, 119, 120, 122,
    128, 135, 136, 140, 143,
    144, 155, 160, 161, 183
    members
        brother 87, 140
        daughter 105, 110, 114,
            124n.25, 163
        father 49, 66, 69, 120,
            140
        father-in-law 140
        mother 28, 75, 97, 110,
            127, 136, 138, 139,
            142, 175; *see also*
            queen mother
        son 29, 49, 64, 65, 72,
            73, 75, 127, 163, 178,
            180, 183
        uncle 140
farmstead 104, 105, 106, 107,
    108, 109, 124, 158; *see also*
    agriculture
feasting 15, 29, 106, 124, 125,
    128n. 32; *see also* food
feminist criticism 40
fertility 3, 29, 39, 41, 75n.58,
    110, 111, 113, 114, 121,
    142; *see also* infertility
festival 66, 89, 108, 110, 112,
    114, 123, 124, 125, 126,
    137n.2
    Booths/Tabernacles 112, 124
    new moon 125, 126, 128
    Passover 5, 37, 112, 124
    Sabbath 124n.23, 125,
        126, 144
    Weeks/Pentecost 112, 124
food 83, 91, 105, 125, 111;
    see also feasting
    bread 83, 87, 111, 124n.24
    drink 15, 111, 128, 130;
        see also libation
    eating 15, 122, 125, 126,
        130
    manna 125
    meal 83, 84, 89, 125, 126,
        137n.2, 142, 143, 181
    meat 83, 84, 125, 126
    production of 122
    regulations about 5, 144
foreignness 26, 46, 47, 68, 76,
    86, 87, 88, 108, 155, 156,
    157, 163, 164, 178

fort(ress) *see* warfare
funerary rites *see* death

Gad 162, 179; *see also* deities
Galilee 93, 94
garden 75, 110
garrison *see* warfare
gate cults *see* cult
Gaza 25, 96, 98
gĕbîrâ 4, 75–6; *see also* queen mother
gender 4, 41, 44, 159, 160
genealogy 32, 62n.5, 119, 161, 175, 180
Gerizim 107, 182, 184
Gezer 64n.12, 107
Gibeah 65
Gibeath-elohim 84
Gibeon 68n.25, 84, 90
Gihon 71, 110
Gilead 84, 161, 167
Gilgal 65, 66, 84, 85, 88, 90
god(dess) *see* deities
griffin 64, 65n.16

hair *see* body
Hamath 68, 178, 179, 184
harvest 18, 112, 114, 124, 125
Hazor 64n.12, 92, 107
head *see* body
healing 41, 74, 128, 129, 130, 136, 142n.12
health 29, 128
heathenism 191
heavens 14, 15, 16, 17, 20, 21, 29, 31, 71, 109–10, 181
Hebron 24, 44, 67, 70, 83, 84, 90, 111, 150
henotheism 176n.4
Heshbon 63
Hesiod 73
Hezekiah 39, 85, 87, 88, 107, 112, 130, 157
high place *see* bāmôt
hills 25, 44, 84, 92, 97, 111, 142, 165, 182
home 1, 4, 5, 37, 41, 48n.6, 108, 109, 112, 118, 119, 124, 137, 180, 183
Horus *see* deities
Horvat Qitmit 96, 97, 98
Horvat Radum 94, 96
Horvat 'Uza 94, 95, 96, 143
Huldah 113
husband 42, 110, 111, 156; *see also* marriage; wife
hypostases 181
Hyrcanus 183

icon *see* iconography; image
iconoclasm 26, 191
iconography 11, 16, 18, 39, 65n.16, 71n.37, 76, 97, 99, 127, 151, 158–60, 161
identity 27n.8, 49, 108, 120,

121, 123, 126, 130, 144, 150, 156, 159, 166n.25, 167
ideology 2, 4, 26, 27, 42, 43, 48, 61, 62, 63, 64, 65, 66, 71, 75, 76, 109, 111, 113, 114
idolatry 86, 111, 112, 114
Idumaea 6, 175, 182
image 4, 12, 15, 18, 29, 32, 65, 66, 71n.35, 72, 86, 93, 110, 128, 140, 158–60, 192
figurine 4, 29, 97, 122, 127, 142
statue 25, 29, 32, 74, 86, 89, 110
impurity 21, 26, 45, 86, 87, 88, 111, 129, 130
incantation 143
incense 29, 37, 83, 84, 95, 96, 98, 122, 142, 152, 181
individual 5, 12, 13, 14, 16, 19, 46, 48, 119n.8, 120, 130, 135–6, 137, 139, 140, 141, 142, 143, 144, 145, 191
infertility 126, 129, 138
initiation 12, 16, 71, 161
'Iraq al-Amir 182, 183, 184
Isaac 83, 107, 175, 176
Isis *see* deities
Islam 3, 127, 192

Jabbok river 83, 167
Jachin 71
Jacob 13, 62n.5, 104, 107, 110, 160, 163, 167, 175, 176, 183
Jason 183
Jebusite 62, 67, 68
Jedidiah 73n.44
Jehoiachin 179, 180
Jehoshaphat 111
Jephthah's daughter 114, 163
Jericho 63
Jeroboam I 61, 65, 66, 67, 70, 85, 156, 158, 159, 160, 161, 167
Jeroboam II 179
Jerusalem 4, 5, 31, 32, 43, 62, 63, 65, 67, 68, 69, 71, 74, 75, 82, 83, 84, 85, 86, 87, 88, 89, 90, 93, 97, 98, 106, 107, 108, 110, 111, 112, 114, 118, 124, 137n.2, 140, 152n.4, 158, 162, 180, 183
temple 1, 4, 5, 11, 17, 31, 32, 42, 46, 66, 69, 82, 85, 86, 87, 88, 97, 111, 112, 113, 118, 124, 125, 143, 157, 183, 191
jewellery 127; *see also* amulet
Jezreel 107
Jordan river 89, 91, 93, 94, 161, 162, 166, 183
Josephus 66, 183
Josiah 32, 39, 70, 85, 86, 87, 88, 112, 143

Judaism 3, 5, 6, 16, 11, 21, 50, 82, 83, 112, 127, 144, 145, 179, 180, 181, 183, 184, 191, 192, 193

Ketef Hinnom 46, 143
Khirbet Beit Lei 31, 46, 152n.4
Khirbet el-Qom 24, 30, 46, 111, 136, 140, 141n.8, 152
Khnum *see* deities
kingship 4, 5, 24, 15, 16, 17, 21, 25, 29, 32, 49, 61–76, 83, 85, 86, 87, 88, 107, 109, 110, 111, 112, 113, 137, 143, 157–8, 159, 180, 191
Kinneret 61–76, 94, 107
kinship 105, 109, 119, 120, 130, 140
Kiriath-jearim 84
Kirta 64, 65, 71
kispum 74, 75
Kronos *see* deities
Kuntillet 'Ajrud 4, 24, 30, 31, 32n.11, 96–7, 111, 113, 136, 137, 140, 150, 152–3, 165, 167

Lachish 63, 92, 93, 94, 107, 122
lament 128, 136, 137, 138, 139, 140, 142, 144
land holdings 92, 104–5, 107, 120, 124, 128, 135n.1
land of the dead; *see* underworld
law 5, 70n.33, 87, 108, 109, 112, 162; *see also* Torah
Leontopolis 183, 184
letter *see* writing
Levites 14, 15, 87, 107, 113, 158, 160, 161
libation 29, 89, 93, 98, 122, 136, 142
liberation theology 40
liturgy 5, 70, 74, 108, 112
local religion *see* religion
lotus 65n.16, 91

Maccabees 88, 183
magic 16, 18, 30, 41, 43, 113, 123, 127, 129, 136, 142, 143; *see also* incantation; spell
Manasseh 63, 85, 87, 88
Marduk *see* deities
marginalization 3, 37, 40, 41, 44, 46
Mari 23, 25, 69, 176, 177–8, 184
marriage 26, 29, 75, 126; *see also* bride
maṣṣēbôt see standing stone
meal *see* feast; food
medicine 127, 129
Megiddo 63, 92, 94, 107, 122

Melchizedek 62n.8, 83
memorial monument 46, 83;
   see also standing stone
Merneptah 25
Mesad Haseva 96
Mesha 163, 166
Mesopotamia 6, 15, 68, 72,
   110, 127, 136, 159, 179,
   180, 184
messenger gods *see* deities
Micaiah 15, 16, 17
Midrash 13
miracle-working 113
Miriam 14
Mizpah 84, 85, 90
Moab 5, 27, 63, 141, 157,
   164, 175
Molech *see* deities
monolatry 6, 192
monotheism 3, 6, 31, 39, 40,
   74, 67n.20, 72n.38, 73, 109,
   1150, 154, 191, 192
moon 29, 125, 126, 128, 142
   see also festival
morality 27, 38
mortuary rituals *see* death
Moses 14, 15, 25, 71, 72, 87,
   107, 127, 160, 161, 166n.26,
   175, 176, 191
Mot *see* deities
mother *see* family
mountain 15, 18, 30, 31, 72,
   84, 91, 94, 150, 182, 184
mourning *see* death
mouth *see* body
music 70, 96, 125; *see also*
   lament; singing
mysticism 3, 12, 13, 16, 17
myth 17, 18, 19, 24, 29, 30,
   43, 63n.10, 65, 66, 70,
   72n.40, 73, 74n.51, 75, 76,
   108, 109, 110, 111, 113,
   114, 159, 165

Nadab 15
names *see* personal names
Naram-Sin 72
Nathan 65
nature 3, 16, 32, 38, 39, 113,
   123, 130, 140, 158
Nebuchadnezzar 180
Necho 88
necromancy 3, 30, 44, 74; *see
   also* death
Negev 24, 97, 98
netherworld *see* underworld
Nineveh 23
Nippur 180
Nob 84, 90

offering 29, 66, 71, 74, 83,
   84, 86, 89, 90, 96, 112,
   212, 122, 124, 125, 127,
   128, 129, 142, 181; *see also*
   incense; libation; sacrifice;
   votive

official religion *see* religion
oil 69, 105, 111
omen 13, 20, 30, 129
Omri 107, 164
Onias III 183
Onias IV 183
oracle 14, 19, 21, 67, 68, 75,
   76, 110, 136, 138, 139n.6,
   144, 162n.22pi
orientalism 44
origins 5, 25, 32, 62, 66, 67,
   68, 72n.40, 75, 76, 105n.3,
   106, 112, 118n.2, 123n.22,
   124, 160, 161n.20, 164,
   165, 176, 181, 182, 184
orthodoxy 3, 38, 45, 47, 109,
   111, 112, 163, 191, 192,
   193
orthopraxy 193
Otherness 3, 17, 26, 44, 46,
   47, 86, 164, 167
Othniel 85

pagan 38, 39, 47, 72n.38
palace 16, 40, 43, 64, 69, 70,
   75, 105, 107, 108, 109, 183
pantheon 19, 28, 31, 63, 65,
   68, 73, 159
paradise 110, 114
paranormal 3, 13
Passover *see* festival
Pataeke *see* deities
patriarch 4, 13, 25, 26, 67, 82,
   83, 84, 136, 160, 191
Peniel 83
Penuel 161
Persia 19, 27, 82, 83, 93, 108,
   181
personal names 6, 67n.22,
   110, 127, 136, 137, 138,
   139, 140, 143, 153–6, 175,
   176, 177, 179, 180
personification 109–10
Philistines 21, 25, 62, 150, 152
Phoenicians 23, 25, 27, 91,
   141, 155, 156, 163, 175,
   178
piety 5, 6, 40, 44, 88, 120n11,
   130, 135–45, 152, 153, 155,
   193
pilgrimage 112, 124, 137n.2,
   158, 167
pollution *see* impurity
poly-Yahwism 1, 31
polygamy 75
polytheism 1, 3, 28, 31, 39,
   40, 47, 67n.20, 73, 75, 140,
   154, 175, 191
pomegranate 94
post-colonial criticism 40
prayer 6, 69n.32, 87, 127, 129,
   136, 138, 142, 144, 153
pregnancy 127, 136, 138, 139,
   142; *see also* birth
priest 14, 15, 16, 17, 21, 32,
   29, 32, 40, 43, 65, 66, 70,

83, 84, 86, 87, 96, 105, 107,
   110, 112, 113, 114, 118,
   125, 129, 136, 144, 160,
   161, 163, 178, 181, 183,
   192
   high priest 70, 110, 183;
      see also cult
primitive 38, 44, 47
procession 65, 110
prohibitions 32, 128, 136
Promised Land 23, 26, 83, 85,
   98, 137, 163, 166
prophecy 5, 13, 14, 15, 16,
   17, 19, 21, 38, 65, 70,
   104n.2, 113, 129, 136, 140,
   142, 144, 192, 193; *see also*
   divination; oracle
protection 26, 28, 29, 30, 42,
   46, 69, 98, 99, 105, 109,
   110, 113, 127, 139, 140,
   141, 142, 143, 144
psychology 12, 13, 123, 130
Ptah 73n.44
puberty 126
purity 15, 16, 21, 129; *see also*
   impurity

queen 75
queen mother 4, 75; see also
   gĕbîrâ

racism 27
Ramah 84
Ramat Rahel 107
Rationalism 39
reform 39, 66, 70, 75, 85, 87,
   88, 138, 143, 156, 157, 160,
   191
Rehoboam 66, 85, 161
religion
   book religion 3, 49–50,
      70n.33, 82, 87, 108, 192,
      193
   centralized 4, 11, 12, 21,
      32, 38, 83, 84, 85, 88,
      99, 111, 112, 124, 135,
      143, 192
   family 40, 43, 44, 46, 48,
      49, 119n.5, n.8, 120,
      122, 125, 128, 135, 136,
      138, 139, 140, 143, 144
   folk 3, 38, 39, 43, 44
   household 1, 5, 29, 40, 41,
      42, 43, 45, 46, 48, 108,
      118–30, 137n.2, 152, 191
   local 1, 4, 5, 6, 27, 37, 40,
      41, 43, 48n.6, 63, 68, 82,
      90, 91, 114, 118n.2, 125,
      137n.2, 140, 142, 149,
      150, 151, 152, 153, 156,
      158, 161, 163, 165, 167
   men's religion 42n.4
   national 5, 6, 40, 43, 66,
      70, 109, 112, 118, 119,
      121, 122n.19, 123, 124,
      130, 140, 150, 175, 191

religion (*continued*)
    official 37–50, 135, 136,
        137, 138, 140, 145
    personal 5, 12, 16, 17, 18,
        30, 40, 66, 120n.11, 130,
        135–45, 193
    popular 3, 4, 11–12,
        15, 18, 20, 21, 37–50,
        64n.14, 108, 111, 125,
        143, 149
    rural 1, 4, 5, 12, 43, 86,
        104–14, 119, 121
    state 29, 37, 38, 40, 42, 43,
        46, 48, 49, 138, 140
    urban 90–4, 104–14
    women's religion 1, 3, 4, 6,
        38, 41, 42, 43, 44, 124,
        127, 128, 142, 143
reproduction 126, 127, 128;
    see also birth; conception;
    fertility
revelation 50
riddles 14
ritual 2, 5, 12, 15, 16, 20, 21,
    24, 29, 30, 37, 38, 41, 44,
    45, 46, 47, 64, 65, 66, 69,
    70, 71, 73, 74, 76, 83, 87,
    89, 90, 110, 121, 122, 123,
    126, 127, 135, 136, 140,
    142, 143, 144, 161
river 20, 83, 89, 91, 93, 94,
    165, 167; *see also* stream;
    water
Romans 192

Sabbath *see* festival
sacred space 11, 20, 45, 90,
    91, 98, 99, 114, 122, 153,
    167
sacred time 5, 29–30, 66,
    124–6; *see also* calendar
sacrifice 38, 65, 66, 71, 83, 84,
    86, 89, 96, 118, 124, 125,
    126, 127, 129, 137n.2, 142,
    143, 181; *see also* offering
    child 162, 163–4
    human 27
saint 155, 161
Salem 83
Samaria 1, 4, 31, 32, 64n.12,
    65n.16, 84, 86, 87, 90, 97,
    107, 108, 112, 113, 119n.3,
    142, 150, 152, 153, 154,
    155, 159, 167, 181, 182
Samaritans 82, 181, 182
Samson 124
Samuel 21, 66, 74, 114, 161
Sanchuniathon 178
sanctuary *see* cult
Saturn *see* deities
Saul 3, 21, 62, 63, 65, 66, 70,
    74, 75, 155
saviour 13, 61
sceptre 71
scribes *see* writing
Scripture *see* writing

scroll *see* writing
seer 12, 14, 15, 16, 18, 19, 20;
    see also divination; prophecy
seraphim 16
sex/sexuality 75, 104, 129
Shadday *see* deities
shamanism 71n.35
shaving rite 128; *see also* hair
Shechem 63, 68, 83, 85, 104,
    105, 106, 162, 165
Sheol *see* underworld
Shephelah 62
Sheshonq 107
Shiloh 84, 85, 90, 107, 114,
    119n.3, 161, 162
Sidon 63, 66
Sinai 15, 39, 72, 96, 111, 112,
    124, 137
singing 16, 128; *see also*
    lament, music
Sippar 71
sociology 32, 40, 42, 44, 76,
    113, 162
soldiery *see* warfare
Solomon 32, 62n.7, 65, 66,
    69, 70, 71, 73n.44, 75, 85,
    106, 107, 108, 114, 157
son *see* family
sorcery 142, 143
spells 136, 142n.12
sphinx 65n.16
standing stone 88, 89, 91,
    92, 99
    maṣṣēbôt 92, 94, 95, 98, 99
    memorial monument 16,
        83
    pillar 71, 85
    stele 25, 67n.7, 72, 93
state formation 105, 106, 107
stream 110
sun 23, 28, 64, 65, 71n.35,
    92, 142
supernatural 71, 121, 130
superstition 23, 38
Susa 64
symbolism 12, 13, 14, 17, 18,
    19, 20, 29, 32, 41, 64, 70,
    71, 89, 92, 106, 109, 111,
    127, 140, 143, 159
syncretism 143, 154, 157, 192

Taanach 63, 68n.25
Tabernacle 118
tablet *see* writing
Tabnit 66
teaching 49, 87
Tel Aroer 97
Tel Dan 62n.7, 92, 94,
    165n.24
Tell el-Yehudieh 183
Tell Halif 122
Tell Mardikah 176
Tel Rehov 91, 95
Teman 31, 96, 150, 152, 153,
    160, 167
temple, *see* cult

tĕrāpîm 128
theology 6, 11, 20, 26, 31, 37,
    38, 39, 40, 44, 45, 47, 70,
    72n.41, 73, 74, 76, 89, 114,
    135, 138, 140, 143, 144,
    145, 150, 156, 157, 158,
    160, 168, 193
theophany 19, 20, 83
Tiamat *see* deities
Titans *see* deities
tomb *see* death
Torah 38, 40, 49, 72n.40, 136,
    145, 162
trance 13, 17
transcendence 17
transfiguration 72
travel 74, 98, 113, 114, 118,
    165, 167
tree *see* cult
tribe 3, 48, 62, 84, 85, 107,
    119, 162, 163
Trojan War 178
Tuthmosis III 71n.35
Tyre 63, 66, 110

Ugarit 4, 23, 25, 31, 63, 64,
    65, 67, 68, 71, 73, 75, 122,
    178, 184
    texts 6, 15, 30, 64, 66, 71,
        72n.38, 74, 111, 122,
        127, 159, 176
underworld 11, 13, 20–1, 28,
    29, 30, 74
    land of the dead 3, 12
    nctherland 18
    Pit 20
    Sheol 3, 11, 20, 21
urbanism 25, 104, 105, 108
Uriah 67
Urim 21

vision 3, 6, 11, 12, 13, 14,
    15, 16, 17, 18, 19, 20, 21,
    162n.22; *see also* dream
votives 89, 127, 142; *see also*
    offering
vow 129, 130, 136, 138, 142

Wadi Daliyeh 182
warfare 15, 27, 42, 62, 64,
    66, 69, 83, 107, 113–14,
    180
    army 1, 15, 16, 89, 105,
        108, 113
    fort 4, 83, 90, 94–6, 98,
        107, 113, 181
washing 29, 71, 89, 127, 129
water 16, 71, 89, 97, 111,
    129
weather 3, 28, 29, 30, 31,
    150
    rain 28, 109, 111, 113
    storm 17, 111, 159
weaving 41, 42, 97, 108
Western culture(s) 39, 40, 44,
    46, 47, 48, 126

wife 42, 68, 109, 110, 111, 124n.25, 127, 139, 157, 181
wilderness 72n.40, 75n.52, 82, 104, 106, 112, 114, 118, 124, 160
wisdom 13, 141
witchcraft 44
womb *see* body
women 1, 3, 4, 6, 21, 38, 41, 42, 43, 44, 96, 104, 114, 124n.25, 127, 128, 142, 143; *see also* religion
worship 1, 2, 3, 4, 5, 6, 29, 30, 31, 32, 37, 38, 39, 40, 42, 43, 44, 45, 46, 47, 69, 83, 85, 86, 87, 88, 89, 97, 98, 111, 113, 150, 152, 153, 154, 155, 156, 157, 163, 165, 166, 167, 175, 176, 178, 179, 180, 181, 183, 184, 191, 192, 193

writing 4, 6, 20, 39, 49, 50, 71, 96, 108, 113, 136, 177
    archive 25, 63, 64n.14, 67n.21, 108, 113, 180, 181
    book 3, 49–50, 70n.33, 82, 87, 108, 192, 193
    canon 13, 82, 85, 86, 88, 108, 145, 167
    documents 61, 96, 145, 156, 181, 193
    inscriptions 24, 25, 30, 31, 44, 46, 66, 71, 93, 97, 111, 136, 141, 150, 152, 153, 162, 164, 165, 166, 179, 182, 183
    letters 25, 63, 83, 91, 96, 106, 181
    ostraca 92, 236, 153, 154, 155, 182
    papyri 30, 96, 136, 159,

180, 182, 183
    scribes 4, 20, 26, 40, 49, 82, 88, 105, 108, 113, 136, 145
    Scripture 13, 18, 21, 145
    scrolls 110
    tablets 72, 111, 176, 177, 179, 180

Yamm *see* deities
Yhwh *see* deities

Zadok 65
Zaphon 31
Zedekiah 16
Zerubbabel 61
Zimri-Lim 69
Zion 31, 109, 110, 137, 138, 143, 144, 150
zoomorphism 122, 142
Zoroastrianism 192